Robert Hemphill

Goats Ate Our Wires

Robert Hemphill is the author of two previous business and travel memoirs, Dust Tea, Dingoes and Dragons and Stories from the Middle Seat, both available on Amazon.com.

He lives in Encinitas, California, where he writes occasionally on local and state politics, engages in intermittent philanthropy, and attempts to train two cats to sit on his lap. Not at the same time.

www.rfhemphill.com

To Libby —
With all best wishes —

Goats
Ate Our
Wires

Bob Hemphill

Stories of Travel
for Business and Pleasure

R. F. Hemphill

Published in the USA by

 Strelitzia Ventures

Copyright © 2020 Robert Hemphill

EDITED BY
Andrea Susan Glass, www.WritersWay.com and Shelley Chung

INTERIOR AND COVER DESIGN BY
Victoria Vinton, www.CoyotePressGraphicCommunications.com

FORMATTING, ARTISTIC INSIGHTS, USEFUL INFORMATION,
GENERAL GUIDANCE AND THOUGHTFUL ADVICE PROVIDED BY

Jared Kuritz and Antoinette Kuritz, www.Strategies PR.com

ISBN
978-1-948792-06-6 (IngramSpark Paperback)
978-1-948792-07-3 (KDP Paperback)
978-1-948792-09-7 (Kindle eBook)

Contents

Dedication

This book is dedicated to

S. David Freeman,

a leader in energy for the last sixty-five years,

one who has been right far more often than he has been wrong.

But right or wrong,

he continues to lead the charge on renewable energy

And the fight against climate change.

And to everyone who worked with me

At AES Solar and Silver Ridge Power

As we walked point on the solar revolution.

Introduction

This is my third published book, which proves that you can't always learn from experience.

It is made up largely of letters I have written describing my business and travel experiences. It covers the period from 2008 to 2019. The letters are written initially to my dad, and after his death in 2010 to his sister, my aunt Janet. She is now ninety-seven and lives in Lincoln, Nebraska, where she has lived all her life. She is still healthy, physically and mentally. I hope to do as well when I am ninety-seven.

This book covers anecdotally the surprising rise of renewables, principally solar panels and wind turbines, as providers of clean electricity. It is a remarkable story that has resulted in the demise of coal and oil-fired plants all over the world and their replacement by a cheaper, cleaner, and in every way better technology. I am delighted to have had a part in moving this revolution forward, after serving in the fossil fuel army for twenty-five years of my career. But enthusiastic as I was, I never foresaw how quickly prices would decline and how rapidly the questions I got would change from "Isn't that solar stuff too expensive" to "So when will we get rid of all the coal plants?"

If I had to make two guesses about the future of electricity in the world, I would say:

Sometime before the end of 2021, some reputable developer will win a bid in an auction with a price of $.01 per kWh in his long-term contract. The lowest bid I have seen to date is $.0149 from an auction in Macedonia.

The last utility coal plant in the US will go out of service by the end of 2030. As I write this, coal is down to 19% of US electricity supply. It peaked in 2006 at 60%. It's not much of a leap to continue that decline linearly, and it's likely even to speed up.

So what about the title? During the five years starting in 2008 we created and I led a solar company that was rapidly developing and building utility scale solar plants—big arrays of solar panels on metal frames supported by posts, but sitting in large fields, not on rooftops. One of our better locations was in southern Italy, mostly in Puglia, the province that is the "heel" of the boot, and a really great and beautiful place. At one of our monthly progress meetings our country manager handed out to each of the thirty or so attendees a neatly wrapped, individual package of goat cheese. Because we designed the plants with the panels laid out in rows, and because there had to be enough space between each row for maintenance access, we ended up with a lot of grass and weeds growing in the rows. His clever idea was instead of using a noisy mower to keep the grass down, he went to a local farmer and rented a herd of goats. The goats were trucked over and ate all the grass, then went home and the farmer made us cheese from their milk.

We all thought this was brilliant—inexpensive, environmentally delightful, contributing to the local economy, and we even got some cheese for our contribution. Applause for all of those involved.

At the next monthly meeting, everything proceeded normally except there was no cheese distribution. "What happened?" I asked. Well, the goats ate all the grass and then, because they were goats and had been left unsupervised for a bit, they began seeing what else was around. They ended up eating the electrical wiring that connected each solar panel with its neighbor. Fortunately we ran a low voltage system. Unfortunately eating the wires was not really a good thing, not for our electricity production and probably not for the goats. The law of unintended consequences for sure.

So, this isn't really an electricity textbook, it's just stories about business and travel. And all the craziness and strangeness recounted herein really happened. I hope you enjoy it.

Robert Hemphill
Encinitas, CA

Section I

Letters to My Dad

I continued my practice of writing occasional long or some-times short letters to my dad to explain to him what we were doing, where we were traveling, what we were experiencing. He was at this point long retired from the air force and living in Olympia, Washington, a small, wet, grey city that I do not recommend other than as a suitable background for personal despair. He moved there to be close to his partner (my mom had died some twenty-five years earlier) who had moved there to be close to her two daughters, each of whom had then moved away. Ah, families.

I visited him frequently during this time as I was on the board of several small and ultimately futile venture companies, both headquartered in Seattle. These are the letters I wrote to him during this period, from 2005 to 2010, when he passed away at the age of ninety-two.

[1]

Boats in Paris Are a Bad Idea
Unless They Use Electricity

October 2005

Dear Dad,

L's mother had decided that she would go on her church's trip from Houston to France, to include Paris and the Normandy beaches, an appropriate itinerary especially since the parishioners who signed up were all well past retirement age, and thus not too young enough to remember D-Day. I suspect you do as well, although at that point you were on some crap hole of a small island battling your way toward Japan. But she wanted a family member to come with her, which was reasonable given her limited ability to walk long distances and her occasional confusion and failure of short-term memory. But as both of us were working this was not very convenient. We split the trip and I got the second shift.

Sometimes it's not so much fun. I spent the day that I was to leave in the AES headquarters in Arlington, with a "strategy" meeting led by a consulting firm called CERA, which stands for Cambridge Energy

Resources Associates. They are highly regarded and are a pretty big-time group, founded by a Yale guy two years behind me named Daniel Yergin. He received a Pulitzer Prize in 1992 for writing a very good book about oil. At least I am assured it was good, I never actually read it since it was all oil, and electricity and oil do not mix. Nice fuel but too expensive and too unpredictable and controlled largely by countries that don't like us much. The consulting firm puts on an annual convention of sorts in Houston, called modestly "CERA Week," and they invite all their clients to come speak on panels while other clients listen in the audience, waiting impatiently to speak on their own panels. I went once and found it to be a bit disjointed and besides I was too low on the energy totem pole for people to seek me out and ask for my business card, and I was too annoyed with the whole process—mostly because I wasn't on a panel—to seek out others and ask them for their business cards. I am pretty sure I didn't stay the whole week.

Of course, I didn't know Yergin at Yale since I didn't know anybody there really. It's hard to pick up a raft of friends for life when you're studying and also working twenty hours a week at several jobs so you can pay your tuition and assorted stuff.

The output of this long day sitting in a conference room with no windows looking at slides of graphs and charts was that: 1) energy is important; 2) future energy price and supply curves are difficult to predict; and 3) if you pay us more money, we will share these remarkable insights with you in even greater detail so you can incorporate them into your corporate strategy.

We were too embarrassed to tell these smart and polished guys, all wearing better suits than us and Hermès ties, that we didn't actually have a corporate strategy. Or rather, our strategy was simple: find places where they need electricity and we can either build something or buy something that makes electricity cheap enough to make money, and where somebody there has enough money to pay us. Dennis Bakke, the AES COO who was even more antistrategy than I was, once phrased it thusly: "We try a lot of things, and we keep the ones that work and call them our strategy."

The meeting ended, it was raining hard, I was already late, but I hurried home to deal with the dogs before heading to Dulles. The dogs, who had been outside all day, were glad to see me and jumped wetly all over me in happiness and anticipation of food. I got to United at Dulles even more late and somewhat muddy. No upgrade, but at least they put me in "premium economy," which is something of an oxymoron. It is said that this gets you more legroom than "economy" (plain old economy? Economy for cheapskates?). If so, then you probably need to be well under five feet tall to be comfortable there.

We flew overnight as one always does, landed at Heathrow, and changed to BMI to fly on to Paris. This is a run-of-the-mill airline that used to be British Midlands and served mostly guess where, but then it got convinced that it had a larger vision, perhaps even a strategy, and no, I don't know the difference between a vision and a strategy and a mission statement except I don't think most businesses go on missions; I believe that is left to Mormons and evangelical parties. Anyway, they changed their name and now won't tell you what it means. Just like AES was originally Applied Energy Systems but we quickly found that that meant nothing to anyone starting with us, so now we say that it doesn't stand for anything. This isn't very satisfactory but maybe it's our strategy.

I got a small rental car that was OK and is a good thing since there really aren't any large rental cars in Europe anyway, and drove into Paris. This was a mistake since I was trying to go to Rouen to meet up with the mother-in-law and group. I figured that if I just drove around on the freeways long enough I would see a sign for it, and besides I took French at Yale long ago when I was not meeting Daniel Yergin, so I had uttered those fateful words, "How hard could it be?" This is the second stupidest thing in the world to say about anything and is always followed by the God of Bad Luck looking down on you and saying with a smirk, "OK, Mr. Smart Guy, we will show you exactly how hard." Just so you won't have to ask, the first stupidest thing to say in the world is, when confronted by an officer of the law who is suggesting that you have committed an infraction, you retort, "Don't you know who I am?" Once you realize this mistake you can't back away from it by saying, "Really, I'm sorry, I have forgotten who I am, I was hoping that you would know."

Because it's now 0830 in the morning, there is much traffic. I am both driving and trying to find signs that will get me out of here (miscellaneous bits of Paris not recognizable as the Eiffel Tower) and on the way to Rouen. After realizing that I am about to start my second circumnavigation of the *périphérique*, which I have realized is the French designation for beltway, I take the next road west as I am pretty sure it's in that direction. Yes, I didn't do much homework for this trip, I was too busy worrying about whether we had a strategy.

The French system of roadways doesn't let me down and I do get to Rouen. But wait, there is still much driving around to do as I have to find the *Hôtel de la Cathédrale*. Not so many signs. I find one correctly named and stop, go in, only to be informed that this is the aforementioned hotel but there's another one and since I don't have a reservation at this one, I should probably try the other one. The real one is near and easy to find, they treacherously tell me, and I am given all sort of directions, most of which I cannot understand. Perhaps starting with my limited French of *"Où est la hôtel de la cathédrale"* was not the best choice, it fooled them into thinking I really was French. OK, maybe not, I still had some dog-deposited mud on my pants.

I was successful in finding the district de piétons, but you can't park, as this is a pedestrian district. Fortunately I didn't. Unfortunately I wasn't really looking for the *district de piétons*. Eventually I did find the hotel, which was sort of beside the cathedral (well, *quelle* surprise) but not exactly since Rouen isn't really that big—blind pig, acorn, etc., and it was the *Hôtel Mercure Rouen Centre Cathédrale*. I felt a small sense of triumph. Very small.

The mother-in-law and the touring party arrive having spent the day at the cathedral (well, remember, their church organized this party), we go to dinner, and of course there is no steak frites on the menu. But I finally get to change my clothes.

Just in case you find yourself in Rouen, which I do not recommend, note that there actually isn't much to do there once you've seen the *cathédrale*. The *cathédrale*, by the way, is named the "Cathedral of Notre-Dame of

Rouen" in an attempt to trick you into thinking that you're in Paris. You are not. The list of "Ten Best Tourist Sites" on the Internet, this one put together by the local chamber of commerce, includes the cathedral, another cathedral where Joan of Arc was tried and sentenced to death but not the site where she was barbecued, an old street, and a big clock that doesn't do anything but tell time—no priests or witches or panda bears rotating in and out and around the large clock face. Since the group has by now exhausted the entire panoply of Rouen sights, we go off by large tourist bus to Honfleur. This is a very lovely and almost Disney-quality picturesque fishing port with the boats all tied up in rows in a rectangular marina, which in turn is surrounded on three sides by small restaurants. All the fishing boats are there in the marina. This always makes me wonder—if this is a fishing town, why aren't these guys out fishing? Do they only catch fish by night? That would make a risky business even less attractive, unless for some unknown biological reason fish are attracted to fishing boats more easily in the evening.

There is not so much else to do after you have walked around the marina and looked at all the restaurants, except to pick one and eat lunch. I order chicken with *frites* since I am betting all the fish on the menu comes from Chile or someplace where they still really do fishing.

Then to the "peace museum" in Caen, which is actually all about war but doesn't have any good T-shirts, and finally to an inn. It is on a farm in Crépon, near Omaha Beach and the Omaha Beach Golf Course. The latte r seemed strange to me but no one else in the group appeared offended. Maybe they were just old and not veterans.

The next morning L leaves in the dark with the car and many written instructions to me. I wish her good luck, but finding Paris from Crépon is probably easier than the reverse. I suggest she just head east but she does not seem to cherish this advice. We spend the obligatory day at the beaches—Omaha, Utah, Pointe du Hoc. There are lots of rusting tanks and gun emplacements. I think about *Saving Private Ryan* and how enormously brave the US troops were to make this difficult and bloody landing. We go to lunch in Sainte-Mère-Église (*dinde avec frites*). A life-size but not at all lifelike dummy in US uniform is displayed on the local chapel, hanging from the church spire where his parachute is caught. This was one of the drop zones, and some poor airborne trooper did get hung up when his chute caught on the spire. The explanation is that the loyal French rescued him, but I wonder. I remember at Fort Bragg that all the drop zones had the names of European places where paratroopers made combat jumps in WWII—this one, Luzon, Normandy, Salerno, Nijmegen. I jumped onto most of them when I was there and only got caught in trees, not church spires. Then on to the US cemetery and a wreath laying, very solemn and moving, really. How they keep all the white crosses so perfectly aligned is very impressive.

The next day, having had enough death and bravery for a time, we get back in the bus for the long ride to Chartres, complete with several traffic jams, no lunch, but two sandwich stops before and after at very nice roadway 7-Eleven equivalents but since this is France they are much nicer than that. We blow through the cathedral, see great windows, get on the bus to Paris for the last two days of the trip.

Paris by bus tour is about what you would expect and what you would not want to experience. Essentially drive-bys with curt descriptions—"This is Notre-Dame on the left, a famous cathedral, coming up on the right is the Hôtel de Ville which isn't really a hotel, ha, ha." We do stop and do the Louvre in two hours, one of which was devoted for some reason to the Egyptian collection, but we also buzzed by the Venus de Milo, Winged Victory, and the *Mona Lisa* so you could say that you saw the three biggies.

The group farewell dinner was on one of the *bateau-mouches*, a set of medium-sized barges that cruise up and down the Seine and lure unsuspecting customers onto them for a "champagne dinner" and seeing the sites by evening, said to be all lighted up. But the Seine has been long since turned into an urban river with large stone walls to control it. So you cruise by the "sights" and if you're lucky you see the tippy tops of them but mostly you look out the windows and see the stone wall fifteen feet away. Not wonderful—both the food and surely the "sights." And there was a noisy piano player. Ugh.

Right now I can almost hear you asking longingly, "Hey, hotshot, I've been to Paris, so where's the energy part of this letter?" OK, OK, we're getting to that. I got on the 9:40 p.m. flight to Brazil on a Monday night, four days after getting back from Paris. The nice thing about going to South America is that they don't trick you like flying to Europe. There's only a couple hours time change, so if they say you take off at nine and land at nine in the morning, you get your full ten or twelve hours on the plane. Plenty of time to enjoy the luxury of fine airline cuisine, the swell reclining seats that in other times have been used for below-the-knee amputations, and the flying Petri dish of bacteria, many of them not your friends, into which each airplane has been changed by the reduced air changes per hour the airlines have decreed in the name of saving money. I arrived grumpy, with a sore throat, but all my luggage, in the pouring rain. Welcome to São Paulo, a really big city of almost no charm whatsoever. Even less in downpours. But lots of traffic. Swell.

After the two hours in from the airport, we roll right into meetings. It's why I'm there, it's my life, I live for meetings. About six years ago we bought in a three-way deal with some partners, both the São Paulo electric distribution business (Electro Paulo) and the Rio de Janeiro electric company, wonderfully named "Light." I am here as the AES rep for a quarterly progress review meeting.

Some background: as you know, we got these electric utilities that come with wires to the houses of all the customers, over which we deliver our wondrous product. How does that work, you may ask. Let us consider for a moment another operation where they sell things to customers, say Nordstrom, and how we are different.

The CEO of Nordstrom, I have it on good assurance from Elika—my daughter who used to work there—has all his stores and all his cash registers connected to an IT/communications system. Hence, he can tell every day just how much each register has sold, and what, and probably to whom and by which salesperson. So if Register 17 in Tysons Corner has sold eighty-seven pairs of jeans, he knows it. The merchandise is bar coded, and the machines are networked. He can control inventory, he can compile records on who is selling and who is not, he can spot goof ups and mistakes and fraud, he can reorder, shift merchandise, decide to put stuff on sale, etc. Now I don't think that he actually looks at each register each day, but he can. Plus he has a bunch of staff to do that. And so can all the other folks in the organization who have a reason to do so. You can bet that the store manager checks all his registers every day. When Elika ran a department there she certainly checked hers. He has data and he has a system that lets him collect the data, analyze it if he wants, and then take whatever actions he thinks make sense.

Let us now think about selling ele ctricity, a noble and time-honored profession if ever there was one. It works like this. We pour a bunch of electricity into the top of the system every day. It goes somewhere. Every thirty days or so we send a bunch of guys out to read the meters that have, usually, recorded where some of the electricity went. The meter reader writes down the numbers, usually getting about 10% of them wrong. He takes his sheet of numbers back to the billing office where the numbers are transposed, and another 10% added to the error rate. We then calculate what each customer owes us based on these readings and send out bills and people usually pay us. They can go online and pay us if they are diligent and literate, but they cannot go online and pay us by credit card, only by wire transfer. And who, by the way, does a wire transfer for a thirty-five-dollar bill? Your bank will charge you twenty-five dollars for the transfer. That would be both difficult and silly, and besides only geniuses like Amazon and eBay have figured out how to sell stuff over the Internet using credit cards. Hey, we don't need the money, we're a monopoly, let's make it as hard as possible for folks to pay us.

In the richer areas people send us checks, eventually, so that we're probably getting paid thirty to forty-five days after the commodity has been purchased and used. Giant, my local supermarket don't do that, Freddy Meyer, your own grocery store, don't do that. No sensible person or business in commerce does that. Oh, yeah, this thirty to forty-five days of universal credit that we give everyone. No credit checks. You got an electric meter, you get credit.

Let us explore this odd system in a little more depth. Sure, we have time. How does your utility, Olympia Electric Coop or whatever it is, know when your power goes off so they can come out and do electric magic and climb up poles and say the prayers up there that make it go back on? They must have meters or indicators or signals or some such modern thing—guys sitting in fancy control rooms with computers and big black screens and red and green blinging lights and such like, just waiting for Colonel Hemphill's electricity to go out so they can pounce on the problem and solve it. After all, if your service is out, you ain't using our product and therefore not piling up that big bill that we will eventually collect, when we get around to it.

Uh, no. The way we know you got no electricity is you call us. Yes, absolutely true. This is definitely not Nordstrom. And if you never call us, it is entirely possible that we will never know, and you will never again have electricity. To make matters more interesting, assume you have decided to stop paying and send the money to your local charity. Once we finally figure out that you haven't paid us in six months, we have to send two guys and a truck to your house and one of them does something mechanical to turn off your electricity. And, when you pay your bill, the same thing to get it turned on again.

No one has ever suggested that our brother giant monopoly, the much-derided telephone company, is an efficient business. But the moment your phone goes out, they know it. They can generally fix it remotely, with no truck rolls. And if you don't pay your bill, first they just turn off your outgoing service, but let you receive calls, along with a message suggesting that you might want to pay your bill. And after a couple more days of nonpayment, they turn off all your service. They have a very high incidence of payment, and a very low level of losses for nonpayment.

At our meetings in São Paulo, we talk a lot about these things. The standard industry loss rate in US electric utilities is 3%–4% . In São Paulo, despite essentially the same systems and the same kinds of equipment, the loss rate is running at 12%. This is not good, but it's down from the 15% that it was when we bought the place. It's down to 11% in our utility in Caracas—very equivalent to São Paulo—but in our African utility in Cameroon it's 20%.

OK, I can't stand to write about this anymore, although if you asked of course I could.

Much love, Bob

[2]

The Solar Revolution
Lurches Slowly Forward

October 2007

Dear Dad,

It all started innocently enough. Like all complicated things seem to.

I was minding my own business, and hopefully the company's business at AES, when Paul Hanrahan, the CEO, asked me to come work for him as chief of staff. Nice idea, maybe, but we've never been long on staff positions, and the idea of a chief of staff was wholly new to us and to me. What Paul really wanted was someone to try and make the trains run on time, another part of managing a large enterprise that has grown out of a small one. And, it might be said, an enterprise where we had not developed the skills and practices to do this, since what we were really interested in was making laying more track and making more trains. Hence this did not come naturally to us as an organization. This meant small things, like making sure that all our meetings of the executive office, the real internal decision-making body for the company, had an agenda, that said agenda was prepared well ahead of time, that any decisions that were on the agenda had supporting decision papers, that all the papers to be prepared were delivered to the XO members far enough ahead of time so that they could actually read them, that minutes of the meeting were kept as a record and were subsequently circulated. This could be called good corporate hygiene, or it could be called bureaucratic goombah, take your pick.

Then the same again for all board meetings, except here we were slightly more disciplined, thanks to the single-handed efforts of Brian Miller, our general counsel. And, one might add, part of this task was not just scheduling, it was also trying to assure that the decision papers were well written and that the analysis was correctly and reasonably done. Also, as we are fond of saying in the military, "additional duties as assigned," which meant everything from standing in for Paul in key meetings to making sure the Christmas party entertainment was laid on. Much process in a process adverse company, and all to be done without stepping on the toes of any of the line managers. Right.

So I said sure, sounds great, but I would also like another portfolio, since the chief of staff one is pretty content free, although important. I would like to be charged with examining new technology and its applicability to our business. Paul agreed.

SMALL NOTE OF EXPLANATION: we have never at AES been much of a technology company. For one thing, the technology of making electricity changes very slowly. In many cases—burning a fossil fuel in a boiler to make steam, running the stream through a turbine to make the shaft of the turbine spin, using this spinning shaft in a generator to make electricity in some magical way that no one can really explain, condensing the spent steam, putting the now condensed steam (called "water" how about that?) back in the boiler, and starting all over again—what we are doing has not changed materially in sixty or seventy years. We have one plant in Pennsylvania, called Beaver Valley, which was commissioned in 1943, and is still working perfectly fine today, with an availability of better than 90%. As you will remember, I was born in 1943 and I am not sure my availability today is better than 90%. It is actually a good thing that the technology doesn't change very quickly, because this means that once you learn how something works, you don't have to relearn something new in three years. I doubt that computers made in 1943 are still in service; I am positive that cars and airplanes made in 1943 are no longer used commercially. And the technologies for all these things have changed dramatically, which means industry participants who wish to be successful have to keep up. But not so much power plants. We just have to keep them running, we don't have to redesign them every three years.

Our second reason for not being too interested in technology is that there is a well-established network of suppliers already doing the work and upgrading the existing technologies. Gas turbines, for example, are jet engines reengineered for stationary use in making electricity. As engine technology has changed, thanks to DARPA and the Pentagon, the machines have become cheaper and more efficient. The efficiency gains are particularly startling: the first of these machines that we bought for electricity use had heat rates of above ten thousand Btu/kWh.

OK, now we pause to digress on another of the utility industry's bits of weirdness. When everyone else in the civilized world talks about efficiency, they refer to the ratio of the fuel that goes into the system or machine compared to the work that actually comes out. The internal combustion engine in your car, for example, is about 30% efficient, meaning that you actually turn only 30% of the calories in the fuel that's consumed in the engine into motive power—so the calculation is energy out divided by energy in. But us geniuses in the power biz prefer to reverse the equation and put "energy in" on the top of the equation. And then we don't do the division.

This is further confused by the fact that you have to know what a kWh of electricity is "worth" in Btus, or you can never get to a more universally understood efficiency. For reference, this number is 3,412. So, just to follow this through in mind-numbing detail, if you get 3,412 Btu of work out, i.e., one kilowatt-hour, but you had to put 10,000 Btu of fuel in, then your traditional efficiency is 34.12% (3,412 over 10,000)—not much better than your car. We express it, however, as the Btus in to get one kWh out, so perversely a lower number means a higher efficiency. OK, I promise never to explain this again.

Suffice it to say that gas turbine efficiency has gone from about 34% to better than 55% in twenty years, largely through taking advantage of changes in jet engine efficiency—better materials, better blade design, etc. This is, for the power industry, a huge change. Coal plant efficiencies during the same period maybe have gone from 30% to 35%. But it's bupkis compared to computers, whereas we all know from Moore's Law, things get twice as good and half as expensive every eleven seconds, except for every Microsoft product.

Given all this, AES has never had much interest in new technology. We have no central engineering staff, no labs with scientists in white coats torturing generically identical mice—no wait, that's biotech—and no patents or test facilities and so forth. But our sense was that there were new ideas relevant to power generation that were finally getting to acceptable levels of cost and reliability for commercial deployment, and there were new problems for the industry to confront that would require new technological approaches. This was no better than a sense but sometimes this sort of informal aggregation of data, informed by industry experience, is useful.

After much discussion and fooling around and false starts, we selected four technologies on which to focus our efforts, each characterized by being relevant to what we do, make and sell electricity, and for being likely to experience a big difference in said commercial activity, relatively soon. We started to go to trade shows, read industry literature, visit companies who actually had technologies, etc. Sadly there is no shortcut way to do this, no small pill that you can swallow to become expert on a new industry. Probably the best idea we had was to make a visit to Silicon Valley. And it wasn't even my idea.

We have a board member named Dr. Kristina Johnson, currently the provost of Johns Hopkins University. She is a PhD engineer by training and was previously chairman of the Department of Engineering at Duke University, not a small academic accomplishment. She has also at one point taken one of her own ideas, created a start-up company, gotten it funded, and ran it well enough to sell it to some bigger company. And she got funded by the gold standard of venture capital, a fund called Kleiner Perkins Caufield & Byers. As we began messing around in the technology area, we formed a board committee to help us deal with this stuff, and Kristina was a very valuable member of it. She offered to introduce us to the guys at Kleiner, so we said sure.

Since I wanted to make a good impression, I convinced Paul to come along. People pay more attention to meetings when the CEO is there. We flew to California, spent the morning in a pointless visit to Stanford, and then took off down Interstate 80 to Menlo Park and the sacred domain. Note the first: in VC land, there is a definite hierarchy, with about ten firms being at the top level, and then a very large separation between all the remaining two thousand or so various-sized funds who call themselves venture capitalists. Most of the ten have made money in computer hardware and software, and most of them are located, not just in Silicon Valley, but many are at a singular location called Sand Hill Road. This includes Kleiner Perkins, but also Mohr Davidow and NEA and Draper Fisher Jurvetson. These names don't mean much to the average American, but these are the folks who financed Amazon and Cisco and Microsoft and Apple and Intel and many, many other household names. And did very well for their investors and for the principals of the funds as a result. They are pretty close to royalty in the venture community. No, that's not right. They ARE royalty.

So it was with more than a small amount of trepidation that we rolled our rental car into the parking lot of 2750 Sand Hill Road. I fully expected a thirty-minute meeting with some junior associates, who would be polite but disinterested, and that would be that. But note the second: the venture community has discovered "green." Interest in environmental things and energy things is now fashionable, especially interest in "renewable" energy. This is variously referred to as clean tech or green tech or what have you, newsletters and websites have sprung up, conferences are being held. The definition is fuzzy, but all the major VC funds have begun moving aggressively out of their traditional investment areas of IT and biotech and into energy and related venues. This is a major change, and, when you think about it, one that is not made quickly and easily. I know a lot about energy, but if you asked me to start investing in the food processing business, almost none of the technical stuff and the commercial stuff that I know, or the relationships I have, would apply. Same is true for these guys—iPods ain't solar panels, and laptops aren't electric cars.

We show up, they are expecting us, we are taken into a nice conference room. The offices are in a beautiful modern building, lots of glass and wood, and surrounded by small but gorgeously landscaped grounds. Exceptionally bucolic and serene. And then six of the firm's total of twelve partners, and two senior associates, come into the meeting. This included one of the name partners, Brooke Byers, and a man named John Doerr, who is probably the single best-known VC in the world. He consults with the governor of California, etc. He is a very, very big deal. And for two hours they tell us, all of them, over and over, how glad they are that we have come, how much they would like to work with us, what a great reputation we have in the industry, how much value we could add to what they do. And we discuss and debate over the whole range of new technologies. Thank God we have done some homework. This is not at all what I expected—not a drop of arrogance, not a drop of condescension. And these are people who have earned the right to be arrogant. It is quite possibly the best meeting I have ever attended, and completely different from what I expected. Remarkable.

As we subsequently float back to our hotel, Paul allows as how that was pretty good and maybe we are on to something after all. And he is not a person who effuses readily.

Now back to reality. What do we concentrate on now that we have this wonderful access and this commitment from the CEO that maybe my idea to look into some technology stuff is reasonable? We select four areas:

Energy storage, which really means batteries. This is actually the holy grail of the utility industry, and especially of the renewables part of the industry. Remember that electricity is kind of like a kiss—wonderful, but it has to be made anew each time. There is no good way to store the supply economically, other than as water in dams and most of the good dam sites have already been built by us industrious humans. And the demand for electricity is unpredictable and again instantaneous. You needy customers seem to want your lights to come on when you turn the switch. The need for storage is particularly acute when you begin to think about renewables and using more and more of them in the power grid. Take my word for it, but of all the renewable technologies, only two are really worth much to the utility, "worth much" defined by me as being plentiful and of reasonable cost: electricity from wind and electricity from the sun. Forget geothermal, too limited a resource. Forget ocean waves, etc. And biomass, if we were able to master the technology, should be used for liquid fuels to replace petroleum, not burned in stationary power plants.

But the two big problems with the wind and the sun are, obviously, that the wind blows whenever it wants to and the sun doesn't shine at night. Hmm, hope that wasn't too technical. Hence the electricity from these resources is currently made whenever we can and injected into the grid and sold on an "as and when made" basis. This is not ideal, like the season for fresh asparagus at the supermarket used to be limited to around Easter, before we discovered the southern hemisphere and airplanes. So batteries would be nice, and ones that are not like what we currently have, whose problem is basically cycle life. With the traditional lead acid battery, once you cycle through three hundred or four hundred charge/discharge cycles, it's done. If we are to use these every day when the sun shines or the wind blows, a useful life of a year or so doesn't work. Fortunately there are, we find as we dig into this, newer chemistries with higher costs but way better cycle life—ten thousand or even forty thousand. Now we're getting somewhere. I won't bore you with the details but as we pursue this, we find interesting technologies and profitable applications.

Coal to something. For quite a while, energy folks have recognized that coal is plentiful and widely distributed. We aren't that clever, but fortunately this is obvious. We have also found that it is a solid and hard to burn. Determining this was in fact not too difficult. And technically it is less "BTU intensive" on a cubic foot basis than most other energy sources, so transportation costs become an issue. Here's the comparison.

A barrel of crude oil is 42 gallons, a weird standard, since most of us think of 55-gallon drums as a "barrel," but not in the oil industry. This barrel has 6 million Btus of energy in it, and weights about 275 pounds. To get the same number of Btus from coal requires almost twice that much material, 578 pounds to be exact. Gas is harder to compare by weight since, well, it's a gas. But gas has roughly 92% of the Btus that oil has per pound. Wood as a fuel is even worse, about 8,600 Btus per pound, so less even than coal. This in part helps to explain why oil sells for such a high price and is such a valuable fuel—it's more concentrated as a Btu source, it's way easier to move around, and it's easier to burn cleanly.

But we coal fans are undeterred; we think there should be a way to turn coal into something closer to oil or gas and thus widen the uses for the fuel by increasing ease of use. This thinking has been around for some time, starting with a couple of German chemists in the 1920s who developed something called the Fischer-Tropsch process, which they modestly named after themselves. What this does is, using a lot of steam and high temperature and pressure, convert coal into a not very good gas, and after several more steps, a sort of expensive oil substitute. It is interesting to note that the two places where this has really been pursued energetically, pardon the pun, are in Germany during WWII, and in South Africa during the embargo of the sixties and seventies. Both places had very little native oil, lots of native coal, and had their other people's oil cut off due to bad behavior. But as oil prices spike, interest in converting coal into something better always arises. And it would be useful in the power industry as building new coal plants and burning coal directly has become more and more problematic. Hence our focus.

Carbon separation and sequestration. If CO_2 is a problem, then more coal plants are not the answer, and it's not just the Sierra Club saying this any longer. It would be very cool if we could separate the CO_2 out of the exhaust of our coal plants, and then put it somewhere where it wouldn't bother us. This is not, however, quite as easy as it seems. For starters, the exhaust from a power plant is a lot. And the combustion products are all mixed together with the unburned oxygen and the completely useless nitrogen that make up more than 80% of what goes up the stack. To grab the 15% to 18% that is CO_2 you have to process the entire volume of gas. Not impossible, just lots of fans and blowers and pipes and duct work and vessels. The second problem is that CO_2, being the result of a chemical process, is quite stable and nonreactive. So to find some chemical to react with it in a way that then allows physical separation from the rest of the gas stream, as a precipitate for example, is not so easy.

Assuming that you solve this nontrivial problem, then the even larger problem is, "Now what?" Where do you put the damn stuff? Current thinking is you stick it down into oil fields or inject it somewhere into the ground and hope it never comes back to visit you. My personal opinion is that this is flawed thinking. Number one, there aren't nearly enough depleted oil and gas reservoirs to hold all the CO_2 we make, and number two there are all sorts of questions about the physical integrity of these reservoirs. Remember, what we have been doing for seventy-five years is poking holes in these reservoirs and fracturing them and horizontally drilling through them and doing other nasty things to them with the express purpose of getting stuff OUT of them, not of keeping stuff in. And because CO_2 is odorless, detection is not simple. Finally, everyone cites the example of Lake Nyos in Cameroon where in 1986 a large bubble of CO_2 emerged from the bottom of the lake and drifted into a nearby village. Since carbon dioxide is heavier than air, it basically asphyxiated the sleeping villagers. Probably what we should do, if we can in fact separate the CO_2 economically, is convert it into some sort of solid and then put it somewhere that we can keep track of. But that's a story for another day.

Finally, the point of this tedious and rambling introduction: The fourth area that we picked was solar photovoltaic technology. Clean, safe, no toxic components, no air or water emissions, harmless, easy to build, long lasting, easy to maintain, easy on the eyes. And phenomenally expensive. And everyone at Kleiner Perkins was especially interested.

Once you have done the clever intellectual work of setting priorities and identifying promising technologies, how do you gather the information you need? You have already gone to Northern California, naturally now you go to Southern California. Thus in September I found myself at an annual industry conference in Long Beach called "Solar America 2007," and also known as the Attack of the Name Badge People.

The attendance was said to be ten thousand persons, the most ever for this particular conference, and the conference declared itself "sold out." I saw some large fraction of these souls at the conference sessions and on the floor of the trade show as I dutifully visited each booth and tried to get smarter. I did see all ten thousand people Wednesday night at the reception at the Aquarium of the Pacific and was standing behind about five thousand of them in the line for the bar. Not so many appeared to be interested in the fish. The solar people only come out at night? Oh, yeah, there was free food and free booze. But we do all wear our name tags so we can get into the party. And so that when you meet someone you can already see his or her name and the name of his or her company so you know if you really want to talk to them. This is actually quite helpful except when the names on the badge are written like the size of this type-face. And then you have to peer closely into the chest of the party to whom you are speaking, which is not really a good thing to do for so many reasons. But we soldier on, badges on our lapels and business cards at the ready.

We do wonder about whether this is a real industry or not, and how much we are actually going to learn here, when we find that the keynote speaker for the third day of the conference is Larry Hagman. He is old. I have to acknowledge that *Dallas* the TV show was a long time ago, and I did see a couple of episodes, might have been in black and white. He is not so much of a solar or energy expert as perhaps one would wish. He is here, apparently, because he has put some solar panels on his house. And probably because he couldn't make the cut on *Dancing with the Stars*. His solar views are not as sophisticated as one might wish either, to wit, "The price of oil is gonna double, and then so is the price of electricity." Note that we dummies in the electric industry use oil for about 2% of all power generated, as it is too expensive. Hence the price of electricity has precious little to do with the price of oil. Then he said, "I read this book and it says we're gonna run outta electricity in twenty years, done, that's it." Huh? But electricity is a manufactured product, made from something else... oh never mind. Despite these scholarly remarks, certain members of the audience line up to ask him questions, such as: "Do you think we should go beyond net metering rate schedules to tariffs that force utility buyback at average wholesale prices?" and "What do you think the rate of growth in solar panel production over the next five years will be?" Larry does not give convincing answers to these questions. The best question was, "What about you and Barbara Eden?" I guess she was the *Dallas* costar, and I further gather that this question did not refer to whether they played volleyball during breaks in the shooting. Larry's answer was enigmatic.

Despite his strong support for the solar industry, and the location of the conference in Long Beach, the governor of California did not make an appearance, so we did not get a chance to ask him about Barbara Eden and compare his answers with Larry's.

There were approximately five hundred exhibitors at the conference, split about one-third solar cell or panel suppliers, one-third ancillary hardware/software suppliers, one-sixth installers/system integrators, and one-sixth folks who seemed to have wandered into the wrong show (residential wind turbines, for example, lead acid batteries, smart grid hardware, and the University of North Carolina).

First and most important, it was a very disappointing doodad harvest. As we all know, doodad quantity and quality is a very important measure of trade show excellence. There were many, many pens; some Post-it notes; a couple of squeezy rubber things (a yellow star and, of all things, an elephant); no baseball caps; one exceedingly cheap tote bag; no T-shirts; and only one coffee mug. And to get the coffee mug you had to take a survey (Q1: Did you know before coming to this show that Mitsubishi made solar panels? Q6: Are you satisfied with your Mitsubishi solar electric panels?" I am not sure there were right answers but they gave me a coffee mug anyway.) Very little food was being handed out (crappy little hard peppermint candies, Tootsie Rolls, and stuff like that) although at one Italian panel maker's booth they were pushing small cups of red wine along with slices of parmesan and prosciutto. At two in the afternoon. Now I know why we are doing solar in Italy. Their booth was well patronized.

At one booth you got to spin a wheel with symbols of stuff on it, but if you landed on most of the symbols you got nothing. If you won, which I did, you received a bright orange sack, with inside it a rather thin and thus not very air-worthy Frisbee with a printed logo on top saying "Solar is future." I took this to mean, by extension, that syntax is past.

Attendees were mostly middle-aged white guys in casual clothes (60%), young Chinese wearing dark slacks and slightly dazed expressions (20%), aging hippies, the odd person in a dark suit and tie, bright-eyed Indian entrepreneurs, etc., for the rest. Much intense conversation was going on, although by a random sampling it seemed that the visitors to the booths were in many cases trying to sell the booth occupants something, rather than buy what the occupants were interested in selling.

Only a couple of recognizable names were present—GE, Chevron, Mitsubishi, Sanyo, Sharp—and the first two had only very small booths. And the last three had no one who could answer any questions, you had to have some vice president call you back. This was not a problem with just the big guys, however.

A large number of Chinese panel suppliers showed up, usually with very unattractive booths and names like "Taiyuan Shingua Mei Xin Solar Enterprise Unlimited STD" and interesting misspellings, i.e., "Manufacturing Plant in Outer Mongoloian." But no one is immune. The Sanyo people have printed on their business cards: "Think GAIA for Life and the Earth." What in the world does that mean, and who is GAIA anyway, and why does he or she have a name full of capital letters? And how exactly does one "think GAIA?" Maybe they meant "Thank GAIA?" But that doesn't make much sense either.

But even the Americans are starting to run out of good names. I stopped at the booth of a new amorphous silicon solar panel maker with the unlikely name of "xsunx." Someone is already using "Xunlight"— really—so I guess this was the best they could do. But I could not tell if the first X is capitalized or not. Does one pronounce this "icks-sun-icks?" Or "ex-sun-ex"? And why would you want such a name anyway? Why not just call yourself the Jim and Bill Solar Company?

The peculiarly named "Solarfun" company of China has as their US president the equally peculiarly named Ocean Yuan. His real name is

Hai-Yung Yuan which, he assured me, does translate as "ocean." I thought longingly of the days when the Japanese selling stuff in the US all decided to put "Sam" as their first names, regardless of what their real names were. There is also a booth for Canadian Solar. This, too, is a Chinese manufacturer. And no, they didn't get confused about either the name of their country, or where their manufacturing plant actually was; the founder, although indeed Chinese, went to school in Toronto. Well, why not.

But to the substance. Because we are still trying to learn about this stuff, and because this is what you do at trade shows, I went around generally and doggedly asking every panel/module supplier two very hard questions: 1) What is your manufacturing capacity in Mw on an annual basis? 2) If we wanted to buy 10 Mw delivered to Italy in Q3 or Q4 of 2008, would that much supply be available, and what would be the approximate price? I would argue that these are just the kind of questions that a company sales representative who has to sit all day in a trade show booth would want to hear, and for which one would have a rehearsed answer. Or at least a cheat sheet to consult in the unlikely event that someone wanted actually to buy some of your product. But no.

Why are these important questions? The short answer is that all our diligent research, which required reading the trade press and the *Financial Times*, has uncovered the fact that the generous Europeans have put in place large subsidies to be given to anyone, even crass Americans, who show up and build solar plants in sunny places, especially Spain, Italy, Greece, and France. Also Germany, which is about as sunny as Montreal. But very dedicatedly green. And if they are strewing twenty euro notes on the ground in Andalusia and Puglia then it is our duty to our shareholders to bend over and pick up as many of them as we can. But to drive the analogy to its illogical conclusion, the bottleneck is the availability of solar panels. You only get the subsidy in the price you are paid for the solar electricity you make, and you cannot make any without the panels.

The results of my trade show floor research were peculiar, although interesting. In maybe one-third of the cases I got actual answers. These answers were generally 15 Mw to 100 Mw, and the prices uniformly were in the range of \$3.60–\$3.75 per watt for modules only, usually factory gate. This compares, unfavorably, with the price of a coal-fired plant (\$1.00–\$2.00 per watt) although you do have operating costs. In one-third of the cases I was told to call someone else for an answer for this question, but the contact information for the someone else was not provided, as in "You should call our representative in Germany for that information." After a while I got irritated and my feet hurt, so I began to respond, politely, "Well, as it is that I am a potential customer, perhaps you should have your representative in Germany call me." Most folks said that maybe that was possible, although many seemed surprised by such a concept, if not downright suspicious. I choose to interpret this as yet another sign of tight supply, not commercial idiocy, but I could be wrong. Even GE said, "We'll have to talk to our people on the East Coast." Sanyo suggested, "You should call us every quarter and then we'll let you know if anything is available and what the price is." Several of the few knowledgeable people asked what month in the quarter, and allowed as how they were fully sold out for 2007 and 80% sold out for 2008, but for a really good potential customer they could probably squeeze in 10 Mw. One person, but only one person, actually uttered the remarkable words: "I really want your business." I wanted to kiss him.

One-third of the people I talked to were clueless, really. Two examples: Siliken Power (a Spanish panel manufacturer) said, "It is impossible to know the price."

"Ever?" I asked, but got no response other than, "Is impossible."

It is an interesting concept to sell a product where one cannot know the price. How do you know if you have gotten paid enough?

E-Village Solar had a small booth with two attractive blondes sitting in it, each wearing white knit tops that were cut remarkably low for a business function, or for any function not involving fun and games. Despite this, I asked my standard questions. The response: "We don't work for the company, they just hired us to provide information."

"Fine," said I, "what is the information?"

"We don't have any idea what you're talking about," they cheerfully responded, although not in unison.

I saw only two thin film PV manufacturers, and neither was First Solar or Nanosolar, the acknowledged leaders. The first it was a small company located in Tucson called Global Solar; they have a massive 2 Mw of capacity, which would really have to be considered experimental or pilot stage at best. They are building a factory and should have 40–80 Mw in 2009, and they use CIGS technology—a thin film (hence the name) of copper, indium, gallium, and selenium laid down on a substrate, usually glass. The other was the aforementioned Xsunx, who is developing their own amorphous silicon technology, but not using the AMAT or Oerlikon factory in a box—two capital goods manufacturers who have cleverly put together complete manufacturing systems that allow you to be in the solar cell and module manufacturing business, if only you give them money. Xsunx, too, is building a factory and expects to be ready to produce 25 Mw per year starting in 2009. They plan to price at $3.00 per watt.

What do we conclude out of all this rather random information gathering and conference-going experience? That 90% of the players remain focused on rooftops, and the need for legislative subsidies, tax credits, etc. Almost no one is talking about grid parity—producing electricity from PV installations at a price that can compete with other, nonsolar technologies, without subsidy. I even had to explain global warming and the Kyoto Protocol and CO_2 offsets to the Sunpower chief salesperson, who had never heard of them—and these can be generated and sold by every solar installation in a Kyoto signatory country. And Sunpower is really one of the biggest and best of the polysilicon panel manufacturers. And they want to do utility-scale projects.

The few people, mostly from Europe, who understand about the subsidized feed-in tariffs in Spain and Italy are having a devil of a time with the classic question: Who among all the countless small developers has a real project, and who does not? One did mention that Pirelli is getting into the solar project business in Italy. What this has to do with tires we know not.

Polysilicon panel makers are selling everything they can make, but to put on roofs. Charging $3.75 per watt is not competitive at all with thin film pricing—which is currently $2.40 but heading down. No one seems to care at the moment, and everyone is rapidly expanding capacity. There is a real crash coming, or at least a market shakeout. And we are not wrong in focusing on thin film almost exclusively for our panel supply.

One should remember to wear more comfortable shoes when walking the floor at trade shows.

Overall, the strategy we are developing seems to be correct: We need to run as fast as we can in southern Europe to build projects, but we are not too late. And we need to do everything we can to nail down long-term solar panel supply arrangements with thin film manufacturers, who will unquestionably be the panel suppliers of choice for utility scale installations. And we should not hire unknowledgeable blondes to represent us.

Love and kisses, Bob

Afterword: Of our four strategic initiatives, two were unsuccessful. We never found anyone doing anything remotely sensible to capture CO_2 from an exhaust stream, and then put it somewhere. It is startling to note that this was fourteen years ago, and since then people have continued to spend money on this, with nary a success. We spent no capital, just some of our time, and were wonderfully unsuccessful, but at a very low cost. The current status of the "technology" is nowhere.

We did make a small $3 million investment in a coal to gas technology company, but the low price of gas, then and now, never really made this into an economic proposition.

We ventured into storage, stayed after it, and benefited as the auto people pushed the costs of batteries down, what with "megafactories" and the like. The AES storage portfolio and related development activities, led by capable people like Chris Shelton and John Zahurancik, has become an important driver of AES's business strategy going forward today.

As for the results of the solar photovoltaic initiative, read on.

[3]

It's Christmas
So Give Us Some Money

December 2007

Dear Dad,

Why am I here, you may ask, in dark and cold and rainy London two weeks before Christmas? It's not because the shopping is so great. The guy that writes the mysteries known as the 87th Precinct series, Ed McBain, has a line that one of the homicide detectives repeats in every book: "It's always about sex or money." And since we are talking energy here and not mayhem, you can pretty well write off the sex part.

As you may remember from previous letters, I have become or am in the process of becoming . . . Solar Boy! Hero to the carbon constrained, patron saint of the petroleum afflicted, succor to the green, the near green, and the wannabe green. My darling wife, in hardheaded reality, asks why I am the right guy for this after years of being, in her view, "antisolar." I explain patiently (as any good husband would, patience being a virtue) that my views have always been consistent on this matter, to wit, as soon as solar energy makes sense economically, then I shall be all for it. I will admit that ever since I put one thousand solar water heaters on Nashville rooftops when I was at TVA I have been skeptical, given that at least a third of the solar panels were put up facing north or shading each other by the crackerjack installers. It at the very least soured me on the business of putting things on rooftops.

However, three things have changed that make this a much more interesting business now. First, of course, is the fact that oil seems to be expensive and the producers of it all seem to be countries who are not our friends and operate in places where you would not want to take a vacation. Although fine for having a war. As a good energy analyst, however, one has to note that the price of oil is remarkably unconnected to the making and selling of electricity. We haven't used much oil in the electric industry since the first oil embargo in the seventies. But the high oil price does alert people to the general need for alternative sources of energy, hence the slightly disconnected but nonetheless sincere view of the sun. Ah, but you say, haven't I heard this song before? Didn't renewable energy have a big burst of popularity in the late seventies and early eighties, the very period when someone was financing solar water heaters on Tennessee rooftops?

Yes, indeed. We have been popular before, and then we became less popular, and this was largely tied to the fact that oil spiked at about $30 a barrel and then suddenly dropped back down to around $10, taking the price of natural gas with it. The market, darn it, responded to price signals, the OPEC cartel was not able to control production or else chose not to (the Saudi's, mostly, who were then much more the swing producer than they are now), the spigots were opened. People also began to find and deploy substitutes, conserve more, buy smaller cars, momentarily. I even had a diesel-powered Rabbit. But the price drop that persisted through the nineties pretty much screwed the solar business.

Second, we have the legendary and much-heralded global warming. Probably little need for explanation here. If in fact carbon and CO_2 and the other greenhouse gasses are a problem, then burning fossil fuels (which are, of course, hydrocarbons) to make electricity and run cars probably is not a good long-term idea. The science supporting the issue is not terrific, but the problem is increasingly accepted by the political community, as is the need for some action. Supporting and even subsidizing solar energy is a popular policy choice to help cope with this problem, especially in Europe and the US.

Third, and to my way of thinking most important, the technology is in fact getting better and cheaper. This is the result of a lot of federal research support over the years, as well as some significant recent actions in Europe to create subsidized rates at which utilities must buy solar-generated electricity from those of us clever enough to be making it. This is particularly true for photovoltaics, the type of solar machine that has traditionally relied on extremely pure cells of silicon which, when photons strike them, have their electrons dislodged and scoot around. With the proper engineering, these electrons are channeled into circuits and become, voila, electricity. There is more physics to it than that, but not much more. In fact, the propensity of light to create electric current when it strikes silicon is one of the problems in making computer chips, which are also, it turns out, made of this same, "microelectronic grade" silicon. This is much purer than Ivory soap, which was only 99.44% pure, as you may remember from the advertisements, but was not used to make either computer chips or solar cells. One does wonder what the other .56% was, but we digress.

Over the years much work has been devoted to making the crystalline silicon designs cheaper and raising conversion efficiency, the latter being, as you could probably guess, a measure of how much of the sunlight that strikes a cell or a panel actually gets converted into electricity. More is better, in accordance with general American beliefs. Conversion efficiencies are now in the order of 14% to 20% for these cells and panels. This may seem low, but the equivalent measure for the engine in your car is probably 33%–36%, although unless you have done something weird to it your car does not make electricity. I am instead talking about the efficiency of converting gasoline to motion. A final comparison is that we can now get efficiency on the order of 45%–50% in combined cycle natural gas-fired power plants. Which is helpful as natural gas prices continue to rise.

Since I can't help myself—the ardor of the new convert—I should note for completeness that there are also a set of technologies called "solar thermal" that are also used to make electricity. This involves the use of mirrors to focus the sun on a collector, usually a glass tube containing either water or, more often, a "working fluid" like a thick oil. The fluid is heated to a reasonably high temperature, 500°–700°C, and then sent off to a heat exchanger, where the heat in the oil is transferred to water, which makes steam, which is in turn run through a turbine generator to make electricity. And there are naturally losses all through the system as a result of all these transfers and conversions. I do not like these designs, as they violate Hemphill's First Law of Engineering, the "too much stuff" rule, i.e., good engineering design for machinery and plants and processes does not use too much stuff. By the way, nuclear plants are classic examples of a violation of the "too much stuff" rule, as are most coal gasification plant designs. If you think about it, all I have probably done here is reinvent Occam's razor as applied to engineering. I am sure he would be proud, or else sue me for copyright violation.

Last month we put together our thoughts on solar energy to present to the board for their blessing. We have been working on this pretty seriously for a year or so now, so we think we know something, although that is always a dangerous presumption in life. We gave a nice presentation along the lines of the following: solar power plants are just the same as what we have been doing for twenty-five years, but completely different. Let me clarify:

» A coal plant is a big and expensive bunch of machinery.

» Coal comes in and eventually electricity goes out.

» We sell the electricity on long-term contracts to credit-worthy entities.

» Because we have a nice customer, we are able to raise the enormous buckets of money that we need to do all this, then pay back the banks and have something left over for the shareholders.

And the proposed solar biz is the same and different because:

» The sun comes in to our solar panels and electricity goes out of these very same solar panels—the equivalent of all that complex magic and complicated equipment that converts coal into electricity is squeezed here between two thin pieces of glass.

»   We sell the electricity at highly subsidized rates to credit-worthy entities. This is because of two problems: a) the solar panels are still much more costly than a coal plant on a dollars per Mw basis, although prices are coming down, and b) we can't do much with them at night. Thus you get very expensive machinery that only cranks out kilowatt hours at about 20% of this capacity. This is not a recipe for cheapness, especially when coal plants run at above 90% of capacity, in general.

»   This part ("Please, Mr. Banker, give us money!") is the same as above, except that we need even more money as the plants are more expensive.

The differences are pretty interesting:

»   Solar plants are way simpler and quicker to build. We explain this to the board as equivalent to building an electric fence.

»   We don't burn coal or use any water, and thus permitting should be very much simpler. Essentially this is the same as permitting a small strip shopping center, except without the HVAC or plumbing.

»   Everyone loves a long-term contract at a very high price with a very good customer. What's not to like? And such contracts are sadly not the rule in the traditional electricity business anymore. However, the clever and generous Europeans are subsidizing this technology and it is our duty to save the planet and help them spend their subsidy money.

»   Because they are not totally crazy, the Europeans have also said that they aren't going to do this forever, and they expect this subsidy program to help the industry drive prices down. So we need to move quickly while we can.

The board is very pleased, they like this, we have a convincing case, every single board member says something positive about the idea and the work etc., and then they vote unanimously to approve this as a new "line of business," something that is required as a part of our corporate governance.

"Thank you," I say, blithely adding that now they need to give me seven billion dollars. There is a sudden intake of breath. I sense unease. Could it be that I no longer have my audience in the palm of my hand? Hey, I said this stuff was expensive.

"I recommend that, given the giant capital costs of these projects, we get a partner for this new endeavor," I say brightly.

"Yes, partner, good!" is the response. Exit stage left and on to London.

The purpose of the trip is to rendezvous in London with the Carlyle folks who run their renewable energy fund. Carlyle is a very big, private equity group, started in of all places Washington, DC, by some gentlemen who had worked in the government, in the Carter White House. Over the twenty-five years of its existence it has become very big and very successful. The chairman of AES, Dick Darman, is one of the small group of original founders, as well as a good friend from ever since we worked for Elliott Richardson in the old department of HEW. God, that really does date me, doesn't it? Anyhow, Carlyle has set up a new $4 billion fund to do deals in renewable energy technology, and Dick has been nice enough to introduce us to this group so, thinks I, why not? If we are to plunge into the solar biz, it is likely to take a lot of capital and some risk, and maybe we should find some clever folks with money to help us share the risks and reap the benefits. Besides, the board told me to find a partner, preferably one with large piles of money to fling around, and these guys qualify.

I went directly from the plane to their offices in Mayfair in London. Four of us sat around and ate those funny little triangular sandwiches that the Brits make and discussed our plans for the business and why we were pushing such and such a technology and such and such a company, and if we were to do a joint venture with them, what would it look like. It was wonderfully civilized—there was even tea and biscuits, not the America kind of course, what we would call cookies—and we all seemed to get on well. The team are all refugees from BP, a very large and well-regarded oil company formerly known as British Petroleum. Its former CEO, Lord Browne, has also left and is now heading up this Carlyle renewable fund. At one point in the meeting he came in and we exchanged views and pleasantries. He is very British (two of the other three are good old 'mericans) as one would expect of a person whose first name is Lord. He is distinguished looking and has a lovely and elegant accent, as would also befit a lord. He is about the same size that I am, which I think is a good thing. Neither of us is likely to play point guard for the Celtics anytime soon. I think I accomplished my mission which was, of course, to sell them on the scheme and on our obvious capabilities therefore. So they would like us and give us money. We shall see.

And if you happen to find even two or three billion lying around the house in Olympia, maybe left over from the grocery shopping, be sure and let me know as we have a great use for it.

Love and kisses, Bob

Afterword: We were about to play seriously in the nascent solar industry developing in Europe, but playing required money. What was happening in a nutshell: many European countries had decided that global warming was a serious enough problem that steps should be taken to replace coal as a utility fuel with something else. And the something else then in favor was solar. They enacted what were generally called "feed-in tariffs" that provided any solar project built in their respective country a twenty- or twenty-five-year contract at a generous rate. All you had to do was show up, build a solar plant, connect it to the grid, and they payed you. In the case of Spain, it was $.63 per kWh. This was about ten times what we were getting in other settings for making wholesale power. We found this irresistibly attractive, especially as the traditional European utilities, each probably for a different set of reasons, were not interested in this new market.

By March of 2008 we had put together an equity commitment of a billion dollars. We had no projects in construction and certainly none in operation, we had never built a solar plant, and no one on the AES board had ever even seen one. Sometimes things go your way.

When You're In a Gold Rush,
You Should Rush

June 2008

Dear Dad,

Here it is Friday and so it is off to Tel Aviv we go again after a week in Europe trying to establish the solar empire. Came over on Monday evening after a board meeting of the new solar company where the board members asked, reasonably, why we were rushing around trying to build more plants quickly when we might instead try to figure out what we had learned from the first five. I hate it when boards ask sensible questions to which I don't have ready answers, but I guess that is the reason for them in the first place. As you probably remember, Riverstone (recommended to us by Carlyle) is putting up half the money for this venture, and AES the other half. Hence, I have six board members, three of each flavor, and they all have to agree on anything of consequence that I propose to do. So far, they have.

Actually the Riverstone/Carlyle board members have been excellent—involved, quick to respond, sensible, and helpful. I am very lucky, as they are also on point—they don't ask silly questions or wonder why we are not investigating the opportunity to launch a satellite and collect solar power in space and then beam it back to earth on a microwave beam. Yes, that old clunker of an idea is still around—sigh—and resurfaces every time there is a serious price problem with energy. I think I answered letters on this when I was at the Department of Energy many years ago. The only problems with this daffy idea are: 1) It probably costs about a billion dollars a kilowatt. This is far more than even current land-based solar technologies cost by a factor of 10,000, which is saying a lot. Hence it would make $100 per kWh electricity. You currently pay about $.08 a kWh. 2) There is no design to do this, so I am no doubt off on the price by another order of magnitude. Has NASA ever come in under budget? So that's now $1,000 a kWh. 3) My favorite—the idea of a very focused high-energy beam of microwave radiation coming down from a satellite to a ground-based receptor station where it will be changed back into electricity—which by the way is not all that easy to do either, you ever get your microwave oven to make your lights turn on?—means that you had better not have a bird or an airplane fly through the beam or you have exploded goose or cooked passengers. And if you are off just a hair in aiming for the receptor station, then all the neighbors are up in smoke. I do not think that this will improve property values. And never mind the liability insurance. So there.

And on Tuesday we had a long session with the Spanish team on our new projects. But perhaps I get ahead of myself.

We started the business with a nice pipeline of projects, some very favorable government tariffs in selected locations (Spain and Italy principally), a ragtag band of twelve solar believers recruited from both inside and outside AES, and a billion dollars. I have both done and funded start-up businesses before. Usually you have some of the above but funding more like one to three million dollars. AES, for example, started with a million dollars and six of us barely able to spell "electricity." Starting with a billion dollars, twice as many people, but a more complicated word to spell—"photovoltaics"—is more than a fair trade-off. And since I have done this before, I think that I know what to expect. At least I have convinced the investors, bless their hearts, that I know how to do this. We shall see.

Honestly, we don't really have a billion dollars. It does have a nice ring to it, though, doesn't it? What we have is a commitment to invest a billion dollars, $500 million from the Carlyle Group as represented by Riverstone, their affiliate that does energy deals, and $500 million from AES. But if the situation changes or we turn out to be idiots in developing and operating solar plants or one or the other of the two investors falls on hard times, then we don't have a billion dollars, we have, as one says in Yiddish, "bupkis," which when one looks it up in general means nada, although in specific terms it means goat feces. I love Google. We have to perform, and we have to continue to have a supportive environment, and our investors have to remain financially healthy and continue to think that we're cute. Or at least fashionable. On the whole, however, having a billion-dollar commitment from these two entities is way better than less money from less interested persons.

My job as CEO is to make sure that the money goes off and does interesting things that lead other folks to think that we are, at some point, worth way more than a billion dollars. The good news is that Paul Hanrahan, the AES CEO, and I have, in fact, done this before, just not in solar. We did it in China where we did an IPO based on six memoranda of understanding for projects in China, all in a language we couldn't read—Malaysian, no just kidding, Chinese—and none of them legally binding. This was fully disclosed in the cumbersome documents that go along with an IPO that no one thank God reads, at least no investor. Your lawyers read them, in fact they write them, and charge you a pretty penny for this function. We sold a slug of the Chinese company and had at the closing of the IPO a market value of $200 million. We had spent maybe $10 million to get there, and we kept 30% of the company. The math works out to be that we turned, at that moment, $10 million into $60 million and we had not one project built, not one kilowatt hour generated, and certainly not one RMB of revenue received. I love capital markets. Who wouldn't?

This time around we have actual stuff on the ground and being erected very quickly. Soon, we will have 18.8 Mw of power being fed into the grid whenever the sun shines. And if my most recent three days is any indicator, it shines a lot in southern Spain in the summer. Never mind all that *My*

Fair Lady crap about the rains in Spain. Mostly it's sun.

Since this is an interesting new area of business, and since we are making progress in actually building stuff, this week we had two AES board members come over to Spain for a visit, another good reason for me to be there. It was really useful. Sven Sandstrom, a former head of IFC and Phil Odeen, our current board chairman, came to Madrid and were at our disposal for a couple of days. After first giving them a thorough briefing on the solar program in Spain and our plans for the future, we took them around Madrid on Wednesday, meeting with our bank and with the American ambassador.

On Thursday we all got up very early. In Spain they have a quaint custom called "let's eat dinner really late," which probably has a romantic name in Spanish. None of the restaurants are open until nine o'clock, so if you want to eat earlier, forget it. Really, they're just NOT OPEN. I am not sure about McDonald's, but I don't think I should take board members to McDonald's. Besides they're probably not open either. This time thing might be some sort a federal law on restaurant administration, I can't tell. The other quaint custom in Spain is called (by me) the "law of *jamón*." As you no doubt remember from your studies of Spanish at the University of New Mexico when we all lived in Albuquerque, *jamón* is Spanish for "ham." Only in Spain this is not quite the same creature that you find in the US, not what you encounter even if you go to upscale places like honey-baked ham stores. Spanish ham is, thank God, not "sugar cured." Actually since sugar is not a preservative in any food-related situation, nor is it much of a refrigerant, one is at a loss to figure out what exactly "sugar cured" means. Well, the sugar is clear, but what is the nature of the "curing" process? I guess if you have a sugar deficiency you can be cured by the application of sugar, but who in the whole US can possibly have a sugar deficiency, given that the stuff is found in every last prepared food in the grocery store? L has recently been on an "organic" kick so she brought home some expensive upscale "organic" chicken broth in one of those nice square cartons. But when we used it, it tasted kind of sweet. Then we read the label, and the third ingredient listed was honey. Holy tamales! Somebody put honey in "organic" chicken broth? Is nothing sacred? Even if one presumes it is "organic" honey (which ignores the question of how could you make honey that is not "organic" assuming that you use bees and not little flying robots) why would you want sweet chicken broth? I am not quite as rabid on this matter, but even I was pretty stunned by the honey thing. So we fed it to the dogs. They seemed to like it, but were quite hyperactive for a couple of hours thereafter. And given that they are border collies, that is saying a bunch.

Where were we? Oh yes, ham. Spanish ham is by and large air cured and not smoked like most US hams are, nor is it salt cured, which is another way of curing. If you do the research you will find that salt curing is the most prevalent, then smoking. All of this is to draw the moisture out of the pork and make it keep longer at room temperature. Air curing takes longer. No, I don't know why the ham doesn't get moldy and full of deadly bacteria, I need to do more research. What you get is a nice deep red meat, not boiled pink like in "ham sandwiches" at the deli in the US—which they do call boiled ham, and I don't know if it is cured first then boiled, or how it gets that uniform color and mushy texture and tasteless flavor; no wonder someone invented mustard. The *jamón* has striations and layers of fat and actually looks like it could have resided at one time on the leg of a pig, as opposed to having mistakenly emerged from the bubble gum factory, which I am convinced is where they make "Danish" ham.

In Madrid, *jamón* is one of the most prevalent appetizers served at any dinner. Actually as far as I can tell, all the dinners start (when they finally start) with a whole slug of appetizers shared around the table. I suppose this is the same thing as tapas and it is actually nice except if you are a stupid American you eat all the appetizers and don't realize that these seven or ten or fifteen dishes are merely the beginning. But since this is usually accompanied by very good white and red wine, it all seems so chummy and sophisticated that who cares. I have been to dinners in Spain where there were three or four different kinds of ham as part of the appetizers. In truth it's very good, and there are different special names for each kind of ham. My current favorite is *bellota* which means "acorn," which is what the pig eats in this case. It also has to be the famous black

Iberian pig eating the acorns, and no, we don't know who really keeps track of the black pigs running around in the forest and makes sure that they only eat acorns as opposed to grubs, blackberries, and the odd plastic bottle left behind by hikers. Since in all the American literature about rural folk they are forever feeding "slop" to the pigs, one presumes pigs are not fussy eaters. And don't acorns have a season to them, so what does the pig eat in the spring? OK, never mind all that. Anyway, we take our two intrepid directors out for a lovely dinner or two with ham, and it is great. They are both good sports and interested in what's going on, and the Spain team is attentive and communicative and not awed by dealing with directors, so it all goes very well.

On to Granada! When I was in the special forces reserve, and assigned to the Atlantic Command in Norfolk, we used to say this a lot in semi-jest as the evil Cubans had arrived in Granada the island, not to be confused with Granada the site of the Alhambra and capital of Andalusia in southern Spain. We were hot to kick them out, given the Monroe Doctrine and the strategic importance of a Caribbean island with a population of twenty-two thousand folks and an area of probably nineteen square miles and an international runway of five thousand feet, suitable to land Russian helicopters on. If they made it from Minsk. But that was then, and we really did invade the island and kicked off the Cubans who turned out to be merely civil engineers but bent on extending the airfield and creating another Cuban Missile Crisis only this time one presumes with airplanes. And not in Cuba. Otherwise the same.

Our mission to this Granada is different, as we are going to see two of our five solar plants and I don't think there are any Cubans around. Like many things in life, seeing this stuff is far better than trying to describe it in words or even showing people pictures of it. At the risk of descending into the carnal, think about the difference between describing sex to a person, seeing a picture of sex, and having sex. I rest my case, although visiting a power plant is, I am told, not nearly as good as having sex. Personally, I wouldn't know.

We roust everyone out early, take them to the airport, and fly to

Granada. On to the big van/bus thing, and away we go to the first site, called Iznalloz, being constructed for us by a German company called Phoenix. They specialize in solar but I don't understand why they have this name since they are clearly not from Arizona and the mythical bird of the same name kept getting dropped into the fire and being reborn, not the sun.

Some more background—we have five plants in construction in Spain, each small, averaging 3 to 5 Mw. Bear in mind that the current average size for a coal-fired power plant is probably 600 Mw and you will get an indication of relative size. So far, this stuff is small from a utility perspective. But it is very not small from a land use perspective. The first one I ever saw, before we convinced the AES board to let us embark on this adventure, was also in Andalusia. I asked to see a plant in construction, not one of ours as we did not have one yet. I was at least smart enough not to want to go ask the AES board for a bajillion dollars to build a lot of somethings that I had never even seen one of. Our obliging contractor says I can see his 2 Mw site. He takes me into the backwoods of Andalusia, and then off-road along an arroyo. I am sitting there in the car getting hot and dusty and going, "Jeez, I am a big important power executive, they are taking me to this tiny-ass solar site, grump, grump, don't they know what a big deal I am, why couldn't I see something of a normal size."

We come up over a rise in the ground and there, spread out in front of me, for what seems like miles and miles, is row after row after row of solar panels.

"OK," I said to myself, "this is bigger than I thought." And it was, and they are. It is useful to remind oneself from time to time that the sun, while widespread as an energy source, is also very, very diffuse. So you have to use a lot of hardware to collect it and concentrate it into usable amounts of real energy. Our rule of thumb is it takes about 3 hectares per Mw. And since I always have to look up what a hectare is, I will helpfully add that it is 2.47 acres. You may prefer to think of it as 10,000 square meters, or as a square 100 meters by 100 meters—say three football fields side by side, including end zones. So not small and it thus takes nine football fields for us to make one megawatt. Or you may not prefer to think of it that way and just remember when you are a contestant on *Jeopardy* that one megawatt takes ten acres. There, isn't that easier?

We take the board members to our site and (thank goodness) all the workers are wearing hard hats. And lots of panels have been put up, and more are being put up. And the sun is shining. Many pictures are taken, the German site manager and his Singaporean number two give a very good explanation of what is going on, we poke around and everyone likes what they see.In truth it's hard not to like a power plant that can get built in three months—not three years—has no moving parts, no rotating equipment, no hazardous chemicals, and actually no operating personnel. The sun shines down, it hits the panels, the electricity squirts out into cables, and we send it to the purchasing Spanish utility—with whom we have a twenty-five-year contract to take everything that we can produce, whenever we produce it. They are required by Spanish law to take it and to pay us, and the price at the moment is highly subsidized—€.42, which translates into $.65 per kilowatt hour. In comparison, we get paid in other jurisdictions with other technologies anywhere from $.04 to $.12—$.65 is better.

Now the sharp thinkers in the group are probably asking, "Yes, but what does it cost to make the electricity?" Well, also a lot. At the moment the capital is very expensive; probably we will pay around $6,000 per kW. In comparison, I could build a gas-fired combined cycle power plant for under $1,000 per kW, and even a fully emission-controlled coal plant for under $3,000. But that is not all the story. The second bad part is that the sun does not shine at night, and it also does not shine straight down on your panels other than at noon, and the stupid earth insists on having its axis be at an angle other than ninety degrees to the plane of its axis around the sun so we have longer and shorter days. And then there are sometimes clouds. The upshot of all this is that you have a very expensive piece of capital equipment sitting there making electricity the equivalent of 15% to 25% of the time, on an annual basis. This makes the kilowatt hours currently expensive.

Two last points on solar economics: it's getting better. There is reason to believe that as we get smarter about building these, and as the solar panel manufacturers build more efficient factories with higher utilization rates, and as the research raises the efficiency of conversion of the panels, capital costs will come down per kW and thus the cost to make each unit of power will decrease. Oure engineers are working on having the sun shine at night, which would be really helpful, but progress is slow. Second point: this is not really just solar rah-rah and speculation. I cannot name another electricity technology where I can have a long-term contract for the output of a capital item at a guaranteed price, and the replacement of said capital item if required will be cheaper than the original construction price. I do have such a contract for panels.

And yet one final point on the economics of electricity. I am neither a fan for nor a detractor of nuclear power. I worked at TVA for four years and they were a serious nuclear utility, so I know a little about it. What I know is that we don't seem to be able to make it cheaply and safely at the same time. The Russian-designed plants at Chernobyl were cheaper to build than US designs, and the safety results seem clear. There is much talk in the industry of a "nuclear renaissance," which is what it would be since we have not built a new nuke in the US since 1983. Several people are proposing them, however. The most recent public submission that I have seen on costs is for a two-unit plant being proposed by Duke Energyfor a location in North Carolina that already has a nuclear plant there. The estimated costs for this plant have risen to more than $6,000 per kW, and I can promise you that this number is low as they have underestimated construction interest. Makes you feel a little better that your costs are $6K but coming down. And never mind about all that pesky spent fuel storage problem, and the risks of diverting the plutonium, and the risks of accidents, etc.

Fortunately for the board members, they do not have to listen to much of this. The visits end successfully, we fly back to Madrid, and enjoy another evening of *jamón.*

I Visit the Energy Minister of Turkey

Our local partner, a firm called IC in Turkey, where we have a joint venture doing small- and medium-sized hydro plants, called and said that the energy minister wanted us to visit and give him a proposal to build 1,000 Mw of solar energy in Turkey in the next twelve months. It was on a sole-source basis and he would pay a lot for it as Turkey has great sun and was running out of conventional energy. Since I had planned to be in the area anyway, I sat down and put together eight PowerPoint slides in about half an hour. If you know your business and you can spell Turkey this is not hard to do, particularly since you have almost no information to work on, like "Where would this be exactly?" and "Who owns the land?" and "Who buys the power?" and "Who pays the bills?" Little things like that. All solved in the proposal by making grand assumptions. And so off to Ankara I go and my new 1,000 Mw project.

Well, the meeting was not the great success we had hoped for—probably a "seven" out of a scale of . . . a thousand. The minister did not appear to have any clue that he had "asked for" 1,000 Mw, nor did he understand why it would be so expensive. This was made clear in the first several minutes of the meeting. We never got past page two of the presentation—too bad, as it was a pretty nice one if I do say so myself—pictures and all. After this wonderful start, things actually got worse. We heard the traditional line we used to get in China, "You must understand that we are a poor country, we cannot afford these prices, etc." No particular concerns expressed about running out of power. He was not well briefed; he was surprised that Turkey solar resources are not far better than elsewhere in Europe—no, they are about as good as southern Spain and southern Italy. At one point he said, "We have the capacity to generate 350 terawatt hours from solar." This is a nonsense number that someone who doesn't know anything told him and he unfortunately remembered. Yes, I replied, but that would require putting collectors on every square kilometer of the country, and then all the people here would have to move to Bulgaria. I don't think he was amused.

The last two-thirds of the meeting were conducted entirely in Turkish between the minister and Firat, our partner from IC. Afterward Firat told me that they had discussed some scheme that I did not fully understand that would have the government change a law, whose result would be that AES would avoid $100 million of acquisition fees for some wind sites, and then we could apply this to a demonstration solar site to get the cost down. I am completely unclear on what he meant or how this would work. Firat did say that we would need to brief the prime minister on this and that his father would need to be involved. I think that the minister wants some solar project—maybe 50 or 100 Mw—but he doesn't want to pay for it. But I really could not tell. Perhaps I am not cut out for sales.

What about solar panel manufacturing?

One part of our strategy for world dominance through solar electricity is to focus on what are called "thin film" panels. Solar technology, like everything else in the world, is more complicated than it looks, once you get to the second level. There are basically two types of panels at the moment: ones made of the pure, refined silicon, and a second variety made of a thin film of photo reactive or "semiconducting" metals. This can be either a cocktail of cadmium and telluride (an oxide of the element tellurium or a ski town in Colorado, take your pick), or a mixture of four metals—copper, indium, gallium, and selenium. The former are called "cadtel" panels by us experts, and the latter are usually abbreviated as "CIGS." Both of these basic formulations were developed at one of the DOE national labs, the one called the National Renewable Energy Lab in Golden, Colorado, where your tax dollars have been happily at work since it was established during the first energy crisis in the late seventies. The lab guys not only work on solar stuff, but on wind, geothermal, ocean or wave power, etc. Budgets for all this declined precipitously in the 1985 to 2000 period, but they have developed some good things, most especially the two thin film technologies. These technologies are quite similar, and they share the same advantages and disadvantages.

As a baseline, it is useful to understand the manufacturing process for pure silicon panels. First you take sand, since it is largely silica, which is silicon dioxide, which is fortunate since you were looking for silicon anyway. Oh, yes, this is also the third most widely distributed element in the world, I think maybe only nitrogen and oxygen are more plentiful, so it would seem a real head start. The problem is that silicon only works as a semiconductor and generator of electricity when it is quite pure, "eight nines" as the fabricators say, or 99.999999% pure, which sand ain't. Hence a complicated and expensive refining process involving melting, remelting, adding reactants, creating differential cooling, and so forth. Suffice it to say that this is very capital intensive and in fact quite electricity intensive. The result is an ingot that looks for all the world like a loaf of Wonder Bread, except it's an unattractive smoke-grey color and about two feet long.

This ingot is then cut into thin slices, and after some front and back contacts are pasted on, you have your basic silicon solar cell. The refining process makes this into "polycrystalline silicon" but I am not sure exactly why this is important. The cells are then arranged in a metal frame, connected together, covered top and bottom with glass, and you have a solar panel. At least you have a solar panel made of polycrystalline silicon. This panel, depending a little on how the connections are made and how the cells are treated, has a conversion efficiency of 14% to 16%, which means it turns somewhat less than one-fifth of the energy of the sun that hits it into actual usable electricity. But it is expensive because the silicon is expensive to make, and because you use, comparatively speaking, a lot of it. You can only cut the slices off the ingot so thin, or you lose structural integrity. In human speak, this means they break. And all the processing is not as automated as one would have thought. There is much transferring the cells between stages by stacking them up and putting them on little carts and rolling them to the next machine and putting them into the machine one by one by hand. And not just in China, also in Frederick, Maryland, where I have been through the BP solar panel facility. Not nearly as high tech and full of robots as one would have thought. All this explains the high cost and, to my way of thinking, the limited likelihood of cost reductions for this technology. You just can slice this stuff only so thinly.

The thin film alternative is complicated but in a different way. You use what are printing techniques to put down the active chemical mixture very thinly on a substrate, which is a fancy name for a big roll of thin plastic. There are three or four different technologies for doing this— screen printing, evaporation, chemical deposition, etc.—and the jury is still out on what the winners will be. We have placed our bet on screen printing, but on a big roll, while it is moving rapidly down a line. I have attended several board meetings and it is not easy to tell how the process is going or when they will have a commercial product that we can use. The key is getting the material to lay evenly but very thinly on this fast-moving sheet of plastic. It is more difficult than we originally thought. This last sentence could perhaps apply to 50% of all human experience, but that doesn't make me any happier.

By the Way, Bulgarian Fashions

I stopped in Sofia, capital of Bulgaria, on the way back from Turkey. When I checked in to the standard, undistinguished, boring, business-friendly Hilton on a Wednesday about four, the entire lobby had been taken over by a stage and runway and lighting and sound system for a fashion show, and you could barely wedge yourself past the cables and fixtures and mysterious black sound equipment to get to the check-in desk. There was loud music ("Can I have a room on an upper floor, please?"), there were young women with very elaborate eye makeup—I had no idea you could have two-inch-long eyelashes—strutting up and down the runway, hips jutting forward, while a guy in very tight jeans and what I presume was a fashionable T-shirt (black with silver overprinting of what might have been a picture of Charlemagne if he were Bulgarian, which I do not believe he was) shouting orders or coaching or compliments over a handheld megaphone, just like I used to use when I was a coxswain on the Trumbull College intramural crew at Yale. Some technologies don't change.

"What's this?" I asked, since the logo behind the stage said "Triumph," which I know only to be a motorcycle or an obsolete Brit sports car or the title of a movie about black soldiers in the Civil War—no, wait, that was *Glory*—and none of these choices coincided with thin twenty-year-old women doing *America's Next Top Model* knockoffs in Sofia.

"Is fashion show," helpfully explained the desk clerk, which information was not in fact helpful.

"What kind?" I asked. Although in truth there aren't that many kinds of fashion shows, and I don't think Yves Saint Laurent has been here lately, especially as he is dead.

Calmly the clerk said, "Bulgarian design ladies' underwear."

Sadly, Aneliya Erdly, our very capable country manager, had with a great lack of cultural understanding arranged a dinner with several power plant developers for the same time as the show, so we will never know what cutting-edge Bulgarian design ladies' underclothing looks like. Maybe they have a website.

Love and kisses, Bob

[5]

India Has Fascinating Caves and Less Fascinating Banks

March 2009

Dear Dad,

Why do I always wait this long to make important decisions? Why have I waited until the doggone tournament is almost starting to make my picks? I already gave my five dollars to Leith Mann, the corporate secretary at AES as well as betting pool administrator, but I didn't give her my picks—and I can't really find a bracket form that I can fill out and send in. The alternative is electronically listing game by game who wins, in an email, which is a little, umm, tedious. Besides there's probably now some Sarbanes-Oxley requirement that office betting pools be disclosed to shareholders and the top five winners have their winnings added to their salary and duly taxed.

This is the beginning of March Madness, the important NCAA college basketball tournament, for goodness' sake. Not everyone thinks this is important, or even interesting, but nations all have peculiar customs. In India, for example, they have some exotic holidays that no matter how much you read about them you cannot make sense of, like Holi, where celebrators go around and throw (or blow?) colored powders, like fine chalk dust, all over each other and innocent bystanders. Why? Is this toxic? Does it wash off? This is a "celebration of spring." Which of the pantheon of Hindu gods, or of the numerous Buddhist bodhisattvas, or of the nine incarnations of Vishnu does this refer to? Who is the god of colored powders? Maybe it's talcum powder and not chalk dust. As so often in India, there are questions and there are not answers.

One year in March I found myself in western Australia during this crucial annual period, in the primitive times before email, if you can remember back that far. I couldn't even find the brackets anywhere, listing who was in the tournament and who was playing whom. And the Perth *Herald* really didn't care. The faxed copy that someone kindly sent me was unreadable because the print was so small. So I sent a fax back to Leith and said, "The team whose name starts with the later letter of the alphabet wins." Thus Duke beats Arizona, but loses to Kansas, for example. Actually I did quite well, and came in third out of more than a hundred entries. Unfortunately I picked Xavier to win everything.

I am informed that there is also a school of betting in the tournament wherein you determine the mascot of each team and then you pick whoever's mascot would beat the other mascot. If it's the tiger vs. the jackrabbit, no problem, although I don't know any teams with a rabbit for a mascot. The Fighting Rabbits of South Alabama? But what if it's not so clear? What if you're the Tennessee Volunteers vs. the Duke Blue Devils? Or the Portland Sea Dogs vs. the Oklahoma Sooners? What is a sooner, anyway? Does he or she beat a sea dog, but what is a sea dog? This system is too complicated. I think I shall have to tell her to go with the seedings in each bracket, and then for the final four probably the good old alphabet strategy again.

Why is this important other than the potential loss of five precious dollars? Why can't I just sit down, print out the brackets, and walk over to Leith's office and hand them to her, on one of those few days when I am in town? If you are reading carefully you will have noticed several casual mentions of India above, which may seem mystifying taken in context. Here is the secret: I am about to arrive in India for a ten-day visit, to join a US-sponsored solar trade mission and to spend a couple of days doing something I have always wanted to do, which is visit the rock carvings in the caves of Ajanta and Ellora in the state of Maharashtra. Thus here I am in an airplane soon to land in Mumbai, fretting about college basketball rather than cultivating the calm and ethereal world view that we Americans usually associate with Indian religion, about which of course we know nothing. "The Buddha teaches that everything is nothing, or slightly more."

Friday, Mumbai: the last time I came here it was pretty gritty—crowded airport, you were assaulted the moment you got to the terminal, lots of people importuning you to take their taxis or to let them carry your bags, the arrival hall poorly lit and not all that clean, many officials in various kinds of uniforms standing around mostly doing nothing that one could determine. So when I arrived last night I did not have high expectations. However . . . it is much, much better—new building, polished marble floors, quick baggage delivery, luggage trolleys readily available without people offering to sell them to you even though they are free, everyone not directly involved with traveling kept outside by very serious-looking Indian army soldiers with very serious-looking automatic weapons with twenty-round magazines inserted. I remind myself that this is the city where the Pakistani terrorists killed a bunch of people in November, so you can appreciate the security. It still smells slightly smoky and spicy, and it's still hot outside and muggy, but we are after all in the tropics, even if it is only March.

I am staying near the airport at a Grand Hyatt that is lovely. But I know little of Mumbai geography except that the city is on the ocean and it rains like a bastard during the monsoon season, which fortunately this is not. In a recent year Mumbai recorded in one twenty-four-hour period one meter of rain. Yes, 39.37 inches if I remember my high school math correctly. Needless to say, things broke down, even in a city used to rain.

My plan for the day is to do a warm-up cave in Mumbai, then the big deal ones the next two days. Plus, naturally, I have a business meeting since the business is, after all, paying the freight on this trip. There are a series of five rock caves on an island called Elephanta in the Mumbai harbor. The concierge explains that one goes to the Gateway of India next to the Taj Mahal Hotel, both of which sit on the seaside, and then one gets a ferry out to the caves. It takes an hour to get from the hotel to the Taj, and a half hour on the ferry to the caves, I am informed. This, of course, is not true. Well, the geography is true but the Mumbai factor must be applied to the timing, i.e., double it or maybe on a really good day multiply it by one and a half times.

This is a subset of what I subsequently detect in many dealings in India, which is the wish not to displease, or maybe it is the view of how things should be vs. how they are. A number of times during the trade mission we asked reasonable questions like "How long will it take the tax office to grant us the land allocation?" since solar plants, although they do have many virtues, do have to be put somewhere, generally on a piece of land. The answer inevitably is "It will be no problem" or "It will be done immediately" or "There is no difficulty." In the south this is even accompanied by that weird bobblehead doll sort of head waving that is disconcerting, although a sign of respect. At least they tell the Americans it is a gesture of respect; who really knows?

The cab ride to the Taj Hotel/Gateway of India is in fact one hour and forty-five minutes although the distance is maybe twelve kilometers but it's OK as you get a lot of time to check out the urban surroundings. And you are generally moving slowly enough so that you can read every sign and observe the dress and activities of every person you pass, sometimes several times if they are walking in the same direction as your cab, since walking is frequently faster. At various points one is approached not by beggars, but by kids attempting to sell books to the passengers in the cars. This is a bit novel. And the book selection is limited: *Slumdog Millionaire* (no surprise there), Obama books, and Paulo Coelho books in Italian. Really.

Observation number one: There are still a lot of people in India, and they still walk not only on the sidewalks but also in the street, and apparently much business is still conducted on the sidewalks. However, many,

many of them no longer ride bicycles, but have upgraded to motorbikes and motorcycles. It's always hard to notice what is not there, but what is not there in Mumbai is bicycles. In terms of economic development, this is a good sign. In terms of air quality, not so much.

Observation number two: It is nice to know English, and even though we blame the British for much bad stuff, the fact that they unified India via language is very important. You can read all the signs. Again, things not seen. Traveling through China or Saudi Arabia or even Italy is much different as you cannot easily figure out what the signs say. Mumbai is said to be the commercial capital of India, and all the signs reinforce this. The financial system has been opened up to competition, and what you notice for sure is that there are now a ton of banks—Axis, Advantage, Avancis, I stop trying to keep track after the *A*'s—all with billboards, where there were only a handful of state-owned banks before. And cell phone networks—Indiphone, Virgin, ALLTEL, Tata phone, both international carriers and a lot of Indian carriers. And Indians have clearly adopted this technology every bit as much as Euros and Americans. Which is good, as my BlackBerry works everywhere I go. More than I can say for Japan.

Observation number three: The ones that don't have motorbikes go everywhere in three-wheeled small motorcycle vehicles, which one might call "rickshaws" except that this ain't China; and that are called "tuk-tuks" in Bangkok; but here are called "autos," which is short for "auto-rickshaw." They are open on the sides but have shiny curved black carapaces covering the driver and the two or three or four passengers. In Mumbai they are exclusively shiny black and look for all the world like large beetles scurrying through the traffic.

Observation number four: We blame the British, which is always handy since they're mostly not here to defend themselves. The traffic is obviously up, but the roads are the same as they've always been. And so we get the "four lanes of traffic on a two-lane road" phenomenon. Lane striping is for reference only, although we don't know reference to what. Spacing between vehicles—side to side, front to back—is way closer than I am comfortable with, and it's not even my car. Much lane changing and darting about. Fortunately all the animals that I remember from before, sacred cows and all that, seem to have figured out that walking droopily down the road is not a survival strategy here. Plus there's almost no vegetation to eat, so why bother? There is now a Mumbai subway, and I briefly contemplate going really native and taking it, but wisely decide no. Besides, there's no station near the hotel.

Observation number five: On the tour boat over to Elephanta, it is mostly Indians—families, couples, stray adults—and four other westerners. The westerners are a mom; a spiky-haired twentysomething boy; and two twentysomething girls, one in a completely inappropriate pinafore with plunging neckline and cell phone surgically attached to her ear, and the other a fat girl (sorry, there's no way around this, it was a fat girl) with blonde hair with blue tips—yes blue—also wearing blue leggings. I do not believe that *Vogue* or even Helen Gurley Brown (is she even still alive? Goodness it's been a long time since *Sex and the Single Girl*) would approve. Plus aren't leggings hot? I have not recently worn teal blue leggings so I would not know. The three young persons have very dark eyebrows, are talking loudly, poking each other, manically changing seats, eating small foil-wrapped cheese squares, and casually throwing the trash into the harbor. Since I have had the bad judgment to sit across from them on this very small boat that is moving very slowly and with occasionally disconcerting tippy-ness toward the island, I get to observe far more of this than I want. And I cannot quite figure out the language, although it sounds sort of like Italian with a German accent. Finally I ask them where they are from, and they tell me Bucharest. Romanians are the new Germans.

The island is modest sized and green and quite hilly; as we finally approach we see that there is a long straight concrete jetty leading out from the base of the island to the place where the boats dock. Weirdness we cannot blame on the Brits: running along the jetty to the point where the path to the caves starts is a narrow-gauge railroad track. And, lo and behold, sitting on these tracks is a kid's amusement park sort of Toonerville trolley, a little engine painted red and blue as if it were a real train, pulling a series of open passenger carriages. For ten rupees (twenty cents at current exchange rates) you can ride the massive distance of maybe two hundred yards from the boat dock to the path. And since there is no roundhouse, the engine pulls on the trip in and pushes on the trip out. And makes a lot of nasty diesel smoke each way. I elect to walk.

The caves are not located conveniently at the train stop. Possibly because the carvers did not anticipate the jetty and the train, which does mean that their powers of vision were limited. The caves are, in fact, about two-thirds of the way up the hill. The path up to the caves from the base of the hill is paved, with a series of steps and then a flat landing, then more steps, etc. The guidebook says that one should be prepared to climb a lot of steps, although really it's not that big a deal. The path is covered over with the ubiquitous blue polyester tarps that have replaced the red and blue and white striped tarps and bags that one used to see everywhere in Asia. What the guidebook does not say is that this is something like an Indian version of the (North American) Indian version of running the gauntlet. The path is bordered on each side by wall-to wall-souvenir stands. And rather than leanly muscled (North American) Indians wanting to hit you with clubs, we have languid south continent Indians wanting you to buy stuff. Except it's hot and most of the pilgrims on the path are Indians who are clearly not in the market, so the focus is on us few westerners, but even that is desultory.

The good news is that one is in shade, sweating and laboring up the hill, and trying to be polite in declining the offers to buy postcards, replicas of the Taj Mahal (why here?), images of Ganesha the elephant-headed deity not found in these caves, African-looking carvings (did giraffes really live here, or Masai warriors?), T-shirts that at least seem to have Shiva's image and say "Elephanta Island" and the like. I fantasize briefly about suggesting to the hawkers that the Romanians are really rich, but desist. The one disappointment is that, as usual, no snow globes. If there had been an Elephanta Island snow globe with the image of Shiva inside it I would have bought one for sure, or even five. Or a Shiva coffee mug. But no luck.

Even with all this reasonably routine and predictable commercial stuff, there is something worthwhile here. The island was discovered by and named by the Portuguese. We pause momentarily to think about the concept of "discovered." The caves are clearly a man-made feature. Some

Indians carved them. I don't want in the least to sound like a granola-eating, earth-shoe wearing (do they still make earth shoes? Never mind), bleeding-heart, politically correct one-worlder, and in fact I am a rapacious capitalist with reasonably strong first world credentials, but didn't the guys who were doing the carving, and the folks who came here subsequently to worship, already know it was here? Were they blindfolded? You can see the darn island from the shore of the bay, how hard was it to discover? I don't want to descend into the swamp of semantics but to say that the Portuguese "discovered" it seems strange. Tombs buried in the sands of Egypt that no one had heard of or seen or visited for two thousand years, yes, them you can "discover." Big fat islands in the middle of a harbor, I don't think so.

And let's not start on Columbus discovering America. It is also interesting to note that the reason that it is named Elephanta is that when the Portuguese first landed here they found a large sculpture of an elephant sitting near the shore. Which they then threw into the bay, history does not say why or even how, since this would not have been easy to move. They subsequently used the images in the caves for target practice. Lovely people.

The caves are great. Actually they are remarkable, although only cave number five is spectacular. It seems that these were not really caves; they might have been small crevasses in the rock of the island, and for some reason not known, resources were mustered to go in, dig and carve out the rock, and create sanctuaries with elaborately carved pillars supporting the cave roof, and then along the sides and back of this rectangular and generously sized space, probably fifty meters wide by fifty meters deep by at least twelve to fifteen feet high, are a series of Hindu religious carvings. In the back at the center is a twelve-foot-tall carving of Shiva with three faces: the serene face, the instructive face, and the contemplative face. Because this is a large and deep sculpture, but essentially a bas relief, it is said that the fourth face is in the stone and is the scary face. Just as well not to be able to see it.

We now pause for a moment of religious contemplation. The Hindu religion is hard to figure out. I think about what venture capitalists call the "elevator pitch." Say you want to start a company, you have a great idea or technology or both, and you find yourself in an elevator with the head of Kleiner Perkins or Sequoia Capital. You have him for thirty seconds. Unless he pushes the "emergency" button. How do you explain your business? Nice concept, and I would argue that religions probably need an elevator pitch. For Christians, the Apostles' Creed works— "I believe in God, the Father Almighty, maker of heaven and earth, and in Jesus Christ his only Son our Lord, etc." I have not timed this but I think you can get through it in thirty seconds. Add the Ten Commandments and the Golden Rule, and you've got it. So what is the elevator pitch for the Hindu religion? Or for being a Buddhist? I cannot tell, and I have been hanging around the Orient for some time. Not that there aren't second and third level confusions—in Christianity there are saints and martyrs and apostles and really nice guys like Johnny Appleseed, no wait, I don't think he's a religious icon. But it's hard to understand the basics of being a Hindu.

There's Shiva, the creator and the destroyer, although probably not simultaneously; and there's Vishnu; and there's Ganesha with his elephant head who is the son of Shiva I believe; and there's Shiva's wife Parvati, even though Shiva is sometimes a woman; and there's the guy in Sri Lanka, Ravana, who has twenty heads and twenty arms and keeps trying to bring down the whole enterprise. Perhaps he is mad as he has not been invited to G20 meetings, for which he is obviously suited. He could hold them all by himself. And we haven't even gotten to the Buddhists and the difference between Mahayana and Theravada and Hinayana Buddhism. And what about the Jains and the Sikhs? And never mind the Muslims, they don't much like graven images. Although they're a clear factor in Indian history, since they conquered something like half the place, they are not found in the caves. It's confusing without a playbook.

Because I am curious, and because 950 million Indians can't be wrong, I research this briefly on Wikipedia. Initial description of Hinduism:

Hinduism is the predominant religion of the Indian subcontinent. Hinduism is often referred to as Sanatana Dharma, a Sanskrit phrase meaning "the eternal law," by its adherents. Hindu beliefs vary widely, with concepts of God and/or gods ranging from panentheism, pantheism, monotheism, polytheism, and atheism with Vishnu and Shiva being the most popular deities. It is formed of diverse traditions and types and has no single founder. Other notable characteristics include a belief in reincarnation and karma, as well as personal duty, or dharma.

I have to pause to look up "panentheism," which means, according to a Bible website, "essentially a combination of theism (God is the supreme being) and pantheism (God is everything). While pantheism says that God and the universe are coextensive, panentheism claims the God is greater than the universe and that the universe is contained within God." So now you know.

Further research only clarifies that there are many, many forms of this religion, which perhaps explains why us westerners cannot effectively encapsulate it. Again we quote:

The characteristic of comprehensive tolerance to differences in belief and Hinduism's dogmatic openness makes it difficult to define it as a religion according to the traditional Western conceptions. Although Hinduism is a clear practical concept to the majority of adherents, many expressed a problem arriving at a definition of the term, mainly because of the wide range of traditions and ideas incorporated or covered by it. Sometimes referred to as a religion, Hinduism is more often defined as a religious tradition. It is therefore described as both the oldest of the world's religions and most diverse in religious traditions.

Given some of the results of the history of Christianity (quod vide, the Inquisition) perhaps "comprehensive tolerance to differences in belief" and "dogmatic openness" are not such bad things.

One other interesting note: there are a lot of monkeys around the caves, and they are tame enough that you can approach them. There are many signs saying in what I believe is clear English: "Do not bother or tease the monkeys. They will bite you." Taking this as a challenge, several of the westerners do in fact tease the monkeys—holding out food, pulling it back. I watch with interest, rooting for the monkeys, but unfortunately no one gets bitten. None of the many Indians, including the small kids, teases the monkeys. Perhaps their English is better than that of the westerners.

Having done the caves, I return to the real world and go to a meeting with a bank in order to beg for money. Naturally I am late, but not horribly late. Yes √ Bank (the logo has a square around the check mark but I am not sufficiently skilled to reproduce this on my computer, alas) is one among the wave of new banks enabled by liberalized Indian banking legislation. Fortunately they do not seem to have bought any crappy US mortgages given by banks in a fit of kindness to people who cannot make the payments, and then sold on to sucker banks who do not understand what they have bought, so they have money to lend. Great—I am a potential borrower.

Small world department: the head of the bank, one of the bankers I am meeting with, has been a banker for a while, and while we are busy each discussing credentials, he mentions that he led a tranche of the financing of the first big foreign-developed power plant in India, Dabhol. If there are two names everyone in the business community knows about with regard to India, it's Bhopal, where Union Carbide poisoned a bunch of people in 1984; and Dabhol, a big Enron project of the early nineties that ran afoul of the weirdness of Indian religious-based politics. The financing for Dabhol, which was an enormous accomplishment at the time, made all of us at AES very envious. This fine gentleman remembers the Enron team, many of whom I know, positively of course. Dabhol was a 2,400 Mw gas-fired power plant and several billion dollars, and I am only talking about a 5 Mw solar plant and maybe twenty million dollars, so we all agree this is easier. The bank is trying to carve a place for itself as a leader in financing for renewables and has enough lending capacity to do the whole project without bringing in another bank. So this turns out to be a very good meeting, although really, most first meetings are pretty good. Then again, see below.

The guidebooks blithely say that the Ajanta and Ellora caves are "near" Mumbai. So I don't bother to look on a map, but when I check with the concierge—"Can I just take a taxi?"—he looks at me as if I were daft. You can take a cab but it's a ten-hour drive over bad roads. The caves are near Mumbai as Aroostook County in northern Maine is near New York City.

Aha. And the caves are really not "near" each other, either. It turns out that you have to fly to Aurangabad, visit one on Saturday and one on Sunday, and then come back to Mumbai. Good thing I am flexible. And as usual, you have to get up at zero-dark-thirty to catch the plane. Which I do.

Arriving in Aurangabad one notes a very lovely and new and spacious airport with one— count them, one—plane there, that being the one that I am on. Well, you get your bag pretty quickly. I check into the Ajanta Ambassador Hotel, an actually decent hotel but not a Four Seasons. The restaurant menu, when I eat there later, offers lobster thermidor, chateaubriand, and chicken in a basket, all on the "Western food" page. I stick with the Indian items. However, as promised, they have a car and a guide ready, so I pee and wash my hands, scoop up a bottle of water, and off I go. Old India rule: always use the bathroom when available, always carry your own bottled water. This may be a universal rule for travel outside of everywhere but maybe Switzerland.

So, the caves—first you drive two hours outside of the city, at a moderate rate of speed over decent two-lane roads, but now that we are not in Mumbai you do see oxen and oxcarts and bullocks and assorted rural stuff, but not so much people. Well, that's relative, there are still lots of people but nothing to compare to Mumbai. Hold it, Mumbai is a city and this is the countryside—dang, that explains it, cities have more people! It's pretty flat and brown as we are only a month away from the monsoon season. This is cotton country and nut orchards and so forth. And as we are on the Deccan Plateau, the largest basalt outcropping in the world I am informed by Ram, the slightly portly and balding guide, the hills all look like they have flattops. We would call them mesas in the Southwest but they don't have steep sides. Very interesting. At one point we pass a caravan of probably twenty oxcarts loaded with a lot of people and a lot of stuff. This is migrant workers going on to the next location for agricultural work, say Ram. OK, they really do look poor. And like so much of Indian culture, the poorest folks have the darkest skins. Sound familiar?

The caves are hidden in a horseshoe canyon, about halfway up the side of the outer canyon wall, and not actually very visible from anywhere but the top of the canyon on the other side of the stream, the Waghur River, which formed the canyon, and which at this time of the year has zero water in it. These were discovered, well I would say "rediscovered," by a Brit named Captain Morgan of the Madras Regiment in1819. He was, of course, out hunting tigers rather than searching for cave-based religious art. He probably told someone, but it was another seventy years before they really came to the notice of the world at large. And they are wonderful! There are about thirty, and like Elephanta, they are caves that only exist because artisans came in and carved caves out of the solid rock. And this all happened in the 700 BC to AD 400 time frame. Since that was the heyday of Indian Buddhism, the iconography is all Buddhist. And apparently a series of rulers had these carved over time, each one trying to have a bigger shrine/monastery than the former ruler. Is this really what the lord Buddha taught us, or is this yet another example of the well-known human (and perhaps male) trait of "mine is bigger than yours?" Why here? It is a peaceful setting except for the Indian schoolkids, but not especially dramatic. There are no answers, of course. About three-fourths of the caves were actually used as small monasteries, and have rooms, small cells really, carved in the side walls for monks. The remaining caves are higher and more church-like and were clearly places of worship. Most of the caves have reasonably well-preserved paintings on their walls of incidents in the life of Buddha. Without a guide this would be hard to interpret, and it's not so easy with a guide. And there are many statues of Buddha, large and small, throughout the caves. In one of the sanctuaries there is a seventeen-foot-long reclining statue that takes up much of one wall. It is all wonderful and impressive, and not at all crowded. There are few westerners, maybe five, in addition to me. No Romanians.

After three or four hours of cave viewing and walking up and down steps and along the paths of the canyon wall, one is hot and tired and hungry. There is a grubby restaurant at the entrance to the canyon. Ram recommends that I not eat the food, but says the cold drinks are OK. So I order a beer and they bring me a large Fosters, one of the fine beers of Australia, along with a plate of *papadums*, the crispy tortilla-like crackers made with lentil flour that do in fact go well with beer. I gratefully drink the lager and consider several things.

Consider number one: no one in India seems to smoke. The hotels all have no smoking floors, but you see almost no one on the street smoking. And it is forbidden in all the restaurants. I can't remember if I ever noticed this before, but it is really remarkable. And very different from China, where just about everyone smokes.

Consider number two: the restrooms are uniformly reasonable, even out in the sticks like where I am. This is a definite change. I routinely carry toilet paper with me, but this has not even been necessary.

Consider number three: I have ordered nothing but Indian food, and I continue to do so the whole trip, but it seems less spicy than I remember. Can this be, or have my taste buds just burned out?

As I am now out of beer, we head back for Mumbai. However, along the way Ram insists on stopping and showing me two other "sights." The first is the mausoleum of Aurangzeb, a Muslim ruler of this area at some time in the past that I can't quite understand, who named the town after himself. The tomb isn't very impressive, but the story is nice. It seems that late in life King Aurangzeb adopted a modest style of living and insisted that when he died he should be buried in a very simple manner. And he was. In the 1920s Lord Curzon was the British ruler of the country. He heard about this and insisted that this was not an appropriate burial for such a great ruler, and had it rebuilt in a much more grandiose fashion. I am bemused to see that outside the tomb, which Ram informs me is a Muslim area, the refreshment shops are selling Mecca Cola.

Closer to town we make one last stop, this time at another tomb which, Ram says, is a "small version" of the Taj Mahal. Well, it is, except it is made of plaster and not gleaming white marble, and the four minarets on the corners are too tall so the proportions are off, and it doesn't sit on the edge of a river so it somehow doesn't have the majesty of the original since you can see a bunch of the city behind it. What we have here is the K-Mart version of the Taj Mahal.

The Ellora caves, the next day's target, are only an hour outside of town, in a different direction. These did not have to be rediscovered by any tiger hunters, as they are much more accessible from the plain. There are about thirty-six of them, more spread out than Ajanta, carved later, and in three distinct groups—a set dedicated to the Jain religion, one to the Hindu religion, and a Buddhist set. There are no wall paintings, but much more elaborate carvings, which I actually like better. Probably the best one is the Hindu cave that really isn't a cave at all, but a massive three-story monument cut into the hillside and carved entirely out of one original piece of rock. Ram informs me that it is larger than the Parthenon and indeed it is pretty darn big. It is elaborate, with carvings of Hindu deities everywhere, on every surface. Some carvings are eroded but most are not. It is a stunning site, and I spend an hour just wandering around remarking at the elaboration and the beauty and the effort that went into creating all this—the rooms, the bridges and porticos, the sculptures large and small. Building it from the ground up, with large chunks of rock, would have been remarkable enough, but to carve it literally from the top down is truly a wondrous accomplishment. And again only two or three other west-erners are here. This in itself is completely worth the trip.

I fly back to Mumbai from the still completely empty airport, empty except for the one plane going back to Mumbai. After all, I have a trade mission to go on. I am a little sorry to leave as Aurangabad is a nice, relatively clean, and pretty modern town. King Aurangzeb would be pleased, except for the tomb thing.

What exactly is a "trade mission" you're probably asking yourself, since I don't believe they have them in the US Air Force. It wasn't clear to me either, but now that I have been on one, here is the short version. The organizer, in this case the commercial attaché at the US embassy, decides on a particular theme, makes up an itinerary of places to visit and people to talk to, and then somehow assembles a group of American companies to come and see what the business opportunities are in his neck of the woods.

For us this meant solar energy, and we ended up with a group of eleven companies. Some were developers like us, interested in building and oper-ating plants in India and selling electricity here; most of the rest were suppliers of one sort of another, interested in selling things to Indians who were interested in building solar plants. It was, to be honest, a sort of a mixed bag, with the participants being by and large the sales and business development people. I was initially not keen on participating, but I am glad that I did. The principal value was the meetings with senior energy and renewable energy ministry officials, federal and state, that the embassy had set up in each location. It would have been difficult for us to access these gentlemen on our own, and being with an official delegation made it all easier and somehow more, well, "official."

We have been working in India for more than a year, with a very good guy named Srinivas Nagabhirava, an AES person who formerly was doing IT implementation in Ukraine for us. But he has decided that it would be more fun to be a solar person so we gave him a shot, especially as he was willing to relocate to Hyderabad and take on India. It has taken a while, but both the central government and several of the more progressive states have announced programs to subsidize a certain number of solar installations in their locations. We have been awarded one five Mw project under the Rajasthan program, and there were two hundred applicants, so that is pretty impressive. We are told we will receive 20 Mw under the Gujarat program, which would also be good. And both of these will now be a lot of work to pull off—be careful what you wish for. Note that India has an electric system of only about 185,000 Mw for a population of more than a billion; the US, with 300 million people, has 900,000 Mw. So there is clearly room for more electricity generation, especially as many of the states are in such bad shape that they have to cut off factories from time to time. But the existing generation is pretty traditional stuff—coal and gas and hydro. There is a grand total of 2 Mw of solar. And that 2 Mw is currently in construction in West Bengal, so the real number is zero.

It was a hectic week of listening to government officials explain their programs; of asking questions and being told, improbably, "It will be no problem"; of meeting with lots of local Indian companies who either were of the "I have a project in Ranakpur" variety and wanted a partner, or wanted to sell us something. About one in twenty of these meetings was useful, but the government meetings were generally good. It may well be possible to get something done here, although the barriers remain large.

Since the first solar plant is just now being built, there are not lots of contractors with the experience in how to build these; there is one, and he's busy in West Bengal. Panels are made here, but by a firm that is just starting into the business, so no one knows if these panels will actually work, and therefore they can't be financed so we cannot use them. The local distribution companies, who will have to buy this power under a long-term contract, have never done so, thus a model contract does not exist. And for all these reasons the template for financing does not exist—no bank has financed one. Perhaps you begin to get the picture. The good news is that no one is ahead of us. I guess that's good news.

One final anecdote, characteristic of breaking into new markets. On one of the days of the mission we had two individual meetings set up in Delhi, both with financial institutions, since to do this, as always, we need money. The first was with the Infrastructure Finance Corp, an Indian government agency set up as a bank to provide additional and longer-term financing to infrastructure projects—power plants, ports, roads, etc.—with the understanding that most banks don't like to lend for as long a term as these projects need. The chairman, a sad looking Sikh in a pink turban, explained his attractive-sounding program, and then assured us that our project, at $20–$25 million, was too small for his bank. Aha. Then we trotted off to the eleventh floor offices of the Power Finance Corporation, another Indian government institution set up to finance, you guessed it, power plants. Our guys had had preliminary and quite encouraging discussions with the head of renewable finance for this institution, and he was enthusiastic about our project and assured us the bank was as well.

So we troop into the office of the chairman, also a Sikh, but bigger and this time with a white turban. After introductions, he said, "Why would I ever finance something like this? Why would Rajasthan buy your fifteen-rupee power when they could buy four-rupee power from someone else?" It became quickly clear that this was not a rhetorical question.

"We will have a power contract with the utility," we answered politely.

"Nonsense," he said, "they will never buy this power and I will never finance such a project as yours."

That all took four minutes. We asked the question a couple more times and received the same definitive, not quite rude answer. Five minutes had now elapsed. Unfortunately tea had been ordered. There was something of an awkward silence. I didn't think Chairman Sikh would like to talk about the Final Four, and my stockpile of Indian small talk is not large—"So, how's the cricket going this year?" I was reminded of a woman friend of mine who tells the story of going for a job interview that went bad from the moment it started. The interviewer did not like the school she went to, he dismissed the degrees she had gotten, he had little regard for the place she worked, or the nature of her experience. And on and on, with nothing about her making the grade. Finally she stood up and said, "Well, most people think I have pretty good legs. What about my legs—do you at least like my legs?" I don't think you can do this today. Anyway I was pretty sure if I asked him, the chairman would not have liked my legs either.

Love and kisses, Bob

Afterword: Why spend so much time worrying about Indian banks? The problem is currency mismatch. It works like this: if you borrow money from Citibank, you borrow dollars and they wish to get repaid in dollars. But you have a contract in Rajasthan with the electric utility who wishes to pay you in rupees for the power you sell him from your project. But the payments to the bank you agreed to make are in dollars. So you have to change your rupees into dollars. Your economic calculations justifying the project assumed an exchange rate wherein everything would work out fine. But exchange rates fluctuate, especially over longer periods of time, like the twenty years of your power contract and the period of your bank loan. You can do better than you thought—then bully for you! Or the opposite, but the bank still needs to get paid. In dollars.

If you are dealing in major currencies—dollars or euros or yen principally, perhaps UK pounds—there are hedges you can purchase to limit this risk, but of course they cost money. In third world currencies like rupees there are no long-term hedges.

But—aha—what if you borrow in rupees, you get paid for your power in rupees, and you pay back the bank in rupees? You have eliminated at least one of the many risks that can screw up an otherwise good project. Hence my interest in Indian banks. And we were successful in arranging just such a transaction, to my surprise and delight. One less thing to worry about.

[6]

If You've Seen One Temple . . .
You Only Have Five Thousand to Go

October 2009

Dear Dad,

There is a very famous location in Burma, the "temple city" of Bagan. Except you have to be careful now, as the country is sometimes, by some people, called Myanmar. But the people who changed the name are the current ruling military junta who none of us sensitive liberals like, so should we use their name for the country? Or not?

I don't think you should go around changing the name of your country back and forth. Maybe once you're independent from the rapacious Belgians you can decide not to be the "Belgian Congo" anymore. Umm, wait, the rapacious Belgians? Those guys in that small, wet, cold country with a trivial seacoast and no port, brown beer, and the statue of the little boy urinating? Hardly comes across these days as rapacious. And the first shot after the Belgians left was just to call it the Congo, but this would not do as the French also had a similar territory called the Congo, independent about the same time and just across the river. The Congo River, it turns out, which has never had its name changed.

For one brief shining moment in time both countries were called the Congo, but the Belgian one was known by the initial of its capital, formerly called Leopoldville and named originally after guess who (you don't have to guess, King Leopold, the ruler who sponsored the original colonization); the other capital, on the north side of the Congo River, was named after the French-Italian lieutenant who discovered or captured or expropriated it (stories differ), Pierre de Brazza, on behalf of the French, and hence Brazzaville. Thus the Belgian one was Congo L and the French one was Congo B, which seemed clear enough. But then the name of Leopoldville was changed to the much more African sounding Kinshasa, which is some Lingala dialect word meaning we can't find out, although there appears to have been a small fishing village named Kinchassa that originally stood on the site. We don't know what that meant either.

Then the whole country had its name changed to Zaire. There was a lot of that going around, and thus this is not to be confused with Zambia or Zimbabwe, two nearby African countries of distinctly different temperaments but names also starting with Z. It is said that Zaire comes from the mispronunciation of the Kongo *word* nzere or nzadi, which means "the river that swallows all rivers." However, our reference for this arcane piece of info is a website called "Baby Names Hub" that also informs us that for the last 130 years, according to US census data, the number of babies named Zaire has been zero until 1997 when this number shot up to about two hundred, where it has stayed since. Thus we speculate that the information is of questionable value. At least something about rivers makes more sense, given the extremely large river wandering around the vicinity—yes, the Amazon. No, just kidding, the Mississippi.

Congo B ground along being named Congo until it became, at independence in 1960, Republic of the Congo. In 1970 leftists took over and it was for a while People's Republic of the Congo but then later went back to being plain old Republic of the Congo, while at long last Zaire, after

Mobutu, became Democratic Republic of the Congo. Which certainly cleared everything up. I think Brazzaville and Kinshasa's names remain unchanged but this cannot be judged to be a permanent state of affairs. Fortunately, both locations fall into the "really distressed African country where not much is going on except stuff of interest to the United Nations or students of genocide" and certainly not much of interest to electric utility executives.

Actually, at one point some African power officials had a plan to dam the Congo River in a number of places and create a 40,000 Mw hydro system and export the power to, um, where exactly? The whole area south of the Sahara uses maybe 20,000 Mw not counting South Africa. And not a single country there has any credit to speak of except maybe Zimbabwe, so who would have paid for the electricity? But fortunately for you this is not a letter about that.

As noted, this letter is about my recent trip to Burma, or perhaps Myanmar. Personally I do not believe you should call a country something that sounds like a kitchen wrap—try the new Myanmar for all your food preservation and leftover wrapping tasks. But the junta did not consult me. Maybe they were mad that there were all those Burma-Shave signs along the US highways, except the generals in the junta probably have not been driving down many US highways recently, given that there are some sanctions which apply to them personally. Tough restrictions, like, if you are a high-ranking military dictator of a miscellaneously named south Asian country, you cannot rent a car with a GPS in Kansas, or you have to have a middle seat in coach if you fly on a US airline other than Delta. And about as effective. And the sad part is you cannot put those wonderfully silly signs on freeways anymore either, as Lady Bird Johnson made it illegal, so all the Burma-Shave signs have now been given to the Smithsonian. And Burma-Shave, after due consideration by its board of directors, has elected not to change its name to Myanmar-Shave. The "Burma" part comes from mysterious "secret ingredients from the Malay Peninsula and Burma." No further explanation. Ingredients apparently not subject to the embargo. Or FDA disclosure requirements. I brought some Burma-Shave shaving cream with me, but it was by accident.

Day One: Friday—Singapore to Yangon

I was in Singapore for an AES development meeting where Paul Hanrahan, the CEO, gets all the developers together and we each display our budgets for the next year and our plans and so forth, and then, putting aside all our parochial interests and thinking only of the greater benefit of the company, we sort of discuss and ask probing questions and sort of vote and decide how to allocate to the $250 million dollars of projects the $100 million of allowed free cash flow for next year. Fortunately there are some bad ideas that are easily recognized, like building small nuclear plants, and unfortunately there are some bad ideas that are only slowly recognized, like trying to do $5 billion coal projects in India in the face of global warming and a meltdown in the finance system that hardly allows you to raise $50 million, let alone one hundred times as much. And some good ideas like, *ahem*, the solar effort that is trundling along nicely, thank you very much. But as soon as this meeting ends on a Friday, I head for the airport. I have wanted to go to Myanmar, and specifically to Bagan, city of ten-thousand temples, for a very long time. It is said to be as interesting a site for ancient religious edifices as Angkor Wat, my all-time favorite in the category, and this conference presents a perfect jumping-off point to go there for a long weekend. Sadly, by myself, as L has committed to speak at an important stem cell conference in Korea.

The following theme will recur ad nauseum in this letter—Myanmar is about thirty years behind the rest of Asia. Or forty. Everyone says that, and it's true, but in patches. I land at the capital, a city of five million people in a country of sixty million, and note that Yangon International Airport (the Brits called it Rangoon but we won't go through all that name stuff again) has four gates. Chattanooga Airport in Tennessee, an airport serving a city of 175,000 in a state of six million people, has eight gates.

My guide meets me at the airport as planned. He is a nice and understandable Burmese named Yann although I initially think his name is Jen as he is wearing a skirt. I have not attempted to arrange all this running around Burma stuff myself, as: a) I do not have the time and b) I do not have the knowledge and c) I fortunately do have the money, so I am in the hands of Golden Lotus Tours and Travel. Yann/Jen and the driver take me to the Governor's Residence, which turns out to be a lovely hotel in north Yangon, terrific room with dark wood, blue-tiled pool, beautiful outdoor bar overlooking a large, wraparound fish pond filled with carp, all complimented by gorgeous tropical landscaping. Very strong impression of somewhere the last governor should have lived, if he actually didn't.

All the guidebooks that I had time to find (one) and all the material from Golden Lotus (one and a half pages) said over and over: no Internet, no cell phones, no BlackBerries, don't be looking for any contact with the outside world while you're here. Carrier pigeons maybe. But at check-in the hotel desk agent politely says they have a Wi-Fi network and hands me the access code. While I have schooled myself for this weekend of intense deprivation outside the electronic womb that surrounds us—well, maybe not surrounds you, since you refuse to use your email account—now a glimmer of hope arises. "Ha," I think, but nothing else as I have an appointment with a pagoda.

Shwedagon Pagoda, or *Paya* as the Burmese say, is said to be taller than Borobudur, a beautiful and impressive Buddhist monument in Indonesia that I visited two years ago. It is also said by my guide that this is the tallest pagoda in the world even though Borobudur is bigger in terms of area. Shwedagon is in fact pretty darn big, you can see it from many places in the city. But maybe the Burmese exaggerate, and anyway who cares except *The Guinness Book of Records* and the odd Indonesian.

Borobudur, for reference, is a triumph of serene high craftsmanship. Executed entirely in dark stone, it has for ornamentation only stone carvings of Buddha, in his sitting pose, approximately four hundred of them, in niches surrounding its three levels and four sides, as well as in cupolas on top. Consistency of theme, unified focus of execution, artistic balance; a remarkable and moving monument. It sits at the high point in the middle of a flat agricultural plain, where serenity seems the natural state of affairs.

Shwedagon, different. For starters, it is in downtown Yangon, with traffic all about. And the large, really very large upside-down, turnip-shaped stupa is all covered in gold. As one begins to realize after repeated examples, in Burma if some gold is good, more is better. So we have very big and very golden. There is a further difference: supporters and believers and pretty much anyone who can afford it has been allowed to put up on the temple grounds all manner of smaller shrines, all Buddhist of course, but in varying sizes and with quite varying styles. Some are appended to the stupa, some are freestanding. And they are not built of grey stone, nor is there any particular thematic unity.

Not only do we have Buddha, we got Disney morphs—the seven dwarfs into Asian spirits and animals—but the genetics gets goofed up. Images all over the place of Garuda (large predatory bird, sometimes with portions of a human body incorporated in his architecture), chinthe (a combination of lion head and dog body), naga (a sort of cobra only weirder), woman lions, chinthes with split backsides so they can crouch easily on corners, kinnara (woman's body, bird's feet), a sea dragon called Makara, etc. These ceramic monsters in very bright colors are in large supply, placed in front of or at the sides of or on top of or crawling around the edges of the small shrines, all protecting or announcing or doing who knows what for their particular Buddha.

The Buddhas are also all over the place, generally sitting down and doing with their hands the "earth touching position." Which means connectedness to the earth, although why exactly this is important is not made clear. The Buddhas come in all sizes. They all have pure white skin, big lips, big grins, gold robes, and hands way too big for their bodies. And their fingers are all the same length. Perhaps this is the result of meditation, perhaps of something else. There are more than three hundred images here of said party. My favorite, however, is that found in several of the smaller chapels. The Buddha image has been arranged with a neon halo, kind of like disco lighting or a badly designed pinball machine backdrop. While you're standing there contemplating the eternity of the universe and the meaning of nirvana, the backdrop to Buddha's head keeps lighting up, then spinning around and changing color, shooting off sparks, etc. Yann, who seems pretty mellow about the whole thing, says that this is new in the last ten years and even he thinks it is a bit much. On the other hand, the rose window in Notre-Dame was probably thought gaudy and inappropriate by some early Christian believers.

Two gigantic and brightly painted chinthes, each easily one hundred feet tall, stand guard at the south gate, but once you are past them, you take an elevator to get to the plaza level. Shoes and socks are removed to go into the complex. Despite groups of volunteer young folks busily sweeping the marble and washing it down, your feet get pretty dirty.

At one point Yann points out to me that the Burmese divide the week into eight days, one for each compass point, and that when you are at a pagoda, you should go to the compass point of your birthday. There you will find a small image that is the zodiac equivalent symbol for your day of birth, and you should pour water on its head. Apparently they like this. To get to eight, they have decided that Wednesday is two days. So much for Western linear thinking. The animals are, starting with Sunday: Garuda, tiger, lion, elephant with and without tusks (the two days of Wednesday, if you are keeping count), rat, guinea pig, and dragon, in that order. I don't know what day of the week I was born on, and need to go on the Internet to check. I am worried that I am a guinea pig.

The pagoda is renewed annually, regilded due to the wear and tear of the two hundred inches of rain per year that Yangon gets, which peaks in August at almost sixty inches. These numbers are amazing but verified in several places. Note to self: do not go to Yangon in August. Because of this maintenance, UNESCO has turned it down as a World Heritage site. Apparently UNESCO believes in genteel disintegration. This lack of designation does not seem to bother anyone attending the temple.

Final difference: Borobudur, in the middle of the countryside of Java, does not any longer seem to function as a real place of active worship. Few people visit it. Shwedagon: lots of people—young, old, couples, families, monks male and female. Some praying, some sweeping the floor, some of the younger citizens walking around checking out the opposite sex. I would not have thought that the local *paya* was a good place to pick up chicks, but who knows?

By the way, where are the jewels? The book says that the top is supposed to be not just gold but encrusted with many emeralds, rubies, and so forth, but it sure doesn't look that way. Yann says that lots of stuff has been stolen, and now no one can sleep in the pagoda area at night. But this is recent. It doesn't seem to be the fault of the British.

The central pagoda structurally is made of bricks covered in plaster covered in gold plate or leaf. It is solid inside, unlike temples, of which more to come. Except for the lack of doors to get inside—which might be a clue—you would not necessarily know this, and apparently no one did until the earthquake of 1975 that significantly damaged the stupa. No, I don't know why no one asked, "Hey, what's inside here?" before then. During the restoration process there were of course no "as built" drawings, and after some investigation it was determined that this was the tenth construction iteration, and that each new pagoda had simply been built on top of the previous one. This is exactly the same process followed in Central America, where pre-Columbian pyramids are not hollow, and where each new one is built on top of the previous one, and there are no rooms inside and no treasure. Remarkable parallel.

Other interesting matters not having to do with Buddha or temples or the Internet: everyone drives on the right-hand side of the road in Myanmar, and this has been the requirement since the junta changed the rules in 1980. However, almost all the cars have right-hand drive. Such cars are made for those few countries (UK, Australia, Japan) where one drives on the left-hand side of the road. Apparently the wily Japanese have kept sending used Toyotas and Hondas to Burma, so most of the cars are still right-hand drive. This was either a diabolically clever part of the sanctions, or the Japanese don't care. It may also have something to do with affordability. Fortunately traffic is light, especially light for a major Asian city. And I am being driven around on a Friday afternoon, not a holiday, at rush hour.

There are no motorcycles or bicycles on the streets. None at all. I have never seen a south Asian city with no motorbikes. Once I finally realize this and ask, Yann says that, again, the junta decided that they gummed up traffic, so that in Yangon they are simply prohibited on all the major streets in the central part of the city. It does mean the busses do a good business.

Favorite commercial enterprises discovered so far:

» Energy Horse Co Ltd.: don't know what they do, but it's a great name. Wish I had seen the logo.

» Godzilla mosquito coils: but the mosquitoes, against which the guidebook was quite clear in warning one, do not seem that bad.

Favorite "east meets west but it's not a perfect fit" moment: In the Shwedagon Pagoda, I come across a group of Thai monks clad in orange robes, a brighter and different color than the burnt sienna robes of the Burmese monks. They sit cross-legged in a row of two, roughly thirty monks in all, with another fifty or so Thai citizens, on a pilgrimage, all reverently kneeling and clumped behind the two rows of monks. The monks are chanting in unison in Sanskrit, an impressive set of sounds, atonal but rhythmic, a barrage of candles on the marble in front of them. A long white thread ran through the hands of each monk and then stretched back behind them to connect to the other worshippers in a serpentine fashion—a touching scene of traditional belief. While I watched, feeling a little intrusive as a faithless westerner, one monk in the second row held up at arms-length a small digital camera to get a flash picture of himself and the other chanting monks in this swell surrounding.

About monks: The male Burmese monks wear reddish brown robes, while the females wear pink. Both have shaved heads and live in monasteries side by side with their communities. There are far fewer female than male monks. They do spend most of each day begging for food, successfully it seems, as all Burmese feel an obligation to feed the monks. Numbers are not clear but it could be as much as 2% of the population. And while some monks spend their lives dedicated to religious service, you can leave if you want to without stigma, and you can come and go. This is a remarkable degree of flexibility and perhaps explains how they are both so well tolerated by and integrated into the society. "There goes Charlie, he's decided to be a monk this month."

I return to the dark teak, open architecture, good French food, and attentive help of the Governor's Residence. Everything about this hotel is terrific, and it is acknowledged to be the best in Yangon. I should add that although they say they have Wi-Fi and an Internet connection, and even give out the encouraging little bit of paper with a password on it when you check in, it's a lie.

Sitting on the covered veranda in the gathering dusk and trying pointlessly to get my computer to work, I notice bats flitting around the high ceiling and over the swimming pool. Geckos are climbing the white support columns and edging along the roof, looking for the bugs to eat that the bats miss. There were lots of bats and geckoes, which I rather liked. At dinner, small, brightly colored flowers and flower petals have been sprinkled tastefully over the white tablecloth and are being eaten by small ants on the tablecloth, also tastefully. It is the tropics, after all. Because you should always drink the wine of the land, although in some cases no more than once, I ordered a glass of sauvignon blanc from a winery in the Shan State in northern Burma, at Taunggyi to be exact, 2008 vintage. I had no idea that they made wine in Myanmar. It was surprisingly good. And Buddhists don't believe in drinking alcohol. Maybe the Shan are pantheists. Although as my guide said when I asked him about this and vegetarianism, "I am fifty percent Buddhist."

Yangon looks like Japan in the late nineteen fifties. Some new buildings, mostly old ones, lots of busses and trucks but not really very much traffic. No Western establishments at all, no Starbucks (eek!), no KFC, no McDonald's, no Coke or Pepsi ads on billboards, no Total gas stations, nothing. Even in Cameroon you see some commercial evidence of the West. There is plenty of billboard advertising for soft drinks and cosmetics and food and the like, just none of it mentions Western or international brands. The rural areas around Bagan resemble Vietnam in the middle sixties during the war—crumbling infrastructure that the colonial power built, and nothing repaired since, due in the case of Vietnam to the continued war, and one supposes in the case of Burma due to the sanctions. But since they only started seriously in 1988, mostly to prohibit foreign investment as well as exports of native products, this cannot be the whole answer. The infrastructure seems frozen in time, roads and bridges are crappy and eroding away at the edges. The telecom system is crappy, Internet access is nonexistent—have I mentioned this before? Except the electricity system seems fine, even in the small villages where the houses are built of woven mats. Why is this? The universal answer seems to be that the junta likes things this way.

As to the financial infrastructure, the guidebooks all say forget credit cards and traveler's checks. But bring lots of US dollars as they are the preferred currency, in fact the hotels won't settle their bills in other than cash, US variety. And they look at each bill carefully, rejecting the worn or torn ones. One is charged a 20% premium to use chat, the local currency. I ponder the fact that the US is one of the most unrelenting proponents of the embargo and the sanctions that must to some degree be keeping Myanmar frozen in the undeveloped state/time warp in which it finds itself. Yet the dollar is openly used and accepted everywhere. And English is one of the two official languages of the country, taught in all the schools. The junta does not seem to be as good at mind control as one would have thought. Peculiar, has nobody here read 1984? George Orwell served as a colonial officer in this country, for goodness' sake.

Day Two: On to Bagan

Before breakfast, like a junkie seeking a fix, I try the much-heralded Internet access again. I am reminded of ISDN, an early Internet network protocol and the wag's explanation of what the initials really stood for—"it still does nothing." As a consolation prize I have wonderful Burmese coconut noodle soup for breakfast, and a croissant. And good coffee. The ants appear to have decided to go elsewhere as there are now no flower petals on the table. Too bad, they would have liked the soup.

On the road to the airport, Yann points out the first university in the country, started by an American priest who came here in 1905. He was a dedicated teacher who spent his entire life in Burma. You might have thought that monkish modesty would have made him name the school after a saint or something, but I am charmed that he named it after himself: Judson University.

At check-in, a sticker with Yangon Airway's red flying elephant symbol is attached to your clothing, which is a good thing as flights and gates are not announced at the spartan "domestic terminal." So you look around to see if some of the other red elephant people are getting into the rusty bus on the tarmac and heading for the plane. It's kind of like a family run airline, except run by your least competent relative. "Air Yangon has its entire fleet ready to serve you," which is two airplanes. I don't ask about spare parts.

The group boards, including some obvious tourists from Europe (the faux photographers' vests are a giveaway, I suspect), a bunch of shifty young Chinese (probably smuggling opium or heroin, although Bagan is not a great place for that, as it is too far south) and a really fat Burmese, at least that's what I think he is, as he is wearing the traditional lungi, the skirt thing. This does not seem to me to be a sensible garment. It is like what you wear at the locker room when you wrap the towel around your waist, if you are a guy that is, I don't know what women wear in their locker rooms I am sorry to say. Only those locker room towels don't stay up too well but the Burmese have perfected how to keep them up. They are essentially long skirts, and probably 90% of the men are dressed this way. But this guy on the airplane is really large and is sitting across the aisle from me. When the stewardess tries to get his tray out from his armrest, it won't fit over his stomach, so he sits there with his tray at about twenty degrees above horizontal, but he does help himself to the strange box "breakfast" of an odd triangular piece of turnover-looking thing and eats it all. He does not eat the box in which it came, to my surprise. He could be Samoan, but I do not think they wear long skirts. And he has a three-day growth of beard and all Samoans are clean shaven. This is a strange country.

On the flight I take a little time to see about the language. It may be syllabic, but the writing seems as if it's all "*o*'s", although some have curlicues and hyphens attached to them. I think they bought too many vowels but Vanna White won't take them back. I do try and learn hello and thank you (*ming-ga-la-ba* and *cezu-tin-bah-deh*, respectively) and everyone seems very surprised to see a tourist who knows even this much. More than that I do not have time to attempt.

We land at the small town of Nyaung-U, where I am met cheerfully by another Golden Lotus guide, this time named Toto. Somehow I avoid asking him how's Dorothy. Lonely Planet, which is the only guidebook I have found, says that the hotel to which I am taken, the Thiripyitsaya Sanctuary Resort, has "too much landscaping." I think they are being snobs; the landscaping is again fabulous and verdant and of course tropical, and besides the place is so expensive why would any backpacker stay here? He would not. I have a three-room villa on the second floor with a canopied bed, fridge, coffee fixings, and a balcony overlooking the Ayeyarwady. Damn, it's only instant coffee. Despite this deprivation I decide to stay.

Lunch at the Green Elephant Restaurant overlooking the river and a golden pagoda consists of fried spinach leaves, curry, lentil soup, and, what the heck I'm on vacation, Myanmar beer—a fine light lager. The French tourist group behind me sure thinks so, as they have consumed about twenty-five bottles of wine and are speaking really loud French. There are no other guests. Shortly, the French leave.

Our first stop is the King Manuha Pahto, "pahto" apparently meaning temple, which is something you can go inside of, unlike stupas or pagodas. We pause for a moment to think about how the whole place started. The area around Bagan in AD 1075 was the Pyu kingdom, ruled by King Anawrahta. Disturbed by his kingdom's traditional name—would you want to be known as King of the Pyu?—he decided to become a Buddhist. But not just any Buddhist, he appears to have wanted to be a really big deal Buddhist, with the whole thing—monks, relics, temples, etc. He achieved this by conquering the neighboring Mon kingdom and seizing the monks and the holy scriptures and the holy relics and the king himself (the afore mentioned Manuha) and taking them all back to Bagan to put in place serious Buddhism for all. This religious zeal and accompanying successful empire building triggers the largest construction boom ever seen in the country, as around four thousand temples and stupas and monasteries are built within about a sixteen-square-mile radius in the space of five hundred years. These amazing structures are all built due to a religion which teaches that the notion of self is merely an illusion and which has four principles:

Life is *dukkha*. I always wondered about that. I do think that some of life is *dukkha*. Very well, I can't hold out any longer: *dukkha* means "unsatisfactoriness," which although cumbersome as an English word has a nice feel. I experience *dukkha* in life from time to time, like when I'm stuck in traffic. Or my Internet access goes down. That is certainly *dukkha*.

The reason why life is *dukkha* is *tanha* (selfish desire, ego, striving, the need to see what day of the week you were born on). To eliminate *tanha*, you should behave yourself (proper behavior—don't kill, steal, lie, or drink beer).

This will establish *kutho* (merit), which is sort of like frequent flyer miles, only religious. I don't think you get a monthly statement, however. If you do all this and get enough *kutho*, you move to a higher state and eventually some more good things happen, although this part gets a bit more confusing ("scholars disagree") as to how to get to wherever this is and what to find there.

And thus, children, we find that the adoption of a religion that emphasizes the end of striving and competition and the abnegation of the self as the path to virtue has had, as the policy wonks say, unanticipated consequences. Each of the forty-five kings of the reign built bigger temples than the previous guy to perhaps emphasize how they had overcome the need for striving and how clearly they had sublimated the ego into the greater pursuit of something. Thus was it ever so? Cf. Europe, my cathedral is bigger than your cathedral.

Back to Manuha, the captured Mon king. He lived out his life in Bagan and was even allowed to build his own temple. Inside it he placed four large Buddhas, three sitting and one reclining, each in their own interior worship room. But the space is far too small for the large images, it all feels cramped and almost claustrophobic and I am not troubled by said feeling much. If temples can be expressionistic, this one is of sadness and discontent.

Next we go to Gubyaukgyi Temple where there are great frescoes illustrating either the 350 previous lives of Buddha or the jatakas (anecdotes from his real life) or possibly both. I am not clear if this is all set down carefully. However, even the Sermon on the Mount has a couple of different renditions in the gospels, so who are we to criticize? The 350 lives do seem a bit much, even if the iconography and artistry is pretty neat. The frescoes include a very dramatic row of monks looking up at Buddha, about half preserved. The beautiful ceramics on the outside of the temple are also inconsistent and fragmentary.

Then to Ananda Praya, the first temple built with four entrances and not one but four central Buddha images, one for each direction, in a core of four rooms. The building is laid out in an open cross format, with large windows and thus good lighting, lots of inner halls with many small images of Buddha set in niches in the walls. If one is good, four are better, and sixty-seven are terrific.

Finally Toto takes me to visit a small temple whose name I don't get, where you can climb up a constricted, very steep stairway and then look around and see within easy eyesight temple after temple and stupa after stupa. Sadly, the modest image of Buddha in a niche on the roof has been looted; the head is gone and the chest ripped open. "Looking for jewels" says Toto. This was not done by unbelievers, Christian missionaries, or Islamic zealots, but by looters. There was a legend that the image makers deposited jewels inside the statues, which was largely untrue. I find this depressing, but the view is great—you can see easily several hundred structures from here, all sizes and most shapes—I lose count after 150. One even looks like a Maya pyramid with the stepped slopes. Several look like the giant 1950's Palace of Culture and Science building in the center of Warsaw, probably the world's ugliest edifice. The Soviets deserved to be tossed out based on their taste in architecture alone.

GENERAL NOTE ONE: It's hot. Very hot. Really very hot, and I like hot weather. The guidebook recommends renting a bike and pedaling around to see the temples. I recommend not doing this unless you wish to get heat stroke in about twenty minutes. I recommend instead an air-conditioned secondhand right-hand drive Honda. There is very, very little traffic and one tour bus at our biggest stop (Ananda). The sites are virtually empty, no picnickers, very few tourists. And the ones who are here seem to be pilgrims, really, not garden-variety sightseers like me. This must not be the season, thinks I. But the guidebook says it is, and Toto agrees. The other seasons are hotter.

GENERAL NOTE TWO: After many repetitions, I am beginning to figure out that the position of the hands of the Buddha image is important. Meditation is both hands in lap, only flat on top of each other here, different in Japan where the fingers butt into each other. There are other hand positions for defending, teaching, probably calling a cab; it's hard to get the complete alphabet.

That evening I sit at the hotel's lovely but empty bar, watching the setting sun play through the colorful liquor bottles, drinking a cold beer and watching the Ayeyarwady (you may know it by the British spelling, Irrawaddy) River, large and brown, slow and empty. Remarkably empty. I see maybe two or three boats of any size in my three days in Bagan. It is also muddy. To the south of the resort, women are beating their clothes on the banks, really, just like in *National Geographic*. But not many and not energetically. And how does this get clothes clean anyway?

A Thai tourist group is also staying at the hotel, and so there is entertainment after dinner, including something really impressive: the elephant dance. It's like the old vaudeville skits of the two guys inside the horse suit, except here the coordinated movements are graceful and compelling, and a little dangerous, as the dancers start on a raised platform and then move up onto smaller and smaller platforms. At each level the "elephant" either does handstands or raises up on his back legs. I try and determine what the people inside are holding on to when they do this, but fail. At the end of the performance, several people go up to the elephant and pin bills to his trunk. At first I am surprised, then I think about the fact that in ethnic weddings in some US communities, each male guest pins money to the dress of the bride as he dances with her. The cheap guys pin five dollars, the big spenders twenty dollars. I also remember when you took me to baseball games in Albuquerque, New Mexico, to see the Albuquerque Dukes. I think this was Class C ball, but they had a former big-league guy who used to hit home runs. And when he was through running the bases, he would make a circuit past the folks in the good seats just behind home plate, and they would roll up dollar bills and stick them through the chicken wire and he would collect them as he passed by. This made me very embarrassed and I don't know quite why. We never gave him any money, of course, but then we were in the cheap seats. At least we were there.

This time I give the elephant some money. He earned it.

Day Three: The Secrets of the Nats

We start our long circular road trip by driving through an old oil and gas area, some small parts of it still producing. Small pipelines are just running along the ground, not very "engineered" but with no evidence of seepage or oil spills. The occasional pump is still working. Our immediate destination is Chauk, a medium-sized town, and its market. This is a serious, colorful, working market. It has all sorts of produce, some recognizable, some less so: tomatoes, peppers, coriander, flowers, fresh meat and chickens with fly squadrons flying cover, cooked food and noodle stalls, dried and salted fish, bundles of branches for the bark that makes the cosmetic facial paste/sunblock. Everything is displayed in bulk, in huge open bags, or arrayed on the round woven mat trays, but once sold it goes into the inevitable plastic bags. Made in China perhaps? It is big and crowded and I am the only westerner. I am not wearing a skirt and I am wearing, yes, I'll say it, a baseball cap—the only person wearing a baseball cap. That's how you can tell I am a westerner. The people at the market are curious but very polite; there is little staring, no begging or pushiness, little pointing.

We leave Chauk and continue to drive through this resolutely agricultural landscape, with occasional very small and poor towns—houses of split bamboo walls, not brick, thatched roofs, not corrugated tin. Crops in the field include sesame, shallots, cotton. All work is being done by hand. There is absolutely no machinery, not even small tractors or tillers.

As we drive, we pass trucks stacked three times their height with goods, frequently with a young man riding perilously on top of everything. The road base is bumpy, rutted, with many potholes, essentially one lane. It becomes all sand when we cross the riverbeds, so it is good thing this is the dry season. There are no bridges, almost no culverts, certainly no signs for speed limit or "Twenty-four kilometers to East Psawsaw." Cow herds, goat herds, ruts for oxcarts running parallel to the roadway in most cases. Is this the Burmese version of the diamond lane? At one point we cross a single-track railroad. The train actually takes longer than driving, says the guide, fifteen hours to get to Yangon while it takes only thirteen hours to drive. On these roads that seems hard to believe. Besides us, I see four cars all day.

After a long drive over the lousy, narrow but very lightly trafficked roads, we arrive at the Salay Monastery, built in the eighteenth century and known for its carved teak scenes from Buddha's life that decorate the sides of the facility. They all have useful but enigmatic explanatory signs—"Abstaining Sensuality," "The Daughters of the Family Li," "The Buddha with the Deer of the Forest." Again, I think if this were Christian iconography and the carving showed a guy tearing apart a bread roll and the sign said "Loaves and Fishes" we would know immediately what it meant. This must be the same.

We then go to a nearby set of temples to see the "World's Largest Lacquer Buddha." It's pretty big but not as big as a number of the other Buddhas. But far more interesting is the image at the nearby temple: a sizeable concrete Daruma doll, with the traditional red paint and white face. I am surprised—World's Largest Daruma Doll—and I have never seen these outside of Japan. The story of Lord Daruma I eagerly tell to my guide. As you may recall, the legend is as follows: Lord Daruma was a Japanese noble who converted to Buddhism and decided to meditate as a way to seek enlightenment. He sat cross-legged and arms folded, staring at a blank wall in front of him, for twenty years, at which point he became enlightened. He had also become blind and all his limbs had atrophied. In Japan he is now a folk item, a red roundish doll that you can knock over but rights itself due to its ovoid shape and weighted bottom. We have inflatable bozo the clown dolls that do the same thing when you punch them, which shows how spiritual we are. In Japan, the dolls can be readily purchased. You paint in one of the two blank eyes and make a wish for good luck. When you get your wish, you reward the Daruma by painting in the other eye so he can now see. I did this when I was going to the Rhodes Scholar interviews, thinking that there was no sense in turning down luck, no matter where it might come from. However, the folklore is unclear as to what one does if the wish is not granted—maybe split the doll's head open? I don't know. The Daruma image here in Myanmar has both eyes, which seems more humane.

Toto is not especially impressed with my level of Buddhist scholarship. But this Daruma is really big, set up as a gateway to walk through to get to the temple. Very strange and interesting. I am certain that this is evidence of trade between Japan and Burma. However, I fear that this link has already been discovered by other scholars, probably the used car dealers.

We drive past a British-era fertilizer plant—the only even remotely industrial facility seen on the whole eight-hour tour of the countryside. There was an explosion two years ago, and the plant has sat idle since. And it's a big plant, lots of tanks and round pressure vessels with curving stairways climbing up them. I start to ask more questions, then think to myself that nitrate fertilizer is a very useful ingredient in homemade explosives. So maybe an unhealthy interest in such a plant by a foreigner is not a smart idea. Back to discussions about temples.

Soon we turn onto what is advertised as the main road from Mandalay, the largest city to the north of us, and running south to Yangon. There are several dogs sleeping in the middle of it. This might be a sign.

We eventually reach our destination, Mount Popa. This is a granite plinth sticking up from the side of the larger mountain range, and it is quite dramatic. Lunch has been arranged at the Popa Mountain Resort, yet another impressive hotel whose open-air dining room overlooks the valley and Mount Popa. Said mount is important as it is the home of the thirty-seven official nats, not gnats or the Washington, DC, baseball team. The nats are something like lower-level deities or local supernatural guardians, but not part of Buddhism. They also have their own museum/shrine at the base of the mountain. Images of all thirty-seven are there, and it's an eclectic crowd, which includes several with six arms. Also Shiva and Ganesha and several miscellaneous Chinese. Each is said to have specific powers. But their powers can't be that great because atop the mountain are only Buddhist temples, and new ones at that. However, Burmese are careful not to offend nats, especially local ones.

It's a long drive back, which may be what the Washington Nats felt about losing 103 games this year, but with (as usual) little traffic. At the hotel I swim in the pool to cool off. The hotel doesn't even claim to have Internet, and the rooms don't have TV sets, a fact that I have just noticed. There is an old computer hooked up next to the check-in desk, but you can only get Gmail and Yahoo, not a direct connection to the AES Internet web email site. One dollar a minute, but you don't have to pin it to anyone's clothing—or perhaps you pin it to your own.

Day Four: More Temples, Please

Toto, after consultation with the Wicked Witch of the East, wants me to go to a market again, and then to go to a local lacquer factory and see lacquer being made and then no doubt, my head clouded with lacquer fumes—it's painted wooden bowls, right—to buy several sets of lacquer as Christmas presents. Since I have always really disliked lacquer ware as a form of food container, ever since you made us go to lacquer stores in Japan, I suggest instead that we should really see some more temples, since that is what I am here for. So temples it is we see:

Dhamma Yazika: I ask if the Japanese mobsters come here often, but this weak cross-cultural pun—the Yakuza is the Japanese mob—gets no response. Large temple, well maintained, with a very nice bell.

Shwezigon Pagoda: similar to Shwedagon in Yangon, and lots of gilt. Very impressive and slightly more human scale.

Thatbyinnyu: big and white and imposing, it is Bagan's highest pagoda, but it's kind of boxy. Not all temple architecture is wonderful.

Sulamani Pahto: nice grounds, better internal lighting, generally lovely.

Dhammayangyi: I look around for Gwen Verdon and the ball players in the traditional pinstripe uniforms, but nothing. And I have no one to share this clever observation with, since really old American musicals do not appear to be allowed by the government. This is also the largest of the temples, and the one that looks a bit like a Maya pyramid. Its inner sanctum rooms are filled up with brick fragments, so far unexcavated. I like this one a lot, although by nature I am a Dodgers fan.

At the end of the day we go to another temple, Shwesandaw Paya, for the obligatory "look at all the temples at sunset" that is best observed by climbing the extremely steep steps to the fourth and highest platform of this temple and then watching the sun, yes, set over the low mountains across the Ayeyarwady to the west. It's OK, but not so clear to me why this is any better than watching the sun set from the resort's lovely terrace, which also borders the river, with perhaps a cold beverage to hand, rather than with fifty-seven other mostly European tourists and a lot of Burmese kids hawking statues of elephants. Of which animal we have seen neither live ones nor any images in any of the temples, so why to buy one as a souvenir is not so clear to me.

The sunset ritual is clearly a part of every "tour" and I can only conclude that, yes, you can see a lot more of the temples that populate the near landscape when you are this high up, and yes, they are pretty although harder to see as the light decreases, and yes, it's hard to come up with new ways to look at the temples you have already seen up close. I suggest to Toto that they try "temples at dawn" or "temples at ten-thirty in the morning" or "temples standing on your head" but he does not seem interested in my marketing insights. I decide that I really don't need to wait until it is really dark to climb down the steep stairs with no railings, so we depart.

Day Five: To Yangon and "Civilization"

Upon landing from Bagan, I am met at the Yangon airport by Yann who suggests seeing another temple. Dedicated to the sport as I am, I demur. I return to the lovely hotel and find, magically, that the Wi-Fi access now works and I can get my email. I refuse to think about how dependent I am on this electronic tether. Hey, I can quit anytime. I do note that now I won't have to sit cross-legged, meditating for twenty years by staring intently at the blank screen of my computer, waiting for something to download. Thus I lose my chance to become the first Western, Internet-age Lord Daruma.

Most important of all, I can finally check on which day of the week my birth date fell, never mind all the business stuff waiting for me. I do, and find that I was born on Saturday, which makes me a dragon, thank God. And only one day away from a guinea pig. Good work, Mom and Dad!

Love and kisses, Bob

Afterword: This was a great trip when I took it, even though the military was in charge of Myanmar, the US and other sanctions were in place, and Aung San Suu Kyi was under house arrest, Nobel Prize and all. That has changed significantly, in ways that initially many thought were for the better. This has proven not to be true. I am glad I went when I did. It would now require a great deal of convincing to get me to return.

<hr />

My father died in June of 2010, after a long and full life. He was ninety-two years old. For his memorial service, my brother and I composed an appreciation of his life, with David doing most of the work. I read it at the service.

Given that he was the focus of so many of these letters, I decided to include this piece both as a tribute to him and as an answer to any questions about what sort of a man, professional air force officer, and father he was. We loved him and we miss him.

He was buried with full military honors at Arlington National Cemetery. I visit his grave site from time to time.

An Appreciation
Robert Frederick Hemphill

by David F. Hemphill, his son

Our dad was an interesting, clever, witty, bright guy. Our favorite picture, one that we used for his obituary, shows him as a brash young air corps lieutenant in the early 1940s—a bit smug, confident of his skills, and no doubt certain that he was the smartest guy in the room. It's possible that he may have passed this latter trait on to his two sons. . . .

Dad was a fortunate son of the Nebraska middle class. His father was a dentist, and Dad grew up not much affected by the Depression in a classic, warm nuclear family in the charming small town of Blair, Nebraska, just north of Omaha on the Missouri River. In the last few years of his life, as his brain aged, Dad focused more and more on his childhood and what it was like to come home to his mother's freshly baked cherry pies, play golf with his father on the local golf course with the Nebraska sand fairways, watch band concerts in the city park as all the cars lit up the bandstand with their headlights, play with one of his family's endless series of dogs—all named "Spot," go sledding with his Flexible Flyer sled on Waterworks Hill in the winters, or fight with his younger sister, Janet.

Dad was smack dab in the middle of the World War II generation. He graduated from college just before Pearl Harbor, and was in pilot training as an air corps cadet the day the Japanese bombs fell in December 1941. He married his college sweetheart—our mother, Betty Roach—soon after he got his flight wings at a tiny airfield in Dalhart, Texas, and the two of them began an odyssey across the South as he was assigned to an endless series of small air bases. His oldest son—that would be me—was born outside one of those bases in Walterboro, South Carolina. Ultimately Dad saw service as a combat pilot, operations officer, squadron leader, and group commander near the end of the war in the Pacific with the decorated 507th Fighter Group, flying his beloved P-47 (nicknamed the *Flying Erector Set* because it was constructed from salvaged aircraft parts from other damaged airplanes). Here's what some of Dad's fellow pilots recently had to say about him when they learned of his death:

> *As a member of the 507th Fighter Group, I soon became aware of his many great qualities and talents, and I have to say that if someone were to ask me to name the one individual in the group whom I most looked up to and admired, it would have been Bob.*

> *He was a great guy and fine pilot. He was our group commander when Art Rice moved up to wing and he was a good one. He will be missed.*

> *The greatest honor awarded to a fighter pilot is the respect of his fellow pilots. He was respected by all of us. His intelligence and wit will be missed by all of the members of the 507th.*

Dad returned from the war to greet his newborn second child, Gia, in 1945; and youngest child David was born a few years later in 1949. Already at the rank of major by his mid-twenties, he and Mom decided to stay in the service instead of return to the life of a small-town lawyer in Nebraska or Colorado. As he explained it to us later, they both wanted to travel and see the world—and they wanted this experience for their children. And travel they did. At one point Dad served under Dr. Ralph Bunche on a diplomatic assignment with the UN to supervise armistice arrangements in Palestine during the formation of the State of Israel, and this gave him a taste for international diplomatic work that he later pursued. Dad also spent time in the Strategic Air Command (or "SAC"), going on regular alerts as a bomber commander and base commander under the leadership of the legendary General Curtis LeMay. Subsequent to this, Dad got his first assignment to Japan in 1954 serving with the US Far East Command in Tokyo, and he fell in love with the culture, language, and people of Japan, as did Mom.

Dad taught us a number of lessons, but two important ones come to mind. The first one was this: do not pursue rank for rank's sake in your career; instead focus on what interests, inspires, and motivates you—and makes unique use of your talents. To illustrate this, he made a key decision in his career in the early 1960s. In terms of rank, up until that point he was a "fast mover"— a major in his mid-twenties and a full colonel while still in his mid-thirties, he had a good chance to make it to the rank of general if he pursued the right assignments. However, the "right assignments" would have meant more years in SAC in god-awful locations (frozen airbases in North Dakota, endless alerts on flight lines at all hours of the morning). That's how one moves up in the military—with combat command assignments.

Instead, he chose to move in the direction of diplomatic, international work, knowing that these assignments probably would not help him attain higher rank. But he also knew that he would be doing significant and rewarding work that made far better use of all his talents, and would provide a much more stimulating experience for his wife and family. Thanks, Dad. Tokyo, Japan, instead of Minot, North Dakota. Good choice! He did this, and as a result he attained the most rewarding assignment of his career serving as air attaché at the American embassy in Tokyo from 1964 to 1967, under the universally respected Ambassador Edwin O. Reischauer. In his prime, Dad was an impressive presence, smooth socially, and a polished diplomat. He could give a speech in fluent Japanese at the drop of a hat. He was so successful in his attaché position that the entire general staff of the Japanese Air Force came to the airport to see him off when he left Japan at the end of his attaché assignment in 1967. So on the matter of career choice, point taken, Dad.

Another lesson Dad taught was delivered to David one day while driving home from a rewarding day of wine tasting in the Napa Valley of Northern California. Possibly under the influence of the fine California cabernets that he loved, Dad observed that if he had it to do over again, he would have spent a lot more time with his family and a lot less time on his air force career. He observed passionately that the time he lost by doing air force paperwork instead of watching his kids grow up could never be reclaimed, and he was sorry for that. Again, point taken, Dad.

Dad was an interesting father, probably different for each of his children. Some of his initial childrearing instincts seemed to have been drawn from his military training. Thus, we had Saturday morning inspections where he would drop a quarter on the bedspread to see if it bounced—this reputedly measured whether the bed was properly made. The knowledge of how to make proper "hospital corners" on bed sheets also remained with each of his children as a result—a useful life lesson, no doubt. Dad also maintained what was called the "Allowance Book" for his three children, and in it he meticulously documented each child's behaviors—the good, the bad, and the ugly—by means of careful notations and deductions from the modest weekly allowance we all received. Among the notations in the Allowance Book were such things as: "Gia, talking back, debit five cents," "Bobby, failure to clear table, debit five cents," or "David, failure to clean room, debit five cents." To be fair, Dad also occasionally noted good behavior on those rare occasions when it occurred: "David, helped Mother take in groceries, credit five cents," "Bobby, got straight As, credit fifty cents," or "Gia, joined church choir, credit ten cents." Although our home was not exactly like *The Great Santini*, there were some pretty memorable shouting matches between Dad and his two eldest children.

For some reason, however, by the time David came along, Dad must have let his guard down a bit, or maybe he tired of playing the stern disciplinarian. So David has lots of warm fuzzy memories of Dad as a warm and consoling figure— giving comfort and drying the tears of playground insults or schoolroom injustices. Dad talked to David about emotions, happiness, and sadness, and how one could expect to expe- rience a wide range of emotions throughout life. Heavy stuff for a ten-year-old, but it stuck. Dad also made fourth-grader David burst with pride when he showed up at one school career day with his jet pilot helmet and flying suit to wow classmates with fighter pilot exploits. Another time, Dad was the guest speaker at David's High School Honor Society induction, and read a poem to end his speech from an anonymous author that he later revealed to be none other than himself. Mom and David were suitably impressed.

Dad was fortunate in his long and rewarding years of retire- ment—first five years in Japan, then twenty years in Hawaii, followed by another twenty years in Washington State. He was also fortunate in his romantic relationships. Dad had two great loves in his life: first, our mother, Betty Hemphill; then later after Mom had passed away, his dear friend Mary Jane Van Buren. Dad was well aware of his good luck in having quality relationships with both of these remarkable women. Even in his final days, we found unfinished poems where he wistfully mused about his good luck in life and love.

Dad was also a very funny guy, a great storyteller, and a clever wordsmith. He used to tell us bedtime stories that turned into interesting serials. One set of stories was about two characters called "Oscar and Philip," who lived on "Ice Tea Lake" and drove a "spaghetti-cycle." The most memorable stories were about Harrison the Bunny and his buddies who comprised the "Black Mysterious Gang," including Herman Otter, Billy Raccoon, and Junior Mouse. With our mother's help, the stories were tape-recorded (high tech for the fifties), transcribed, and eventually self-published. Harrison the Bunny had wide-ranging exploits, including an all-time favorite where Harrison mistakenly took the family garbage to lunch instead of his own lunch, since there were two bags on the kitchen counter when he left for school. High humor indeed for the minds of children, hearing about Harrison opening up his sack of garbage at lunchtime in class!

In more recent years, Dad entertained his granddaughters, Lydia and Bizzy, by playing endless card games of Hearts, Go Fish, and Fan Tan on summer vacation visits. Dad had names for everybody: he was "Colonel Sharp Eyes," Lydia was "Slick Card Sam," and Bizzy was "Little Friend." The family had other silly names for Dad at different times, including "the Jolly Colonel" (sometimes "the JC") and "Mango Bob" (because he had the world's largest mango tree in his house in Hawaii). Dad also loved to laugh; at times he'd laugh so hard that tears would roll down his cheeks, and he'd eventually get hiccups that would last for several minutes before subsiding.

Dad was also a good musician. He sang in several church choirs, was a second-generation trombonist, and dearly loved listening to his beloved big band recordings—as they evolved from shellac to vinyl to audiotape to CD. He also never tired of telling stories about how he had met and chatted with famous big band leaders Woody Herman, Jimmy Dorsey, and Stan Kenton by approaching them at breaks in clubs when he was a young fan. Dad had a sweet, "gee whiz" sort of naiveté when recalling these experiences.

And then there were the dogs. As a kid, his family had mutts—all named "Spot," and when he and his sister, Aunt Janet, talked about them, they'd refer to "Spot the First," "Spot the Second," and so on. But it was the beagles that commanded his attention in the last few decades of his life. There were a total of five: Oscar, Philip, Linus, Schroeder, and Charlie. Those of you who are *Peanuts* fans may detect a pattern in the naming of the last three of them. The first two beagles were named after his "Oscar and Philip" bedtime stories. Dad loved each of the beagles dearly, and he must have thought it was "inhumane" to train them, for they were surely among the worst-behaved dogs the world ever saw. But he adored the beagles and indulged them, and they returned his love with doggy affection in full measure.

On our 1999 millennium trip to Asia, Dad asked Jennifer if she knew why he had such clean ears. When Jennifer allowed that indeed she did not know why Dad's ears were so clean (politely refraining from adding that she did not particularly wish to know why), he explained that Charlie, his last and beloved beagle, always licked Dad's ears clean when he was picked up from the kennel. Beagle hygiene, it turns out. Although he later denied it, Dad also had two cats when he lived in Hawaii—charmingly called Miss Boo and Little Boo. How far the tough old squadron leader had fallen. . . . Late in his life Dad developed what some would call an overly soft spot in his heart for all animals in need, to the extent that his house was filled with solicitations from every "save the animals" charity on the planet. Who knew that there was an organization in Tennessee devoted to saving retired circus elephants? Or a group in LA that rescued feral donkeys and cats? And on and on. Well, Dad knew about each and every one of them, and he supported all of them with his characteristic twenty-five-dollar donations.

On the technology front, Dad was not a real handyman, not a "fix the car in the driveway" kind of guy. Perhaps his career as a pilot taught him that someone else called a crew chief handled things technical or mechanical on the airplanes he flew. But he did come up with some creatively strange gadgets to solve household problems. For example, he labored intensively with several generations of beagles to construct barriers to keep the dogs in the kitchen when he was out of the house—because due to their lack of training, they always messed up the house when they were left alone. None of Dad's dog barriers ever worked, but they grew in size and complexity with each dog, ultimately to include large pieces of plywood sheeting with handles, hasps, locks, chains, grommets, and God knows what—all of which had to be put into place each time he left the house.

In Hawaii, he also displayed his technological savvy when trying to control the fly population in his yard. He bought a mail-away device called a "Big Stinky," which was a large plastic container that hung from a tree and attracted flies to a narrow, irreversible opening with a piece of rotting meat placed at the bottom of the receptacle. The Big Stinky was actually pretty good at killing flies (and it had a great name), but unfortunately Dad could never figure out how to empty the thing once it was filled with dead flies and rotting meat.

Dad also introduced us to an interesting approach to cleaning our garbage can one time when we were living in Alexandria and Mom was away on a trip. He brought the trash can into the house, set it on top of the stove, filled it with water and detergent, and turned on the burners. Then he got on a chair and stirred the pot with a toilet brush until he decided it was clean. Doubtless Dad's military training was at work here, and some distant memories of KP had kicked in.

It was also around this time that Dad invented his famous

"meat loaf and weenies" recipe, which involved embedding hot dogs in meat loaf. Once baked and sliced, the meat loaf slices looked up at the diner with two strange pink eyes. The word "appetizing" scarcely describes the experience. Somewhat later, with the invention of the microwave, Dad quickly became a fan and generated entirely new uses for the device. Instead of throwing away perfectly good dry dog food that had been infested with ants, for example, he microwaved the dog food. The ants were not killed, but they emerged from the oven wobbly and radiated—sort of walking sideways. And presumably the dogs then ate the food. Which may explain a lot about the dogs' behavior, come to think of it.

And finally, there was Dad's poetry. Although we joked a lot about it, he used poetry to express emotions that he could not otherwise articulate. His mother, Lola Taylor Hemphill, also wrote poetry, and Dad followed her path in this. He loved to expound on his poetry-writing "process" and on the virtues of finding the exact word to use in his poetry—including waking up in the middle of the night to scribble down an idea, only to find the "great idea" illegible or nonsensical in the harsh light of day. It also turns out that Dad took his writing quite seriously: when packing up his house recently, David went through shelf after shelf of rhyming dictionaries, thesauruses, poetry compilations, and even a valuable manual that is commended highly to all—it is entitled *Air Force Writing*. There is one tearjerker of a poem that Dad wrote when his last child, David, left home to go away to college at Berkeley in 1967. It exemplifies his use of poetry to figure out his feelings—and it's still a little hard to get through.

THE CHANGE

And so it comes, the terminal day when the last one goes.
Feel now that chilling wedge of loneliness of parents
when the youngest has departed.
How fleeting these years—
were they full enough?
Did we suffice?
Were your days at home all that you had hoped?

You lad, fast become man, whose feet have known
the soft Hakone moss, the Bowery cobble, and the jet craft's aisle
through time—
Have we measured up?
God knows you have, so well that this empty space we call
your room hollowly mocks my footsteps,
sees my fingers touching ancient coins,
themes marked "A," battered music stand.

This resisted admission that a chapter has closed because it must
is a precursor of changes yet too vast to know.
It is not goodbye and yet it is, for lad and time have moved on,
and the man obtains—
he who was exceedingly loved and loved bounteously in return,
and left a magic memory—
he who knew trial and pain, fear and anger and God,
who persevered and found ancient wisdom in his grasp.

You know the love and pride we hold for you.
You will know it even more when, tomorrow,
you stand clutching after the last to go.

To close, our dad was a good father, a good husband, a good pilot, a good leader (military and civilian), a good writer, a good musician, a good food and drink appreciator, a good friend to many—and probably lots of other good things that those who knew him from different walks of life would add. We hope that each of you will treasure your individual memories of this smart, interesting, devoted, clever, funny, talented guy—we certainly shall.

Section 2

Letters to My Aunt

After my father passed away, I continued to write letters detailing my travel and business adventures, only sending them to his sister, my aunt Janet. Those letters follow. She lives in Lincoln, NE, where she has lived all her life since college at the University of Nebraska, with the exception of the last several years of WWII when she was one of the inaugural class of Pan American stewardesses and was based in Portland, Oregon. Which, by the way, she completely enjoyed. But love came along and at the end of the war she married Pete Jenkins, a blond, crewcut naval aviator. And a gifted choral teacher, singer, and musician. Pete got a job at the university and Janet birthed and raised four kids, my cousins.

I still see Janet at least yearly in Lincoln; she is smart, well read, and has the pleasant and occasionally challenging directness for which midwesterners are legitimately known. I love her dearly. I see the cousins there as well, usually at the Fourth of July celebration at Cousin Jim's house. He annually constructs something out of more than a thousand bottle rockets, called auspiciously the Redneck Rocket Launcher, and somehow avoids blowing off one of his fingers or setting anything important on fire when he ignites it at the end of the evening.

[7]

Hi, Bulgaria, Good to See You; and India, How You Been?

July/August 2010

Dear Aunt Janet,

You may be asking yourself right now, "I wonder what happens when a big 'xecutive in the energy business takes a trip abroad?" Or, more likely, you're asking yourself, "I wonder if I should have a ham and cheese sandwich for lunch?" But on the off chance that your mind is occupied with the fascinations of question number one, I am here to give you the answer! Or at least my answer.

I just finished a two-and-a-half week around-the-world trip to some of the various places where we are trying to develop and build solar plants. As a part of that trip, I wrote "field notes" to send to my board of directors so they wouldn't wonder why I was spending their money flitting about to pleasure spots like Bulgaria and Wuxi, China. What follows is "field notes with explication." A great word, explication, sounds like it should be associated with spitting in the street in a time of great sickness, but fortunately is not. Because the board already knows a bunch of the jargon found herein, I will both try to explain that, and add the more interesting bits that they don't care about. Maybe this will work, maybe not. The actual notes that I sent to the board will be italicized.

Boring background: I left Sunday night, a couple of days after Dad's interment at Arlington National Cemetery, on an overnight flight to Paris. Overnight is the only way you can get there unless you are Bill Gates and own your own jet. I used to take the early flight, leaving around six, and arriving in Charles de Gaulle Airport (hereinafter CDG, which is what everyone calls it) at six in the early morning. Many things in France are named after the famous general, including an ineffective political party, but then we have Reagan National Airport in Washington and the Republican Party, exact analogues. "Oh six hundred hours" is not a good time to arrive anywhere, especially Paris where they do not get up early unless the Germans are attacking, and probably not even then. This is a good thing about France and Europe in general.

The problem with the flight is the ugly conjunction of time zone change and flight duration. It only takes six hours of flying time to get to Paris, but there is a six-hour time zone change, hence if you leave at six in the evening you arrive at midnight your time. And then the day starts. Besides, the airline tricks you, serves you dinner, offers you a movie ("Wow, *Shrek the 16th* again? Great!") and generally lulls you into thinking that you will arrive at six a.m. your time, and so you have all the time in the world to get whatever sleep one can get on an airplane. You finish dinner and half the movie and nod off and then they immediately turn on all the lights and insist on giving you airline breakfast, which fortunately does not involve meat, something airlines do not do well. And then you land. All day you walk around feeling like someone has deposited sand in your eyes.

So I don't do that anymore, as they have invented a flight that leaves at ten o'clock at night. It's still six hours, and it's still the same time zone change, but at least you get on, you go to sleep, and you arrive around ten in the morning when you can have reasonable meetings with people, since they have now all finally come to work, or just about, in Paris. Not great, but better. Why it took me twenty painful years to figure this out we cannot say.

Okay, here comes the first set of notes that I sent to the board. This is the last time I will make such a labored transition.

Flew overnight from Dulles to Paris, then took train in from CDG to La Défense. Note careful economical approach to transportation, €8.75 for the subway vs. a cab cost of probably €60. Plus you get to meet a lot of real French people on the metro. They appear to be largely Moroccan or African, except for the odd tall Swedish blonde with the backpack and wimpy boyfriend. Maybe I was going through that area where they burned all the cars a couple of years ago, but I don't think they burned any subway cars.

I met with David Corchia, COO of EDF-En in his new office, with a lovely view of La Défense. Which is lovely only if you like modern architecture viewed from above, which I rather do. And no trees. Which it has none of. La Défense is like a miniature Brasilia but with no cars and lots of concrete, glass, modern sculptures of enormous size, frequently by Calder, and the Grande Arche whose purpose and symbolism we know not. Shouldn't the Arc de Triomphe be enough? One would have thought so. And for those enamored of geometry, the Grande Arche, which is in fact pretty big, is on a straight line, heading west, from the Arc de Triomphe. It also has no curves. An "arche" with no arches in it. A triumph of French determinism or something.

Brief explication: Électricité de France (EDF) is the national French utility, the second biggest utility in the world. Only the Russian one is bigger. No longer entirely state owned as of five years ago, they still basically run, control, and dominate the French market for electricity despite the ineffectual mewling of the EU competition bureaucrats in Brussels. EDF-En is a 50% owned subsidiary of big EDF, stands for "EDF-Energies Nouvelles." This company was put together a couple of years ago by Pâris Mouratoglou, a successful energy developer of traditional coal- and gas-fired power plants, who decided that it was time to do wind and solar. He started doing this with his own money, found it to be quite capital intensive, and then brilliantly sold a 50% interest to EDF, probably at a big markup to whatever money he had in the business. We do admire this sort of thing and are striving to emulate it. They are probably our most effective competitor in the solar business, but since the solar area is so new and so small, there is plenty of room for all of us. And, frankly, having someone like them who actually understands that this is electricity we are making here, not model airplanes or rooftop decorations, is good for the whole industry. David Corchia is the number-two guy of the place—chief operating officer or COO—and a former banker.

David was voluble and charming, as always. We discussed the swap idea. He is still interested, wanted to know only who would control the construction of the projects. I said that it made the most sense for the original sponsor to control construction through COD, and have the actual exchange take place at that point. The EDF response to our initial paper had been that they needed to swap at NTP for tax reasons. It may still be necessary to have the swap take place at this point, but to hand over control at COD. No doubt this can be structured around. We agreed that we would proceed on evaluating some specific swaps, and I would provide him three things: 1) our paper on what elements went into the valuation of the projects to be swapped; 2) a model for a typical project, using the variables in 1.; and 3) a short description of several of our Italian projects for his team to look at as a superficial check to see if they were interested, and that we aren't bozos.

Jargon alert: I have found that when you decide to learn a new industry, there is always a mountain of jargon and acronyms to climb, and no one ever gives you a dictionary or climbing tools. "COD" is commercial operations date, the point at which you have completed building your plant and are actually hooked up to the grid, have finished all the testing, are making electricity and—thanks be to God—actually getting paid for it. "NTP" is notice to proceed, which is a formal instruction you give to your construction contractor, the company who is building the plant for you. You generally negotiate the construction contract (referred to below as an "EPC" contract—stands for engineer, procure, and construct, the functions that the contractor performs) and sign it beforehand, but do not activate it until you have the money to pay for it. Doing otherwise makes the construction guys really testy.

The swap idea is this: the weird French have decided that they don't want solar plants to be too big. Blight on the landscape or something; makes no sense to me. And in puritanical École Superieure, "we know everything" fashion, they have decreed that 12 Mw is the largest tolerable size. Now in the real world, parcels of land don't happen to come in nice tidy 12 Mw sizes. In fact they come in hectares, a snotty Euro/metric word that means 2.47 acres. Or if you really are metric, it means 10,000 square meters. Isn't that handy? In general, 12 Mw requires a plot size of about 120 acres or 48.5 hectares, although it depends on how good the sun is in the particular location. Not surprisingly, you can make more electricity with less land if you have more sun.

All the land in France except possibly the Champs-Élysée in Paris seems to be zoned for agricultural use, and although some of my colleagues call what we're doing "solar farms," agriculture this is not. If you find a nice piece of ground that you would like to use for a solar plant, nine times out of ten it will be "agricultural" and thus you have to request that the authorities change the zoning to "light industrial" or some equivalent before it is legal for you to use it. This process is very process heavy, involving probably an environmental study, many forms, much consultation, a public input process, etc., and takes usually a minimum of a year— even if everyone in the whole area agrees that this is a good idea. There is literally no way to foreshorten the process, and the size of the parcel being rezoned doesn't matter. So you might think to yourself, "Self, we got here a lovely 200 hectare plot of land that the owner wants to sell to me and is ideal for a solar plant as it's full of salt and rocks so nothing can grow here. And in fact it could accommodate about a 40 Mw plant. And it is just as much time and trouble to get a 48 hectare piece rezoned as a 200 hectare piece. What say we go for the whole thing, then just grid it out into 48 hectare pieces, call it four different but contiguous solar plants, and we have complied with the rules and their stupid 12 Mw limit."

Ah, but you misjudge the cleverness of the French authorities, *ma chérie*! Any individual solar plant must be separated by a 500 meter corridor if it is to be in the same ownership as the plant next door. So you can't just have a checkerboard of 45 hectare squares, you have 45 hectare squares with wasteful and expensive and vacant 500 meter (five and a half football fields in width) corridors between each plant. Maybe you can plant marigolds. This is pretty silly and a bad use or nonuse of land. You have thus only one real choice, and that is to divide the large piece of land into contiguous plots, and sell of enough of the plots to others so that you can keep most of it. The plots you keep are now separated by at least the requisite 500 meters, but the 500 meters is also a solar plant, just owned by someone else. It is an interesting topographic exercise if you like such things.

What piqued my interest in all this was an article I read that announced that EDF-En was in the process of selling off some pieces of a larger solar plant they had developed, to satisfy this boneheaded 12 Mw limitation. But they are not really in the "develop and sell" business; they, like we, would like to develop, build, own, and operate plants and make electricity and then sell that. And we have lots of projects in development in Italy where they do not have this stupid rule, but not so much in France. And EDF-En is heavy on France, light on Italy. Hence, why not swap projects with EDF-En? Then they don't have to sell Mw, they just exchange some of theirs in France for some of ours in Italy, the French noncontiguity rule is settled and off we go. The mechanics are more complicated than this but conceptually it's reasonably straightforward. Long explanation, simple concept. Whether we can work through the details remains to be seen.

The discussion then turned to Bulgaria. They have a 22 Mw project in the southeast of the country that has all its permits, and has financing arranged with the IFC, and is ready to close. However, Corchia is not comfortable with the tariff risk and has held up closing, although the development team wants to close and begin construction. It turns out that IFC is not really ready either and has put in a condition to drawing down the financing that requires the tariff to get fixed (see below). IFC would still like to close and get its closing fees paid, however. David's response was "Why should I start paying fees for a loan that I may never be able to use?" I agreed to give him some feedback after my trip there. During the Bulgaria discussion he asked his international (by this I believe he meant outside of France) development executive to come in, a woman named Fabienne Demol. She echoed his sentiments although seemed less concerned about tariff change risk. But hey, she's a developer.

EXPLICATION: More on Bulgaria below. Much more. More than you ever hoped to know about solar projects in Bulgaria. You are so lucky.

IFC is the International Finance Corporation, an arm of the World Bank that works with private companies and helps finance their projects in the dodgier parts of the world. Having them as part of your financing structure gives you some protection from bad behavior on the part of the dodgy government where your project is. If one screws around with IFC, as in not repaying them or nationalizing a project in which they have invested, then the World Bank will never lend one's government any more money. Most third world governments run on borrowed money, and since they don't have the luxury the US has—at least for now, who knows about next year?—of going to the private capital markets and selling government debt to the Chinese, then getting your government cut off by the World Bank is a big deal of the negative sort. Unless you are Argentina who for some reason routinely stops paying off its government debt and no one seems really to mind. The flip side of the coin is that the IFC knows it has this clout and is also really the only game in town making these sorts of loans, so they are not particularly customer friendly.

When my colleagues complain about how hard the IFC is to deal with, I say to them, "Remember, they have the money and WE want it."

Meeting over, I board the subway again, head back to CDG, and catch a flight to the capital of Bulgaria. This is the $400 question on *Jeopardy*, category "Small Capitals of the Former Soviet Union," answer, "What is Sofia?" The $1000 question is no doubt "What is Ljubljana?" and if you can pronounce that I will give you a hundred dollars. It is the capital of Slovenia, not to be confused, as I have done in the past, with Slovakia. I have never been there but I long to. Think how great the snow globe would be. And what are the residents of the capital called, Ljubljanaians? But we digress.

Desperately seeking deodorant: There is no worse feeling for an international traveler than being in a slightly odd foreign city, late in the evening, standing at the baggage carousel, alone, so very alone, with every other passenger having secured his or her baggage. Except you. And then the carousel stops, and you know you're doomed. This happens to me with depressing regularity. And happened in Sofia. I go to the "baggage office" and let them know that there's a problem, and please, God, please find my luggage soon and send it to my hotel.

Why is this more of a problem in Sofia than Albuquerque, you may ask? Not having your suitcase is a pain anywhere, for sure. But in New Mexico, the airline folks all speak English, as do the hotel people probably. And, more important, if you now have only the clothes on your back and the many interesting papers in your briefcase, at least you can go to Walgreens tonight and probably Target in the morning and buy toiletries and a clean shirt and some underwear. Ever try sorting out European sizes? Incomprehensible, and the clerks are no help as who cares what American sizes are. Then check out the cosmetics. The razors are pretty straightforward, but I cannot even begin to be sure which boxes and bottles and otherwise strange-shaped containers are the deodorant. I am pretty sure that Europeans now use deodorant, but perhaps they get it at special deodorant stores, no labels on the doors, and hidden from us normal travelers, kind of like speakeasies. This is not the best part of the trip. I go off to my hotel feeling very tired, gritty, and grumpy.

Because they have not "fed" me on the plane from Paris, by the time I get to my hotel, it is too late for room service. Yes, I know that the causality implied in the previous sentence does not follow, I am talking cosmic causality here. Is three small pieces of chocolate cake, each with a raspberry on top, a small bag of Lays potato chips and three glasses of wine from the minibar a good dinner? Well, I guess it all depends. That is what is available in the Radisson in Sofia. That and a really great view of the cathedral two blocks away, golden dome and all.

I believe, based on a substantial number of observations, that in hotel school they teach the managers to leave each new guest three things: a lovely letter of welcome, a small odd pastry (the aforementioned three pieces of chocolate cake, which were actually pretty good given that I had not really had any food since before getting on the airplane on Sunday), and the ever-present fruit basket. I don't care about the letter, they all say the same thing, I will never meet the guy who writes this, I will only have problems late at night when he is not around anyway, and what he does not say in the letter of welcome is which number on the stupid phone do I punch for the front desk? I need a wake-up call since the airline has my alarm clock.

But the biggest mystery is the fruit basket. Why do people who manage hotels think that their guests are suffering from a fruit shortage? Do they all have scurvy? I cannot even begin to count the number of hotels I have been in where they have waiting for you a fruit basket, usually laid out with a napkin and a knife and fork. Two apples, an orange, a banana, a kiwi fruit. I am staying one night. This is a lot of fruit to eat even if I skip dinner. And no one eats it, really. You want to try peeling a kiwi fruit with a dull dinner knife? Besides, other than looking kind of green and pretty, a kiwi fruit doesn't really taste like anything. This is a triumph of New Zealand marketing. What I would really like is a Doritos basket full of chips and Slim Jims, but does anyone ever send that up to my room? Forget about it.

I go to bed in a bad state of mind, wondering if I am such a big deal CEO of a hot solar company, why am I washing out my underwear in the sink?

I warned you there would be a lot about our business in Bulgaria. As a partial introduction, I should note that when I left the government, lo these many years ago, after helping to write and pass energy legislation and other really interesting stuff like that, I had some reservations. I did think to myself that while I could probably make more money in the private sector, I was unlikely to be as intellectually challenged as I had been in government. This was completely wrong, as so many youthful observations are. Business problems are every bit as difficult and interesting as public service ones, and if you get them right they pay way better. If you like you can skip the italicized part but some of it is pretty cool. I will add small explications as we go along.

I flew late on Monday to Sofia [as you already know from reading the whining above]. Our country manager, Aneliya Erdly, had arranged meetings with key ministers: Minister Traikov of Energy, Economy, and

Tourism; Minister Plevneliev of Regional Development; as well as Prime Minister Borissov and three different legislators. Also the head NEK transmission guy. In addition we met with the US ambassador and participated in a press conference that he arranged. It was a quick two days.

Or a long two days if you didn't have a clean shirt. NEK is the National Transmission Electric Utility of Bulgaria. They are key as we have to connect into the grid once we make the electricity, and these are the guys who own the grid and are responsible for moving electricity around the country, and paying us. Fortunately, they are pretty reasonable.

The situation on tariff revision is more complicated than I had previously understood, mostly coming from recent ideas to introduce competitive bidding in parallel with the tariff regime. The process of changing the law, however, is pretty clear: the executive branch submits a proposed law, or in this case a revision, to the parliament; the parliament does a couple of "readings" of the bill, makes such changes as they see fit, and then passes the bill. Since the system in Bulgaria is the same as that in the UK, the executive branch is controlled by the same party as the legislature, so getting things passed is not as difficult or contentious as in the US.

The current law allows for a twenty-five-year power purchase agreement, signed at the time of receipt of the operating permit that is effectively COD, for all projects under 5 Mw. The tariff is currently set at €0.37.3 per kWh. This tariff will be valid until March 31, 2011, after which it may get reset. It is composed of a renewable premium (currently about 90% of the total) and a wholesale component that is based on actual costs for the previous year. The law allows the renewable premium to be reset each year on 1 April—downward by no more than 5% or upward with no cap. The intention was that this reset would only apply to projects whose tariffs had not at that point been set, i.e., new projects, and not to existing projects— ones in construction or operation—but unfortunately the law is drafted poorly and can be read to give the regulatory body authority to decrease the tariff of both existing and new projects. So, theoretically, one can have a project whose tariff goes down 5% a year for each of the twenty-five years of the contract. We cannot finance such an arrangement, and it also shoots the economics. As evidence of this disability, it is interesting to note that only 6 Mw of photovoltaic solar plants have actually been constructed in Bulgaria in the one year since the law went into force. During the same period, Germany, with less sun, a lower tariff level, but a workable law, has constructed 4,000 Mw.

More electricity background: I may not have noted this before, but us utility guys think in terms of megawatts (Mw), which is a thousand kilowatts, which in turn is 1,000 watts. Your light bulbs range from 40 to 100 watts, and your whole house uses maybe 2,500 watts, or 2.5 kilowatts. The total US generation capacity is around 900,000 megawatts. Bulgaria, a much smaller country, is about 11,000 megawatts. Your hometown Lincoln Electric System has about 800 Mw of generating capacity.

We sell electricity in the US, on average, at $.10 per kilowatt hour (kWh) retail, and make it for around $.04 to $.05 wholesale, so for us to get something like $.35 is a big deal. And note that this is in euros, so depending on the exchange rate, currently around $1.30 per euro, this is really more than $.40 USD per kWh. I love this business. But in order to get banks to loan us the money for the plants, we need the tariff to be guaranteed for a long period of time, twenty or twenty-five years, as that is the duration of the loan and banks seem to like to get repaid. Thus the problem in Bulgaria—we can't have the price going down 5% every year. A PPA is a power purchase agreement, a long-term contract for us to sell electricity to the grid—a critical document which both governs how and assures that we get paid.

In previous trips, I had been assured that this matter could and would be corrected quickly and simply. And the good news is that local banks are sufficiently unconcerned about this as to be willing, contrary to IFC's position, to close and fund projects, like our Kalipetrovo 3.9 Mw one, while taking the risk that the law never gets corrected. While I was in Sofia, we received news that our financing with the local Société Générale bank had in fact been approved by the credit committee of the bank in Paris, and thus we could expect to close in a week or two.

Unfortunately, this need for legal revision has opened the gate to a broader reconsideration of the entire renewables law. Aneliya has seen at least ten different drafts of the revision, and in the latest draft from five days ago there have been conceptual changes to the entire program. The most troublesome of these has been to introduce competition into the program while having the feed in tariff regime in parallel, although there has not yet been enough thought given to exactly what this means or how it would be done or what the impacts on existing vs. new projects would be. In our meeting with Minister Traikov and with one of the legislators, this idea of competition, although again with no details or understanding of impacts, was put forth strongly. In our other meetings there was a general under-standing of our position: we have a project ready to go, we have financing arranged, we can be in construction within two weeks of changing the law, Bulgaria needs FDI, can you please get on with it.

MORE LOCAL COLOR: FDI is foreign direct investment. As in, we build a power plant in your country using our money. We already at AES have made big power investments in Bulgaria: a 660 Mw coal-fired plant in the southeast of the country, and a 150 Mw wind plant in the east. The coal plant is late but about to come online, and the wind plant is already up and running. AES is now the largest single foreign investor in Bulgaria. This was not a corporate goal, it just kinda happened. But this explains why a dinky little solar plant commands this level of attention from the political hierarchy.

On Wednesday morning, Peter Lithgow, the AES country manager, and Aneliya and I met with the prime minister in his office. He is a big, bluff guy with a burr haircut, and a reputation for action. Although it was only nine o'clock in the morning, he was smoking a large cigar, one of his trademarks. The meeting started with a discussion on how the PV electricity tariff prices will affect overall electricity energy prices in Bulgaria—not a great beginning—but then it quickly evolved into how fast we can make the investment. After some initial sparring about why Bulgaria should buy this expensive power, he finally got the message that we have a project ready to go and that they have a commitment to renewable energy that they have to meet or the EU will fine them. He also recognized the issue with the fluctuating tariff and stated, "The thermal coal-burning plants have their tariffs fixed so it should not be a problem to do the same for renewables." In fact, the Bulgarian budget for next year has an allowance for fines to be paid to the EU, which are the consequence for Bulgaria's failing to meet its renewable generation target. He called Traikov (who wasn't there) and the CEO of NEK, who was, and he called someone else while we sat there. He said, in essence, I have some credible people here who want to invest in a solar project, we need to make this happen. That was a good result, although it is still not entirely clear how this can be carried out absent the legislative revision mentioned above.

The icing on the cake: Ambassador Warlick, with whom we met on Tuesday, advised that we should hold a press conference on the issue, and volunteered to lead it. So immediately after the PM meeting, we all trooped over to the "American corner" of the American Chamber of Commerce office and spent an hour educating the TV and press folks on our message, which the ambassador ably trumpeted. His message: "Get moving, you Bulgarians. We got Americans here with money to invest in your country!" I was pretty glad that he was in the lead on this.

MORE EXPLICATION: almost every country I have been to where we are seriously considering an investment has an American Chamber of Commerce, an "AmCham" as they are called, a group of the American companies who have invested in the country. This is a useful organization, you can commiserate with your fellow Americans about how badly you are being treated, swap stories about who is the most incompetent government official, and so forth. These are generally good and professional organizations, and they always work closely with the US embassy, no surprise there.

We are now presented with an interesting problem: what is the range of possible outcomes on the tariff, and how should we proceed with the Kalipetrovo project that is fully ready to go, with a 9.5 million euro approved nonrecourse loan (plus a VAT facility) ready to be signed and an accompanying four million Euro equity commitment which requires no additional cash, given that we have already purchased the panels and they are sitting unproductively in a warehouse in Bulgaria. And a signed EPC contract, all construction permits obtained and a signed interconnection agreement.

Oops, MORE JARGON: a nonrecourse loan is an interesting kind of financing where the bank has only a security interest in the assets it is financing, in this case a solar power plant, and the sponsoring company is not on the hook. This allows you to do more borrowing, as our corporate credit rating is not very good. I don't know why banks invented this, but we like it. VAT is the value added tax, in this case a giant sales tax of 17%. But we are exempt from it as the Bulgarians have decided that solar plants are virtuous and should not be taxed. Only what they actually do is charge you the tax and then make you apply to have it refunded. It may not surprise you to know that this does not happen overnight, and cannot happen until the project is completed. Hence you give them your money and eventually they give it back to you, without interest. To make up for this, the kindly bank gives you a separate loan (the "VAT facility") secured with a pledge against the government's obligation to give you back your own money.

There are a range of outcomes to the renewables law revision process:

» The law is never changed and the renewables premium goes down by 5% every year, although there has been enough commotion on this issue, and the record of nonaccomplishment on getting projects built would seem to mitigate against this result. This is a very low probability outcome.

» The law is changed to provide a fixed tariff at some point in a project's development or construction, as we have asked. The proposed "fixing" points have been at PPA or at FIA (final interconnection agreement) as per the latest draft of the law. Subsequent tariff revisions would only apply to new projects that do not have their FIA or PPA by March 31, 2011.

» The law is fixed, as in two above, but only once, and only for the limited universe of projects that have attained some particular milestone in the development process by some specific date. Projects that have not, or that are conceived and executed subsequent to the revision of the law, would receive whatever treatment or tariff is concocted for "new" projects, some form of which could include competitive bidding. Obviously, what the grandfathering milestone is, how it is measured, and what the cutoff date/definition is for existing vs. new projects is critically important. Again, as per the drafts we have seen, the milestones will most likely be a signed FIA or PPA, which works fine for most of our project pipeline and certainly for Kalipetrovo.

»   The old tariff is thrown out and some new process/set of incentives is established for all projects, existing and new.

I would handicap these outcomes, respectively, at 5%, 30%, 50%, and 15%, but that is based on gut feel as well as on all the drafts we have reviewed, conversations with the government, and the assumption that the Bulgarian government will be reasonable in their actions and serious about achieving their 16% renewable energy EU-mandated target. What is clear is that we should proceed to mount an enhanced lobbying effort, both with the government and with the parliament, to get our position heard and some variant of it adopted. We are doing so, and EDF-En has agreed to join the effort. We need to be sensitive to the possibility of a case #3 outcome, and while not pushing ostensibly for it, have it as a fallback. If we can protect our 80 Mw Saint George project still in development and a couple of our other ones in advanced development, we could end up with a portfolio of about 100 Mw's grandfathered under the "old" program/tariff. That might be quite enough to keep us busy for a while as we determine what to do in response to the "new" program conditions.

The hard issue is how to proceed, or not, on Kalipetrovo. There are basically three options:

Do not do any further work on the project: don't sign the loan agreement, don't start construction, don't make the final payment for the project to its local developer. We have told the government that we "cannot" build the project without the law changed, but that is not actually correct. We have been clear that we cannot build Saint George, our large project. The largest risk with this course of action, especially if we do not pay the developer his €530,000 fee that is due in two weeks and is not dependent on any tariff change, is the loss of the project. This course of action underlines and supports our political argument, but it endangers our relations with the bank, with our developer, and with our EPC contractor, Biosar. The

EPC contract with Biosar is technically the least problem because it has been executed, but it has a generous window for notifying the contractor to commence construction. Biosar has, however, been doing the advanced design work for the last month on its own nickel and has already ordered the inverters to secure their availability for the project. They have now spent more than €1 million on this project. If we were to delay the project, this would be the second Biosar project to be deferred (Pchelarovo was the first), raising serious credibility issues with one of our key contractors. Biosar is important to us in Italy; they have worked at risk on Iktinos and now at Kalipetrovo and I suspect they'll be strong candidates for future EPC work.

The local developer, Parvi Mai, we really do have to pay; but that is not a visible signal, i.e., trucks and excavators don't show up on the site and dirt doesn't start flying. The execution of the loan documents is more complex. The local branch of Société Générale went to a lot of trouble to push our loan through their credit committee in Paris at our request. Technically again, we can sign and pay commitment fees (about €60k), but the upfront loan fee (2% or €200k) is not due until the initial drawdown of funds. Just how long the bank would continue to reserve capacity for our loan is an interesting question, as is whether they would be willing to do this at all, given the underlying possibility that it will never be drawn, especially if we don't even execute as planned.

Get halfway pregnant: We could pay the developer, close with and pay the bank commitment fees and the initial loan fee, but not drawdown any funds, and have the contractor start on-site preparation without fully activating the other parts of the contract or going ahead with any long lead time equipment procurement beyond what has already occurred. This would be an equity exposure of close to €1.2 million. The construction effort would now be physically visible, so it undercuts our argument of "we cannot build" and thus our strategy would have to change subtly. Our new story would be "We have been assured that the law will be changed, so we are willing to take some risk that this is true and begin construction. So don't screw us. But we can only build this one small project." What happens if we get the site cleared and the law has still not been changed is not clear, and this could easily happen, i.e., we could find ourselves forced to stop construction and demobilize, lose our inverter allocation and redirect our panels to other projects, which would be expensive and disruptive. And if we have a case #4 change, we stand to lose the €1.2 million if we elect not to proceed to full construction.

Go for it: As above, but we make the initial drawdown and release the contractor. This is a bolder move than two above, and relies more clearly on the "good faith" of the branches of the government. However, by the time the bill gets to the parliament we will be putting up panels, so we have a much stronger case for grandfathering. The team in Bulgaria will do the analysis but argues that we will have an asset of some value if we complete the construction; the issue is only that the returns may not be what we would like.

I am inclined to recommend the third course of action, but I need to review the numbers first. The local team, which is very good by the way, argues that we should go forward because:

It is a strategic investment in a new market which could turn out to be a good one for us; permitting is quicker and easier than France or Italy or Greece; there is a relatively low equity exposure; we have something of a first mover advantage—if the tariff is fixed perfectly, everyone will be in the market; relationships matter (Biosar, Parvi Mai, SocGen); we have reliable and capable Bulgarian developers and additional pipeline; this adds an additional 3.9 Mw in operation by the end of the year to our portfolio; building gives us a case to grandfather Saint George or at least doesn't take away from this argument; it is a robust project (€3.46 kW in cost, lower than most of our Italian projects) with a worst-case scenario of achieving an 8% levered IRR if the law does not change and the tariff is decreased each year by 5%.

We will flesh out the situation and the arguments a bit more and send the matter forward to the board for a decision within the next couple of weeks.

Back story number one: Sometimes it's good to be an American. Ambassador Warlick passed on to me that the US is now in reasonably high regard in Bulgaria, because the FBI recently discovered a serious plot to assassinate Borissov. This information was passed on to him by the ambassador, and the bad guys were thwarted. Nothing about this ever became public. The world is sometimes an uncertain place and it's about more than just investment and economic development.

Back story number two: We have a really wonderful young woman in Bulgaria leading the solar efforts, Aneliya Erdly. She is Bulgarian by birth, a US citizen by marriage, and a pit bull by DNA. She has a US MBA from Georgetown, from whence we recruited her, and she worked for four years at AES doing mergers and acquisitions, so she has good deal experience. I snatched her up when we stated the solar biz as I needed someone for Bulgaria and she was a star. She is smart and fearless and charming when she needs to be charming. If we are successful in Bulgaria, it will be largely due to her skill and hard work. And the wonderful part of starting from scratch with access to the AES talent pool is that I get to select the best people and ignore the less good ones. At one point Paul Hanrahan, the CEO, got annoyed with me and said no more running off with the best developers without my personal approval. OK, I said. What else do you say to your CEO and board member? But it has been a wonderful luxury.

There were more meetings and more discussions and much plotting and strategizing with the country team while I was there, but the notes to the board encapsulate where we came out as to choices. Predictably the country team led by Aneliya wanted to go ahead and build the darn project. When I got back to Arlington, we put together a formal board paper recommending approval, and I am pleased to say that the board relented—they had previously refused to allow us to go ahead, which was why I went to Bulgaria in the first place, to get a more up-to-date feel for the political terrain—and approved the project. We should close the financing and start construction at the end of August. This will be our fifth country with a solar plant.

I am high on Bulgaria, but it is not Paris. In particular, there's this Bulgarian taste thing. On the second day there, basking as I was in the luxury of having finally had my luggage recovered and, after much discussion, delivered to my hotel and thus wearing—finally—a clean shirt, I was standing in front of the hotel waiting for Aneliya to meet me for lunch, as it was a lovely day. The data one collects in watching the passersby supports the conclusion, I got to say, that Bulgarians do not read *Vogue* and are not clothed by Ralph Lauren. The standard outfit is wildly mismatched. Not just plaids and stripes together, although there is that, but more. My favorite outfit among many contenders: a skinny young woman with loud red hair (a color not found in nature) wearing bright yellow jeans, a gold and brown overprinted Esprit T-shirt, and a tan hoodie sweatshirt. All this in just five minutes of people watching.

On Wednesday in the late afternoon I left for India, flying via Munich, once again an overnight flight, this time seven hours and little sleep. I arrived around seven a.m. Delhi time at the absolutely brand-new modern terminal at Delhi, named after Indira Gandhi, another famous non-American political leader other than Charles de Gaulle. If they were really smart they would sell the naming rights to Google or one of the big Indian companies like Tata or Reliance. I don't think Indira paid them anything as she is dead. Stadiums in the US get upwards of $10 million a year for selling naming rights, and this would be way more visible than a baseball field in Houston. No one has asked me, however.

India smells like lemon pickle tastes—a blend of smoke, curry, and tamarind. It is unlike anywhere else in the world. You could be blindfolded getting off the plane and you would know where you were. Visually there is one word for the India you see driving to the hotel or to your business meetings: disorderly. People in the streets, traffic not staying in its lanes, people sleeping, people pushing carts with nothing in them, lots of folks sitting around. Chaotic is probably too strong. And it's not a busy disorderliness, it's just endemic disorganization. They are building a new metro system in Delhi and we pass by lots and lots of construction, with many people, but no one who looks like they are doing real work. How do they ever get anything done here?

Because we have an early meeting I have no time to change my clothes, so off we go to meet with the power minister. I am getting used to this slightly grungy approach to business dress, I just hope the people I meet with don't notice. At least the luggage showed up.

India
Thursday and Friday, 29 and 30 July
I flew in overnight from Sofia via Munich to Delhi. Srini had arranged for meetings with two ministers—power (that one seemed clear) and "new

and renewable energy"—which energy is "new"? I thought we already knew just about all the energy forms there are except possibly cold fusion. And a meeting with the principal secretary of the Ministry of New and Renewable Energy (MNRE). Note that this, too, is the UK system, where the top political appointee is the minister, but the person immediately below him is a permanent civil servant and is called the principal secretary. Usually a member of the Indian Administrative Service (IAS), this is the person who actually runs the ministry although he does not "set policy." The difference between setting policy and administering it is a fine and variable one, as anyone who has ever been in the government or been subject to the government will well appreciate. In addition, these guys rotate frequently among ministries and overseas, serving as chief of mission at Indian embassies, for example. They are very well respected; it is difficult to get into the IAS and the people are generally very bright and hardworking. It is sort of an elite civil service that does not exist in the US. They can also be, I have found from time to time, overbearing and very certain of their own brilliance.

We have just signed the MOU and made the $270k bank deposit, steps that finalize the selection of our 5 Mw project near Jodhpur in Rajasthan as a part of the National Solar Mission, the Indian scheme for stimulating solar energy—20,000 Mw by 2022. This is an admirable goal and one not lacking in ambition. So far, the rules of this central government initiative are attractive and even thoughtful. As a sort of a jump start, the MNRE offered to accept some modest number of projects from state programs into the "mission." Several states, including Gujarat, Punjab, Maharashtra, and Rajasthan had already set solar incentive programs in motion, accepted applications, done a certain amount of screening, and awarded PPAs. But in all cases, the mission pricing is more generous than the state level pricing, so being in the federal program is a benefit to a project. Also from the state's point of view, the subsidy element in the tariff is now picked up in the budget at the federal level, or "center" as it is usually called. Of the four states listed above, all but Gujarat submitted their projects, and ours was among the Rajasthan projects selected. This should mean that we get rapidly financed and built. But little in India is characterized by the adjective "rapid" or the adverb "rapidly."

JARGON WATCH: An MOU is a memorandum of understanding, a nonbinding but very useful written agreement that you sign with someone else and that lays out in writing all the things that you think you have agreed to and they have agreed to, and frequently some surprises as well. It's an intermediate step between marketing where everyone agrees on the buying and selling of whatever is being discussed, and the legally binding contract that really should be done correctly because it counts. The same document is sometimes called a term sheet or a letter of intent (LOI) or a "heads of terms" if you are trying to be British.

A PPA, as noted briefly above, is a power purchase agreement, the key document to our whole business. It lays out what we are going to do, how much, how often, with what regularity and predictability. What we are going to do, essentially, is make lots of electricity. The other party agrees to buy same, for a price, with escalation usually, and payment guarantees and lots of other stuff. The first one we ever signed was eleven pages, and ever since then they have been longer. This document is key as it is what the banks rely on when they loan you the money. They do want you to get paid so they can get paid. Funny how that works.

The process for finalizing the 84 Mw worth of projects (three solar thermal projects of 10 Mw each and thirteen PV projects of 1 Mw to 5 Mw size) is first to sign an MOU, and next to sign a PPA. Once the PPA is signed, we have three months to secure and close the financing of the project, and twelve months to put it into operation, or we lose our deposit. Not quite clear how "close the financing" is defined as we have not seen the final draft of the PPA that we will be asked to sign with no changes. The goal of our meetings was simple: express appreciation for being in the first wave of central government projects, and request a chance to look at the PPA before it goes final. It won't be good if it has provisions in it that the banks won't like, and this is an area where we know quite a bit. And of course we need to be fawning and obsequious (I have finally learned to do obsequy after all these years, I have no shame) to these high government officials, as they have in fact carried out their program in about as efficient a fashion as I have seen anything in India executed.

Meetings one and two, with the two ministers, went fine. We all congratu-lated each other, and both men said we should certainly have a look at the PPA, just contact so and so (not them). Minister Abdullah, the MNRE minister, even said, "Let's get on with it, let's get these plants built. I want to be able to take the prime minister to the inauguration, and point at a light bulb and tell him, 'There's your renewable power.'" This didn't quite follow since you need light bulbs at night when we don't make much solar power, but we liked his enthusiasm.

LOCAL COLOR: these meeting were in each case conducted in what looked like nice one-story houses, with gates and security, but not in big official office buildings. Strange locations for important government ministries. They are all in the downtown government area of Delhi, but very suburban. The power minister was pleasant but a bit unfocused. The renewables minister, a large guy wearing a white linen overshirt, is from Kashmir. He was eating lunch while we met and is said to have three wives. I didn't know you could do that in Islam, but in India many things are possible. The wives, not the lunch.

The third meeting, with Secretary Gupta, went not fine. We got yelled at for thirty minutes for even suggesting that there was any improvement that could possibly be made in the ministry's work formulating the PPA. The fourteen first wave developers who had each signed MOUs (including us of course) had subsequently sent a joint letter to Mr. Gupta pointing out that it was a very one-sided document, and asking that we as a group be allowed to review and comment on the PPA that we are about to be required to sign. This has had a bad effect on Mr. Gupta. "If I had received this letter before, I would never have even had a migration program! This is a benefit to you, it is not a benefit to us! You have received something many others now wish that they had and you are complaining! If you don't like this program you are free to drop out!"

I haven't been in a meeting quite this bad in some time. We never, in the whole thirty minutes, got to utter a single complete sentence. It was so bad as to be silly. I thought at one point of just getting up and walking out. Then I thought of asking the secretary to be more clear, I really wasn't getting his message. Then I thought maybe I should ask if he at least liked my tie. Finally I opted for mostly silence, as attempts to answer any of his statements were immediately interrupted. Ah well, it's not always sweetness and light and little kittens as we build the solar empire.

The good news is that despite this less than useful interchange, the meeting really didn't matter. They will come up with a PPA, we will sign it, and we will most likely get it financed. Or if not, we will organize a cabal of all the developers plus the banks who want to finance these plants and go back and get the changes that we need. This is a high central government priority, and already there has been much press coverage of these initial selections and the signing of the first round of documents.

We have also made significant progress on our two projects. In Rajasthan, we have secured the land, we have the environmental permit, and we have the electric grid interconnection agreement, all signed. We have some initial quotes from EPC contractors and they make the economics work with the tariff rates in the program. We also have done an initial round with Indian banks and they are very interested in providing debt to these projects, although at higher pricing and shorter tenors than we would receive in Europe. But we can build, finance, and get paid in rupees, so we avoid currency risk, at least for the project. If we really wanted to, we could hedge the equity returns, but this would be expensive, and is something we can decide later in any event.

YET MORE JARGON: as explained briefly above, an EPC contract is for engineering, procurement, and construction. There are generally these three steps to building anything of serious industrial nature, and they are most cleanly performed by the same guy, like a Bechtel or Parsons or Black and Veatch. You design the plant, which usually involves some engineering calculations, and specify which and how much equipment you will need—the "engineering" part. Then you go buy it all, the "procurement" part. Then your contractor mobilizes a bunch of guys and equipment on the site and starts digging holes and pouring concrete and installing the equipment and hooking it up to other equipment, and finally you turn it on—the "construction" part. Having one well-capitalized contractor to take the responsibility for this whole task, and to do so while guaranteeing the price, the completion schedule, and the output, makes the project financeable. This is the second most important contract for banks—they want to make sure when they loan you the money that something actually gets built. Something that works, that is.

And what about Gujarat, mentioned above as the careful reader will note, but only in passing? This state is generally thought to be the most business oriented in all India, and I have no data to contradict that. It is also for the moment in the control of the BJP, the opposition party to the Congress Party who controls the center. Hence the Gujarat government, when asked about migrating its projects, simply said "No thanks" and did not propose any. We have received a 15 Mw allocation in their 500 Mw program, signed the PPA, put up another bank deposit as evidence of our seriousness, and can probably meet their deadlines for construction that are similar to the mission ones, but less rigorous—only a COD deadline, no financial close deadline as in the federal program. Our project activities currently hinge on getting the real estate nailed down, but we have been offered three sites, each of which would work, and are close to finalizing this land transaction. We need then to go out for bids on the construction—hard to do that when you cannot tell a contractor just where the site is or what the conditions of the land are—rocks or no rocks? Flat or not flat? As with Rajasthan, we already have significant bank interest. Environmental permits should not be a problem, nor should interconnection as long as we choose the site intelligently. Memo to self: Do not select sites far from power lines. Do not select sites in tiger sanctuaries. This project is a month or two behind the Rajasthan one, but in good shape.

The real miracle of all this is that we have all of one guy in the solar business working on this. He is a pretty good guy, but his background is as an IT project manager, working for AES in Ukraine. However, he is Indian, which helps, and he had the good sense to wish to get out of the IT world, and so we hired him and moved him to Andhra Pradesh, one of the southern states in India. He has received excellent support from the cadre of AES people in Delhi who work on thermal and wind projects. The Delhi group is about to close the financing on a 40 Mw wind deal in Gujarat, and all this experience will be quite useful in financing the two solar projects. I met the team members and we spent some time with them, and they are capable and confident. Nonetheless, we will need to strengthen the resources in India so we can manage two projects simultaneously while continuing to expand the pipeline and the footprint. Karnataka and Maharashtra are obvious next states to target, and we continue to see interesting opportunities in Thailand and Sri Lanka. But first we need to get the two India projects financed and into construction.

MORE LOCAL COLOR: while I was in India I had several long discussions of strategy and implementation with Srini, the one solar guy on our payroll noted above, and the AES local team in Delhi—what to bid where, how does it all work, do we need more resources. India has concocted a pretty good program, whose second-round details had just been released on the Sunday before I arrived. And since we have just signed the MOU on that Saturday, we are among the 86 Mw of projects that are now official, and the first ones in the program. One pernicious problem looming on the horizon: local content. This is a potential requirement that your project procure some portion of its equipment from Indian manufacturers. The Indians don't necessarily want to subsidize all this solar stuff only to have all the money go off to the Chinese who make the panels. This is a general reaction in most countries, not exclusive to India. There is no local content rule for those of us in first, but it starts with next 150 Mw, so we need to figure it out. It is complicated but interesting, which seems to characterize India.

I leave Saturday morning and fly to Singapore, stay overnight at an airport hotel, have room service for dinner, and do email. See how romantic this is? On Sunday I fly all day to Beijing. But that's another letter.

Love and kisses, Bob

Afterword: We were never able to work out the "swap" idea with EDF-En— project development is full of challenges, and difficult to accomplish in the best of circumstances. Adding one more negotiation to the already long list of things to get done proved to be too much, so we just let it die. Good ideas don't always win, for many reasons.

We decided to build the Kalipetrovo project in Bulgaria, regardless of changes in the support laws. It was successful and went into service nine months after this letter was written, and the project continues to make electricity and the Bulgarian utility continues to pay for it.

We did not build anything else in Bulgaria as the change in laws made the economics of new projects much less attractive, and we had better places to spend our limited development dollars and talent.

We built the 5 Mw project in Rajasthan successfully, but we were not able to build anything else in India. It remains a theoretically attractive market, but a very tough one in which to function honestly.

How to Appear Knowledgeable While Looking at Something About Which You Are Clueless

August 2010

Dear Aunt Janet,

This is my third Beijing Airport, and a vast improvement on both number one and number two. I first started going here on business in 1991 which, now that I stop and add it up, was almost twenty years ago. There is no place I know of on earth that has changed so dramatically in so short a time as has this country. And largely for the better. I am traveling with two other members of the solar team and I immediately avail my colleagues, Tim Montgomery, our VP for engineering and construction, and Dave Amico, our head procurement guy, of these perceptive observations, and equivalent others. After a while, however, I realize there is a good chance that I will degenerate into irrelevance if I keep saying, "When I first came here, none of these buildings were here." Perhaps I already have. Very much like saying, "When I was a boy…"

We don't actually go to Beijing; we get into a van and drive for two and a half hours, around the outermost of the six Beijing ring roads. It's late afternoon and grey and hot, but the roads are beautiful and the traffic light. We are headed to Baoding for the first of five meetings in five days with five Chinese solar panel manufacturers. We are short of panels for next year, so this is something of a sales pitch—"We're a real company, you can count on us as a customer, how about some of those lovely and cheap solar panels?" Everything in business, I figured out a long time ago, has an element of selling to it. You would think that because we have money and would like to buy panels, we would be purchasing, not selling. Not so.

To amuse myself on the drive, I start counting building cranes once we get past Beijing. And only the ones that I can see from the road. I am not sure I got them all, since there were new buildings going up on both sides of the highway, nearby and not as nearby. Between Beijing and Baoding, a road time of two hours and fifteen minutes, I counted 175 cranes. What economic crisis?

We got to the hotel, checked in, and went to the hotel restaurant for dinner. Chinese of course; Baoding is not an especially cosmopolitan place. At this point my notes to the board begin—but with an introduction on the whole issue of food, a matter that no serious traveler to China can avoid, or avoid from thinking and commenting about. At least I can't.

This is the second installment of a letter based on and including the "field notes," a report that I sent to my board of directors, covering a recent two-and-a-half-week trip abroad. This installment recounts the China portion of the trip. The field notes are in italics.

Day One, Monday: Baoding

We all (Tim Montgomery, David Amico, and I) flew in to Beijing on Sunday, where we were met by Eric Han, a very good guy and member of the AES procurement team in China. Also Chinese, which has been a help. He had assisted very generously in making all the arrangements for our supplier visits. We drove in a van to Baoding two and a half hours south of Beijing, checked in to the Yingli Hotel. And then dinner.

GENERAL OBSERVATIONS: lots of Chinese food for breakfast, lunch, and dinner (well, we ARE in China after all), much of it very good, some of it not so good; some of it recognizable, some of it not, none of it what you would find on the menu of the Peking Gourmet in Falls Church. I have developed my theory of food preferences. Westerners see and eat food in a normal distribution, with the traditional meat/potatoes/vegetables/apple pie dishes in the center, with generally well liked but more expensive/exotic things, and thus less consumed, on the right tail (caviar, lobster, saffron), and things not to everyone's taste on the left tail (snails, pickled beets). The Chinese, it seems to me, see food as a rectangle, and are happy to eat the same amounts of, and enjoy, almost anything that even comes close to the definition of "food." On this trip we didn't really get very challenged. No sea slugs or camel hooves, although we did have one dish that was actually very tasty, where the main ingredient turned out to be a brown semigelatinous cross between noodles and bread that had been soaked in a pond. I did think at first of camel snot.

All the meals had more dishes than you could eat, which is unchanged from 1991 when Paul Hanrahan and I first began coming here. This has been explained to me simply as generous Chinese hospitality. However, my darker suspicion is that there are many, many people still alive who remember directly, or whose parents told them stories of, the Great Famine in 1958–1961, caused by Mao's ill-conceived Great Leap Forward, when thirty million Chinese died of starvation. This was out of a population at that time of probably five hundred million. I remember all my dad's and mom's stories of the depression, where a lot of people were out of work but very few starved to death, certainly not 7.5% of the population. Had to make an impact, even down to today.

Once you get outside the cities you can see more clearly that there is "old China" and there is "new China" (see below) but some parts of old China and new China are the same. Say you are hooked up to the Internet with a modern high speed connection, sitting in your extremely modern Hyatt hotel room, on the 78th floor of an extremely modern glass building, in the extremely modern Pudong section of Shanghai, and looking down on the Bund just across the river, and you decide to look up "Mao famine" on Google so you can be sure of the dates listed above. You quickly get an impressive list of sites. Not a single one of the sites can be viewed on your computer from this location ("Internet Explorer cannot display the webpage"). Not one. None. Old China with new equipment.

Yingli is one of the top three solar panel manufacturers in China. Monday morning we had a wonderful tour of their manufacturing facilities: they are highly automated, with some refining of silicon into ingots, then slicing ingots into wafers, etc. All the workers wear tan uniforms with name tags and the Yingli logo, including the chairman. We gowned up (the booties, the hairnets, the gowns, and thank God no pictures allowed—I used to think this was to protect trade secrets, but it may be to keep your customers from being recorded digitally looking like dorks) and went through air blower rooms before being allowed into the manufacturing areas. Very clean, very orderly, lots of signage of what the goals are, how the production has improved in efficiency, in output, in decreased breakage, etc. In both Chinese and English or I would not have known what they said. This could be a world-class manufacturing facility anywhere in the globe, it just happens to be in China. They currently have 1,200 Mw of production in Baoding (roughly 50% polycrystalline/50% monocrystalline) and are building another 600 Mw in Hainan Island, (all but 100–200 Mw of this 600 Mw expansion will be monocrystalline) which should be ready mid next year. By the end of 2012 they expect to add even more capacity and be at 2,200 Mw.

JARGON BREAK: making solar panels is in some respects simple. You start with sand, which is largely silicon, silicon dioxide to be precise. I think I discussed this all in boring detail in an earlier letter.

Yingli has elected to do most of the refining and all of the manufacturing steps themselves, but others have different approaches. One interesting note: in the refining process for the silicon to go into your panels you can stop at the correct purity, bur with mixed crystal sizes and types, or you can go one step further and make silicon with all the crystals of the same size. The first is called "polycrystalline silicon" and the second "monocrystalline"— poly and mono in industry shorthand. The

NOTE: it's still a poor country. This is a manufacturing facility that employs 12,000 people. Much of that is shift work (they run 24/7) but the "parking lot" had maybe two hundred cars in it. Lots of motorcycles and motorbikes, and lots and lots of bicycles, however.

latter, for some reason of physics that I can't explain, makes slightly better panels (16% efficiency rather than 14%) but is a more costly process. The industry has not yet come down clearly on which is the better product, but my sense is that most customers are happy to buy panels with "poly" rather than "mono" silicon. We ourselves will take anything we can get right now.

We had several hours of commercial discussions with Chairman Miao, who speaks no English, joining the commercial team, all of whom speak very good English. It started a little strangely with the chairman saying that his next good idea was for Yingli to make trucks with giant flywheels in them that could drive into the desert to a solar plant making electricity (presumably off the grid for some reason), use the electricity to fill up the flywheel, and then drive back to the city and plug in and off-load the electricity. It didn't seem the right time to give him my "flywheels will never work" speech. Later that evening at the bar, Tim mused on whether a truck with a giant flywheel would ever be able to turn a corner—think gyroscopes.

But then we got down to business. A reminder on the background here: last year we went through a whole big exercise to find a dedicated supplier of polycrystalline panels for us, and Yingli was the most responsive. We signed an exclusive contract with them and gave them forecasts of our needs that over time turned into smaller orders than initially forecast, as projects slipped. For 2011, however, we gave them an indicative 80 Mw actual order, which they initially agreed they could supply, only later to come back and say that all we could get was 30 Mw. This was not quite what we had anticipated when we made the arrangement. Hence several discussions have followed, whose basic themes were repeated here.

Over the course of the meeting, it became clear that there was not much that they could or would do to meet our needs, although they have now agreed to go to 44 Mw, 24 for the US (our Puerto Rico project) and 20 Mw for Europe. Their reasoning, expressed much more politely and indirectly: "Yes, we signed an agreement with you, but you gave us all these big talk numbers of what you needed, and then in reality you only bought 20 Mw from us in 2010. All of our customers are asking for more Mw for next year and we could easily sell twice what we think we can make. You are the only guys who are not being held to 2010 volumes for 2011—you are getting more than twice what you ordered in 2010. If we have more production toward the end of the year as a result of running our machines better and at higher throughput rates, we will be happy to add to your allocation, but we cannot really count on that, although we expect it."

So there you are. All the more reason to be visiting other potential suppliers. Other interesting tidbits:

—They are moving their production break between mono and poly to favor more mono. Given its slightly higher efficiency—about 200 points—they see this as a more cost-effective use for the other stuff that goes into a panel—glass, aluminum frame, ancillary materials.

—They make/refine about 30% of their own silicon at the plant, and thus are reliant on outside suppliers for the majority of their ingots and/or wafers. This, and not manufacturing of wafers into cells and then into modules, is the real constraint on production. They said that the Chinese government in 2009 closed a number of silicon refineries that were in various stages of construction, both due to fear of oversupply and because these are heavily polluting facilities. This turns out to have been a mistake. It takes about two years to bring a silicon refinery online, vs. maybe nine months for a wafer to cell to module line. A 100 Mw module line costs $100 million—but it was not clear if that number included any silicon refining.

—A rule of thumb for going from silicon refining capacity to kW is six grams of silicon equals one kW of panels, although some people use seven as the translation factor.

—They sold 200 Mw in China last year for "strategic reasons" at a price 30% lower than they could have gotten in Europe. Old China.

—Module price in the US next year will be $1.65 to $1.80.

We got in a van and drove back to Beijing, then flew to Shanghai and checked in to the Sheraton downtown—a very elegant glass and marble high-rise hotel just slightly north of the Bund.

ADDITIONAL LOCAL COLOR: since I had counted cranes on the way down, I decided repeating that exercise was not so interesting. I did notice, however, clear signs of the End of Chinese Civilization As We Know It: as we were driving across the hinterlands we passed three different and distinct construction sites, each of which boasted a sign which read in English "Outlet Mall Under Construction." Oh my god, the virus has crossed the ocean and infected China! Wait, doesn't all the outlet mall stuff come from China in the first place? This is so confusing. . . .

If you were dropped in the middle of downtown Shanghai, perhaps across from our fancy and modern and glitzy Sheraton hotel, preferably around nine o'clock in the evening when the neon is at its finest, and you were allowed to turn around and simply observe your surroundings—the buildings, the traffic, the people on the street, the stores—and then asked where you were, you would know that you were in a modern Asian city, but you would not know if it was Taipei or Tokyo or Singapore or Hong Kong. This was not true of Shanghai, or of any mainland Chinese city, twenty years ago. You would also not think you were in Delhi or Mumbai. They still look largely the same as they did two decades ago. This is a remarkable change in twenty years. Definitely new China.

Day Two, Tuesday: Shanghai, Then On to Hangzhou

Tuesday morning we went to the Shanghai offices of Solarfun. Old China briefly intruded before we left the hotel in the form of no hot water for the shower. A Sheraton-expensive hotel. God, I hate cold showers. Designer soap and shampoo, though.

Solarfun (second-worst company name of the trip) is a fairly large panel maker (currently 900 Mw) who does a lot of OEM work for others, including Q Cells and other German solar panel suppliers we don't know the names of for sure. They noted that the quality must be high for the product to pass, and thus they have German engineers stationed in their plant 24/7. We did not get a chance to visit the plant as it is a good deal farther away from Shanghai than we had time to go. It is interesting to note that Q Cells was one of the original high tech/green tech manufacturers in Germany, the wave of the future and the salvation of East Germans. They did put a large complex of solar plants with large subsidies from the German government in east Germany, near Leipzig, and called it "Solar Valley." And now, not so much. Q Cells (and others) have laid off a number of German workers, and are making all their cells outside of Germany—it actually looks like Solarfun is making all of their cells!—and their *company's value has dropped substantially. In November of 2008 before the fun really started Q Cells was worth $15.5 billion, and today you could buy the whole place for $600 million—a 96% decrease in market value less than two years.*

JARGON WATCH: an OEM is an "original equipment manufacturer," which means the guy that really makes the thing that you are selling. The OEM for the tires on your car is clearly not GM or Ford, as they don't make tires. Sometimes this matters, and sometimes people keep it unclear. I am willing to bet that fewer than half the customers for the "German" panels know that they are made in China. Maybe there's a labeling requirement, maybe not. I don't care that my Izod shirt is made in Honduras and not France, but the origins of a sophisticated piece of electrical equipment might be different.

Solarfun seems to have had the epiphany that all OEMs have at some point: "Hey, we could sell this stuff under our own name, we don't need the Germans." They are of questionable bankability, but the more we learn about them the more we like them and think that we may have been grading them too severely. We have proposed to them an arrangement whereby they defer 20% of their purchase price until we have financed a plant built using their modules, which no doubt means until six months after construction when we have enough data to verify that they work as promised.

We met with the president, Peter Xie, and Gareth Kung, CFO, both young Chinese with good English. We discussed the bankability problem and the opportunity openly, and they are understandably not so eager to do this. "Our board is very conservative, we have never done anything like this before, etc." All legitimate responses. They probably would not be keen on this in a less robust market but in this market, the question they are surely asking themselves is: "Why do this now with guys we don't know, when we can sell all we make to guys we know?" We all agreed that both of us are looking for good customers and repeat business, but then all customers always say that to all suppliers. And all suppliers always say that to all customers. I'll respect you in the morning. We came away with the feeling that we would probably be able to work something out on a small (5 Mw?) project, and then we would have to go from there. They did agree to send us a list of projects where they have been approved for nonrecourse construction financing. It's a start.

A couple of days later while we were still in China a news story was released indicating that the Korean chemical company Hanwha has bought 50% of Solarfun for $350 million. One would think that this would make it easier for them to do a "risky" transaction like the one we are proposing. Good Energies, a competitor/colleague of ours, is also an investor here, so we may be able to encourage them through that channel. This also means that, at this valuation, Solarfun is worth $100 million more than Q Cells. Sic transit gloria mundi and so forth.

We got in the van and drove for three hours to Hangzhou. Dave and Tim broke out their computers and did email and I concentrated on not getting carsick.

Day Three, Wednesday: Hangzhou, Then On to Suzhou

Hangzhou is one of the two "garden cities" of the Shanghai region, with its major feature being West Lake, said to be the most beautiful lake in China. We were there to visit Chint Solar, an arm of plain old Chint, a $3 billion electric system hardware manufacturer, NYSE and the like. Chint Solar has decided, for reasons best known to themselves, to become "Astronergy," which I thought was "Astroenergy" and thus reminded me of Astro Boy, the Japanese cartoon character of indeterminate sexual orientation and miscellaneous superpowers.

But it's really Astronergy, pronounced like you would pronounce astronomy if you had a speech defect. Yes, worst name of the trip.

We were taken to a "provincial guest house" right on the lake (Xihu State Guesthouse). I have been to "guest houses" before in various parts of Asia and it is generally the last choice short of sleeping under a bridge. But wow, this one was different.

INTERJECTION: So, why was it different? If you're a board member, these notes will never tell you. First, it's on West Lake, the most beautiful, etc., right on the lake side, wonderful real estate. Second, it's got uniformed and armed guards standing at attention at the entrance, saluting smartly, and so forth. It is actually state property, and many of the Beijing officials (Mao included, they have his picture on the wall) have come and stayed here. Third, it's lovely, elegantly designed, beautifully appointed, and a nice blend of Western and Chinese. As we have time, we all elect to go for walks along the lake. You clearly have to be connected to get in here, it's not on Hotels.com. Astronergy is trying to make a point about how well connected they are. Nice, but a bit old China.

This company has interesting people and they are quite different from Yingli. They have a very capable president, Liyou Yang, PhD from Rutgers and good work experience at Exxon, and a very good head sales guy named Alan Yuan. At several of the suppliers we visited, the salespeople have adopted "Western" first names for doing business, just as the Japanese did in the early eighties. Sam Nakagawa indeed.

We toured the factory and learned a lot, including a number of differences from Yingli:

» *This company is smaller, probably 200 Mw of polycrystalline silicon and a 75 Mw Oerlikon amorphous crystalline thin film line. They plan to expand the amorphous production substantially, by building their own new lines and using only the deposition machines from Oerlikon. So much for the "factory in a box" concept that both Oerlikon and Applied Materials have been pushing, although AM has recently stopped selling this product. Yang claims that by going to individual vendors directly, and doing the integration themselves, they can reduce capital costs by two-thirds (!!). We told them that we were not that interested in the amorphous product, and that we believed it would have significant bankability problems, but they seemed undeterred.*

» *They are the OEM for Schuco and Conergy, other German "module manufacturers," now in name only obviously, so they have the same story on quality as Solarfun, same 24/7 on-site team of German engineers—well different engineers, I imagine.*

» *They are also planning on doubling their silicon line to 400 Mw and believe that this new line will be more efficient and take their total manufacturing costs down from $1.20 to $.72 per watt. They expect this second line to be in operation by October.*

» *They use a lot more labor than Yingli. Lots of crews of women as far as we could tell, but all the workers wear full gowns, head nets, and face masks so it's not entirely clear; all of them soldering the three aluminum wires onto each five-inch square wafer, putting it in the tray of finished goods, then picking up and soldering another one. Plus labor to take the strings of wafers and place them on the glass substrate before they are laminated. Dr. Yang argues that he could use machines but they have found that there is too much breakage of the expensive wafers and the women do a more careful job. Plus he has a very careful and thorough pre- and post- inspection quality control system with all sorts of checks along the way, so errant cells or modules don't get through.*

» *They buy their wafers, they don't refine silicon or slice ingots. Reasoning: this is not a high value part of the business, making wafers into cells and modules is, so that's where they should specialize. This does, however, leave you reliant on the silicon refiners and wafer makers.*

» *They see more market demand for poly modules and are shifting away from making mono modules—complete opposite of Yingli.*

» *They indicated they have an independent insurance provider that backs their module warranty, Swiss Re I think. This is both interesting and smart.*

JARGON WATCH: amorphous silicon is yet another way of putting silicon on a substrate, in this case glass, but this time the process is a "thin film" one, relying on vapor deposition to deposit a very thin, but noncrystalline layer on glass. Maybe cheaper than refining silicon, but the panels made this way are also lower efficiency—they convert at best 9% of the available sunlight into electricity vs. 14% for polycrystalline silicon. My concern with it is that anyone using one of these systems is a brand-new manufacturer and thus has no experience running the machines he has bought, and making the panels. Most banks won't finance such panels from start-up companies, no matter how good the equipment is that is used to make them. And in truth I don't blame them. It is entirely possible to make "bad" panels with good equipment, and we have some at one of our plants.

Another intermission, this one for a visit to the Zhejiang Province head-quarters and "lunch" with the vice governor. This is not just a few guys chatting over tuna fish sandwiches, this is a demonstration for us of the Chint/Astronergy political connections. The chairman and founder of Chint is a member of the Chinese Peoples Council and thus something of a politician although not a full-time one. Upon arrival at the imposing headquarters building (Hangzhou is the capital of the province) we were introduced to ten local officials including the deputy governor, and then we went into a "meeting room" familiar in style to all who have had political meetings in Asia: upholstered arm chairs complete with lace antimacassars arranged in pairs in a U shape, and a little table in between each pair of chairs. The head of the room is for the DG and me. But of course, since we are both sitting facing the open end of the U, and the TV camera, we really can't see each other unless we turn uncomfortably ninety degrees.

The DG makes a long speech. Part of the refrain was the "we are a poor country" leitmotif, which will also not be new to China/Asia vets, but a lot of it was energy, energy conservation, renewable energy, etc. He remarked that he was glad to see that we all had worn ties and jackets to the meeting, as we had been carefully instructed to do, but since they were running the AC at a higher setting for efficiency reasons, none of the province employees were required to wear ties in the summer. And sure enough, none were. After probably twenty-five minutes the DG came to an end, and I made polite responses about how glad we are to be here, how important solar energy is, and so forth. We adjourned to lunch, again the traditional round table, and lots of individual courses. There was a menu and nothing truly weird was included, well maybe fat balls in fish maw soup, but all in all it was the best food we had during the trip. There were also some obligatory toasts, and much Chinese joshing of each other, 90% of which went over the heads of the three westerners as it was not translated. So we kept our heads down and just ate. Always a wise course of action.

New China: at all the "banquets" that Paul Hanrahan, the AES CEO, and I went to when we were first getting established in China in the early nineties, there were always lots of people smoking, usually everyone but us. While there is still some smoking going on at lunch, and at the other dinners that we had, it's much reduced. Thank God.

There is still much toasting of each other, to friendship and coopera-tion and working together for the common good, although usually not to ending world hunger. This is still not done in compositions that will be treasured over the ages as gems of literature, but it was thus ever so. It was also customary to drink these toasts using a really vile Chinese rice brandy called Maotai. Awful stuff that has now generally been replaced with cheap red wine. Believe it or not, this is an improvement. Double thank God.

We reconvened after the lunch, and the Astronergy team basically agreed with our proposal to defer 20% of the price of their modules until after we financed the project in which they were used, starting with a modest-sized pilot project. And without a lot of whining and complaining. We did mention the possibility of a 25 Mw follow on order, but no commitments until we determine bankability. It seems that our visit and the good prep work down by our team was convincing. Or maybe the fact that we can all now pick up individual peanuts with our chopsticks. Tim even picked up two peanuts holding them side by side. He did this twice to show off.

We left and drove to Wuxi, in a light rainstorm and yet another van. We finally got there and checked in to the I Park Hotel, which is part of the massive Suntech campus. Suntech is the largest panel manufacturer in China, and thus in the world, and a real pioneer in the business.

Dinner at the I Park Hotel Chinese restaurant: this time we had an illustrated and multilingual menu, à la Denny's, but with no chicken fried steak with sausage gravy, alas. Key offerings included: sliced donkey meat with brown sauce, fried chicken gristle with peanuts, lamb guts with sweet sauce, and many sea slug recipes. We avoided the above and had things less challenging to Western sensitivities and were well fed. Lots of Tsingtao beer helped.

All five of the hotels in China that we stayed in, even in Wuxi, which is pretty far off the tourist track, have high speed Internet connections that are free. They all worked for me and my computer. This is good. They also all have adopted the pernicious Euro idea that the top cover on your bed should be a down quilt inside a duvet cover. I doubt that there is a character in Chinese for "duvet." So you have two choices when you finish doing your email and decide to go to bed and see if you can sleep past two-thirty (answer: no, not until the last night before you go home—this time zone change thing is challenging). You can really crank down the AC to a very cold number, probably less than twenty degrees (remember, we are operating in centigrade here as does all the world—metric system—other than the backwards US and UK) and then crawl under the covers and be warm in your artificially cold room and wake up with frost on the window, while the outside temperature is pushing ninety. Or you can disassemble the quilt from its sheet like cover, and then use the cover as a sheet, turn the AC to a reasonable number, and be comfortable as well as environmentally responsible, sleeping in a twenty-five-degree centigrade room with just a sheet to cover you. They have to change these covers anyway, well I suppose they do, so the poor cleaning crew has to disassemble the duvet and you're just giving them a head start. This bugs me. What happened to sheets and blankets?

The somewhat strange I Park Hotel also has a different take on the fruit basket. I find, while looking for the shampoo, that they have instead some things that appear to have to do with sex, and not only condoms, in a basket in the bathroom. For starters, there are two small boxes, labeled in each case "Private Parts Lotion," but one is sublabeled "Only for Man" and the other "Only for Woman." Can you use them both together, assuming you have a willingly participating man and woman, and if you do is it additive or multiplicative? Even more interesting is a slightly larger package containing a condom with a vibrator. The title on the box is "Vibrated & Condom" and the helpful instructions on the back of the package are (and I quote):

1. With its vibration, this kit can make your sex a more pleasant experience. Besides, you can DIY while your sex partner is absent.

2. Wrapped into high-quality food-grade materials, the vibrator should be more agreeable and safer to use.

3. The design separating the vibrator from battery can effectively avoid the battery leakage. This product can be used for duration of forty minutes after battery installed.

So many questions—can I turn the battery on and off or do I have to use all forty minutes at once? What is "battery leakage" and will it electrocute me? Or important parts of me? Where do I put the vibrator, especially given the food-grade materials wrapping? Am I supposed to eat the vibrator? That would seem contrary to general vibrator protocols. Does the condom itself vibrate, or just the vibrator? Note: the box also has a very small picture of a small blue tire looking thing—could be the condom, although it looks hollow—and attached at the top is a pink rectangle, about 75% the size of the condom. Is it attached? Does orientation matter, sexual or otherwise? Does it go on the top or the bottom? There is so much to learn in China. In a rare burst of good judgment, I don't take this fascinating item with me. Not sure what I would say going through customs.

Day Four, Thursday: Wuxi, Then On to Suzhou

In the morning we walked over to the Suntech offices, across the street from the hotel. We were greeted with an electronic sign announcing our visit: "Eagerly greet the great American company AES Solar!" How nice, if surprising. We were more or less eagerly greeted by a young woman waiting at the door who served as our tour guide. Wait, how did she know it was us? Oh, we're the only big noses in Wuxi. Aha. We got a not very satisfactory canned tour of one of the module assembly plants that is in the same building as the headquarters. But it was all viewed through windows so we couldn't get close to the equipment, or in some cases even see very much, and the guide really couldn't answer any technical questions. However, we have by now seen a few of these facilities, so we pretty much got the picture.

We then went to the seventh floor and met for several hours with Chairman Shi and two of his senior guys: David Hogg, who is transitioning from head of European sales to chief of operations, and Jerry Stokes, vice president of strategy and business development, who seems to be assuming David's old responsibilities. The meeting with Suntech was the best in China. Dr. Shi is smart and articulate and speaks good English, and his two senior guys who are both Aussies are experienced, smart, and candid. We like Australians; they are just like Americans but without the political correctness. They have built an interesting and large business in ten years. Seventy percent year-on-year growth is both impressive and hard to sustain. Thus they have problems and opportunities and see the market much the way we do—it will consolidate, big players who know what they're doing will dominate both supply and development, and the choosing of who to play with and who to ignore is very important and very hard. Plus the whole area is immature and not at all transparent.

One interesting anecdote: they had a developer come to them with a request for modules. He sent them a signed contract as evidence that he was real and serious. The Suntech guys checked around and found that it was forged! At least we don't have that level of problem.

They have no more insight into whether the industry is building into a surplus or a shortage than we do, although they ask us somewhat desperately. And they are getting squeezed by their suppliers (they do not make their own poly or monocrystalline silicon, so they buy the wafers from other suppliers—this surprised me) and from the downstream by their customers as subsidized tariffs go down.

"We have contracts with Chinese suppliers. But someone offers them another three cents a watt and they go there, forget our contract!" I am secretly delighted that Chinese companies are doing to other Chinese companies what they have done to Western companies for years. However, I have the good sense not to say this.

We also discuss intermittency the future direction of the business, and a lot of other very interesting things. They are candid in acknowledging their shortcomings and what they are doing to correct them, which is hugely refreshing in a week of "we believe in quality, we are ISO 9001, we make only the best modules, etc." and the bottom line is that they are at 1,500 Mw this year going to 2,500 Mw next year, and are thus the biggest in the world and likely to stay that way. One module leaves their factory every four seconds.

We also discussed their downstream plans. Suntech uses their downstream interests to secure demand and to stabilize swings in their revenue. They indicated they don't have long term or expanded interests in competing with their customers.

We plan to buy 15 Mw from them this year and we suggested 50 Mw next year once we get the first deal done satisfactorily. They seemed amenable and impressed with our seriousness or something. However, we are clearly not the only westerners who have ever come to visit them.

We retrieve our baggage from the thirty-dollar-a-night I Park Hotel ("Worth every penny," remarks Tim, who is not a big fan of Chinese breakfast cuisine) and head up the road to Suzhou.

We arrive in midafternoon and check in to the Pan Pacific hotel, the best hotel of the trip. It does not cost thirty dollars, but it has an Italian restaurant that is a welcome break from a nonstop diet of Chinese food. Suzhou is particularly known for its gardens, and there is a lovely one directly behind the hotel, complete with a seven-story, thousand-year-old pagoda. Dave and I spend an hour exploring the paths and waterways and greenery, although it remains as before breathtakingly hot and humid. Very few people other than us are in the gardens, proving once again that Chinese have good sense.

INTERESTING SIDE NOTE: Chairman Shi has asked Paul Hanrahan, the AES CEO, to join the Suntech board. I think this would be a fascinating experience and am strongly supportive, but only if the potential conflict stuff can be worked out. Otherwise he will have to keep leaving the meetings when they discuss anything interesting.

Day Five, Friday: Suzhou and Then Back to Shanghai

Tim announced at dinner the previous evening that he liked the Pan Pacific hotel so well that he was considering never leaving. We were sympathetic, and the I Park was not a great hotel. But like the trooper he is, he did show up in the morning and off we went to LDK, our final panel maker visit. Had he but known what was to follow, he might have reconsidered. . . .

We spent a really tedious session with their crack sales team: Wilson Hu, manager of Suzhou module sales department; Jerry Hu (biz cards simply said "Sales Department") and it turns out that she is a girl, androgynous name and all; and Dr. Seok-Jin Lee, vice president/ sales and marketing. Wilson was making the presentation wearing a grey T-shirt with the words "Los Angeles" emblazoned across the front of it. I wondered idly when was the last time that I had been in a real business meeting, not a conference at a resort, and one of the key participants was wearing a T-shirt. Never, I concluded.

They went through their canned presentation on the company. Many of the slides had misspelled words on them—"We have very string quality standards"—and several more had numerical mistakes or things that, and when we asked about them, they said, "I don't really know the answer to that."

My favorite: we asked, really more to be polite than anything else, "What

*does LDK stand for?" Since this is the name of the company you would think
there would be an easy answer. No.*

*"The founder used to be working in Europe and he was very fast with things
so his customers called him Lightning something." Huh?*

*Tim asked about one of the data sheets for their panels, where there seemed
to be a remarkable number, an output too high for the size of the panel. Response
by head sales guy: "Oh, that number doesn't look right, I have to check."*

*Note that the data sheet is the key document by which customers decide to
specify your panels and then order them. It has things on it like how big they are
and how much electricity they make. Kind of important. If you walked into a
store and saw some jeans with a label that indicated a waist size of two hundred
inches, you would ask the clerk if that was really true. Probably he wouldn't
know, but the vice president for sales of the jeans company might be expected
to. The whole thing became a little embarrassing as confusion piled up on top
of ignorance on a foundation of lack of clarity, misspellings, bad syntax, and
general incoherence. They did give us coffee when we arrived and got started,
which was just about the only good thing we got out of the meeting.*

*We went to inspect the factory following a dirt pathway through some over-
grown grass and across a very big street. You got the sense that people didn't walk
between the two buildings very much.*

*I have developed a theory about Chinese manufacturing. There seem to be
two approaches, and choosing one or the other is closer to theology than rational
economic assessment:*

> » *Approach #1: use labor for every step in the process unless it cannot
> be done by humans, and then use a machine. Example: laminating
> the cells and other layers of stuff onto the glass substrate. This has to be
> done in a big machine where a lot of heat and pressure is applied. You
> cannot use a hand iron and iron the cells onto the glass, like my mom
> used to iron a patch onto the knees of my jeans.*

> » *Approach #2: use machines for every step in the process unless it cannot
> be done by machines, and then use labor. Example: junction boxes. The
> electricity in a solar panel is generated on the front of the panel, but
> then it has to go somewhere. The panels are constructed to collect and
> funnel the electricity to the back through four wires. But these wires
> need to be hooked up to something, and that something is a junction*

box, a small black plastic thing about the size of your hand that has cable connectors that will ultimately on-site be hooked up to other cables and the electricity led off eventually to go to your hair dryer. These plastic things are glued on to the back of the panels by hand, and so far no one has come up with a machine that is able to do this satisfactorily.

Yingli is a believer in Approach #2, and ultimately so am I, based on the old IBM mantra that machines should work and people should think. Machines are good at simple, repetitive tasks, where doing exactly the same thing exactly the same way one million times is a good thing. Machines are not good at complex tasks where judgment is necessary and the task varies from case to case and has to be adapted to fit each situation. Yingli believes in machines.

LDK believes in people, and lots of them. Their factory was the least automated of any that we have seen. As long as the labor is cheap and abundant and the anonymous woman in the hairnet and face mask doesn't one day get sick of soldering the same three strips of aluminum in exactly the same place to the unending supply of square polysilicon wafers in the same pattern for eight hours a day for $45 per month, and instead goes home and jumps in the nearest deep lake, this works. LDK has grown from zero to twenty thousand workers in four years. Think about that—recruiting, checking references, screening resumes, training, just giving the unending procession of people uniforms . . . this is a remarkable, even startling accomplishment. And they have substantial polysilicon refining capability and big plans. But their quality control systems are pretty low quality and it is very hard to feature buying their panels for our projects. There are no German engineers on-site 24/7. They are at least a year to eighteen months away from being a possible supplier. This was, by the way, the only instance where we were not required to gown up to make a factory floor visit.

After an hour we had seen more than enough. But the weather outside had turned dramatically from hot and muggy to threatening. There were no umbrellas in the foyer of the factory. We walked back across the highway in the pouring rain, getting very wet. Tim remarked, "It's important to be able to calibrate your observations." We now had one end point for our calibration.

We drove three hours back to Shanghai, checked in to the Hyatt in Pudong, had a drink at Cloud Nine, "the highest bar in the world" on the eighty-ninth floor, and decided that it should be called "the highest bar in the world with the slowest service." The next morning Tim and Dave departed for the US and I went on to Hawaii. For more business meetings but less Chinese food.

Love and kisses, Bob

Afterword: We built one 15 Mw project in Puerto Rico using Yingli panels, but nothing else in our portfolio with Chinese panels. A competitor to the Chinese, First Solar, was a US company although with manufacturing in both the US and Malaya. They used a slightly different technology, thin film panels of cadmium and telluride, and they were cheaper than silicon panels and just as efficient. Plus they were a US company, which meant that we had a better chance of enforcing performance warranties if necessary than we would have against a Chinese company. We ended up using First Solar panels on 95% of all our projects.

[9]

So You Will Never Ever Again Have to Read Anything about the Maya

November 2010

Dear Aunt Janet,

Carelessly losing your BlackBerry cell phone in a cab on the way to the airport for an international flight is not a good way to start off a two-week vacation. Who do you call to get it back? The cab company, but you don't know the number of the specific cab. Wait, never mind, how do you even make a call if you've lost your cell phone? Well, pay phones . . . but there aren't any pay phones anymore. There actually are two at the airport, but neither of them seems to work. So you open your computer and boot up and go on the Internet and send your secretary a message of some urgency about calling to get the BlackBerry back. Eventually the cab guy is notified and makes a special trip to the airport to give it back.

This is a demonstration of why going to the airport early is a really good idea. Never mind all that time consuming, superman x-ray vision looking through your clothes security stuff. Of course, a better plan would be not to lose your BlackBerry or forget your passport or go to the wrong airport. It's also not good to go on the wrong day, although better a day early than a day late. All four of the above dumb things I have now done in the last twenty-four months. And we can helpfully add another veteran travel tip: if you are going to be away in Central America from the first of November to the thirteenth of November, don't screw up your reservation and have Continental schedule you to come back on the thirteenth of December instead. More time than you really want to spend looking at Maya sites, no matter how fascinating. If I stayed that long I might have to apply for Guatemalan citizenship.

For no reason that I can explain compellingly, I have always been fascinated by the pre-Columbian civilizations of Mexico, Central America and South America. And by their rapid and complete demise at the hands of a very small number of avaricious and well-armed Spaniards with horses. These native people created some beautiful things and built some impressive ceremonial centers, and so I decided to go visit same when a trip came up that worked. Of course, nothing in today's interconnected age really "works" if you want to get away, and I didn't want to get so away that everyone forgot about me. Or be gone so long that someone took my office. Thirteen days seemed about right, and the sites are in Honduras and Guatemala, so there was not much of a change in time zone challenge. And I figured I could still work in the evenings while my travel mates relaxed and regaled each other with tales of what it was like to be retired. About which I am not interested and have nothing to add other than the often not-welcome question, "But what do you *do* all day?"

Thus on the appointed day my reclaimed BlackBerry and I depart Washington and arrive, finally, in San Pedro Sula, one of the two main cities of Honduras. We have landed in the middle of a flat, green tropical valley; it's eighty-four degrees and humid, and there are palms and banana trees just outside the boundary of the airport, and more palm plantations as you fly in over the low and gentle hills. Well, it's not London.

We debark into a modern glass and granite airport of shiny floors and open, airy design. An airport with not very many gringos around—say five—and only one in a conservative blue blazer—me. This is my standard travel attire, based on the theory that the airlines will treat you nicer if they think you are a business person. I cannot assure you that it works, I think they treat everyone like dirt. I am early, having taken a different route than the others in this tour group, organized by Far Horizons, a tour organization specializing in visiting old sites and ancient ruins. I have time to kill, but I have no lempiras, the currency of Honduras, with an official exchange rate of 18,891 per dollar, only—surprise!—instead you get about 14,000 if you offer up one US dollar. This seems like many lempiras. But wait—there are two side-by-side ATMs at the airport, one that gives you lempiras and one that gives you either lempiras or dollars. Except that neither gives you anything as both are broken. The bank at the airport does grudgingly change money, although at the above rate. So you take your new wads of currency and go to the Wendy's or the Dunkin' Donuts in the airport and get a café con leche and see if you think you are really on vacation.

After about an hour, the rest of our group of twenty has shown up, so we board the bus and go into town where we stop for a quick lunch at a hotel in San Pedro Sula—grilled chicken sandwich and french fries. I wonder idly if this is typical Honduran food. No, it turns out—this is better. I puckishly ask if the restaurant has some of the well-known Maya sandwich spread—Mayanaise. Blank looks all around.

We have all been sternly instructed to bring along metal water bottles with no BPA lining, which we are to fill from a water system at the back of the tour bus. This avoids the scourge of plastic water bottles, and we are concerned about too much plastic in the country; we want to set a good example as conscientious rich tourists. At lunch we are also instructed to fill our water bottles with water from the plastic bottles of water that we have each been served. How this actually reduces the number of plastic bottles in the country is not made clear. Besides, my all steel, not BPA-lined, fifteen-dollar L.L. Bean special water bottle leaks all over my backpack. So much for greenness.

The members of the group introduce themselves, bit by bit. As to raw data, we have (counting me and L, although L is not here yet) six couples (four retired), two single men (one retired), and six single women (four

retired). Professionally there are four medical profession types, three entrepreneurs, one engineer, one lawyer, one museum person, and I can't tell
about the rest. The best ones are a radiologist from Cleveland who turns
out to be a very good guy, with strong and negative ideas on health care
reform, and an attractive Canadian couple who stand out as they order a
couple of beers to go with their sandwiches at lunch. I bond with them
immediately. Cultural note: the local Honduran beer is called Salva Vida,
which means "life saver." A decent beer, and even better as a name for a
beer.

Over the thirteen days of the trip my fellow tourists divide up in my
mind into tiers. We are all white, with one Aussie and two Canadians
and the rest US. The Canadians, the radiologist, and a couple from San
Diego—he a retired immunologist and National Academy of Sciences
fellow and she a PhD medical researcher—are the most interesting. The
second tier is fitfully interesting, and one of the couples is not interesting
at all and besides the wife is mean to her husband. Fortunately, I don't care
and her husband doesn't seem to notice. But no one is truly jerky, and no
one acts like a know it all, and no one is ever late for the bus, making the
rest of us wait. This is quite rare on tours. Also most of them have been
here before and know more about the Maya than I do. I am on a trip with
Maya geeks, but not show-off Maya geeks.

Fed, watered and beer-ed, we reboard our large and quite comfortable Volvo bus, a vehicle in which we spend, by my count, a number of
hours equal to the number we spend at all the sites we visit. The Maya
did not build their stuff close together, and the roads are not exactly interstate quality. But the air-conditioning works and the driver, Tullio, is very
pleasant and very skilled.

The local guide, Jose Antonio, introduces himself. He is right on the
edge of being a *Saturday Night Live* parody of the slick Latino ladies' man.
About forty, good-looking in an up from the barrio, Fernando Lamas (or
Billy Crystal playing Fernando Lamas) sort of way, dark hair pulled straight
back, small ponytail, tight black T-shirts, small medallion suspended on a
leather cord around his neck, jokes about his girlfriends (although married
with two daughters), very good English. But he is also very solicitous of all

us tourists, willing to answer any question asked of him, careful to make sure everyone is comfortable at every meal. He has a decent knowledge of the basics of archaeology and the sites, but he is really not along for this. For that we have Dr. Michael Coe.

Coe is the reason that I wanted to come on the trip. And he was a disappointment. He was a full professor at Yale forever, did some truly breakthrough work in deciphering the Maya writing system of glyphs, and is an acknowledged giant in the field. But he's not much as a trip leader. This is my third trip with an archaeology expert along (a US Southwest trip with Steve Lekson and a Yale trip to Peru with a Yale professor whose name I forget) and Coe was the least good of the three. Rambling, not to the point, often useless information ("my days in the CIA" or "how I caught some fish somewhere"), not really enough structured lectures about the Maya (three in thirteen days), and a lecture on Angkor Wat in Cambodia that was a joke, just a travelogue and promotion for Angkor. And besides, he was rude to L: "Well, if you don't know anything about the Maya, you shouldn't be on this trip." Not a good marketing pitch. He is, as they say in the UK, past his "sell by" date.

As we drive through San Pedro Sula on the way to Santa Rosa, the nearest city to Copán, our first stop, I see my favorite sign of the trip, at a fast food place. A big sign on a tall pole announces: "Power Chicken— *Orgullo Catracho.*" *Orgullo* means proud, and *Catracho* means Honduran. I am not telling what power or chicken means. I wish I could have stopped and got the T-shirt. The chicken itself looked like an avian Arnold Schwarzenegger. Yellow, however.

Guatemalans think Hondurans are lazy. There is not enough data on this trip to determine, although the Honduras landscape we drove through did look less well maintained and energetic. Our local guide, Jose Antonio, who is Guatemalan and the source of this information, says the favorite Guatemalan joke about Hondurans is this: on his fourth and final trip to the new world, Christopher Columbus landed in Honduras. Maybe he brought Power Chicken with him. He looked around a bit, then said to the assembled Indians, "Don't do anything until I come back." And so they didn't. Maybe it's funnier in Spanish. It's probably not funny in Honduran.

My Spanish needs improvement. We drive past many small commercial establishments announcing that they are "*pulperias.*" I am confused as the closest my small Spanish dictionary can get is "*pulpo,*" which means octopus, and there are way too many three-stool cafés along the road for them all to be serving octopus unless perhaps it is the national dish of Honduras. It turns out that this means a juice stand. And maybe some food on the side. No tentacles.

Some geography: we spend only the first day in Honduras, and it seems enough. Most of the Maya stuff is in Guatemala, with probably 20% in Mexico, but we're going to be in Guatemala for the rest of the trip. The country is a rectangle, eleven million population, 65% Maya Indian descendants. The long axis of the rectangle runs north/south, with the Pacific as the bottom border, Mexico at the west and north sides, and Belize and Honduras at the east side. It takes up about two-thirds of the Yucatán Peninsula, with the remaining third at the top, which is Mexico's Yucatán. We drive all over the place.

During the bus ride through Honduras we get into real archaeology discussions, which were welcome. The first and perhaps most interesting question from an epistemological viewpoint: How do we know what we know? It has to be a pain to be an honest archaeologist. The historical record is so limited, especially in those cultures where we don't have writing, or where we had some but some religious nut burned all the books (see below). What we have from the Maya are: 1) a writing system that after seventy-five years of effort we can now read pretty well; 2) a number of large stone monuments, an integral feature of which is some of this writing, always in "glyphs," the word used to describe the Maya script; and 3) lots and lots of vases and bowls and domestic and ceremonial containers, usually elegantly painted and also usually inscribed with these same sort of glyphs around the top or running down one edge. Apparently once you invent writing, you can't help yourself, you write on everything. And we have a very limited number of large wall paintings, at Bonampak and at San Bartolo among others, that are useful for understanding both Maya cosmography and life at court. But that's really it. It is a remarkable feat of scholarship that we have been able to decipher as much as we have.

Eventually we get to Copán, the only site we visit in Honduras. And the first of the sites that we will visit during the intermissions when we are not riding around in the bus. We eventually visited eight Maya sites. The most interesting to the least interesting, in order:

1) Tikal: Probably everyone's favorite Maya site, and less visited than Chichen Itza only because it's not next to Cancún. It probably started up in 400 BC and lasted, with various changes of leadership and conquests of others and being conquered by others, until AD 900, the general time of the society-wide Maya collapse. There are more than 500 structures on the site—it's a big place—and more than 2,500 have been identified in the immediate area, although many of these are individual house mounds. Most of the large sites have not been excavated and restored, so you see lots of really tall and unnaturally steep piles of green, jungle-covered dirt as you wander through the place. There were also more than 100 reservoirs on the site for water supply.

Estimates are that 60,000 people lived at Tikal, which is a very large number for this time in human history. By AD 500 Rome, then the largest city in the world, was around 100,000 inhabitants. Tikal is in the Petén, or southern Maya lowlands, which is confusing as it is the northern part of Guatemala—a low, flat, scrubby area with limited landscape features. South of the Mexican Yucatán, however. You can climb to the top of most of the major pyramids, but this is not for the altitude challenged—the stairs are steep, or the ladders are steep, and it is a long way to the top. The views are incomparable, as you can see the other major pyramids sticking out of the green jungle. And like Angkor, it is so large that it is not really possible to see it in a day if you want to know something about each of the structures. It was, however, great, and well worth visiting again.

Wildlife note: sitting at the top of the first pyramid we got to, we heard an amazing loud screaming noise, a cross between jet engines and really agonized operatic tenors being tortured. It was more than a little startling until someone explained that it was a troop of howler monkeys. Well named. I also finally saw a toucan after all these years of having our investment business named after it, and it was quite handsome, although smaller than I would have thought. The toucan may have thought I was smaller than he expected.

Surprise: there is a museum on the site, and it's crappy. Small, poorly lit, not well maintained. It was something of a disappointment—why do we spend two hours there?

2) Copán: This is one of the six sites Dr. Coe says you must visit if you are serious about the Maya. Unfortunately we only go to two of them—this one and Tikal. Thanks for the expert advice. The other four, for reference, are Uaxactun, Uxmal, Palenque, and Chichen Itza.

Copán is a big, varied, and impressive site, well maintained and restored, and the farthest southeast of any real "Maya" site. It is the only one we visited in Honduras, and probably the only one worth visiting in Honduras. It is best known for its three-dimensional sculptures, almost all in the form of large flat slabs of rock called stelae. There were 20,000 to 25,000 inhabitants at its peak. There are many pyramids and/or temples and/or royal dwellings, all built one on top of the other in typical Maya style, including the especially large one at the south end of the site. And you can clamber all over all of them. Unlike Tikal, almost everything at the site has been excavated and restored, at least to some degree.

As best one can tell, the Maya land area was organized into city states of varying size and power, each with a ruler, and each frequently at war with at least one of the others. When not fighting, they were trading and inter-marrying. This sounds similar to Europe but without the Roman Empire. The thirteenth king of the dynasty at Copán (misnamed "Eighteen Rabbit" as initially scholars read his name glyph as a rabbit when it was really a gopher head but I suppose it wasn't good to refer to the king as "Eighteen Gopher Head") did well and had a lot of stelae carved and erected in his own behalf. However, toward the end of his rule, the nearby city state of Quiriguá, which had been a vassal for a long time, revolted. The Quiriguáns won the war and chopped off Eighteen Rabbit's head. Proving perhaps that you should spend more money on armies than monuments? The place went downhill after that. The stelae are wonderful, however, and are carved in granite and thus much better preserved than stelae in other sites we visit.

The nearby river took away half the site at one point after AD 900 so one can see the levels of building built upon building that have been naturally exposed. After this handy riverine excavation, archaeologists went into some of the levels, tunneled around, and found Rosalila, an entire ceremonial building buried intact for a change. Usually the Maya tore down the buildings on a particular site, filled the rooms with rubble, burned the timbers, etc. After all, they were erecting a new and better monument for the then-current king, so who cared about Grandpa's memorial. For some reason this one building was left whole as it was being covered over and built on. It has been completely recreated at full scale in the courtyard of the museum on the site. This is the best museum we visit, but the highlight is the reconstruction of what is a two-story, probably three thousand-square-foot building, painted red and white and yellow and green, with the heads of painted serpents coming out of the walls, the whole darn thing. It is very impressive.

3) Quiriguá: The site is in the southeast corner of Guatemala, a long morning drive from Copán, including crossing the Honduras/Guatemala border, which turns out not to be a big deal. The site is on low land, very subject to flooding, and in the middle of a banana plantation. Whichever religious planner told the king that this was a good site was wrong. It is a long, relatively narrow site. There is the usual big plaza, with several obvious temples/pyramids not excavated. Many wonderful and very tall trees surround the site, and a fantastic ceiba—"tree of heaven"—stands in the middle of the otherwise clear and grassy plaza.

While the architecture is only moderately impressive, it does have the largest stelae in Mesoamerica, all carved in brown sandstone, dotted around the plaza. But this is not a good material for monuments, and they are seriously eroding. Some are no longer straight up and down, listing at noticeable angles. In several the cracks have been fixed with cement, but given the varying degrees of water absorption and differential rates of thermal expansion of the sandstone vs. the cement, this is not good either. We are told that there is no money for further preservation.

The carving is indeed both large and with wonderful artistic expression. There are also big zoomorphs—large stone animals, kind of mixed toad/jaguar/crocodile beings—also covered with glyphs. And all in honor of the ruler who nailed the thirteenth king of Copán; the glyphs even incorporate the Copán place glyph. The winners write the history.

Afterward more bus ride, then a boat ride to the hotel on the Rio Dulce, a large river draining Lake Itzal and the site of the night's hotel. We make a quick side trip to the Castillo something or other, a fifteenth-century Spanish fort at the mouth of Lake Itzal, built to protect against pirates of which there were many on the coast. The hotel was funky but pleasant, with an interesting old meets new twist: wireless Internet in the room, but no hot water.

4) Takalik Abaj: The site has been around since the Olmec heyday (900 BC to 400 BC). The visit starts in a large and strange resort called Hostal Santa Cruz, which already has its Christmas decorations up. We arrive in the afternoon and after dinner all gather in the conference room for a special lecture by the Guatemalan architects who are in charge of the ongoing excavations. But the architects are unfortunately late so we order more beer and sit around on the uncomfortable chairs. Then they unfortunately actually do show up and give us a seventy-five-minute detailed and largely incomprehensible presentation on the migration of artistic styles and technologies over time at their particular site, which is called Tak'alik Abaj. They note especially that the site was formerly called Abaj Tak'alik but for obscure reasons, that was wrong. Glad we got that corrected, I wasn't sleeping well at night.

The local architects have a problem in addition to logorrhea. This is a major classic site—large layout, many different buildings, good amount of history, nice quantity of small artifacts, but there wasn't any stone around except river boulders, so you don't have the impressive stone pyramids. There were large earthen mounds—qua—pyramids, laid out in generally the same patterns as other Maya sites. And the dirt sides of these mounds had big round stones stuck into them. But these did not fit together like brick works and thus didn't last. No masons or no tools or something. This was not so great when it rained. Plus it's just not possible to reconstruct convincingly. Nonetheless, they have painstakingly labeled every round boulder or rock that they have excavated. Why? Too much free time? The Philistine in me says rocks is rocks, unless they're carved. In which case they become artifacts and are much cooler. This shortcoming of the site does not prevent the head architect from going on and on about her site after our initial walk around. Even our crowd of enthusiasts begins to feel their eyes glaze over. Fortunately there's lunch.

5) Iximche: This is one of several post-classic sites we visit, built after the collapse in AD 900, but at least it is large and well excavated and restored. But it could really be called Mini-Maya; there's nothing taller than twenty meters and nothing at right angles. Clearly the builders exercised less control and had less focus than at the classic sites—things had begun to fall apart.

6) Coatzamalguapa: After a day of visiting museums in Guatemala City, the capital located in roughly the middle of the bottom half of the country, we take the bus down to the coastal plain in the south. The middle part of Guatemala is mountainous, called, appropriately enough, the Highlands, with plains on the north and south. The remaining northern part of the country, a lower but rough amalgamation of hills and valleys and rainforest is called the Petén. The Petén is where the bulk of the Maya sites are, but not all of them. In fact the darn things are everywhere. There are, according to Jose Antonio, our Guatemalan archaeologist and guide, three thousand registered sites, of which fewer than one hundred have been dug and published and reconstructed to any degree.

We are accompanied by Oswaldo Chinchilla, the director of the Popol Vuh Museum, a small but lovely institution we have seen the previous day. He is a very pleasant and relatively young guy who has the disconcerting habit of actually telling you when he (or the profession) doesn't know something. Which, as we have learned from previous trips, is more often than not. Do we know what this is used for? No, we don't. Do we know how the Maya combed their hair? We don't have any evidence in the archaeological record of combs, so we are not certain. He has taken two sites in particular as his specialty, one called Coatzamalguapa. We stop first at the museum that houses artifacts from the site. It is a small but decent metal building, kind of like a barn where you would keep a couple of tractors and a cultivator if you were a not very successful farmer. But it has very nice pieces, the mandatory broken pottery, but especially some very big stone stelae including one out front that is the largest ever found in this region. The Germans dug here in the early part of the twentieth century so most of the really best stuff is in the Berlin Ethnological Museum. But enough remains to be interesting. The iconography is as complicated as ever, but the art is more fluid and less rigid—dancers, positions of bodies that indicate movement rather than the rigid parade ground stances seen at Tikal and Copán. We do not go to the actual site, which apparently is covered over with sugar cane and mostly torn up.

7) El Baúl: After the Coatzamalguapa museum, we go to lunch at another museum, this one housing the artifacts found at a site called El Baúl. It is next to a big sugar cane mill that is rusting out and no longer operating. Jose Antonio notes that this and the previous museum are actually owned by the guys that own all the sugar cane land. The El Baúl museum is an open-air museum, although under roof, and has nothing but large stone pieces, my personal favorite. It has many, many of them, and they are wonderful and well preserved. Most of these, and many of the large pieces at the previous museum, have been found by what should be called farm equipment archaeology. You're out plowing the field and you come across a big rock. It has funny markings on it. You either break it up and push it over to the side of the field, or you plow around it and call someone. We don't know how many times the former happened, but certainly quite a lot. We also don't know how many times the landowner, when called, said, "OK, great, bring this on up to the house." Jose Antonio says he has been in wealthy homes in Guatemala City or Quetzaltenango where there are collections just as good and extensive as in the El Baúl museum—but never studied, never documented as to provenance, never published. These Maya guys really did like carving on stone and they made a very large number of images.

Then we go off to the actual El Baúl site. As frequently happens when there is not enough money, it's just a bunch of small hills, the highest maybe one hundred feet above the sugar cane. These are all man-made and used to be platforms and pyramids. No guards, no boundaries, no gates, no nice stone paths. And completely unexcavated, except there is a big stone head three quarters of which is sticking up out of the ground. The big head appears to make this a "sacred site" which as far as I can tell means: 1) sometimes local Maya come here and burn incense or candles or what have you and do worship-like things, possibly asking for a good harvest or for the army not to come back or for a ride to the soccer game; and 2) you throw trash around everywhere. Styrofoam cups, liquor bottles, cigarette packs, potato chip wrappers, just normal crap. Very surprising way to treat a sacred site. Maybe I am too anal.

8) Utatlán: This too is a "post-classic" site, i.e., one built after everything went to hell in a handcart. Pleasant enough but just a bunch of hillocks, very little excavated, nothing restored. And a well-known but small, smoky cave where present day Indians do ceremonies. I do not find this compelling. At least it doesn't rain.

And finally, other places we went to that weren't so interesting:

1) Guatemala City: We went there to see the National Museum and the Popol Vuh Museum (described above). The National Museum is another indoor/outdoor structure, with a lot of nice stelae, all of them slowly eroding away, and many nice artifacts in dimly lit cases, with relatively little explanatory material. No comparison to the National Museum in Mexico City. No positive comparison.

2) Chichicastenango: This is a highlands town which is famous for its craft market. And on Thursdays they really do have an almost innumerable bunch of small craft booths set up in all the streets selling weavings, embroidered items, figurines, masks, carved stone stuff, and on and on. It was about what one would expect, but not many gringos were there, so how these folks make a living is hard to figure out. And when you get up on Friday morning and look out the window, like Brigadoon the shops are all completely gone. To where, we don't know. What they don't tell you is that it gets cold at night and everyone heats with wood and in the morning you can barely breathe for all the smoke in the air. Don't go here in the fall or winter.

We were also there to climb up to the top of a local sacred mountain, Paschal Abaj, which turned out to be a hill, and watch a local shaman perform rituals said to be descended from the Maya. We are severely cautioned to be respectful. So we have nineteen picture-taking Americans clustering around a flat rock on top of a hill, watching an old guy swinging a coffee can with something smoky in it. Soon another Guatemalan woman comes up the hill, carrying a basket on her back, and sets up a souvenir stand, selling little carved Maya pyramids, frogs, and other junk. We respectfully climb back down the hill.

3) Lake Atitlán and associated small villages: The lake is also in the Highlands. It is nice, as lakes go, and there are a couple of volcanoes that have plunked themselves down around the lake and look volcano-like, and there are a bunch of small towns in the steep valleys leading down to the lake, and the Hotel Atitlán was lovely and had a truly beautiful garden. We were there, however, to see the local Maya religious observances, which turned out to be not much. But first, the obligatory stop at the local weaving place. Introduced as a special benefit, we were to be invited into the home of Doña Perez Celada, only available to us because she is a special friend of our guide Jose Antonio. She is one of the few people still maintaining the traditions of hand weaving in Guatemala. And she is even letting us into her home. Wow, we are so lucky!

We all troop up the hill and down an alley and into her "home." Sure enough, there is the little grey-haired eighty-four-year-old woman sitting on the dirt floor and carding wool into yarn. Gosh, real wool, and real yarn! The tradition lives! It is interesting to note that propped up in front of Doña Perez was a sign, nicely lettered in English, saying that she would appreciate a donation if you wanted to take pictures. And all around the edges of her "home" were wooden benches, convenient for all us big-butt Americans to sit down on and watch her. And there were lots of items she and her team of native weavers had woven, all hanging on hangers from the ceiling, all nicely tagged in English, in dollars, with US sizes. Surprising indeed, since we were among the fortunate few ever to visit her.

But everyone was charmed. I went outside and said to the radiologist (also not a native weaving fan), "Think about it this way. One of those nice Indian capes in there sells for two hundred dollars and takes probably twenty days to make, sitting on the floor of this studio, using a backstrap loom, by hand. So you make ten dollars a day. And that's ignoring any cost of materials, so you actually make less. Why exactly is it that we think it is a good idea to promote this? The Chinese can make the same thing for probably twenty bucks, using mechanical looms. Do we really want these native women to spend their lives kneeling on the floor and making this stuff for one buck an hour? I don't get it." I decided not to buy any woven items.

Maya Notes: what follows are random bits of Maya stuff that one learns during the thirteen days of hanging around with Maya enthusiasts.

M-Note: Maya iconography is really hard to figure out. The best and most complicated is on the stelae, generally a large rectangular piece of granite or sandstone, eight to twelve feet tall, found as monuments at the major sites. But difficult to read. Who is this guy, what is he carrying, why does he seem to have the head of a god in his arm and snakes for a belt, and he's wearing jaguar sandals and there's all this other stuff—ear spools, headdress, breast plate, curlicues, with not so much realism, all carved in eroding stone? Sometimes the figure is in profile, but usually front view in bas relief. Always the figure of a person, and he takes up all the room on at least one side. Frequently he's on both sides, and the same guy. Always a king, as who else had the power and the money to get these things carved and erected?

M-Note: The king got to be named for the two names of his day of birth. Hence Eighteen Rabbit, the unfortunate last king of Copán. The eighteen is the name of the month, and the other is the name of the day. It's sort of like being named Fourteen June if that's when you were born. We don't know why the months only had numbers and the days had names. In our system it's the reverse, that's what makes a horse race. This does rather limit the number of available names, but there weren't enough kings to really make it confusing. Plus I haven't noticed that the English or the French really took much advantage of their freedom to name kings "Sunshine" or "Moon Rock" and instead stuck to Charles and George and Henry and Louis. Anyway, sometimes they didn't use the numbers, as in Spear Thrower Owl, the king who conquered Tikal in the 400s. This is definitely a better name.

M-Note: The fall of Maya civilization, c. AD 900. This is one of the longer running mysteries of Mesoamerican archaeology, now generally cleared up. The evidence is pretty clear that after 900, there was a fair amount of political/social disintegration. While the Maya people continued to live in the area, and grow corn and beans and squash and fight with each other, several things just stopped: no more stelae and no more inscriptions. There is not one that anyone has found that has a date later than AD 900—and almost everything up to that point had one or more dates on it. The Maya were very keen on using their dating system.

No more monumental sites like Tikal. Settlements still have plazas and even ball courts, but the structures are shorter and less monumental, and appear to be sited with defensive purposes in mind. And the fine rectangular alignments of east-west and north-south that characterize classic period sites are gone. It is as if the Maya forgot how to use the north star. Or maybe it no longer mattered. And even the pottery becomes less painted, and no more use of glyphs on the pieces. As if they had forgotten how to write, or the learned classes that knew the system had gotten killed off.

Sustaining the elites in Maya society meant that you needed a very productive worker class to raise enough food for themselves and for all the artisans and stone workers and masons and carvers who are erecting all the pyramids and carving the stelae. During the good times, supporting this was easy. The population grew, monumental architecture was erected, and beautiful things were created. But around 900, there occurs a series of significant three- to five-year droughts. Nowhere that we visited did anyone identify any of the structures on the archaeological sites as being for food storage, which is surprisingly different than in the southwest or the Inca Empire. Maybe it's that Honduras thing again—it's the tropics, you can always just reach up and grab a banana. It is not hard to posit a series of food shortages and famines undermining the legitimacy of the regime in power. We don't know exactly what happened or when at every site, but this general explanation is now widely accepted. Moral: don't outgrow your food supply and save 10% of your paycheck at the Credit Union each month, because ultimately the government won't save you. Or something like that.

M-Note: The Maya used stimulating substances, probably peyote related, which they took in not only by drinking and smoking, but also ingesting them as enemas. Gracious, is "ingesting" really the right word here? One of the archaeologists said "ingesting" although I am physiologically challenged if this applies to enemas. Enough on that subject. On to the bloodletting.

M-Note: Maya invention of writing and ego. Actually I don't think the Maya invented ego, there is a strong case that the Greeks invented it. However, Maya potters and artists actually signed their work, predominantly ceramic as that is mostly what we have that survived, but some of the few extant murals as well. This practice was not known in the West at this time. Ego knows no limits among artists. And Maya artists/scribes were of high status in society, frequently marrying into royal lineages, and getting to hang around the palace and paint pots and stuff and eat for free. The gods of the scribes were represented as monkeys, however, which is some indication that you needed to know your place, no matter how well you could write and paint.

M-Note: Blood sacrifices are pretty common around the world, although I prefer the ones where it's some poor animal who gets it. The bad part about being a Maya ruler was that you had to use your own blood. It dripped onto a piece of paper and then was burned and the smoke patterns interpreted. It couldn't just be from a nosebleed, which would have been OK; no, you had to draw the blood from your tongue or from your penis. Yikes, it makes me uncomfortable even to write that down. I think if I were the supreme ruler of Palenque I would invent a new ritual. There is substantial evidence, again on the vases and pottery, that stingray spines were used to do this. I don't want to know any more about this, thank you very much.

M-Note: The ball game. This is hard to figure out. There are many "ball courts" in Maya sites, but also all around the rest of Mesoamerica, although not in South America. There is a lot of misinformation about this as well, and no one seems to be able to agree on what the rules were, who played, whether the winners got executed or the losers got sacrificed, when and how, how long the games lasted, were there referees, were there TV timeouts, was there a draft, could you take an option on a player, were there free agents, etc. The most sensible thing one can conclude from all this is that there were a lot of different ball games, and that the rules changed over time and over geography. Which isn't so odd when you think about how many "ball games" we have in the West, all played on a square or rectangular court—soccer, basketball, baseball, field hockey—and if you want to stretch it a bit—rugby, football, Australian rules rugby, bladder ball, dodge ball. Anyway you get the picture. Once again we don't really know the details. At least when you get killed in football it's accidental.

M-Note: Little people and *The Wizard of Oz*. Dwarves were objects of respect and fascination at the courts of the Maya elite. We don't know why. And let's not get into that dwarves vs. midgets thing again.

M-Note: Bishop Diego de Landa. My, oh my, where to begin. Cortés came first, of course, and walloped the Aztecs and laid claim to all of the Americas, including perhaps Las Vegas although he had not been there and if he had, he might have carved that out. It's hard to understand the religious zeal that drove explorers—well that and the gold, but the gold is easier to explain—but the friars and the fighters seemed to show up in equal numbers, with the friars right on the heels of the fighters. And they probably did equal damage conquering/enslaving people and converting them to their religion whether they wish to be converted or not, are both fairly wrenching businesses no matter who is doing it to whom. Bishop Diego de Landa came to the New World soon after Cortés and was made religious head of all of the Yucatán, i.e., all of Maya land as then defined—the entire Yucatán Peninsula. Many of the good fathers were eager to convert the heathens, but Landa probably takes some sort of weird good guy/bad guy jackpot. He was clearly a dedicated Catholic with no use for idolatry, graven images, and so forth. He is probably best known for deciding that the Maya books, called codex or codices, beautifully written on papyrus-style paper, were somehow representations of the Maya religion. So he assembled all that he could find and in 1517 burned them up. No one knows how many, but no doubt many, many. Only four are known to survive, and these four tend to be lists of things rather than the Gospel According to Matthew.

The Dresden Codex, for example, is eighty-two pages of lists of things, dates, calendars, omens, and some astrological/astronomical predictions. So much for the historical record as recorded by the Maya invention of writing. Landa was also known to torture the local Indians as a handy way to make them recant their faith and embrace Catholicism. He did so with sufficient vigor that even the local Spaniards were affronted and complained to the authorities, and he was eventually censured and his authority constricted. However, Landa also did substantial anthropological research on native customs and practices, and published the only surviving long and authoritative treatise from that time period, *Relación de las cosas de Yucatán*, detailing what he learned from the locals he interviewed and presumably converted although maybe by this time he didn't have to torture them—"Hey, here comes Landa, start saying that catechism I taught you." Among the many important things he left was a record of what he called the Maya alphabet. But more on that later. Without it, a kind of crude Rosetta stone to Maya writing once someone figured it out, we would probably still not know what all the glyphs mean.

M-Note: The other most important book on the Maya besides Landa's is something called the *Popol Vuh*, a narrative about the origins, traditions, and history of the Maya nation by an anonymous Guatemalan Indian who produced the document between 1554 and 1558, probably with Spanish help. Subsequently, a priest, Francisco Ximénez, copied the manuscript, adding a Spanish translation.

This sets out the Maya cosmography—the seven layers of the underworld, the thirteen layers of the heavens, the almost numberless gods and deities, the two hero twins, the creation of the world and the four worlds that have gone before this one, the death and resurrection of the corn god, the whole schlemiel. I confess to having not read this, but most of the people on the trip had. There seems to be general agreement that the Maya pantheon, in the broadest sense, is the most complicated and difficult to understand in the world. I have sat through several sessions explaining the *Ramayana*, the long and confusing Hindu epic of creation, but it's the *Bobbsey Twins at Friendly Farm* compared to the *Popol Vuh*.

Which reminds me, there were, as everyone knows, two sets of Bobbsey Twins, the older two (Bert and Nan) and the younger two (Flossie and Freddie). If one assumes that "Freddie" was a diminutive for Fred, then was Flossie's real name Floss? Who would name their daughter "Floss," except maybe a dentist?

M-Notes: The Maya go to the movies. As far as any of us on the trip could figure, and we had a lot of time to discuss this on the bus, there are really only four movies where the Maya or really the Maya pyramids, play much of a role. Thanks to the wonders of IMDb, here they are, in order of score according to the website. I haven't seen any of them, and, having read the plot summaries, have no intention of doing so. You'll see why. You will also wonder what fourth grader in ESL class writes these summaries.

Apocalypto (7.9 out of 10; 2006—this whole thing was Mel Gibson's idea, believe it or not, and it's all in subtitles—weird): *In the declining Maya civilization, a peaceful tribe is brutally attacked by warriors seeking slaves and human beings for sacrifice for their gods, as the rulers insist the key to prosperity is to build more temples and offer human sacrifices. Jaguar Paw hides his pregnant wife and his son in a deep hole nearby their tribe and is captured while fighting with his people. An eclipse spares his life from the sacrifice and later he has to fight to survive and save his beloved family.*

The Ruins (6 out of 10; 2008): *While on vacation in a resort in Mexico, the Americans Jeff, his girlfriend Amy, her best friend Stacy, and her boyfriend Eric befriend the German Mathias in the swimming pool. Mathias invites the group to visit the ruins of a Maya temple with his Greek friend Dimitri in an archeological field where his brother Henrich and his girlfriend [nameless we presume] are camped eighteen kilometers far from the resort. They hire an old taxi and when they reach the spot, they are surrounded by Maya villagers armed of revolver, rifle, and bow and arrow that kill Dimitri and do not allow the group to leave the place. They climb a construction covered of creepers with red flowers and remain under siege of the locals. When they hear a cell phone in the bottom of a well, Mathias decides to seek the apparatus using a rope that breaks and he has a serious accident breaking his back. Amy and Stacy go to the bottom of the mine to rescue Mathias and they find many corpses covered by the climbing plants.*

Against All Odds (Jeff Bridges) (5.7 out of 10; 1984): *Terry Brogan, an aging football player in LA, is cut early in the season; he needs money, so he takes a job from a shady friend of his, Jake Wise, to track down Wise's girlfriend, Jessie, who's somewhere in Mexico. She's also the daughter of a very wealthy land developer, who owns Terry's team. He heads for Cozumel, finds Jessie, and promptly falls in love with her. He thinks it's mutual, then without warning, she heads back to LA and Jake. What's going on with her, and what's the connection between Jake's hold on Jessie and the various politicians, lawyers, and environmentalists who seem to be converging on some sort of land deal? Terry keeps looking for answers.*

Alien vs. Predator (5.4 out of 10; 2004): *When a private satellite encounters an unidentified source of heat in Antarctica and it is found to be a pyramid buried deep underground, a search team comprising of top-of-the-line archaeologists and engineers is sent to Antarctica to find out more. Once there, the team comes across signs which indicate that the place is in habited by an unknown alien species. It is not long before the aliens begin to hunt the team members. At the same time, a trio of coming-of-age Predators have arrived to collect the skulls of the aliens as trophies, and the humans are caught between a deadly battle between the two warring species.*

I doubt seriously that any of the movies made any more sense than those summaries. The only really good role any Maya thing has is a bit part in *Star Wars*. When the rebel ships lift off to go fight the Death Star, they take off from Temple 4 at Tikal, which is described in the movie as the fourth moon of Yavin. At least it's not a pyramid buried deep underground in the Antarctic.

Ten things the Maya do better than you:

» Invented a numbering system to the base twenty. This is the only one in the world, so far as I can determine. Our everyday system is to the base ten, but when one examines both fingers and toes, then twenty probably makes just as much sense. But it's not much good without...

» Invented the zero. This is a big deal, it makes real math possible. The only other culture to do it was India, from whom the West borrowed this handy concept. You don't believe me, try multiplying XXLV by MMCCXIV.

» Invented astronomy, but so did Ptolemy and the Greeks and the Phoenicians and probably the Indians and the Chinese and goodness knows who else. They did figure out the solar year at 365.254 days, which isn't bad when you don't have clocks. And they were able to predict eclipses, although Mel Gibson obviously didn't know this or he would have written a better script for *Apocalypto*. And a better name for the movie, while he was at it.

» Invented north, etc. So did lots of people. This might be a subset of inventing the zero (above,) as the north star seems to have been pretty much a giveaway although I have never been able to find the damn thing. No evidence that they understood magnetism, magnetic north, etc.

» CHOCOLATE! They invented chocolate! Now we're talking. This was not easy to do. The cacao tree grows in the Guatemala coastal lowlands, the fruit is a pod that looks exactly like a football except for the laces, and grows right out of the trunk of the tree, which is a little spooky to begin with; how come it's not a disease or something? Break it open and it has a white sweet pulp inside, and in the center are the cacao beans (seeds) but they have to be fermented and then roasted and then ground before they're edible. Lots of hit and miss in figuring that out, one suspects. But they did! There is not only evidence from all the pictures on the pottery, some clever archaeologists even sent newly excavated vases and bowls back to the Hershey chocolate labs where the residues were clearly identified as chocolate. We are so grateful! There is no evidence that the Maya invented Cocoa Puffs, however.

» Invented blood sacrifices from places you shouldn't give blood from, and the Red Cross would never ask you to.

» Invented house paint. Especially red. All the structures were painted, and in bright colors; they weren't all this nice post-modernist limestone white and grey that they are now. At Copán one of the temples, Rosalila, was buried intact. The Maya general practice was to reduce the old building to rubble, for sound civil engineering reasons of compaction etc., and then go ahead and build the next one on top of it. In this case they just filled in all the rooms with dirt and rocks. When it was discovered, and carefully excavated, all the paint remained, in glorious reds and yellows and blue and greens. This was not a people given to subtlety. That much red, even on a building only about the size of a modern three-bedroom house, is startling.

» Invented the calendar. Once you invent astronomy, and you invent the ability to count, it's not a leap to come up with the calendar. In fact, they had three calendars, which is probably two more than a body needs. Let me see if I can explain this: they had the short count year, a period of thirteen months, each of twenty days in length. This is where rulers got their names, as above. There was also another year with a name not clear, which was 360 days in length. Moreover, the Maya understood that the "real" year was 365+ days, so they just left out the last five days of the year, a period of bad omens, and everyone sat home not really doing anything, except chanting and not walking under ladders. Could be the five days between Christmas and New Year's.

Then there was the famous LONG COUNT, which is a period of time defined as 5,016 years and 120 days. It started on 13 August 3014 BC and is the fifth civilization recognized in Maya cosmography. This calendar, too, is a cycle, just a really long one. All the stelae have "long count" dates on them, which are simply the number of days since the beginning of the fifth world on which that particular monument was erected. And (remember the zero and the base twenty) once you figure out the numbering system, and you are given five numbers in order, and you know when time started, it makes translating these dates into Western dates precise and exact. There are many things we don't know yet about Maya civilization, but we got the date thing knocked. Because the fifth world is a precise and cyclical period, we know that it will end on 23 December 2012. Thus the world will end, etc. This is handy to know as you will not have to buy anyone Christmas presents that year. If Bishop Landa hadn't destroyed all the books, we might even know what comes next.

» Invented writing. They did a way better job of this than any pre-Columbian society. It took a while to decipher, but it is now clear that the written symbols of their language included some that were syllabic and some that were ideographic. Plus you could write the same word in an ideograph, or in a set of symbols, and the scribes often did both. The closest analogue is Japanese, where there are two syllabic sets of symbols, Katakana and Hiragana, which have the "ba, be, bu, bay, bo" sounds and can be put together to form words, i.e., Fu-ji-ya-ma—which would take four characters. There is also Kanji, which is ideographic, and where there is a separate single character for Fujiyama. The Maya mixed and mingled, often in the same glyph. They also repeated themselves just so the reader would get it, writing the word once in syllables and then repeating it in ideographs. And once they started writing they went to town.

» It's not just on the monuments, it's on probably the majority of the pottery. What is also interesting is that, when we finally were able to decipher what the glyphs on the pottery said, it was enormously down-to-earth stuff, like "This is the chocolate jar of Thirteen Pakal made by scribe Two Jaguar." So much for poetry. It is also interesting, perhaps even remarkable, to note that the written script was in Chorti, one of the thirty or so related but far from identical Maya languages. Somehow, someway, no doubt through scribes and elites and traders, there was one language that all the literate elements understood when written. Perhaps the use of Latin as a lingua franca for the educated classes in the first 1000 years AD is as close an analogue as we have, but in Europe we at least had the unifying force of the church. Hard to figure. Small interjection: at some point on the trip it was explained to us that one archaeologist has decided to spend part of his time coming to Guatemala to teach the present-day

Maya how to write glyphs. Let us pause on this for an absurdist moment. Why? What will they write on? And who besides other archaeologists will read it, and they won't even read it as it won't be written on stone monuments? Why not just teach them English so they can at least make a living and not heat their homes and cook with wood stoves and die of respiratory diseases at the age of forty-five? Another example of why it's just as well that I didn't become an academic, I would not have made it.

» Invented head flattening. You know, there's just no telling about human standards of beauty. The Maya clearly found elongated and flattened skulls to be breathtaking and attractive, so they bound their baby's heads to boards when they were just born so that their heads would resemble, what, shovels? This seems nutty to us, but then you probably wondered the first time you saw Michael Jordan wearing a diamond earring. But because he was who he was, everyone wanted one. I harbor a secret suspicion that the flattened heads didn't leave enough room for your brains so you couldn't invent some of the really worthwhile stuff listed below.

Ten things the Maya don't do better than you:

» Toilets and toilet paper. We were firmly instructed when using the bathroom to take used toilet tissues and deposit them in the small plastic trash cans found beside every toilet, and NOT to put them into the bowl of the toilet and attempt to flush them, or dire consequences would ensue. OK, we did, but ew. How hard is it to invent sewers? At least they don't make you clean out the toilet like the Euros want you to do, at least I think that's why the put those brushes beside all the toilets, only I don't ever use them. They can pay somebody to clean out the toilets, thank you very much.

» Food. As a treat we were fed a "native Maya" meal at lunch at Tikal. The principal ingredient seemed to be ramon, a small barely edible berry. You can make ramon into soup or into a tart or just serve the little berries that don't taste like much, and the chef did. You look at the soup and think "OK, black bean soup!" and then no, surprise, it's ramon. Or you bite into the tart that is a suspicious brown-grey color resembling some sort of oil field lubricant, but you're hoping maybe apple, and the no, surprise, it's ramon. Finally we were served small dishes of the little berries themselves, which look like they should be capers but they're a dreary orange and have little holes at the stem and great big pits, so the ratio of flesh to pit is about one to ten, kind of like those small stupid French olives that the Mediterranean cooking of France seems to be based on. And beside they taste like slightly sweet bland nothingness. Subsequent research reveals that the Ramones were an early punk group, and each of the group members changed his last name to Ramone when joining the group. They were from New Jersey which may explain this. I do not think they were Maya.

» Poison. They invented blow guns but only used pebbles in them, not like the clever Brazilians who figured out poison for their darts. Besides, think about it, is a blow gun a really good weapon? No range, not much muzzle velocity for the projectile, tedious to reload, single shot only, etc. In fact, they also didn't invent the atlatl, a spear throwing enhancement that their brother Indians in the Mexico area did invent, and then came down and at various times conquered various of the Maya cities. This is curious as military innovation usually travels pretty fast, but the Maya never quite got the atlatl.

» Gold. Nope, no gold, the Spaniards were quite disappointed. They did have jade, but so did lots of people and the Spaniards weren't interested.

» Metal. Nope, no metal. Yes, gold is a metal and we already listed that, but gold is a singularly useless metal except as a store of value. Can't make it into weapons, or chisels for cutting stone, or plow shares, or atomic bombs. Generally it would be better to invent iron than gold. But the Maya had neither.

» Tables and chairs. Well for God's sake, how hard is this? All they did was sit in the grass or, if you were an elite, sit on slightly raised benches, mostly of carved stone. Some even have four legs, so the concept was there at the edges. You can craft almost anything better if you are sitting on a chair at a table rather than kneeling on your knees and weaving or grinding corn on a metate, or if you are painting pots or making pots or ruling your small kingdom. The vases depicting rulers and gods all have them sitting cross-legged on a raised platform, but not raised much. Nobody is leaning back on cushions even. The examination of the bones of the women reveals a lot of calcification around the knees, the result of all that kneeling. Ugh.

» Draft animals. No horses, no oxen, nothing to pull a plow or a wagon. But that's OK because . . .

» The wheel was also not used anywhere in Mesoamerica. This too is remarkable, especially as there are surviving images of toys mounted on wheels. But nothing useful. Not even wheelbarrows, which sure would have been helpful in building all those stone pyramids or large dirt mounds.

» Restaurants in general. We went to a fancy restaurant in Guatemala City. You could tell it was fancy because there was not enough light to read the menu. When I broke out my flashlight I found that one of the selections under "appetizer" was french fries. So I had them, and they were great. Innovation? Mistake? Who can tell?

» Olympic basketball team. Maya people of classic times were really short, and today they still are. Heredity, poor diet, breathing wood smoke, who knows. Very, very short. I could be a dominating center on the Maya national basketball team. Well maybe I could have a couple of years ago.

You know you have been gone too long, and been exposed to too much local culture/ancient culture gobbledygook when you decide that the extensive literature explaining the veneration for the corn god—a significant guy in both Aztec and Maya culture—stems from a mistranslation, and he is really not the corn god but the corn dog. His revered son is, of course, the hot dog. L does not think this is as funny as I do, but agrees it's time to go home.

Love and kisses, Bob

Afterword: Even in 2010 while on this trip there were occasional references to "drug lords" although we saw no evidence at all of this and had no problems. According to current press reports, these areas in Mexico, Guatemala, and Honduras have become more dangerous and difficult. I am glad I went when I did. I would have to think very carefully about making another similar trip. Too bad, because I would really like to see Palenque, the only other site of the consequence and magnitude of Tikal.

[10]

Calling It "Easter Island" Shows a Distinct Lack of Imagination

November 2011

Dear Aunt Janet,

The last time I tried to go on a vacation, I lost my BlackBerry. This time I lost my airplane. But I still had a great time.

That's not quite correct, about the airplane. I am headed to Santiago, Chile, and then on to Easter Island. Easter Island is owned by Chile—did they discover it or capture it, I am not clear, and I think it was named Easter Island by a Dutch explorer named Jacob Roggeveen, who landed there on Easter Sunday in 1722. He was looking for a legendary place called Davis Land but it turned out only to be a figment of the pirate Edward Davis's imagination. Well, of course, what pirate makes a living being an explorer? A slug of Polynesians were already living on the island, which they called Rapa Nui, but they lost out. The whole entire reason this small bit of land sitting unremarkably in the South Pacific not near to anything is at all interesting is that it has wonderful and large and exotic stone sculptures unique in the world and mostly not plundered. I have always wanted to go there. So now I am.

Another somewhat less interesting reason to go is that we own a very nice utility business in Chile called Gener, which is a good name as utility names go, in that it means "to generate" in Spanish. I have some business in Chile about which more on later, but mostly this is a vacation. And it started from San Diego where I was for yet more business, this time of the solar variety. But the Southern California morning dawned foggy and more foggy and when I got to the airport I was informed that we were not flying up to LA to catch the Santiago flight, we were instead riding in a van. So it goes in the world of luxury travel. Gee, you can duplicate this in Nebraska, just get in a crowded white van and ride around for two hours. It will probably cost less and you can pretend about the fog.

Gener, as the name would imply, generates electricity in Chile but does not distribute it, instead selling it on a wholesale basis to a series of local distribution utilities. We make about one-third of the country's electricity. Several other electro-geek facts: Chile is long and thin, and in the north has the famous Atacama Desert, one of the driest and sunniest places on earth. The desert is not heavily populated except by miners. There is much mineral wealth here to go along with the no water, and they need electricity. Mining, it turns out, is more than just steam shovels digging stuff out of the ground. Much of what they dig out is "ore," a polite name for dirt and rock with a small amount of more valuable stuff mixed in, like gold, copper, lithium, etc.

Because it is not intelligent to move a bunch of low-class dirt around more than you need to, the ore is almost always processed at the mine site, so that the good parts get shipped out and the dirt stays behind, although now with a different name, "tailings." I don't know why it is called this. Although it differs from mineral to mineral and from deposit to deposit of the same mineral, the processing generally involves grinding up the dirt and rocks into smaller pieces, then either mechanically or chemically separating out the stuff you want and leaving the rest in a big and generally unattractive pile—a "tailings" pile. The chemical part also involves a lot of water, and in the case of gold, the leaching agent is mercury. Noisy, dusty, destructive, ugly, and full of nasty and hazardous chemicals—what's not to like? I must say, watching a mining operation makes you think that a coal-fired power plant is an environmentally sensitive thing to do.

More interesting from our point of view is that all this brute force activity uses lots of electricity. I am embarrassed to admit that I was talking recently about all this with a gold mining guy who was explaining electric use at his mine in Mauretania of all places. He said something like "and of course the electric shovels are a big source of demand." I pictured digging a hole in my backyard with a garden shovel with an extension cord coming out of the handle. What? Where is the electric part? My puzzled look made him explain that these are big digging machines, what a layman would call "steam shovels" although the days of powering them with steam are long gone. So, steam shovels with big extension cords coming out the back, I guess.

Much of this mining goes on in the north in Chile, and there is an electric grid there, and we have power plants there, so that's all good. What's also good is that the north and the south, where Santiago and all the people are who aren't miners, are not connected to each other electrically. Feel free to use this fact at cocktail parties although it may not be as fascinating to others as it is to some of us. The northern grid has no non-miner people, and in many cases the mines actually have built their own power plants or systems. If they have, then in all cases, they use diesel as the fuel to make electricity on-site.

And now at last, the punch line. You may have noticed that oil is expensive these days, for so many reasons we won't go into here. And making this very high-quality fuel into dumb old electricity is actually not very smart. Energy guys like me LOVE oil. When I am reborn in my next life, I am going to be an oil guy, they have so much money! And that is because oil is the perfect fuel. And it can do anything you want—run cars, run your furnace at home, run factories, make electricity. What it cannot do is be predictably priced.

If we had lots of oil, it would be all we should use. Well, there is that

CO_2 thing. Here's an analogy: if you had lots of money but credit cards and checks didn't exist, you would not want the only available currency to be the dollar bill. Think how much money you'd have to carry around. Oil is the hundred-dollar bill of energy. Natural gas is a fifty-dollar bill, coal is a ten-dollar bill, and wind and solar are probably quarters and dimes. Still money, but more problems logistically.

But oil ain't cheap, and if you are using oil to make electricity and run your mine in a sunny place, we can use solar panels and do the job more economically. Hence our burgeoning interest in Chile. Whew, I bet you're glad that's over. I am.

Day Two, Friday: Santiago

The van to the plane works, and then one flies overnight, as Chile is a long way south. We get in at the lovely hour of 0530 and then it takes a long time to clear customs. Why? Was it a surprise that an airplane showed up? Don't the customs and immigration guys know when the planes are coming in? Not exactly a frigging mystery, says I, buy a smartphone with an app or something and then you'll know. But once out of the terminal the weather is nice and the hotel is ready. I love Marriott's, very predictable on the good side—they do what they say, the room was ready, the elevators work, you get free Internet and a free bottle of water. I send out all my accumulated work from the plane and take a nap. It is a plus-five time difference from the West Coast where I have been, so in my body it's still 0230.

I go to lunch with Felipe Cerón, the CEO of our Gener business. He is an old friend and has run the business since we bought it in 2000. This acquisition was one of the smarter things we ever did, it has made us a lot of money. And now we want to do solar stuff here. The small trick is that I am no longer a "pure" AES person. AES Solar is funded half by AES and half by the private equity fund called Riverstone. To work on solar in Chile it begins to matter how we answer the oldest business partnership questions in the world: who does what, and who gets what. Fortunately this is not all that hard as the solar biz in Chile is still largely one of press releases and not panels on frames. We have a great lunch at a small and wonderful seafood place in downtown Santiago. Felipe has never been to

Easter Island, although he is a native Chilean, and a Harvard grad we should add. That's OK, I have never been to Mount Vernon. Well, that's a small fib, I haven't been there since I was in high school, and it's not a four-hour plane ride from Arlington, it's a forty-five-minute drive.

Over calamari and swordfish and sea urchin (no spines, I note with relief) we agree to proceed slowly and see if the market in the north really develops. If it does there will be plenty of work for everyone and having a joint effort with these guys will reduce our costs and speed up their learning curve. Then I go back to the hotel room and spend four hours carefully drafting a proposal to have a large Japanese corporation buy half of our solar business in Europe. This is actually hard work requiring thought and precision, and I am less than sure that I want them for a partner anyway. I finally give it up at seven-thirty and head out in need of a drink. This global stuff makes my eyes cross.

Cheetos Horneados, or the perils of being without a dictionary: there is a large Walmart equivalent store called Tottus next to the Marriott, so I go there in the afternoon because I am cheap and I need to get a few essentials laid in for when the rest of the group arrives: potato chips, olives, peanuts, salami, white wine, just the basics. They have bags of "Cheetos Horneados." I buy one, but I worry about the Cheeto mascot, who looks like the Pink Panther (does Peter Sellers know?) but is actually "Chester Cheetah." I am not sure that cheetahs eat Cheetos in the wild. But the Horneados part—does Chester, incomprehensible symbol of Cheetos that he is, leap priapically out of the bag when it is opened and chase all the women? Or maybe when you eat them they are a mysterious Chilean aphrodisiac? Lydia, my brother's oldest daughter who is fluent in Spanish, later informs me that *horneados* means "baked." Shoot.

Day Three, Saturday: Santiago

My brother, David, and his family arrive around noon, and L arrives about the same time, so they all get checked in and take a nap. We meet for lunch then go downtown to the pre-Colombian art museum, since we are all fans and Chile is in pre-Colombian territory. It's a good collection but a little dusty and not well lit. We amble around Santiago and decide that it is fine but not Paris—nothing wrong with it, but not many old buildings due to the large number of earthquakes they have experienced, pleasant enough but not so much to look at.

Day Four, Sunday: Trip to the Wineries

Through the hotel we have arranged a vehicle and a guide to take us to visit three wineries in the Maipo Valley, about an hour outside of town. Chile makes really excellent wines and the wineries are easily accessible. It is a lovely afternoon and the wineries are each different enough to be interesting. Santa Rita is our first stop—it has a classic colonial ranchero building and sets of flower gardens, a nicely organized tour, and decent wine. Although we have been encouraged by the concierge to stop there for lunch, we demurred, not wanting to get stuck for several hours at a typical South American lunch. Most of the rest of the people on the tour, however, troop off to the dining room. We next visit a very small winery called Huelken. The owner himself gives us the tour, and then seats us plus a couple of American bicycle tourists in his courtyard at an outdoor picnic table, where he pours the wines himself. This is lovely and warm and sunny and there is cheese and salami and crackers. And the wine is very good. Finally we go to the Concha y Toro vineyard, which is the complete opposite: very big, very organized, very much set to provide all the tourist amenities. There is even a cheesy tour of *casillero del diablo*, the "basement of the devil." At one point the lights all go out and—nothing much happens. No devil appears. It was a legend to keep the help from going to the cellars and sampling the wine themselves on their off-duty hours. Despite this silliness, the wine is very good. We buy a bottle and several keychains. If they had snow globes of the devil I would have bought one of those as well.

Day Five, Monday: Off to Easter Island

After four hours of flying due west from Santiago in a big plane, we land at the airport and debark, along with a large number of passengers including some island kids returning from having won a football tourney. There is only one flight a day, so it's no wonder the plane is full. First impressions of the island are green and brown, pastures only, the land randomly and haphazardly cultivated. One very small town of three thousand. In square miles it's one-tenth the size of Oahu (67 vs. 607 square miles). The terminal looks like the one in Kona on Hawaii, one gate, one baggage carrousel, open and tropical and lots of people milling about. Small-town friendly. We are all pretty excited to be here, in such an out-of-the-way part of the globe.

We are picked up and driven out of town eight kilometers to our fancy hotel. Vegetation along the way is scrubby with mostly cleared fields, a few small houses, no barns. Mostly flat, sloping gently to the ocean, lots of low, black stone walls, and many piles of rocks, made up of the rocks from the fields. Like New England with lava. And there are lots of rocks still left over. Miscellaneous ocean views, cows in some fields, horses in others, but not many of each. It looks like a bit like northern New York except it's volcanic like the dry side of the big island in Hawaii. There are trees in occasional clumps, mostly eucalyptus and acacia—not native. A bright orange small tree is everywhere, the Chilean coral tree we are told (*Erythrina indica*). And in the grass by the roadside a flowering plant looking a lot like lantana except it has one flower head per stem. No one can tell us what it is. More research needed. Very little of the standard tropical vegetation—no crotons, no hibiscus, no plumeria, and, strangest, almost no palm trees.

Explora, our hotel, is one a small chain of ritzy but ecologically sound hotels, so far only in Chile. Three things stand out about this one: The architecture is wonderful. It's very open, all concrete and blond wood and neutral colors, big bathtubs and natural slate walls and lots of windows. The building has a low silhouette, all single story, lots of volcanic rock used for the walls and walkways. No pictures or paint on the walls of the rooms or anywhere inside—it's somehow dramatically plain, nothing to take away from the views. The site is upslope from the shore and from almost every room you have expansive views of the fields and trees and the waves breaking on the rocky and volcanic coast. Number two: They want you to recycle the towels and even the slippers are recyclable. The slippers? Are you supposed to eat them? They do not give you plastic bottles of water, but instead two aluminum water bottles to carry with you, and refill at the water station near the front desk. Less litter. Three: It's "inclusive" so all the meals and drinks and tours and guides are part of the expensive package. The good news is that the food and wine are very good, way better than anything we had in Santiago. Inclusive places always make me nervous because I am never quite certain what is included and what is not, but here it seems that they have it down. This is a great hotel and the perfect place to stay.

They feed us lunch including very good food and a nice selection of wines, and then tell us what the afternoon tour is. Not quite "What would you like to do?" more of "Here's what you are going to do this afternoon." OK, I am willing to turn over the decision making for the moment at least. Did I mention how good the food is?

Good discovery at lunch: when one asks for "local beer," you get it. They make beer here, on the island. It's called Mahina, which means "full moon" and the bottom of the bottle says "Pia Rapa Nui" which means "Beer of Rapa Nui." I suspect Rapa Nui means "our island" in Polynesian but I never get a clear answer on this. We also learn the words for thank you, "*mauruuru*," and hello, which is "*Ioana*." But since everyone here already speaks English and Spanish, this turns out not to be especially useful.

We hike from the lodge down to the coast and Ahu Something. It is great to be outside, although there are lots of loose rocks on the trail and I worry a little about twisting my ankle. This means I focus about half the time on the ground ahead of me and thus don't see as much as I might. There are both horses and cows in the fenced fields along the way, and occasional piles of horse poop or cow poop on the trail. I am unclear on how to discern the difference, but maybe I don't need to know this, I do not intend to become a tracker. There are brightly blooming coral trees and the lantana equivalent bordering the side of the dirt and rocks road. It is windy and cloudy with occasional bursts of sun, and not exactly tropical-island-paradise warm, but we're here and we're doing something.

We eventually arrive at a platform ("ahu") with nothing but toppled-over moai lying around. "Moai" is the Easter Island word for the large stone heads found here. Some are pretty small, maybe as small as five feet tall. And to be technically correct, they are more than stone heads, they are actually heads and torsos, down to about the tops of the hips. All the images at this site were originally on a platform constructed of black volcanic stones crudely fitted together. Apparently no mortar was used— no limestone perhaps, not enough trees to burn to calcify it? Did anyone in Polynesia discover cement? The moai have all been pushed over on their faces so you can only really see the backs of their heads. A couple of the smaller ones have rolled off the platform and ended facing up so you can see the noses and eye sockets. They look like moai all right. At least as far as one can tell. Go lie face down on your bed and see if anyone can really tell what you look like.

HISTORICAL INTERJECTION: archaeologists believe that the Easter Island folks came to the island around AD 500 in small boats from somewhere else in Polynesia, settled in, and began making stone images three hundred years later. This is one remote island—2,000 miles from Pitcairn on the west, itself not exactly the New York city of Polynesia, and 2,500 miles from Chile. And nothing much in the other directions either, so getting to this place if you didn't know it was here was quite a feat, or ridiculously lucky. Even if you believe that Polynesians were superb navigators, you cannot navigate to a place that you don't know exists.

Moai were fabricated at one special location on the island where there was a rich source of the easy-to-work volcanic rock (tuff) from which all the images were carved. They were then each transported and eventually installed on raised rock platforms (ahu) along the coast, with faces facing inward, watching over the settlements of the particular tribe of islanders in that location. The smallest platforms had one statue, biggest had fifteen. Each figure was a memorialization of a person significant to the particular tribe or clan in that location, a chief probably. The images were not worshipped, and they weren't gods, but they were a part of the whole pantheistic/ancestor venerating culture. This moai-making period lasted until about 1600 when there was serious internal conflict. Everyone ran around pushing over everyone else's moais, as well as killing and eating each other. Eventually the moais all got pushed over, thus proving that they didn't have the sort of powers that one would have thought, given how much work it was to make and transport the doggone things. The moai that are now standing up on their platforms have all been re-erected by archaeologists and other outsiders since around 1950. There is of course academic disagreement on what triggered this social and political disintegration—over population, rats eating all the crops, normal human cussedness. The evidence is scanty for any particular explanation over another. Except it's clear that around 1600 all this moai business stopped abruptly.

So much for the facts and the history. What is so amazing about the island is that so few people on such a small place created such large and wonderful figures. There is really nothing else like it that I have ever seen or heard of.

After us "expeditioneers" finish hiking downhill to the ahu, there is an Explora van waiting for us, and a small field table set out with guava juice, cheese and salami, and champagne. My brother notes that, for his money, this is a good way to end a hike. And besides we get to ride back uphill to the hotel.

Day Six, Tuesday: Hiking and Ahus

This morning's expedition is a combined visit to several more ahus and a hike along the north coast. Today we will first see the most famous one, Ahu Tongariki. This site is very impressive. As at every location, the moai (means "ancestor" we are told) are all facing inland. A pretty large tribe all lived around this platform, with the cropland further uphill, and access to the ocean for fishing. In truth all this is pretty speculative as there is no written record, the oral history is largely vacuous, and the first two or three Western visitors made only very limited observations of what was going on, and then took off. What we do know is that when serious westerners came here, all the moai had been pushed over onto their faces. The fifteen restored moai at Tongariki are the most at any one site. They were restored through the good works of the Japanese government and a Japanese crane company. These suckers are made of stone, and the smallest probably weighs twenty tons, so cranes would be useful.

It's a wonderful place, and it is only us and another group of four people. We wander around, take pictures, and listen to the strange local guide named Tito explain that his family owns half the island. And that there was a written language but the missionaries made the people abandon it, and now no one can understand it. The site also contains several petro-glyphs of turtles, tuna, and an odd birdlike creature. We find out later from a more convincing source that something like ten wooden boards remain, with a bunch of glyphs on them, but they cannot be read. No Rosetta stone. Lydia, my niece, remarks that their company policy is now that all documents—budgets, decision memos, briefings, etc.—must be presented exclusively in PowerPoint slides. I am surprised that the missionaries in charge of her company have eliminated the written language and forced all the natives to work only in glyphs.

Data note #1: the small accountant who sits in the back of one's brain, wearing a green eyeshade and keeping track, wants to know just how many ahus there are. As far as the maps can tell us, it looks like sixteen. They are dotted all around the island, but always right on the shoreline. This does make them easier to find. According to the official Explora map:

Along the southeast coast, from south to north:

Ahu Vinapu

Ahu Tahira

Ahu Hanga Poukura

Ahu Hanga Te'e

Ahu Akahanga

Ahu Hanga Te Tenga

Ahu One Makihi

Ahu Tongariki

Along the north coast from east to west:

Ahu Mahatua

Ahu Te Pito Kura

Ahu Nau Nau

Along the east coast, from north to south:

Ahu Vai Mata

Ahu Maitaki Te Moa

Ahu Te Peu

Ahu Akivi (a bit inland, actually)

Ahu Tahai (actually three platforms but all right next to each other)

Ahu Ana Kai Tangata

Two of these (Vai Mata and Maitaki Te Moa) are only accessible by taking a five-hour hike along the coastline of the north, so these we may elect to leave for another time—no road runs along this piece of the island's coast. And using my friend Erik's rule (there is a reason that popular tourist sites are popular—they are the most interesting) one can presume that if these two ahus were hot stuff, someone would have scraped out a road to get to them.

We leave Ahu Tongariki and drive to our drop-off point on the northeastern tip of the island and begin a five-mile hike along the coast. No real elevation changes, but the path is strewn with rocks, small and large. As before, turning an ankle becomes a concern. From time to time one does look up to see the dramatic scenery—the cone of a small volcano and small herds of horses to the left, crashing waves along a rocky and volcanic coastline to the right. At the midpoint of the hike we come to Ahu Te Pito Kura according to one map, or possibly Ahu Keiki'i. This has the standard platform and only one moai, lying face down in the dirt. Tito informs us that this is the largest of the fallen-down moai. It does look pretty big. Good to know. We press on. And on. And on.

We arrive at a small boat harbor, with three wooden rowboat-sized boats in it, and a couple of very small houses or shacks nearby. With three boats moored, the harbor is full. Actually it's more like a boat landing. No one offers to sell us fish. The boats look small, the ocean looks big and choppy. The weather is temperate but cloudy and quite windy. I am happy to be on the land. We pass a small ahu with another facedown moai. No one stops.

The Hike to Nowhere ends at a small beach. Why here? Not clear. Fortunately the van is here also but no champagne. We get in the van anyway and go on to another beach where there are two ahus—this is Ahu Nau Nau. It has a lineup of eight moai standing up, some fragments lying around, and behind it another platform with one moai standing. This latter is the original and first platform to be reconstructed, this one by Thor Heyerdahl who came here in the 1950s, spent a year doing archaeology, and re-erected this particular moai. He also had some theories about the place that have subsequently been discredited, but at least he didn't suspect aliens. The beach is lovely, there are coconut palms and white sand, and the water temperature seems reasonable. No one is around. And at last, after five hours on the trail, there is a toilette. The boys in the group don't seem to need it.

After lunch back at the hotel, we go to what is probably the single best place on the island, called Rano Raraku. This is the volcanic cone/crater from which all the moai were quarried. Remember that this peculiar process of erecting big carved stone figures lasted until 1600, at which time there was a civil war and all the moai were pulled down at all the ahus. And the process of carving same and hauling them to the various sites was also abandoned at this point, as one would surmise. But they left lots of moai already carved or mostly carved, littering the hillside of the volcano, a fair number of them standing up but half buried. You can see their heads but not their bodies. You can get very close to them. It is an amazing and wonderful sight.

Data note #2: according to the manager of the hotel, who seems reasonably knowledgeable, there are 804 moai, by the most authoritative count. She did admit that the surveys are a bit difficult, as what to count as a "moai" is an interesting question. Some of them are broken and only the heads remain, or the bodies are not in the same place as the heads, or there is a weathered piece of stone that could be a head or could be a soccer ball or could just be a weathered piece of stone. Or if one is partly carved and recognizable, but is still anchored in the cliff where it was being carved, does this count? Of these, about 10 are off the island, one in the British Museum, and most of the rest in Chile. Two hundred and thirty made it to platforms and were installed there, and about 170 are scattered around the island, in the process of getting from the quarry to a particular platform when everything ground to a halt. Some 400 are still in the quarry in various stages of completion. It's not clear how many of the 230 have been re-erected, but it appears to be less than 100, maybe less than 50. So far we have seen about 35, although I may not have a precise count. We have also visited 5 of the 16 ahus listed on the map. More tomorrow. I love a vacation with goals and data.

Day Seven, Wednesday: More Hiking, More Moai

Today we are scheduled for an "expedition" called Cliffs and Caves, which focuses on the western side of the island. Easter Island is a fairly regular triangle, one side on the north, another on the west at a right angle to the north side, and the third the hypotenuse running southwest to northeast. Our first stop today is Ahu Akivi, a bit farther up the slope than the other platforms and with the only moai, seven in this case, facing the sea rather than inland. Why? The local lore says this represents the seven original Polynesian islanders who came from Tahiti or somewhere and discovered the island, so the seven moai are their spirits or ancestors or guardians still looking back to where they came from. This makes no sense as these are later era moai, of course. So much for oral history. But they are very impressive and well displayed and erect. Then we go on to the cliffs where we hike for an hour. Less windy but much more cliffy on this side of the island, with beautiful green clear water at the base of the cliffs. You can see it if you get close enough but if you have a fear of heights this is not a great idea. It's steep and vertical. We hike along, find a few lava tube caves and crawl inside them while doing the required bonking of our heads on the ceiling. The first cave smells faintly of urine so I pass on crawling through the second. Caves we have elsewhere in the world.

Then four more ahu, including the only one with eyes. It is said that the eye sockets of the moai all originally had mother of pearl inlays for the whites, and obsidian pupils, although none of this is left. So some genius decided to re-eye one of the moai, and got local artists to do it. They did a reasonably poor job, using white coral that is not iridescent and not even smooth, and red lava for the pupil. The moai so redecorated is not only not fearsome or awe inspiring, he is slightly cross-eyed and appears to be regarding the brim of his hat. Three more platforms, more very good moai, and still no people/tourists at the sites other than us. This is the high season, and these ahu are quite close to town.

After lunch we go back to the quarry and this time hike inside the caldera where the carvers were also busy making moai until work stopped, although getting the damn things out of the inside of a volcano could not have been easy; why they did not concentrate on using the rock on the outside we don't know. There are many more, most standing up although buried up to their chins. And you can walk right up to them and stand beside them—no touching please—and make a funny face and get your picture taken. You are not allowed to put your finger up the nose of a moai, however. Although no doubt someone has. Again, the marvelous nature of the accomplishment of the islanders comes through. Why did they do this? How were they inspired? There of course aren't real answers to these questions, but the site is magical.

An archaeologist from UCLA is working at a small site with two moai. She and her crew have unburied them down to their bases and are now taking what one assumes are long-term measurements of the effects of the wind and rain and sun on the erosion of the statues. I suppose this is useful, although how to preserve these images, if one wished to do so and had the money, is an interesting problem. It hasn't really been solved at Angkor Wat, and the volcanic tuff is a whole lot less durable—that's why they carved it, because they could. Good to see these statues now; they will look much different in a hundred years.

Day Eight, Thursday: Thanksgiving Avoided

This morning I decided to avoid the organized activities, despite disapproving looks from the manager. They want you out and hiking or kayaking or riding on horses morning and afternoon, and have a whole slug of such preconfigured "expeditions" ready to go. It's actually quite a good program in general. The recommended hike was a three-hour climb of a volcano to a reconstructed village from which the famous annual birdman competition started and ended. However, the village is just a couple of small dwellings built into the sides of hills, with stone fronts. And maybe the odd glyph carved in stone. The birdman competition is as nutty as the rest of the history of the island. It pitted champions from each tribe in an annual race. They all left the village site at the top of the volcano, ran down to the shore, swam across to the small island about three kilometers offshore (Motu Nui), braving sharks and currents and such. There the contestants tried to find the first egg of the season of the sooty tern (bad name for a bird, but they probably weren't consulted), and to kill each other. Once located the surviving swimmer straps the egg to his head, swims to the mainland, and runs up to the top of the volcano without breaking the egg. First guy back wins something like his tribe gets to be first in line at the mess hall for a year and no KP; it's not clear. This contest is no longer done because everyone has more sense than this. Somehow this "replaced" the moai. Perhaps this was better than two hundred years of civil war. None of this seems reasonable but that's how oral traditions are. And why they are of limited use in figuring out what really happened six hundred or eight hundred years ago.

Having pluckily avoided this, I spend some time browsing the resources of the hotel. The library is small, and consists of several books on Argentine cooking, three bird-watching magazines, and the last twenty-five issues of *Wine Spectator*. Nothing on Easter Island history or flora and fauna. I suspect they know their clients, but this seems like an odd assortment of titles. Fortunately there is working Wi-Fi and Internet access. I find that the flower I have been regarding is not a lantana at all but a relative of butterfly weed, specifically *Asclepias curassavica*. Boy, that's good to know.

Lunch is advertised as a picnic at the beach, so we all go. It's not a beach exactly, it's a rocky and lava-strewn oceanside site where it's hard to find a comfortable place to sit. And the lunch buffet is set up inside a cave with low ceilings. I confirm this by banging my head into the ceiling. Baseball caps turn out not to be hard hats. I decide to abjure caves for the duration. They do serve cold slices of turkey breast but this is the only reference to the US tradition. Which is fine with us. I don't think a holiday dedicated to eating a lot of food is quite what the US population needs at this point.

In the afternoon we have asked to see the remaining ahus that we have not seen, all along the southeast coast: One Makihi, Akahanga, Ura Uranga Te Mahina, and Hanga Te'e. At least these are the names on the signs in front of the various platforms. The careful reader will note that they do not exactly conform to the names on the map. So much for trying to figure out what you've seen and what you haven't seen. And in truth broken-down stone platforms and big moai tipped over so their noses are in the dirt in front of the platform can get a little hard to distinguish, one from the other, after a while. But this is what we came for, so this is what we're going to see, gosh darn it. And they're still impressive, even prostrate.

As far as David and I can determine, from combing our combined amateur archaeologist memories, there is no other tradition anywhere in Polynesia of the creation/carving of large stone images. Many cultures, maybe all cultures, tend to memorialize their high-ranking dead—the Egyptian pyramids, the Taj Mahal, the Maya pyramids, Inca burial sites, Presbyterian graveyards with headstones—so that part is not at all strange. But what possessed them to start carving large and larger and even larger images to put up as memorials? As fully qualified guys, we can actually understand the bigger and bigger part, but what started this?

The carving and the transportation were truly heroic and signal an island with a substantial economic surplus to support all the carvers and the transporters. All this in rocky and volcanic soil, which doesn't support much agriculture. Plus they had no draft animals, no metal tools, no plows—just wooden digging sticks—and hadn't discovered the wheel. Must have been a lot of fish around so some portion of the islanders could support both themselves and all the artisans carving away madly on the hillside of the volcano and the other guys dragging moai here and there. It is an impressive accomplishment, and largely unlooted unlike many other such sites. Being remote helps.

In the evening we elect to go town to see the native touristic dancers. Sure enough, musicians in the back are playing ukuleles and banging on drums. Women in grass skirts and feather bras and men bare chested, dancing around and every so often shouting "Ha!" or maybe "Kah!" Much singing of what seems like nonsense syllables ("ma nee ke oh a hu a te o pi te la sa a pay oh pa"). Much rapid shaking of behinds. At least they don't pretend to explain each dance, they just do them. There is also a point at which the dancers descend on the audience, select and drag back victims on the stage, and make them dance. The tourists look about as silly as you would expect.

'Day Nine, Friday: Expedition to Town

L and I go into town while David and the family elect a long horse-back ride. We first stop at Ahu Vinapu, the farthest south ahu on the southeastern coast. This is the site of the famous and only female moai. It (she?) is also carved from the red volcanic stone called scoria, the stone used exclusively for the topknots on many of the moai, and not the grey-green tuff used for all the rest of the moai. Curiously, it had two heads rather than one coming out of its neck. The missionaries are said to have knocked off the heads, for secret missionary reasons. Note to primitive cultures everywhere: when in doubt, blame the missionaries. The site also has excellent stonework in its platform, the best in the island. This is the basis for Heyerdahl's claim that the islands were populated by South Americans. The masonry is reminiscent of the best Inca stonework, at Sacsayhuaman for example. Just not quite as gigantic. But this is the only place and platform with such well-executed work.

Our travel book says, "small sleepy beach town," and it's correct, but fun. One or two main streets, one small elementary school, one Catholic church, one priest walking by in a dark cassock, lots of bars and open-air restaurants and souvenir shops. Predictably, many, many, many small stone and wooden replicas of moai for sale—one is tempted to say "mo than the ai can see," but refrains. T-shirts, coffee mugs, coral jewelry, postcards, magnets, but no snow globes. We decide what would be especially nice would be a moai made into a bobblehead doll. Perhaps we have been here long enough.

Day Ten, Saturday

Because this is the way the world works, the day dawns warm and sunny, after five days of cloudy and windy and not very warm weather. Of course today we leave to fly back to Santiago and then on to various home locations. But it has been an exceptional and fascinating trip. I think I have seen at least 90% of all the moai on the island and marveled at them. And that's what we came for.

Love and kisses, Bob

Afterword: AES continues to own significant power assets in Chile, and has built several more power projects since this was written. It also has installed several large "utility-scale" batteries to supplement its generation assets. The government has remained stable enough that our contracts work and we regularly get paid. It is a real success story, although not one without some challenges along the way. But what success story doesn't have these?

Buddhas, Elephants, Fortresses— What's Not to Like?

July 2012

Dear Aunt Janet,

So why do we all hate the airlines? Why aren't we slobbering with thanks that we can fly anywhere in the world except North Korea, and for very little money, and very quickly and comfortably, compared to, say, two years before the mast on a sailing vessel the size of your living room, eating hardtack and salted beef and drinking water from barrels with green goo growing in them. What is hardtack, really? Is it like my first wife's biscuits that she made early in our marriage, economizing by leaving out the baking powder? Is it like matzo? If so that's no help since I don't know what that is either. Is it like Communion wafers, which don't really taste like much as I recall, although it has been a year and a day since I've been through that ceremony? You might go for the wine, although probably not, but not for the wafers. We can only imagine that salted beef is like beef jerky only not the teriyaki-flavored kind. I myself prefer to stick to the classics, i.e., Slim Jims.

We hate the airlines because they cannot seem to run their businesses reliably. I could go through all the stupid details about last-minute disruptions that started this journey. But since everyone who has ever flown even once has the same stories I shall forbear. It's difficult. I want special credit.

We arrived in Colombo, the capital of Sri Lanka (formerly Ceylon) and the only international airport, after many hours on serial airplanes. It was two in the morning. We dutifully but blearily walked through the duty-free shop that was open and selling not just booze and big yellow bags of M&M's, but refrigerators and washing machines. Huh? We eventually emerged from the appliance gauntlet without so much as a blender, and were met by our guide, Ravi, and taken to a nearby hotel.

We are here because the country has eight World Heritage sites and I want to see six of them. The two not-so-interesting ones are forests, and I don't see why they merit this classification, but I guess that's the business of the UN or whoever runs the system. I do not find a bunch of trees interesting. But the other six sites are said to be archaeologically and architecturally significant. Besides nobody much comes to Sri Lanka so that's another attraction. Well, unless they want to buy duty-free kitchen machines and I don't see how that fits in your luggage.

At check-in, I get asked if I am German, then English. Never American, and this continues all through the trip. I don't think we actually see another American the whole time. A sprinkling of Europeans, but no one we can clearly identify as from the US. This is not necessarily a bad thing, but curious.

After a too-short night, we were up and on the road, red-eyed but ready for our first adventure. Elephants were involved. I think this is what L came for.

Infrastructure comment number one: We traveled everywhere in a modest white van, guide and driver in front, us on the bench seats. OK but far from luxe. There is not as yet any domestic commercial aviation, which is surprising even though the country is not geographically enormous. However, it's not small either. Even in Burma one can fly about from the capital to other large cities. This road-bound way of getting around surely does allow one to see more, even though the roads are narrow and in lousy shape. There is only one one-hundred-kilometer stretch of four-lane divided highway anywhere in the country. Everything else is a two lane, very much undivided highway, with lots of potholes and shredded edges. It's generally slow and bumpy going.

Our first destination is the highland city and former capital, Kandy, six or seven hours away. We see firsthand, and occasionally up close, an amazing collection of tuk-tuks (small, open, motorcycle-powered three-wheeler vehicles, usually taxis but sometimes outfitted as trucks), busses, large and small trucks to include petro tankers, motorcycles, some bikes, and very few private cars. Sri Lanka is clearly in the transition from bikes to motorcycles, but if they ever make it to cars, they will have to completely rebuild the cities and most of the highways. Lots of pedestrians are about and at all hours of the day, don't these people have jobs? No sidewalks to speak of, so everybody is walking in the road, crossing the road, hanging out in the road as the traffic roars by. In the towns are lots of schoolkids, all in uniforms, the girls in white pinafores, sometimes with striped ties—it was a British colony at one point but they seem confused about who should wear the ties, here it's the girls—the young boys in blue shorts and white shirts, the older boys in white pants and white shirts. Laundry has to be a problem.

It's the tropics, so the flowers are profuse, some cared for, some just growing along the road or in the drainage ditches. The whole tropical assortment—bougainvillea, red and blue gingers, big orange cosmos, plumeria, allamanda, hibiscus, oleanders, flame trees (royal poinciana), and the pink creeper that took over Hawaii for a while (*Antigonon leptopus*). It's impressive and frequently gorgeous.

Roadside signs abound, but no alcohol, no tobacco, only Pizza Hut (once in Kandy, once in Galle), but lots of profusion and color. No US stuff except Coke. Roadside fruit stands are everywhere—durian, rambutan, coconuts, mangoes, and always bananas—it must be the national fruit of Sri Lanka.

There is very little roadside trash. This is pleasantly surprising. There is a lot of traffic, and the driving standards are random. We get much weaving and passing on curves and hills. Maybe these are not two-lane roads but three or four lane, so long as you can all get by. But this is common in all of Asia and not surprising. Just occasionally terrifying.

We decide that the country has lost twenty-five years due to the civil war between the Tamils and the Lankans, which must have consumed the bulk of government resources and certainly made the country unattractive for investment. It is far behind other places on both commercial infra-structure (i.e., roads) and tourist infrastructure, as in decent hotels. There is very little indication of Western investment, at least at the retail level. No McDonald's (OK, we did see one on the way to the Colombo airport on our last day) or 7-Elevens or Wimpy or Walmart or Carrefour or really anything US or European or Japanese. No adverts for Sharp or Toyota or Ford or Crest. Plenty of shops and commerce but it's all local.

Adventure #1: We Visit the Elephants

Sri Lanka has lots of elephants, more than five thousand by most counts, including both domesticated and wild. Maybe there are more in Laos, where there's an elephant on the flag, but there are sure lots here. The domesticated ones are employed doing heavy lifting of logs and other elephant-like things. I don't think they do plastering or painting, and probably not welding. The rest are still in the jungles and various wildlife preserves in the center of the country. We saw fields near villages with ersatz tree houses from which the residents keep watch at night, waiting for the wild elephants to come to eat the crops, which is not a good thing. The job of the tree house sitter is to scare the elephants away by throwing flaming torches at them. We did not actually see this, and it is not a job to which I aspire.

Some of the elephants have been damaged in the war, some orphaned by other circumstances (villagers with fire sticks?), but whatever the case, they are sent to the Pinnawala Elephant Orphanage, which is on the way to Kandy. It has grown to a herd of some seventy beasts, and they are mostly large, as perhaps one should expect with elephants. The elephants move twice a day from their park to a local river where they bathe and we guess squirt each other with water and so forth. We get there too late for the river part, arriving just as the elephants are coming up the street from the river. We stand there two feet from them and they walk right by us and into their park. Which is startling, as I hadn't really planned to be in the flight path. Fortunately the elephants are herded along by mahouts, young men in curiously bright orange shirts, shorts, and bare feet, carrying long sticks. Which look to me like they would be toothpicks the first time any elephant decided he was tired of being poked.

The elephants finally get into their park, then they stand around and get fed and all us tourists (all Europeans but us) get our pictures taken with the elephants. L is fearless or nuts, and wants to be very close to several of these large mammals. I think about the famous parable of the four blind men and the elephant. Touch one, I suggest, and tell me what it feels like. She does so. She says it feels like an elephant. So much for that tradition.

My favorite visual is of one of the young mahouts, sitting on a log, with many pachyderms arrayed behind him eating bamboo or hay or mulberry leaves or whatever they're feeding them—elephants appear to be omnivorous in a vegetarian sort of way. The kid in his Day-Glow shirt is talking into his cell phone. As so often happens, the pace of development is mixed. But they're not twenty-five years behind on cell phones.

Adventure #2: The Holy City of Kandy, a World Heritage Site

It is hard to take the name of this town seriously. Especially since everything else in SL has much longer and more complicated names, at least the towns and the people do. The president is named *Mahinda Rajapaksa*. A former president was named Chandrika Kumaratunga. You will see more of the city names in a bit. Still, Kandy is a nice town, the third and final capital of the country before the Portuguese and the Dutch and the Brits finally conquered all the island and made it into a colony in the 1700s. It is quite hilly, with a man-made lake in the center, but most important is the Temple of the Sacred Tooth Relic.

Cultural interjection: This is one of the most Buddhist countries in the world as measured by percent of population professing the religion. Maybe Bhutan has more Buddhists, but they are very serious about it here, and have been ever since about 500 BC when the religion came to Sri Lanka. One of the major Buddhist sites is the one in Kandy wherein is housed the "Tooth Relic" as it is generally referred to. Our guide explains this at length and we edit, interpret, and summarize: Buddha said, "Don't worship me when I die, oh, well, OK, maybe just my remains." Then he was cremated. But cremation is not that efficient; it appears that there was a tooth, and perhaps a collarbone left in the ashes. The tooth became a very big deal. It got fought over and stolen and given to Sri Lanka and taken back to India and then taken back to Sri Lanka. All this back and forth had the accompanying good and bad luck following whoever was behaving badly, including at one point the British governor who was guilty of disrespect and thus triggered a big drought. But now finally it's here and being honored.

The religious skeptic might say, however, what with the war and the 2004 tsunami, it is hard to say Sri Lanka has had terrific luck lately. Ah well.

But wait, there's more: Once a year, at the end of July (the beginning of the second monsoon season) there is a weeklong festival honoring the Tooth Relic and the Buddha and requesting a good harvest and the necessary rain. The tooth gets to come out of its temple and it is carried through the streets of Kandy in what people refer to as its casket, mounted elaborately on the back of an elephant. This is the Esala Perahera, which seems to translate as the Tooth Festival, although we had read about it as "the elephant parade." The irreverent among us keep wondering if the Tooth Fairy will also appear, but we keep this to ourselves.

The highlight of the festival occurs in the evening on each of the seven days: a large, logistically challenging and elaborate parade. This honors the tooth, and it is a very big deal. Elephants and dancers and musicians and performers come from all over the country to participate. We are there for the fourth night, and it is hard to believe these people do this every night but apparently so. It is also hard to believe they attract this same large audience every night—reported as 100,000 persons, a big number for even a big city—but apparently so. The place is jammed, which is not hard as the town is relatively small and the streets are narrow. But it's not at all threatening or unpleasant, just quite crowded.

Where you sit really matters. There are modest bleachers at some points, and at the hotels special sections with reserved seats have been set up under the entry porches and verandas. We get there at five-thirty to get our places on the front row at one of the hotels, and it is already crowded. The show runs from seven to ten-thirty, nonstop.

Good thing nobody has to pee; once you sit down you're stuck. There are general hawkers working the crowd, selling small toys, something that looks like popcorn, something that looks like cotton candy. We are particularly amused by some ambitious Pizza Hut guys working the crowd. They take your order, go off somewhere (mobile pizza van?) then they bring back a pizza. The only example of Western fast food we see anywhere except Colombo.

There are also lots of police and some soldiers lining the streets. I am a little apprehensive but then I notice that none of the police have sidearms, it seems that their role is crowd control and maintaining order.

Finally it is dark enough and the parade starts. It begins with lots of young men with whips. The whip crackers wear white sarongs like long skirts and red scarves and are naked from the waist up. They stop every so often and make loud cracks like firecrackers with their whips. Then after four or five cracks, they move on. People toss coins into the street.

Then comes a round of musicians, but not exactly marching bands. Flutes that have but one note, or maybe three, in a scale not familiar to Western music, and drums, drums, drums, drums. Did we mention lots of drums? All men, white sarongs, red scarves, no shirts. And then the fire twirlers, men and boys wearing fire hats, double baton fire twirlers, fire twirlers on stilts, wagon wheel fire twirlers. For those who cannot dance, drum, whip, twirl fire or etc., there are the rows of flag carriers, dressed all in white.

We learn later that the whip crackers are the thunder, the fire guys are the lightning, and the drummers are the sounds of rain on parched earth. The elephants are just there for the spectacle. And spectacle it is—the first elephant appears, dressed in a red velvet cape emblazoned with a repeating large gold lotus symbol. Head and trunk and ears are covered with electric lights! Powered by batteries! Probably not lithium ion. This is all we'll say about electricity, don't worry. Then processions of dancers and then waves of musicians, each wave seventy to eighty strong. The dancers are all in the same variant of white sarong and red scarf or cummerbund, bare chested and barefoot, but the headdresses vary. Good thing that it's warm. We are told that the dance moves are all different and these guys are all from particular regions and this is their local regional dance. "Typical Kandy dancers," says Ravi of a group wearing what look like Wicked Witch of the West hats, but with long cords emanating from the top of the cone, and then a small red pompom on each cord.

Each set of dancers is different. There are sword dancers, dagger dancers with daggers being brandished, stick dancers, dancers with a bunch of sticks. Disk twirlers, disc on stick twirlers. Dancers holding on to a bunch of reeds, dancers with something that looks like a maypole. Dancers with white batons with pompoms on each end, dancers with white scarves that they swirl around, dancers with small cymbals, dancers with tiny drums, fat dancers, thin dancers, kids, old guys. And for reasons not explained, all the dancers and all the drummers and musicians do the whole parade walking backward. Not the elephants. I have not ever seen a backward parade, not even in Tennessee.

We begin to get the rhythm down: elephant in fancy dress, band walking backward, dancers dancing backward, repeat. The parade is lit along its edges by bare-chested men carrying fire baskets of diesel enhanced charcoal on swivels on the top of poles. Smokey but it adds to the atmosphere.

Because I am anal I begin to count the elephants, just to see how many there are in the parade. Occasionally they wear blue capes not red. Sometimes the cape is ornamented with what looks like golden chrysanthemums rather than golden lotus. Sometimes we have two elephants at a time walking side by side, once a couple of baby elephants, but mostly it's one elephant, a band, and then a bunch of dancers.

Elephants #33–35 appear, wearing incredibly ornate capes, lighted shrines on the top of each elephant, the casket of the tooth in the center. Many more dancers and many more drummers. And some big solemn guys with gold hats and parasol carriers walking behind them. These must be parade officials or religious authorities, as they get to walk facing forward. And wear shirts.

Finally some dancers in green, then in teal, then a golf cart made up to look like a peacock. More rows of flag carriers. And musicians, always musicians. These are the Hindus (the ones that survived the war) bringing up the rear.

By elephant #57, discipline has really broken down: we have guys in red plaid short skirts, looking vaguely Scottish, except they also have red tights, and red sleeveless undershirts—Marlon Brando, call your agent. Then dancers wearing exaggerated eye makeup. Finally, after elephant #60, women appear for the first time, these dancers looking like peacocks but with big round fantails affixed to their bottoms. The dancers move the tails with straps. Someone forgot to mention that the fancy tail thing in nature is done by the male peacocks.

Band consistency also goes—the weird flutes are supplemented by horns and clarinets. More shrines on groups of three elephants lumber by, more gold hat guys, more flags, then more girl dancers only this time they are each wearing large gold ears over their normal ears, or maybe these are their normal ears. Makes them look slightly comical. I am sure there is important symbolism here that we're not picking up. Walt Disney?

At last we have four square things like the Arc of the Covenant, each carried by two men. Perhaps they have run out of elephants? Then two police trucks and police with ropes and a surge of watchers into the street as everyone tries to get to their bus or hotel and get home. But it's an orderly and efficient dispersal. Seventy-three total elephants. And probably five thousand dancers and musicians. Wow! And wow again!

The next day we go to the Temple of the Sacred Tooth Relic. The place is jammed, especially with schoolkids since this is a seven-day religious holiday. The temple has much color, much sculpture and bright paint, much visual imagery. There are also some rules, as this is a serious religious shrine. For one, the place is dotted with signs saying, "Please turn off mobile phones." It is also our first of many experiences where you are required to take off your shoes. While you may take pictures inside the temple, which is really a series of buildings within buildings, and a series of large images of the Buddha, you may not turn your back on the Buddha, so you can't have a picture posed in front of the Buddha. And they're pretty clear about this, with guards correcting you if you mess up. Lots of worshippers have brought flowers to be put in front of the images, and there are several signs saying "Please do not stop to smell the flowers."

Throughput is important. In the major building, where the tooth lives (stays?), everybody lines up and is hustled past a small window, which looks like a teller's window at a bank; you have time for only a quick glance inside where you see a gold-covered thing like a bird cage only solid, then on you go.

The courtyard of the temple has a Hindu shrine in it, and next door is a Catholic church. It is hard to decide if this is religious tolerance or hedging your bets. And lots of elephants lazing around, waiting to be dressed up for the evening's parade. Well, they're from out of town, and they had to be put somewhere.

Because we're here and we like gardens, we go to the botanic garden, billed as the largest in Sri Lanka. It's nice and big but is mostly trees and thus technically more an arboretum than a botanic garden. No elephants, but lots of nasty and aggressive monkeys who will try and rip your food out of your hands if you have any. We do not. But we see couple in front of us, and they are finding this less romantic than perhaps they had counted on.

There are also many trees with lots of bats hanging in them, noticeably; seriously, Batman would be right at home here, lots of bats. And not small bats. Large fruit bats. And they don't just hang there passively sleeping and waiting for nightfall or the bat signal from Commissioner Gordon, they squeak and wiggle around and flex their wings and scratch and whatnot. I know we are supposed to like bats as they are good, and we electric people are not supposed to use windmills to kill them, but ugh. I am also careful not to walk directly under any of the trees. At least there aren't any snakes lying around.

Having survived the restive bats and unpleasant monkeys, we ask to go see the really big white Buddha on one of the hills. It turns out that there is something of a competition for the title of World's Largest Outdoor Buddha. The famous Japanese one at Kamakura is a mere thirty-five feet tall. Although it does date back to the twelfth century AD so that should count for something. This one is eighty-eight feet tall and there is a picture gallery at the site that displays photos of the other smaller ones, with the height of each. So there. Because this is still a religious site, we have to take off our shoes and boy, it's midafternoon and the tiles are really hot. And the road to get up to the Buddha is steep and narrow, and it has no guardrails. It was unclear if the car would make it as it kept sputtering, so we had visions of backing down this long, narrow, one-lane road. This does begin to sound like a recipe for religious enlightenment, doesn't it?

Infrastructure comment number two: So how's a guy get a drink around here? When we arrived in Kandy after seeing the elephants at Pinnawala, we were hot and tired and thirsty, which happens when you drive four hours over crappy roads in order to stand around pachyderms for a long time in the sun and then drive some more long time to get to where you're going and don't stop anywhere to have lunch. It's three o'clock so it's after lunch unless you're in Portugal, but the bar is open and serving food. Great! We go in, order sandwiches and french fries and a beer for me and a glass of wine for L. They bring the food, slowly, but then inform us that the bar is not open until four. Hmmm.

We come back from the Esala Perahera that evening, again hot and thirsty. Now the bar is closed, although it's only ten-thirty at night. We are also finally informed that the bar will never be open for the entire seven days of the festival because it's a religious thing. Our room minibar, however, has small bottles of gin in it, but no beer or wine. And no tonic. It does have Sprite. Yes, the shame of it all, we end up having what we decide are Sri Lankan gin and tonics—gin and Sprite. It tastes about like you would expect, and explains why the Brits gave the place independence without a fight.

It is also interesting to note that our hotel in Kandy is built on and right into the side of the hill. A large rocky part of the hill has been incorporated into our room, doubling it in size but increasing it not at all in utility. I guess it's supposed to be natural and so forth, but it just looks odd and dysfunctional since the rock face is jagged and slopes upward. Hasn't anyone here heard of dynamite? We do have a balcony with a nice view, however. It looks out over some more rock. We see a mongoose but luckily no snakes.

Adventure #3: Dambulla

Next morning it's off to World Heritage site #2 (all of Kandy was #1, including I guess the parade)—five caves, full of carved Buddhas. The caves are about midway up a steep hill, and at the bottom is a museum of sorts that forms the base for another very large outdoor Buddha, this one only six years old. And bright gold. I am unclear whether to count the building it sits on as part of its height so it can be entered in the World's Largest Outdoor Buddha sweepstakes. After much walking upstairs, we get to the caves. They are all quite close together, so it's really only a medium-sized site. There are great paintings in some caves, frequently of rows and rows of Buddhas, but occasionally some more interesting scenes of devils and whatnot. But the carvings are the key. There are several very large reclining Buddhas although you don't get the numbers and so cannot conduct in your head the "World's Largest Buddha Lying Down in a Cave" contest. There are, as advertised, many, many Buddhas, mostly life-size to twice life-size and mostly sitting in the classic cross-legged Buddha pose. They have all been carved out of the rock inside the caves, thus making the caves larger. This is a great deal of stonework. The book says there are a total of 174 statues, but I could only count about 100 at most. Once you start counting it's hard to stop. Nonetheless, they are beautiful and impressive. There is also the occasional bodhisattva who has a confusing relationship to things. Ravi explains that in Buddhist cosmography five thousand years after the original Buddha came, then another one comes ("the future Buddha"). This next Buddha is the bodhisattva, and he is carved standing up. And once he comes, the world ends, or else changes into something else (pajamas? No stop that). So take that, you Maya, you have it all wrong.

We head off to our hotel at Kandalama, a famous one designed by Geoffrey Bawa, Sri Lanka's greatest architect. This will be our base for exploring the "cultural triangle" of Sri Lanka—three more of the World Heritage sites besides Dambulla that we have come to see—Sigiriya, Polonnaruwa, and Anuradhapura. See what I mean by big names? We spend the next three days driving to and back from each of these sites. The ratio of driving time to site time is greater than one-to-one, closer to two-to-one, so we become highly familiar with the inside of the van, and we get to hear many things from our guide. There's Buddhism, for example.

Ravi assures us that "Buddhism is not a religion, it is a philosophy." However, they build big temples, have monks, solicit offerings, worship the crap out of pieces of his body, and talk about what happens when you die. And have elaborate festivals to ensure a good harvest. Go figure. He also explains the five Buddhist rules: don't kill and eat animals, don't drink alcohol, don't have sex outside of marriage, don't lie, and don't be jealous. Once you master these, he says, then there are eight more, but he doesn't tell us what they are. We are clearly not worthy.

He also tells us a joke. During the colonial period, a provincial administrator was having a lot of trouble with rats eating his record books. He put in a requisition for a cat to take care of the rats, which was granted. Eventually his books were audited and the auditors wanted to see the cat. Unfortunately the administrator was on vacation and his assistants could not find the cat, so they showed the auditors a small kitten they had retrieved from the village. The auditors were suspicious, until the most clever of the deputies said that the real cat was on vacation with the administrator and this was the "acting cat." Sri Lankan humor? I rather liked it. We decide the roads we are traveling on are not the real roads, they are the "acting" roads.

He also tells us an assortment of what must be local wisdom and cannot possibly be true:

>> Monkeys are the only animals that cannot get cancer.

>> That flower is yellow oleander. If you eat it, then you must eat one teaspoon of sugar in one minute or you will die. [Oleanders are generally poisonous, but really?]

>> This site has not been completely excavated because they are saving it to train future generations of architects. [This is code for there wasn't enough money, a general problem for archaeology worldwide.]

Mr. Bawa's hotel in Kandalama is a wide but shallow structure, built into the side of a hill and with . . . jungle all around. And rocks built into the walls and floors, again. This may sound neat, but has problems. For example, there are lots of monkeys all around, although the hotel finally figured out that having them run down the open hallways made the guests nervous and room service difficult, so they have put electric barriers around the place. Also our room has a very large hornets' nest *right outside the window*. We initially think that the buzzing sound is rain. Fortunately we had not gone out on our balcony to check. Ugh, there's a reason glass was invented, thank goodness.

How does a guy get a drink around here, chapter 2: Not at the bar and not in the dining room, because it's "*Poyo.*" When this is explained to us we immediately wonder what the Spanish word for chicken has to do with anything. It happens that Buddha was born on the full moon, achieved enlightenment on the full moon, died on the day of a full moon, and was not recorded as having anything much to say about chickens. So the full moon, the aforementioned *Poyo*, is a national holiday every month, and one on which alcohol or beef is not served. Plus all the stores are closed. Except for the ones that are open—"Hindu," Ravi explains. And you can get alcohol in your room and they have beef for dinner and lunch. This is not in the guidebooks. Buddhism appears to be somewhat flexible.

Adventure #4: Sigiriya

This is a very impressive site. It was at one point a palace on top of a rock, a really big rock with really steep sides jutting up out of the plains for seven hundred feet. It was, as one might expect, actually a fortress—who builds a palace on top of a rock? Think Masada without the unpleasant outcome, but it is way bigger. There are two rings of moats at ground level, plus the king's baths and his water gardens and his pleasure gardens, all of excellent quality brick or rock work. The inner moat resembles the ones surrounding the Imperial Palace in Tokyo, and were said also to have been filled with crocodiles rather than large carp, which would be a good incentive not to try to cross.

Historical interjection: the history of Sri Lanka up until the colonial period goes like this. Then King X was killed by his son Prince Y, who assumed the throne and killed the other sons, but one escaped and raised an army and came back and overthrew King Y, thus becoming King Z.

Two years later a royal cousin poisoned King Z and his mother and all his sisters and declared himself King A. He reigned for three years until killed mysteriously in a hunting accident, at which point his stepmother put her stepson on the throne, King B, although he was only ten years old—and on and on. Even the guidebook concurs: "Of Anuradhapura's early kings, fifteen ruled for less than a year, twenty-two were murdered by their successors, six were murdered by other people, four committed suicide, thirteen were killed in battle, and eleven were dethroned, never to be heard of again." If you count this up, it explains the premium on high birth rates.

Back to Sigiriya: King Kassapa, who in traditional fashion imprisoned his father in order to become king and just missed capturing his brother. The brother, Moggallana, instead took off to India to raise an army and come back and seize the kingdom. Kassapa's mom was a commoner, so the brother Moggallana was the "rightful" heir. Kassapa has heard the stories so he moves the kingdom to the top of this high rock and builds it out. The whole place was taken from some Buddhist monks who were summarily moved on to the next large and inhospitable rock outcropping to the north. This all occurs from AD 477 to AD 495. Moggallana finally comes back after eighteen years—recruiting turning out to be harder than he thought. Kassapa comes down from the rock to fight him. Why? Kassapa loses and commits suicide. And is awarded the prize for dumbness—hello, stay up on the rock in your fortress, that's why you built it.

The new king thinks Sigiriya is pretty neat but the queen takes one look at all those steps and says, "I am not climbing up and down thousands of steps every time I need to go to the bathroom" and they go back to Anuradhapura, which they reestablish as the capital.

After passing through all the introductory gardens, the climbing begins. There are a lot of steps, many of them cut into the stones around the base of the monolith. As you go higher the steps are supported by posts driven into the rock side. There is some interesting exposure, as they say in mountain climbing, but we persevere.

About three-quarters of the way up we come out to a small flat plateau. Here they hand out the wasp suits. Yes, the next set of steps goes right past a ledge where there are seven very large and visible hornets' nests, the same as the one outside our hotel room but bigger. This particular edition of hornets builds under flat overhangs, and the nests they have constructed, curiously right next to the steps, are dark, black, flattened hemispheres and look like the bottom half of a truck tire, as big as five black trash bags somehow melded together. The helpful signs in English say, "Don't make noise it may cause hornet attacks." The wasp suits are olive-drab full coveralls with hoods, and gloves at the ends of the arms. They look like they're hazmat suits except for the color. And the face is open—huh? And they have to be hot. We're hot and we're wearing shorts.

Good judgment prevails. We elect to stay where we are and not race past the hornets, hornet suit or no. Why they don't just get rid of the nests is a complete mystery, ever heard of Raid? Why put up with all that unnecessary risk and create unnecessary liability and unattractive obstacles for tourists? Some of the tourist ninnies climb past the hornets without suits on. At least they are being quiet. Egad.

Adventure #5: Anuradhapura

This was the site of the first capital of the unified nation and remained so for almost 1,500 years. It is located just about in the center of the northern half of the country. The site is large, but mostly all that remains are foundations and building outlines. In part this is because, like many places, the base of the building was stone, but the sides and roof and upper stories were wood, which has long since disappeared, frequently due to fires. Lighting with oil lamps has its disadvantages. While there are some interesting small buildings dotted around the site, the best thing is . . . STUPAS!

There are three of these structures, also called dagobas, that are really big. What they are takes a while to figure out; they're Sri Lanka's answer to the pyramids. The buildings are very, very large hemispherical structures, built entirely of small bricks, then plastered and whitewashed. They tend to come to a point at the top, but their function was, how shall we say, self-gratification for the rulers who built them. They're solid; you cannot go inside them. You cannot climb to the top of them and look at the view as they are round and smooth and besides they are sacred sites. Mostly they are tombs but not for interment, but for a suitably religious monument to the greatness of the ruler. Sometimes Buddhist relics are inside but they are not meant to be found and removed. In one sense these are magnificent accomplishments—the largest is bigger in volume than the Great Pyramid of Giza. That is a lot of damn bricks.

On the other hand, after you have marveled at the first one, walking all around it in your stocking feet, you determine that it looks pretty much the same from each compass point. That's the nature of spheres. And since the experience is pure shape, no decoration, no altars inside, no images, you begin to wonder irreverently if seeing two or three is really all that fascinating. Answer: no. By the time we get to the last one we do a drive-by. No insult intended but it was a long and bad road to get here, and we have to return to the hotel by the same road. So we do. I think about having been stupa-fied.

Adventure #6: Polonnaruwa

This is the site of the capital that came after Anuradhapura, in its glory during the eleventh to thirteenth centuries. It lied about fifty miles south east, but still in the northern half of Sri Lanka. Because it is obviously newer, there are many more archaeological things here, in much better shape. Also, by the time of Polonnaruwa, the stupa craze seems to have died a natural death. The rulers put any available economic surplus into temples and monasteries—open buildings with many wonderful images of the Buddha. It is a large site and is next to the largest of the artificial lakes, the sea of Samudra, also built by the rulers to solve irrigation and thus agricultural problems.

The buildings are generally wonderful; one has a three-story image of Buddha built of bricks, but carefully and beautifully sculpted—he looks like he is emerging from the back wall of the temple. There is an elegant circular temple with exquisite Buddhas set at the four compass points. Our favorite is a site with images carved right out of the rock face, so that the natural striations in the rock play through the sculptures. Although these are big sculptures—two-to- three stories high, one sitting, one standing, one reclining—they still display the artistry in carving that makes them look both lifelike and religious. This is a hard mix to get right, but the sculptors did. We wander the sites and take many pictures. There are few tourists of any nationality.

Adventure #7: We Drive to Galle

Our last stop is the World Heritage site called Galle, the location of the old fort at a coastal town on the bottom southwestern tip of the island. This name is said to be derived from a Portuguese sailor who, upon first seeing the city, said "chicken" or *galle* in Portuguese. Not clear why—it doesn't much look like a chicken, it's not chicken breeding headquarters; Frank Perdue wasn't invented at the time. It is not close to where we are, and there's no local airport. So we again get into the faithful white van for the ten-hour drive to Galle.

I suggest to L that we play a road game, this one made up and called "I Spy a Buddha." The rule is that it only counts if the image is at least life-size and it has to be visible from the road. I ask if she wants to set the number that we will see or if she wants to pick the over or under. She selects the latter, so I pick six. She immediately takes the "over." What a dummy I am. By the time we are halfway there, we have seen more than twenty-eight large Buddhas, so we stop counting. We also saw a couple of Virgin Marys and one archangel Gabriel but they didn't count. Yes, this is a Buddhist country. We think our guide considers our game to be irreverent.

The good news is that once we get to the vicinity of Colombo around three in the afternoon, we get on the only freeway in the country and for the last one hundred kilometers we zip along, as there is very little traffic, perhaps because it is a toll road. The road is bordered mostly by lovely and green plantations—rubber, palms for palm oil, teak, low-growing tea.

However, we can no longer count Buddhas. So we counted cell towers instead and saw thirty-one. There may be a message here. The modest town of Kurunegala is the midpoint of the drive and the site of a famous "Elephant Rock," a high point visible from everywhere in the town. At its peak sits a large white Buddha, with two cell towers right beside him.

There are two good things about Galle. The second is that it is a suitably fort-like area, commanding the entrance to the port, with big stone walls you can walk on top of, and old colonial buildings of brick and stone and plaster, looking just like you would want them to look—the armory, the barracks, the brigade headquarters, several colonial churches. Most but not all are restored, and there are a fair number of nice shops in the enclave, both tourist stuff and antiques and better-quality clothing. The first good thing is that we get to stay at the Amangalla Hotel, the only Aman chain hotel on the island. It, too, is an old colonial building, beautiful wood and high ceilings and the most impressive swimming pool we have maybe ever seen—overgrown by a large orange poinciana that discreetly drops small brilliant flowers into the water. And the food is fabulous! More than we can say for any of the other places we stayed where the food ranged from acceptable to lousy. This is a nice way to end the trip.

There are also English language newspapers available. One local headline: "Israeli Guards Shoot Dead Palestinian at Check Point." Well, why bother? It reminds one of the headline several years ago in a California paper: "San Francisco Law Now Allows Gay Men and Lesbians to Marry." Well, why would they want to?

On our last day we take a tuk-tuk to the other big hotel in Galle, designed once again by the ubiquitous M. Bawa. Set on a point overlooking the ocean, the sunset is the draw. The hotel is fine but very unpopulated. We have drinks on the terrace and watch the sunset and as we leave we peek into the dining room. It's big with lovely white tablecloths and place settings and zero—count them, zero—patrons, and this is at seven-thirty. Apparently the aforesaid Bawa was not able to do just a plain old nice elegant square hotel, so this one has a circular three-story staircase in the center. For its internal railings it has a helix of life-size rusted iron sculpted figures, mostly of the Portuguese vs. the natives, some horses thrown in, all busy killing each other or being killed by each other, with swords and knives and spears. With three stories of this grisly activity as the highlight of your hotel's entrance, no wonder there's nobody here. I think I liked the wasps better.

The next morning before leaving we go to the government-run handicraft store. There are some interesting masks and thousands of very similar carvings of elephants. Nothing about any of the sites we have visited, no representations on T-shirts or coffee mugs. And no snow globes. You see what I mean about the lack of tourist infrastructure?

Much love, Bob

Afterword: By the second half of 2012, we were in one way quite successful in the solar business. We had developed, designed, permitted, financed, and built fifty individual solar power plants in eight countries, for a total of about 550 Mw of electric capacity. We had a balance sheet of $2.5 billion of assets. We were among the ten largest solar companies in the world. We had invested $900 million of our sponsors' equity in this effort, and raised the other $1.6 billion from banks and other financing sources, all of it on a nonrecourse basis to the parent company.

If we were to continue to grow the business, however, we needed to raise more money. AES and Riverstone acknowledged this, but were clear that they each now had enough solar assets, so we would have to look elsewhere. And at just about the right time, one of our competitors, SunEdison, came calling with a proposal to merge/acquire us. This seemed to make sense, but took some time to work out the details.

I told my board up front that I would support this but I really was ready to do something else. SunEdison had enough talented executives without me, and I didn't want to stand in the way of a successful transaction.

And so in early 2013 I left AES Solar (then called Silver Ridge Power), moved to California, and struck out on my own as a baby author.

[12]

Geezer Rock

April 2013

Dear Aunt Janet,

We went to a rock concert.

At least that is sort of what it was.

I haven't been to a rock concert for, oh, maybe twenty-five years. I think I saw Bob Dylan at Madison Square Garden in 1980. I guess that's thirty-two years. People held up lighters—lit lighters—when he played "Blowin' in the Wind" and the Vietnam War was over but just barely. I went to see the Charlie Daniels Band at a theater in Chattanooga, but that was about the same time period. No one held up lighters, they were afraid of burning the place down.

In the interim I think Nine Inch Nails has come and gone, and Jerry Garcia has died and Michael Jackson has died and some Beach Boys have died and one Rolling Stone has died and John Lennon has died but Mick Jagger keeps rolling on, perhaps with the help of injections of extract of sheep testicles. As does Bob Dylan. And lest we forget, Justin Timberlake has bought Myspace. And Madonna has become a kabbalist, I think. Does she have her own kabbal, and if so what is it plotting? And Lady Gaga has become a Madonna clone. Perhaps every generation needs one?

I cannot recognize eight of the top ten "artists" on the Billboard list of top ten songs. Maroon 5, Owl City, Neon Trees? I cannot hum any of the songs of the two I do recognize, not even one, since I only recognize them from reading about them in People magazine. I may not be the right person to fully appreciate a rock concert. But this did not stop us.

The concert was called the "KPRI Street Beat Block Party." KPRI is a radio station in San Diego that plays middle of the road contemporary rock music, and not hip hop or reggae or rap or that sort of thing. There are probably other genres that it also does not play. Mostly I listen to either country music or old rock and roll, but now it's really old rock and roll. I am pretty sure that both Elvis and Buddy Holly are dead. I fear that Little Richard is still alive, somewhere.

Here are the bands that were featured:

» Tristan Prettyman, who is a girl despite the androgyny of her name. Clearly *Tristan und Isolde* are not her cultural or literary forbears.

» Walk the Moon, a rock band from Cincinnati (!) but wait, is the Rock and Roll Hall of Fame there? Maybe that's Cleveland.

» The Paul Cannon Band, probably named after Paul Cannon or maybe after a cannon named Paul. I don't think most cannons have names, or if they do it's a name like "Big Bertha" or "Nazi Killer," which might not be a good name for a band.

» The Wallflowers, the headliner and therefore the last band to play. Bob Dylan's son, Jakob Dylan, is the leader of this band and they have had a chart-topping hit called "One Headlight." Remember that? I don't. These are all facts that I was told, not knowledge I already had.

The musicians were all young and white and the music was reasonably loud even if you were sitting twenty rows back and in the open air, which we were. The bands all had drums and bass guitars and other guitars and the lead singers shouted a lot. Since I had no idea who any of these people were, I didn't know any of the songs. They all sounded rather alike, but since it was all pretty loud music you could not follow the lyrics, or even hear the lyrics, so perhaps they were all quite different. Every so often you could get a snatch of a song line, usually in the choruses of the songs since you had a better chance as they were repeated. Some of it might actually have been good or at least clever, hard to tell. Snatches that I got included:

- » "Misfits and lovers . . ."
- » "Reboot the mission . . ." Could this have been a song about digital love? Whatever that might be?
- » "I'll never be your valentine . . ." But since the rest of the song was incomprehensible it was hard to get the story line as to why.
- » "Six seconds of [something] . . ." but we don't know what.

There was one band that did play a cover of an old rock and roll song, "Rolling on the River." That one I got. The audience seemed especially appreciative. They got up and danced, respectfully.

The venue was very nice—the city of San Diego had graciously allowed the promoter to block off one entire block of a downtown street. There was an elevated stage at one end, about street width, and a bunch of orderly rows of white chairs taking up a rectangle about three-quarters of the street wide. This was for the higher-priced tickets, which I had purchased, thank goodness. Each ticket cost forty dollars, the second-most costly level, and seemed to me a bargain since it came with a place to sit. Even here it was "stadium seating" so your seats were not reserved, but the house was far from sold out so seating was not a problem. Besides I doubt that sitting up front would have been a good idea, given the decibel level. You got a little color-coded wrist band when you entered that let you in to the seating area. The whole thing started around five so it was light for a couple of hours, and it was over by nine so we could all go home and get to bed by our bedtimes. And even though there were lower prices for standing tickets, very few attendees took advantage of this bargain. Most of us wanted our asses in the chairs, especially if we were going to be there for five or six hours.

It didn't take very long to conclude that this was a rock concert for fogies. There were many clues:

» No one was wearing jeans that had artificially worn holes in them. Many people were wearing jeans, but they were comfort-waist jeans.

» A lot of the men were wearing baseball caps, but they all had the bills pointed forward.

» There were many women in dresses, mostly in sizes north of ten.

» There were lots of Nike swooshes, but on polo shirts.

» There were no visible tattoos or piercings other than ears—and that was exclusively the women.

» There was one woman there using a walker. The mantra of the crowd could have been, "We've come to hear our grandchildren play."

Not only did the "festival" have music, but on the cross street there were lots of food stands and drink stands, so you could leave your seat and wander over to a stand and get a margarita or a glass of OK white wine or a draft local beer and take it back to the concert area and drink and watch and listen. It was warm and it was outdoors and the sunset was beautiful and no one was asking you for money or denying your request for money, so you knew that you were not at work, and it was fine. And given the volume of the sound system, you never missed a note wandering about. You did have to shout at the vendors to make yourself understood. Pointing and displaying money also worked.

The stands included barbecue and steak and cheese and Thai hot fries and the like. My personal favorites were two. At the Sapporo beer stand, if you bought a beer they also gave you a small wind-up Sapporo robot-looking something like a two-inch-high R2-D2. What this has to do with beer we cannot understand because we are not Japanese.

And then there was a stand proudly flying the Swiss flag and selling "raclette in a bun." The buns were soft roles, not sliced, but skewered on a rack with a bunch of shiny steel rods of hot dog length, sticking straight up. The operator plunged a bun onto the rod to heat it, then pressed a button and cheese came out the tip of the erect rod and filled the bun. I am not making this up.

On the other side of the stage from the food and drink area, a local Cadillac dealer had set up six shiny new cars and was auctioning off one of them if you stopped and listened to their advertising and took a survey. I do not think that young persons of the rock-concert-going persuasion are a big part of the Cadillac market. But the cars looked nice with the big grille and sharp-edges style that are currently popular. Plus room in the trunk for your wheelchair.

Once you got past the outfit and food choices, you could concentrate on the behavior of the audience.

Everyone in the audience seemed to have smartphones. The most prominent use was to hold them out at arm's length and take a picture of yourself and your date. There was also a lot of holding the phones up in the air pointed toward the band. I thought this was picture taking but it turns out the users were just getting a better view, using the camera function as a sort of mini-jumbotron. No one was holding up lighters. And there was no smoking anywhere in the area. Maybe we need a "lighter app" for smart phones that you could use at concerts. Maybe I am a hopeless traditionalist.

The place was sparse on African Americans, no surprise there. There was one black guy with a blonde date near us, and he was chewing gum but not in time to the music. Possibly a subtle protest. There was much standing up and politely dancing in place, but it was all "bad white girl dancing." Well, what did we expect? This included a fat girl standing and bobbing up and down from the waist like the toy birds that stick their beak into the glass of water. No sex-crazed groupies were rushing the stage. I don't think anyone was throwing their hotel room keys at the performers. Or their underwear. If they did it would have been big, and thus noticeable. Probably not thongs. Do they make plus size thongs?

The evening was full of unpredictable stuff. Seated several rows in front of us was a chunky girl in a white dress and an all-white clothed man (white pants, shoes, shirt, no tie, jacket) wearing of course a white beret. They got the matching costume award, and seemed deeply involved in the music, nodding and clapping and frequently standing and applauding and generally having a great time. Then they just got up and left halfway through the Wallflowers, in the middle of a song.

Maybe concert standards are different these days, but I would think that frequently checking your email during a concert—you can tell from the scrolling motion you make with your hand, and the fact that you're looking at your lap, not the stage—is probably not a good sign of deep commitment to and involvement in the music. I was more respectful and did not check mine even once, although I did think about it.

Love and kisses, Bob

[13]

There's Way More to China than Beijing

August 2013

Dear Aunt Janet,

When we landed in Beijing, it was Chinese Saint Valentine's Day, which is what our guide said to us the first night. And sure enough the next day, on the special Google website that you get when you are in China, there is a stylized picture of the head and shoulders of a young man on the left, looking slightly uncomfortable, as he views a stylized picture of a young woman on the right, who appears to have just tasted a spoiled frog. Small hearts surround the heads of each person, a bit like spit bubbles, and birds fly between the two, so you know it's love. Probably love of birds, one cannot be certain. And there is a big heart in place of the second "O" in Google. Cute, except I don't think all the Chinese became Catholic, unless maybe when I wasn't looking and thus Saint Valentine is probably not widely recognized. This needs further exploration. Is there chocolate involved?

It was August (perhaps you could tell that from the heading of the letter) and so the whole world goes on vacation and very little gets done in business. My email count drops off from hundreds a day to less than twenty, and 90% of these are offers to sell me enhancements that I really don't want or need, or to send me money from Nigeria. Great time to be away. So we went.

L has never been to China, and I have never been to western China, so we have a combined itinerary that starts in Beijing with the interesting sites that most people have heard of, and then heads west to Xinjiang, which not so many people have heard of. It's a sort of "Silk Road" trip only with adders. We skip Hong Kong and Shanghai and get right into real China. However, "real" China is a whole lot different than it used to be, and it's a little like saying "real United States." Despite my experiences here in business since 1991 (my god, twenty years ago!), I will refrain from making gripping comments such as "When I first came to China there were more bicycles and fewer cars," or I will only say them to L, who is more tolerant. At least so far.

Because we are westerners, we are not sleeping out in tents or riding on camels, but instead staying in nice hotels, starting with the Peninsula in Beijing, which is very nice indeed. The hotel is full of marble, including a giant set of white stairs coming directly off the lobby, and a large break- fast room filled with 95% Chinese who are eating pretty much everything that is laid out on the buffet. Several times over. My modest observation from earlier trips is that Chinese are good eaters, and nothing so far has disabused me of this belief. See food section below. Some things don't change.

Things We Will Only Say Once, but Apply Generally to Our In-China Experience

There are many, many people being tourists at almost every tour site we visited, but they are Chinese. We are frequently the only westerners. The Forbidden City/Tiananmen Square is a case in point. There must have been close to fifty thousand people making the trek to the sites there, and maybe thirty westerners, counting us. We hardly saw any westerners on any of our flights after Beijing. And the Chinese tourists generally included a bunch behaving badly, so we didn't miss the westerners who used to play this role.

HOT: Beijing—hot, hot, hot, and smoggy—90+°C and 85% relative humidity. I like heat but really. Hot everywhere else but not as humid and in Jiayuguan it actually rained. Huh? This is supposed to be a desert.

Where have all the bicycles gone? As we head west, the number of motorcycles compared to cars slowly increases, but except for Kashgar, our last destination, it remains a small fraction of what you would see in any "developing" Asian city. And you see hardly any bicycles anywhere. This is a huge change, and a very interesting indicator of level of economic development.

If you can only say "thank you" and "beer" in Chinese, are you OK? Yes, in Beijing, where English is generally available; less and less as you go west. But we had English-speaking Chinese guides from Cox & Kings with us all the time we were going places.

We felt safe everywhere, cell phone connectivity was available everywhere (thank you, China Mobile), bottled water available everywhere, toilets available at all tourist sites although frequently not Western toilets, beer available and good everywhere, Internet connections available everywhere, even in the not-very-good hotel in Kashgar. There is no escape.

We visited seven different locations, following the ancient Silk Road, or at least one version of it.

Beijing

The Umbrellas of Cherbourg has moved east. I have never seen so many people carrying parasols in the heat, including a lot of men. Maybe every fifth woman had an umbrella as sun protection, perhaps to keep her skin light colored. There was a continuing danger of colliding with someone and having umbrella ribs poking in your face. I have never seen The Umbrellas of Cherbourg; I am just assuming there are a lot of umbrellas in it.

The Forbidden City is big, but repetitive and the buildings all look a lot like each other. And they all have similar names: Gate of Divine Prowess, Gate of Heavenly Purity, Hall of Preserving Harmony, Hall of

Supreme Harmony, Palace of Eternal Spring, etc. And there is nothing in the courtyards but more stone paving, which added to the heat impact. But at least it was not suggested we visit Mao's tomb. Although everyone else is doing so, in long lines. At the end of the journey through the various temples and gates of the Forbidden City you get to a nice back garden, with lots of rocks in it, including the ones with the holes. I confess that I do not understand the thing for big rocks with holes in them. I would rather have a big plant with flowers on it. Maybe I have no sense of history or it is geology?

The Summer Palace is not quite as hot, not quite as crowded, perched on the side of a nice lake named South Lake, but with more Palace of Heavenly Purity buildings. The best part was a Buddhist temple, the Hall of the Sea of Wisdom, set on top of a hill of many steps and no elevators, but once there you were rewarded with a dramatic façade made up of thousands of small images of the Buddha embedded into the face of the temple. And a very hazy view of Beijing, like all the views of Beijing that we saw.

Highlight of the day—we were coming back from dinner to our hotel, heard music, and then came upon the St. Joseph's Church courtyard entirely full of people, mostly women, young and old, stylish and unstylish, doing country line dancing to traditional Chinese music. Yeehaw.

Architecturally, Beijing is not an exciting city, never mind the Olympics. Glass and preformed concrete buildings, straight lines, and right angles dominate the Beijing skyline—very few curves. Sohio and Chinese National Petroleum Company buildings and the three oval-shaped buildings next to the north railway station are the exceptions. It's an architecture that makes only limited use of color. As the city has grown rapidly in the last twenty-five years, the electric infrastructure has struggled to keep up. We frequently saw high voltage transmission towers planted among taller office and apartment buildings, with lines running right between and substantially below the top-level apartments. And then there are the fancy condos with attractive views of a coal-fired power plant next door.

Our second day was a visit to the segment of the great wall at Mutianyu, about one and a half hours north of Beijing, where the wall dominates and traces the very rugged ridgeline of the mountains. There are closer sections but this one is impressive. You have to take a cable car to even get up to the wall, and once there, the wall ascends so steeply in places that there are steps between watch towers, hundreds of steps in some cases. It is not a flat surface. It was hot and sweaty and very vertical, but also wonderfully impressive. The Ming tombs are not so much, except for the line of sculptures. And where was the actual tomb, anyway?

We finished Beijing with two good things. The first was an early morning, well 0830, visit to the Temple of Heaven, which I had never seen before. It is the same size as the Forbidden City but nicer—fewer buildings, same architecture but more impressive, way fewer people, more trees and grass, and they let you actually see inside the buildings and in the case of the entrance hall, walk around inside. The third Ming emperor, Zhu Di (1402–1424), ordered the construction of both the Forbidden City and this equally sized area. He had just moved the capital to Beijing so he and his court needed a place to live, govern, and worship. The Japanese during WWII took over the Hall of Prayer for Good Harvests—maybe holiest place in the entire Chinese pantheon—and used it for headquarters, including putting howitzers up on the plaza so they could shoot at the Forbidden City. Maybe this is apocryphal (it's in the category of "our guide told us this") but I doubt it.

Second, we had the good sense to change our suggested program and avoid a visit to the "hutongs," reconstructed and somewhat fake-looking one-story living spaces with internal courtyards that showed how Beijing people lived in the old time before heating and air-conditioning and indoor toilets. Most of these have been torn down, for good reason, but some saved/refurbished for the tourists to see. This also threatened to include a rickshaw ride. In Beijing traffic? You'll get run over or asphyxiated. I don't think the rickshaw puller runs between two poles like in the old days, I believe he rides a bicycle, and he doesn't wear a coolie hat, and he's probably from Belarus, so what's the point?

Instead, both for variety and because of temple satiation, we visited the 798 Art Zone, a nicely strange modern art neighborhood, a repurposed set of former factory buildings that included street art like three bright red and very large dinosaurs in cages, stacked one on top of the other. There were lots of trendy galleries and cafés and even clothes shops, a girl with green hair, much modern art including a picture of a man lasciviously embracing a tree, another picture of a man with a watering can for a head watering a woman with a potted flower plant for a head. Was there symbolism here? I couldn't figure it out. Modern Chinese art seems to have focused on irony first, art second. I think they are different.

There was lots of graffiti at 798, much of it self-consciously artsy (Keith Haring eat your heart out) but literally none in the rest of the city anywhere that we saw, and we drove around a lot.

More evidence of the wealth of eastern China is there are a lot of boutiques at the Peninsula hotel: Tom Ford, Valentino, Ferragamo, Hermès, Chanel. But there's no sundries store where you can buy a newspaper or a Snickers.

Xi'an

This is a one-trick pony of a city, but it's a great trick.

The emperor Qin Shi Huang, the first emperor of the Qin dynasty, is known for being the first to unify China, and for construction of one of the early "great walls." But what he's really known for is his assemblage of probably the grandest burial site ever seen. The pyramids might be more spectacular as architecture, but his entombment has retired the trophy for "grave goods," for the terracotta statues of warriors he had buried with him. The story of discovery of the site is well known: three farmers digging a well in 1974, etc. The site consists of three separate locations in one area, west of the actual burial site. These three pits hold approximately seven thousand figures, only two thousand fully excavated and reassembled. And only one has so far been found completely intact, the famous kneeling archer. The soldiers, horses, and chariots were arrayed in ranks of four across, standing on a floor made of bricks, with each four-rank column stretching back the length of a football field. The largest pit has eleven such long columns, separated by dirt walls six feet thick that were used for support—in effect long trenches in which the warriors are arrayed. Once the images were installed, logs for the roof were put in place over the trenches. The logs were covered with bamboo mats, then with three meters of earth. There were no doubt serious taxes to support all this work, and the second Qin emperor was not as loved or feared as the first. After five years of his rule, the people revolted and burned the site, or at least burned all the trees supporting the roof, and the whole thing caved in on all the figures. The result was a giant crunch, but no reward for looting.

Architects are on the site, slowly working on excavating and reassembling. You can see them work, and you can also see toward the back of the pit the partially uncovered remains of shattered soldiers, waiting their turn for excavation and reassembly. The three "pits" differ markedly—and there's a fourth one that's empty. The layout of the pits seems to be to protect the emperor from assault from the west—mountain on north, river on south, the kingdom on the east. The four pits are arranged in an arrowhead shape, the first pit at the tip of the arrow, with the arrow pointing west. The smallest pit, number three, has sixty-eight figures includes generals and advisers and an honor guard, not arrayed in battle but waiting for the commander—the buried emperor.

The soldiers differ among the pits. Number one has the most infantry and some chariots; number two has archers both standing and kneeling, and cavalry with lots of horses and cavalrymen. It is thought that pit four would have had more soldiers of differing skills. The figures were each individually crafted, not made in molds, and larger-than-life size, ranging from 1.7–2 meters tall, in an era when people rarely got to be taller than 1.5 meters. And yes, they all do look different. Work began when the Qin emperor was thirteen and continued for thirty-eight years, two years after his death at the age of forty-nine. It's a magnificent site and remarkable evidence of Chinese artistic ability and the capability of the political system to assemble and manage people and resources.

We spend a little time in the city itself, modest sized for China with only nine million people, three ring roads, one subway line running north/south from the three ring roads, another running east/west to open in the fall, several more in construction. Hot, dusty, smoggy—but not as bad as Beijing. It is a center for light manufacturing, textiles, and tourism with a capital *T*. More bikes and motorcycles and motorcycle/cart combinations on the streets, fewer cars, but no draft animals.

This is the beginning of the old Silk Road, and there are one hundred thousand Muslims in the city. We asked our guide if any of these were Han Chinese and she said, dismissively, "No, minorities." She did take us to "the oldest mosque in China" and to the associated nearby market where we bought an image of Ganesha, the Hindu elephant deity, paying in Chinese currency from a Muslim vendor lady with a scarf. We felt very global.

The city's second claim to fame is it is the only Chinese city left with its original city wall intact. The wall is 13.5 kilometers long, 12 feet wide at the top, 16 feet at the bottom, 72 steps, guard towers 120 meters apart—twice the range of a crossbow—and 40 feet tall. It has the four original gates, and twenty-three new gates cut into it to allow for the additional traffic. You can ride bicycles on top but no longer shoot arrows at your enemies. A shame. Then on to the oldest Islamic mosque in China, built originally in AD 742 as a reward for something, rebuilt by the Qing third emperor again for military help against "the animists." This may be an inaccurate Chinese translation of something like "the hairy ones from the north" or "the cow dung eaters" or another sobriquet equally delightful. The Han Chinese have never been hesitant about dismissively characterizing other races.

The temples and other official buildings have a high lintel that you must step over, which keeps out the evil spirits, or at least the ground-dwelling evil spirits not smart enough to get over a twelve-inch stoop. Ground eels? The hotel has mimicked this in the bathroom with a two-and-a-half-inch step that is just high enough to keep out the evil spirits residing in your toes, as you fail to notice the step and jam your foot into it, and then dance around going "*Yow, yow, yow,*" which is a secret incantation to keep out the low-crawling evil spirits often found in upscale hotels.

Jiayuguan

This is a small "new town" of 118,000 people, about fifteen years old, with wide streets, nice parks, little traffic. Its raison d'être is a giant steel mill sitting beside the town along with two large coal-fired power plants and six hyperbolic cooling towers. The steel mill history is interesting: it started construction in 1958, was shut down in 1960 during Mao's Great

Leap Forward when peasants were supposed to make steel in their back-yards and thirty million people starved—"Let them eat steel?"

Construction restarted in 1970 just in time for the Cultural Revolution when Mao again killed no-one-knows-how-many people and you cannot look it up on Google, certainly not in China as the Internet is blocked for that charming little question. It was finally completed in 1990 and started production. But this needed workers and so a whole town was designed and built for them. Most folks work at the steel mill, but as we are not here to apply for a job running the blast furnace, we instead check in to the marginal Holiday Inn, yes a Holiday Inn, although perhaps more in name than anything else. The next day we went to the Jiayuguan Pass, which is the end of the Ming dynasty Great Wall. The eastern end, natch, as the western end falls into the sea near Shanghai.

The travel agency poo-pooed this as a site, but what you see is a very nicely done, big fortress, large towers, walls at least sixty feet tall and twelve feet wide, internal courtyards, all built of mud bricks. And of course there is the Great Wall running off to the east, although here the wall is built of rammed earth and mud bricks and is not as big and impressive as around Beijing. But naturally you would garrison the end of the wall and have troops to both patrol outside the wall and reinforce sections of it when attacked. And a stronghold that any serious attacker would need to subdue or his penetration of the wall would be subject to a flanking attack.

The next morning we drove the 380 kilometers to Dunhuang, since our flight had been previously cancelled about a week before we were to leave for China. Seems that the Chinese airlines have the same passenger-friendly practices as US ones—if the plane isn't full, we ain't flying. This was inconvenient but interesting, and besides there weren't any other options.

You may think that the desert does not start until you get to Xinjiang, but you would be wrong. I don't know how far east it starts as we flew in to Jiayuguan from Xi'an, but it sure starts here. It is the Gobi Desert, which is not really a place since *gobi* is Chinese for "high desert." But desert it is, interspersed with bits of irrigated oases, most of them right along the road. It started impressively barren and got more so as we proceeded. We stopped at a small town two-thirds of the way there, called Guazhou. It is also known as "Melon City" and probably as "Wind City" as it has impressive and nonstop wind. In fact, along the road we passed four very large (400+ machines each) wind farms, most turbines turning. Why not, there is very little else there except small, occasional clumps of dead grass. From then on the agriculture stopped and the landscape was barren as barren can be—flat, brown, no houses or trees or towns or vegetation taller than six inches, one very straight highway, very little traffic in either direction, no billboards or signs of any sort, no nothing—but bizarrely—two side-by-side very large high-voltage transmission lines. Going from what to what we could not determine. Well, I guess the permitting was easy, not many people to show up at the public hearing. Like the desert around El Centro, but without the charm.

We are now driving in/through the Gansu Corridor. Why is this important? Gansu Province is the westernmost province in China (except for Xinjiang, about which more later) and the key part of the Silk Road route. It is shaped like a dumbbell oriented east/west. There are serious mountains to the north (the Black Mountains) and more to the south (the Qilian and the Snow Mountains). To get to Xinxiang and central Asia, you have to go through Gansu and this lovely aforementioned desert. Various locations claim to be "the start of the Silk Road" including Xi'an which, as the Imperial capital until the 1400s, has a fair claim, and Dunhuang as well. In any event, it wasn't just one road, and it wasn't just one cargo, and it morphed over time as tastes and technology changed. But for lots of years if you wanted to sell or trade silk etc. from China in return for lapis lazuli and gems and pasta with clam sauce and other keen stuff from the Stans and Europe, you had to go this way as no boats were available to make the long voyage from Italy, plus most of the world had not yet been discovered by the Europeans, although the people living in the undiscovered lands probably knew where they were. This is a trip roughly organized around the Silk Road, hence the emphasis on getting through Gansu. We have more deserts to conquer!

Dunhuang

An oasis town of 180,000 people, with a long history of being a trade gateway. Not the start of the Silk Road, but an important place as it sits at a "neck" in the Gansu Corridor (sometimes referred to as the Hexi Corridor) and besides was the end of Chinese hegemony, and the beginning of what was variously called Chinese Turkestan, the Abbasid Empire, the Kushan Empire, and who knows what. What we do know is that there were two routes out of Dunhuang to get to the Stans and get past the Taklamakan Desert, which lies directly west of Gansu and is bordered by the extension of these same mountains, except now their names change to the Altun and Kunlun Mountains in the south and the Tien Shan in the north. Taklamakan is said to translate cutely into "place of death" or "you go in and never come out." Successful caravans could go around the north edge or around the south edge of this desert. Whichever you chose, you had to go through an administrative processing area with the Chinese checking your visa, taxing your exports and imports, etc. If you tried to avoid the "gate" then the soldiers hunted you down and said mean things to you. You were, after all, a caravan of one-hundred-plus camels and thus not especially fast moving or invisible. In Dunhuang, depending on whether you were going west or east, you got organized, replenished, and tried to get the sand out of your clothes. It is also an oasis town and the water is used for much agriculture, irrigated of course, even today. The suburbs are filled with small plots of corn and cotton and squash and melons and grapes, grapes, and more grapes.

It's in the middle of a desert, so imagine our surprise to find a large sand dune just south of town and about a block from our hotel. The big tourist attraction is to go over to the dunes and either ride a camel to the top or climb up on foot. And they rent you neon-orange, calf-high foot coverings that keep out the sand and look like moon boots. Fashion statement for the desert. We disregarded, perhaps unwisely, the camel option and climbed to the top of the dune, from which you could see either a) more dunes, whose resemblance to those upon which we were standing was uncanny—sandy, brown—or b) a fine view of the parking lot.

"Great," said L, "another thousand steps." And no staircase. Many fellow climbers were with us, as in almost everything we have done to date. No westerners. We slid back down the hill to go to dinner and see if they had a decent bottle of wine.

The real reason we are here is the Mogao Caves, sometimes called the Thousand Buddha Grottoes. The first was constructed by a devout monk in AD 366, and development and expansion of the site continued to as late as ~AD 1500 when they were abandoned, probably as a result of the sporadic changes in the political and security situation of Dunhuang. There is also a line of reasoning that the Silk Road by this time was diminishing in importance as the sea routes from China to the west became more and more navigable. Note that Christopher Columbus was seeking a new route to India in 1492, which means that there was already seaborne commerce between east and south Asia and Europe, but going the long way around Africa. As the Silk Road became less important, Dunhuang diminished as a wealthy market town. Islam had also made inroads, and religious imagery such as that in the caves is anathema to Muslims.

The site is a series of relatively small caves dug into a line of sandstone cliffs at the eastern edge of the same sand dune, stretching about 1,600 meters end to end. These are widely celebrated and are in the group of the first Chinese sites to make it into UNESCO's list of World Heritage sites—in 1987. There are a total of 975 individual caves, although only 492 of them are "decorated" with sculpture, mural paintings on the walls and ceilings, or both. A total of 2,000 painted sculptures, and enough cave wall murals to equal forty-five square kilometers. They were rediscovered in 1902 by a local guy; the caves had filled with sand and the extreme dryness of the air had preserved them well, with almost no defacing, although with expected fading from where the sun entered—the caves all face east—and oxidation of the lead- based pigments used to paint skin tones, making many of the images look like Chinese in blackface.

Each of the caves that we saw was more or less the same: a central image of Buddha, some with his two acolytes Ananda and Sariputta, some with bodhisattvas on each side, some with both. Some caves had been carved with a square central pillar remaining, and thus four sides for alcove images of Buddha, some have simple basic rectangular dimensions and one Buddha et al. on the back wall. Some had higher decorated ceilings, some had ceilings no more than ten feet high. The ceilings that we saw were uniformly decorated with a repeating motif of the seated Buddha, small in size but with a colored background. With three exceptions, none of the caves are tall or deep, and this makes sense as it appears that each separate cave was excavated and decorated by a particular sponsor, as a gesture of worship or piety or the equivalent. Some are elegant, some are literally the size of small cabinets. Many have the donor's picture at the bottom of the murals.

There are three quite large Buddhas, in three large caves. The reclining Buddha is twenty-three meters long and backed by seventy-two figures representing the seventy-two disciples. It is a great image, lovely and life-like. The disciples are a bit of a problem, as this number appears not in the Buddhist canon, but as the number that Confucius had. There is a certain amount of hedging of bets and religious eclecticism here. Several of the paintings also include Taoist images of various gods: the god of rain; the god of lightning; the god of earth, wind and fire; the god of up with people, etc. The second largest image is a standing Buddha of about twenty-six meters tall. Very impressive and powerful, but you only get to see him at the bottom, so there is neck craning and something is lost by not having a higher view. The third one is really big, almost thirty-seven meters tall and originally had the cave entrance at the top level cut open so you could see his head from a distance. This had predictable effects on preservation, so the whole thing cannot currently be seen and is under renovation. Opens in November, we were told.

We had our own private tour with a young woman who spoke good English. But you are only allowed to see a selection of thirteen caves that are open to the public. And they do hustle you right through. No pictures, of course. The entire place is highly organized. The entrance to each cave has been standardized with cement into a rectangle so that it will hold a lintel with a door and lock for its protection. A piece of stone has also been plastered above the door giving the cave number. Some of the caves were quite small, created by the less wealthy patrons. These too are protected by locked doors, only smaller, and are also numbered. The caves are roughly on four levels, but with the doors and tidy numbers—in order of course—the whole thing resembles nothing so much as a long set of offices or maybe condominiums.

There is much tourist infrastructure present, to include gates and guards and office buildings and ticket buildings and buildings for art reproductions for sale and bathrooms and the like. And a bigger "tourist center" in town is under construction whither it is expected that all tours will start and tourists will spend most of their time. Our personal reaction was that the place is moving rapidly toward the Lascaux model and eventually you won't be able to see any of the caves, just a tourist site with pictures of what you used to be able to see. That will be less interesting. But they'll be preserved. For someone.

Then to the west of town is the anti-Mogao, or the Western Thousand Buddha Caves. Editorial note: the translation of "thousand Buddha" as an adjective is probably technically accurate, but it really means "lots of Buddhas," not exactly one thousand. This site is more caves carved into a cliff along a riverbed, more steep steps up and down, but no road sign for the turnoff, only a gravel parking lot, a ticket taker out for lunch, twelve caves in total, and a guide who spoke only Chinese. The views were more accessible and the whole place way less organized and controlled. The sites were not as impressive and there were no large statues or big caves. By the end of this visit L was suggesting that our trip should be named the Thousand Steps Journey.

Finally we drove west some more, through another hundred km of some more desert—really, that's all there is around town in any direction—and came to yet another "end of the Great Wall," this time the end of the Han dynasty Great Wall. We pause for a short discourse on the Great Wall. Very short. There wasn't just one, there appear to be at least a dozen. They didn't all follow the same route. They didn't all have the same start point and end point, and they were not all built by the same emperor in the same time frame. The fancy and impressive stone one we saw north of Beijing is a Ming dynasty accomplishment (1368–1644) and the last in a large number of "great" walls. The Han dynasty (206 BC to AD 220) is obviously much earlier and the technology much different. The Han wall is about nine feet tall, built with alternating layers of sod and dirt. But lots of it is still there. One might be forgiven for asking just exactly what it was that was worth protecting in the desert 150 km west of Dunhuang, but we're not the emperor.

This particular wall ran all the way to Lanzhou, capital of Gansu Province, and is said to be the longest single one of the several "great walls." Given that the capital of the Han dynasty was Xi'an (then called Chang'an), which was another five hundred km east of Lanzhou, why build it here? It was so remote that the emperors had to institute a one-year draft for all male citizens, send battalions of them off to the various garrison sites along the wall, where they got to become farmers most of the time and raise their own food. Presumably because the place was so inhospitable that there weren't any peasants around to support them. Then they became soldiers when the northern tribes attacked. Although the wall is badly eroded, it is still an impressive site, as are the several watch towers (made of what looks like adobe bricks) that also still exist.

Finally we visited another rectangular clump of bricks structure in the desert, this one the Jade Gate Pass, the northernmost gateway of the Silk Road. Although it would be more accurate to call it a customs house than a pass, since it's sitting in the middle of a piece of the desert, relatively close to the river. You take what you can get in the tourist site business sometimes.

Turpan

We flew from Dunhuang to Urumqi, the province capital and then immediately drove to Turpan, a three-hour drive to the southeast, through a pass in the Tien Shan mountains. The mountains are sere and rugged and dark grey to black, with not a speck of vegetation anywhere. This could have been a tailings pile at a coal mine, except for the ruggedness and the height. It was a lovely road, though.

Why here? Turpan is another key checkpoint/oasis town on the Silk Road. This is where the "road" divides into northern route and southern route to get around the Taklamakan Desert. There was probably not much trading but much reprovisioning and resting up for a very hard slog to Kashgar, a thousand km away through pretty nasty country.

Today it's known for four things:

» Lowest elevation in the world at eighty meters below sea level

» Highest temperature in the world, recorded as 49.7°C in 1997—equals 122°F

» Driest place in China, 20 mm (.9 inches) of rain per year

» Most grapes of anywhere in the world or China or perhaps the province, it wasn't clear. There are a lot grapes here.

Turpan economics are totally tied to grapes and tourism. So they put together just about whatever they have and call it a tourist site. We go to:

» The ruins of Gaochang, the former capital city of the area, obliterated by the Mongols in 1400. This is now largely mud walls, a few well-preserved pieces but the roofs were all supported by wood beams and then probably were mats on top of that so that's all gone. It is the only place we've been in China where there are more westerners than Chinese. And we got our first (and only thank God) ride on a donkey cart. L got flea bites, and not from me. It is clear why this is not a generally accepted form of transport. The site is strongly reminiscent of Chaco Canyon in the southwestern US, although bigger.

» Traditional Uighur village: we tried but got turned away by the police, who were armed with AKs and did not smile. Something about two guys getting killed in a mosque recently. We sat politely in the back of the car and let Nur, our Uighur guide, do the talking. We didn't ask about terrorism or anti-government activity.

» Astana Tombs: largely Han entombment area for the upper and middle class, c. AD 600–1200. Big tourist infrastructure, big fancy gate and office and ticket-taking machinery, plus a marble platform of no clear function except to look out over the not-very-large tomb area and thus see lots of humps of dirt from an elevation of fifty feet. Several tombs have been partially excavated with the back walls to include some lovely paintings left in place. While we are standing on top of the marble platform gazing vaguely at the fields of grapes, three Chinese approach us, the two women wearing such bad hats that ours look like high fashion. They are a reporting team from China National Radio and they want to interview us with the result to be on the air. We consider the downside, then give only first names and plunge ahead. Penetrating questions like, "Where are you from?" San Diego, California, does not register, so we explain that it's the US. First time in China, do you like it, where have you been, did you buy souvenirs. Which site was best? We reply vaguely and diplomatically since there's no reason taking sides and they don't want to know interesting stuff like what Obama should do about Iran or is the one child policy a good idea. We do tell them we'll buy silk and melons, but then we do neither as the silk has become polyester and you can't bring melons into the US. Besides they're heavy.

» Bezeklik Grottoes: a fabulous setting along a gorge in the Flaming Mountains, with a small stream burbling below and austere and very red cliffs on each side. Eighty-five caves dug into one side of the bluff, about seventy-five feet above the river. Originally a royal preserve of Gaochang royalty, similar to Mogao. Only six can now be viewed (see Lascaux syndrome, above). And they are badly beaten up. No sculpture left, most of the paintings defaced or stolen. First defaced after the conversion of the area from Buddhist to Islam, then some friendly Euros showed up and carved the paintings off the walls and took them mostly to Germany, and finally the Red Guards defaced and scribbled over anything that was left. Nice drive, though, with exquisite scenery.

» Grape Land! This is pushing it. You run a road down the middle of a village where there are already lots of grapes planted, put in a parking lot, plant some more grapes on both sides of a walkway that makes a nice U shape and train the grapes to grow over the top of this linear pergola, but so high that no one can reach them, add a couple of fake Uighur houses, and charge admission. Nur says that the traditional mud houses are being torn down and replaced with brick houses, because there's no good way to get electricity into them. This tourist site is actually called "Grape Valley" although there is no valley anywhere in sight. And we're not even here for the annual Grape Festival, held at the end of August. According to the guidebook, "the streets are lined with grapes . . ." I would personally like to see this but consider that it might be messy. Still, there are several hundred Chinese entranced by the grape displays, and also jumping up and trying to pick the grapes despite explicit signs telling you not to.

» Karez irrigation system: an interesting bit of civil engineering, basically underground channels dug from the base of the mountains where the melting snow creates a generous water table, down a gradient to the place where you want the water to come so you can irrigate the crops. The channels are about as big as a man squatting can dig, and they were all dug by hand some 2,000 to 1,500 years ago. Probably five and a half kilometers of them at the peak, and three hundred are still in use. The same system is used in the right places in Iran and Afghanistan. A very large amount of work, but the results are that you have a town and enough surrounding agriculture to support it. And you don't lose any water to evaporation. Outside the town to the east, however, is a very large new Sinopec oil field. And the name of our hotel is the Tuha Petroleum Hotel. A new reason to live in Turpan. And this is so far without fracking.

In the evening we wander the local streets, where even at ten o'clock everyone is out and about, avoiding the heat of midday. L buys a pair of very attractive sneakers for eight dollars. We could buy grapes but decide not. We visit the food market set upon the parking lot on the corner, but bypass the lamb liver kabobs.

Urumqi

The Uighur pronunciation is "oo-rum-chi" and in Mandarin it's "oo-roo-moo-chi." We don't know why. A few quick facts about Xinjiang:

the largest province in China of the thirty-two by a long shot—one-sixth of China's area, but only twenty-two million people, or two percent of the population. Why? The province is dominated by two ovals, a smaller one in the north, the Gurbantunggut Desert, and a larger one in the south, the Taklamakan, both of which are deserts in the serious, nothing-but-sand sense of the word. Surrounding both ovals on all sides are really high mountains, the Himalayas and Pamir to the south, the Tien Shan range running across the middle, and the Altai and Tarbagatai in the north and west. K2, the world's second tallest mountain, is actually cut in half by the Xingjian/Pakistan border.

This is not a place of well-watered verdant valleys or rich farmland. Silk Road travel took place in the very small interstices between the desert and the tall rugged mountains. There were at least three routes from Gansu—one on the south of the Taklamakan, and one on each side, north and south, of the Tien Shan range. The towns including Urumqi are along these routes. In the case of Urumqi, it's on the north side of the Tien Shan mountains and you can see the mountains from the city—rather like Denver, except still snow-covered in August. It's a modern city only recently, having grown from one million people in 2000 to three million today.

We have a great hotel (Sheraton) and good food but not so great for things to see. We go out to the "most famous lake in China" called Heavenly Lake, way up in the mountains, and enjoy the alpine serenity, all of which is organized on buses with the attendant tickets, Chinese music, parking lots, gates, lines, etc. Pretty but we've actually seen a lake before. It appears that none of the five thousand Chinese, with whom we are sharing this intimate moment, have. The province museum in the city is also nice, best known for its collection of mummies, all of whom have been preserved by simply being buried in the desert. Dried out by the heat and dryness before they could decay. Mummies, frankly, are not my cup of tea but others seem to find them fascinating.

The most memorable part of the Urumqi experience is our decision to go to see the native touristic dances on our first evening in town. The entertainment comes with a buffet dinner, always a bad sign. It also comes with an uncountable number of pushy Chinese tourists who are determined to get as much of the food as they can. We end up with watermelon and stale bread, but this is OK because when I look at the "food" on the plates of my close neighbors, I cannot see anything that I can either identify or would be comfortable eating. We also end up with a good bottle of red wine that makes it all tolerable. Barely.

Later we came up with our Han food joke:

Q: What's the perfect Han Chinese dinner and a show type of entertainment?

A: Plenty of food. Oh, was there a show?

The show is loud and glitzy with many costume changes and recorded music. Some of the cast members looked like they were lip synching the songs, but not all of them. The dancing may or may not be "native" as it mostly consisted of arm waving and moving back and forth across the stage in simple patterns—lines, circles, with an occasional twirl added in. Movements were mostly not quite in synch—sort of like a high school presentation of *Glee*. Dances and costumes included Wicked Witch of the West (tall black fezzes on the women, from the top of which sprouted red scarves), *I Dream of Jeannie* gauzy ensembles, Emirates flight stewardess, kris knives or possibly large red peppers wielded by female dancers wearing small organ grinder monkey fezzes, a number with dancers wearing Bobby hats in red and blue. The guys all were in variants of Cossack attire, but in colors. Highlights included the dance of the drink trays (without drinks) and a series of singles or duets: the prom queen singing "Climb Every Mountain" in Chinese, two guys doing dueling bongos, and what looked for all the world like an Elvis impersonator, white jumpsuit with sequins, except he was playing the flute. Our favorite was the lady with the snake, dancing around with the pyramids projected in the background. I did not know that was part of China. The snake was probably scared to death, and should have been, as a number of people in the audience would have been willing to eat it. At the end of the evening the cast members circulated through the audience and selected people to come up on stage, using the criterion that they had to dance worse than the "real" dancers. They were successful.

Kashgar

This is the westernmost city in China. Also clearly the poorest of the cities we have been in. There are more way motorcycles than cars on the roads, less English in the signs, less English anywhere. The motorcycles are all electric and cost 5,000 yuan—about $800. And are ridden by both men and women, Uighur and Chinese. Gasoline-powered bikes and small trucks are not permitted in the city. And our first and only sighting of working donkey carts on city streets. There is minimal traffic, another interesting indicator. The city has no special manufacturing base, just modest agriculture based on irrigation, and not a lot of that. It is known for its pomegranates but they're not ripe yet. And there are many more beggars in the street—to this point we have seen a total of one in six cities, and we saw seven or eight here, men and women. It's the end of the Silk Road in China and a famous oasis town, but then look around for the economic opportunities. Modest. The Chinese government's drive to invest in the five western provinces has not quite gotten here. "Kashgar, Gateway to Uzbekistan." Maybe? Everyone does have a cell phone, however.

It's about 400,000 people, 50% Uighur, 10% other minorities, 40% Han Chinese. Way more women in head scarves, some with faces covered, and a few walking around with brown scarves just thrown over their heads, faces completely covered. I kept waiting for them to walk into something, but one must assume there's a way to see out. Because we are still on Beijing time, the sun comes up at about 0800 and things get started late and then stay open late. More people staring at us westerners than anywhere else, where there was little or none. Lots of soldiers around, serious soldiers in olive drab uniforms, with helmets and riot shields and armored vehicles and AK-47s. We saw several cases where police just stopped young men arbitrarily, to check IDs. Probably they can tell the difference between Han and Uighur; we cannot. But the cash machines work and so does the Internet and it's not threatening or that hot, which is a relief.

Kashgar is home to the largest existing statue of Mao in China. It's right across the street from our hotel and is made of a sandstone-colored brown concrete aggregate, or something similar. Mao has his right hand raised in greeting. No one seems to pay any attention to the statue, or maybe it's the hovering soldiers nearby in the square, sitting on top of their armored personnel carriers that make it seem like a good idea to keep on going.

We visit the Id Kah Mosque, largest in China and not all that large, although pleasant, with many trees in the courtyard and a mosque building that is one story, linear and not deep, and, as our guide says, "humble." We rather like humble in religious edifices, although that tends not to be the trend in any religion that we can identify. While we are there a Chinese group, clearly discernible as the men are wearing shorts and T-shirts and the women have not covered their heads, has one of their number duck under the rope into the prayer area and pretend to kneel, then stick his rear end up in the air and wiggle it. The girls giggle. Our guide, a Uighur named Mohammed, who thus far has been extremely laid back to the point of catatonic, gets mad and yells at the Chinese guy, who quickly retreats. As the Chinese group leaves Mohammed says, "I hate them. They are animals, animals on two legs."

The real reason to come here is the "Sunday Market," which started out as two markets, one outside of town, the livestock market, and the other in town, in a very large covered area, where they sell everything else—but mostly stuff you honestly would not want to buy or cannot identify. The non-livestock market is not particularly interesting—cheap watches, glittery fabric, nuts, unknown spices, rugs, jade jewelry by the ton, more shoes and shoe stores than you can possibly imagine. Except no souvenir T-shirts or refrigerator magnets or coffee mugs or snow globes, we know not why. And not really any measurable "local crafts" and certainly nothing unique to the area or even to Xinjiang.

The livestock market is something else. It's in a big field with hundreds of small trucks coming in to drop off livestock, essentially everything but pigs and feathered animals, to be tied up along rows of rails, and then to be sold to other folks there who arm wrestle the sheep, goats, cows, donkeys, and horses somehow back into the small trucks and with much beeping and honking and discussion maneuver themselves out. No one here has yet invented the ramp. It's crowded and noisy and smelly and quite muddy and really not put on for the tourists. There are probably fifteen westerners present, all of us looking slightly dazed and taking pictures and trying not to get run over or stepped on or to step in something. We especially liked the young woman who had showed up in a long flowing skirt and flip flops. Not a good footwear choice for this venue.

We only saw one camel for sale, but we got to see lots of yaks, my particular favorite. I have in the past confused them with lamas (the animal not the monk) but no more. They look like cows with attitude, mostly because of their quite serious horns, but they're wearing fur coats. They appear to be a bit more docile than the horns implied, but we were careful to keep our distance. I wanted to buy one to take home but since I don't own a ranch in the mountains, or even a yurt, I finally decided it was a bad idea. Besides, I didn't have a motorcycle to carry it on.

And thus having reached the end of China, literally, we turned around and came home.

Food

Chinese have a love-love relationship with food. Each meal at a restaurant involves a great deal of negotiation, generally energetic. And carried out in a loud tone of voice or voices.

Our days usually started with breakfast at the hotel, always (through Dunhuang) a buffet of mostly Chinese but some Western stuff, getting less Western as we head west. There was generally lousy coffee except Beijing, great melons and pineapple, omelets, and some kind of potato—McDonald's equivalent wedges, small quarter skin-on chunks sautéed, and actually cold french fries in Dunhuang. Which the Chinese like and eat with their chopsticks. Past Dunhuang it was mostly unlabeled Chinese food, and toast with jam. And increasingly worse coffee.

Lunch was away from the hotel at a local restaurant selected by the guide. Sort of a crap shoot. Despite having a guide to help us with the interminable negotiations for each luncheon meal, we inevitably ended up with the culinary equivalent of the "point and shoot" camera technique. Generally this worked. In Beijing we utilized point and shoot again for the quick lunch and ordered chicken with peanuts that turned out to be shrimp with cashews, but was fine. This works because the Chinese menus generally have pictures but not English, and the English menus have words but not pictures. The words can be delightful. But what does not seem to work is saying, "How about beef with broccoli?" You would think that this is among the most universal of all Chinese stir-fried dishes. Hell, I can make it. But try asking the waitress about it, and both she and the guide then engage in a long and apparently disputatious dialogue, much page of menu flipping back and forth and finally land on a dish called "donkey stomach braised with winter melon."

Beijing lunch surprise: dumplings that looked like tacos. But pretty good. Other dumplings (second most easy dish in the Chinese repertoire I should think) so far have been too doughy. We persevered, but never had dumplings half as good as you can get at your favorite local Chinese restaurant at home.

Other highlights: Xi'an—great meal for lunch (shrimp with walnuts and lots of vegetables some not identifiable; chicken with peppers and walnuts and celery and garlic and ginger), with the bowl of rice having a sprinkling of corn kernels cooked into it. Great idea for Nebraska.

Jiayuguan: fine lunch of fried pork with fried potatoes in a square dice, and lots of hot peppers.

Dunhuang: excellent noodles with sesame sauce, fried pork spareribs (yes! Make this at home! Who knew you could fry them?), and another one of fried pork with sweet sauce. One might notice a fried theme developing.

Dinner was always on our own, usually at the hotel except in Beijing where we knew more and could get more understandable responses and recommendations from the concierge from using English.

We had Peking duck in Beijing—twice. Well why not? If we had three nights there I would have had it three times. It was consistently wonderful, but with an ever-changing array of accompaniments to put in the rice pancake along with the basics—duck sauce and scallions. Condiments presented included: shredded cucumber, shredded celery, minced garlic—all OK. Then shredded melon, salt, sugar, red pepper, chopped pickled Szechuan vegetable. The sugar didn't seem to add much. And the duck soup at the end was pretty loathsome, and unnecessary.

Best meal in China: lamb with cumin served on a sizzling iron platter, in Dunhuang. And I don't even like lamb.

Worst meal in China: the non-meal at the dance show in Urumqi.

Best rules of thumb: when in doubt, order the noodles, avoid the mutton.

Worst coffee: this is a hard one, but the Tuha Petroleum Hotel in Turpan made coffee that really was black water with no coffee taste at all. Perhaps petroleum based.

The Apartment Building Conundrum

On the outskirts or suburbs of every one of the seven cities that we visited, we observed lots and lots of thirty- to forty-story apartment buildings under construction, or half built, or two-thirds built. There were also ranks and ranks of six-story "garden" apartments outside Turpan and Kashgar. They developments seem arbitrarily stuck on open sites with no surrounding infrastructure, or even other structures of any kind, no services or supermarkets or even traffic, and the built ones mostly don't seem occupied. They remind one of the Bolshevik apartment blocks outside of the major eastern European centers. But these are taller and not occupied

Northeast of Turpan, for example, are row after row after row of five-story apartments, all oriented so that you could put solar on the roofs. Most are three-quarters built, none finished, none occupied. Probably more than 200 individual buildings, probably 30 to 40 apartments per building, so 8,000 units, assume five persons per unit and you have homes for 40,000 people in a 250,000-person town with no suburbs and the entire surrounding area desert. No hinterlands to draw from. Who will move into these? Why aren't they more actively under construction, or more clearly occupied?

Style

Outfit uncertainty: you are a girl, so you remember the perennial question of female travelers—"What should I wear?" We didn't want to look like tourists, although this is a difficult goal because we are tourists, we are going to places tourists go to, we do not look the least bit Chinese, and we only speak English. We don't want to offend any Muslims in the area, but we also don't want to walk around with our heads covered and sweat to death. Our rule of thumb: modest colors, no patterns, sensible shoes. Long sleeved shirts, long pants, no bare arms, lightweight head scarf. Oh, yeah, and dork hats. It is not possible, I believe, to have a decent hat that provides sun protection, is lightweight, is not an offensive color, will stay on your head in a breeze, and still looks cool. Doesn't exist. We looked. So we have round tan hats with chin straps that are assuredly not fashionable but we don't get sunburned. So it goes. But they fold up and we can put them in our small traveling backpack if we get too embarrassed or it gets cloudy.

We worried about being too casual and not respectful enough. Boy, did we overthink this one. China in August has the most informal dress code ever seen except maybe on the Google campus in Silicon Valley. In essence, there isn't one, judging by our fellow Chinese tourists. Anything goes, starting with flip-flops, camo Bermudas, and a nicely matching plaid shirt. It is also OK to wear your backpack to breakfast and eat with it still on. On your back or on your front.

China is where all the unbelievable number of T-shirts manufactured in Bangladesh go to live. All with English writing on them, never Chinese. They're on everyone, old, young, male, female, babies, etc. And in a particularly fetching accommodation to the heat, many of the men we saw in Beijing had their T-shirts pulled up to their armpits, exposing a wide and generally unattractive variety of stomachs—homemade air-conditioning.

Horticulture

Flowers are planted everywhere along the sides of the major roads and freeways, especially in the cities, and they're beautiful. Roses and crepe myrtle and marigolds and zinnia and petunias are in linear beds and espaliered on fences; in some cases it's like driving down a rose tunnel. We first saw this in Beijing, but it continued everywhere we went, and in all the tourist sites as well. The rose is the national flower of China, we were told incorrectly (it's the plum blossom or else the tree peony—opinions differ). In any event, the widespread plantings gave you something nice to look at while sitting in traffic.

Population

Because it was summer and kids were not yet back in school, and because we were going to tourist places, we saw lots and lots of families. Generally they had one child, a mom, a dad, and frequently one or two grandparents, all in conformance with the one child policy. Spoiled brats everywhere. Single kids being raised by parents who were themselves raised as spoiled single kids, and so know no differently. And now you're even getting fat kids. And kids with a remarkable sense of entitlement. Our guide in Beijing complained (at age twenty-nine) that his parents had not yet bought him a car and an apartment. Welcome to the developed world.

Miscellaneous

At dinner our first evening in Turpan, we asked for the "drinks menu." We had long since learned not to ask for the wine list as that did not compute. The young woman waiting on us repeated back, "Drinks menu," which we took as a good sign. She wandered off. We waited. We waited some more. We noticed our waitress standing by the serving station at the side of the room. By some quirk of design, this location was open to the floors above. Suddenly we heard a quite loud *thud-plop!* She picked up the drinks menu, which had been dropped several stories, and brought it over to us, bent corner and all. No sense having more than one of these in the hotel, after all.

East of Turpan, we passed lots of rows of sad little identical brick houses, relatively new looking but unoccupied and falling apart. These were constructed for the Chinese to be relocated from the Three Gorges Dam area. But they brought an initial group out, the visitors took one look at the desert and surroundings, and refused to even go into the houses. Turpan is not eastern China, and they noticed.

Journey to the West is a very famous Chinese novel from the sixteenth century, telling the part true and part folk tale story of a monk's pilgrimage to India that takes him through Xinjiang. He is accompanied by four protectors—a pig, a monkey, a river ogre who is a good guy, and a dragon king disguised as a white horse. The novel was made into a cartoon (the fate of all classics?) and it's very popular in China. And now, there is a *Journey to the West* theme park along the road from Turpan to Bezeklik! No rides. Very small parking lot. And it's sitting in the middle of the desert. No grapes at least, but the Chinese can take pictures of their one child sitting on a plaster pig or horse. Disneyland is still safe.

At the Dunhuang hotel, they advertise on Wednesday nights the "Genghis Khan Fire Pit Barbecue." Given that much of the history of this whole region revolves around keeping the northerners/Mongols out of China this seems a strange choice. L has a different take on it, remarking, "Yeah, like he's really going to show up."

The cell phone carried by our driver in Turpan has for its ring tone a rendition of "Santa Claus Is Coming to Town," played on a xylophone. Really.

Five Things the Chinese Do Better Than Us

One: Build new roads—we were on the road a lot, and all the roads we traveled on were excellent, even challenging ones like the four-lane divided highway from Urumqi to Turpan through some very rugged mountains. Thank goodness. Of course, they're all toll roads, so no access for the peasants.

Two: Build new transmission lines. Really big ones, all along the roads in the west. Connecting new solar and wind plants won't be a problem, they may really be serious about cutting down on the amount of coal burned to make electricity. Although we did see twelve large coal plants located near the wind farms.

Three: Build high-speed rail—these lines are in construction all over the west. When complete, it will be possible to go from Urumqi to Beijing in sixteen hours—2,500 kilometers. With stops at all the provincial capitals along the way.

Four: Organize the tourists and charge admission at every possible tourist site. Well, you do get a colorful receipt as a souvenir.

Five: Connect you to the Internet, everywhere, even in Kashgar and Turpan, although you had to go to the lobby to connect.

Five Things the Chinese Do Worse Than Us

One: Make wine—so they raise twenty-three varieties of grapes in Turpan and they have since forever and they cannot make a decent bottle of wine? It's a much higher-value way to export the grapes, and it only took California fifty years to get pretty darn good at it. Raisins are not a high-value alternative.

Two: Stand in line. For anything. Especially to get on airplanes or into bathrooms or into tourist sites. Maybe they stand in line for something, but we didn't see it.

Three: Make showers in hotel bathrooms that keep the water inside instead of leaking out onto the bathroom floor—we had this problem in six out of seven hotels. You can build high speed rail but not shower joints?

Four: Worry about blocking the view of others. At the show in Urumqi, a number of guys in the front, where we were not, stood up to take pictures of the dancers. Only they used their iPads and held them over their heads and just recorded it all as video, so they just stood there blocking the view. The Chinese guy next to me got so fed up with this that he started throwing lamb bones at these people. This was effective.

Five: Drive. We came across five accidents in our three days in Turpan/Urumqi. Four involved serious smashups (we saw the vehicles); one was an oil truck that dumped part of its cargo on the Turpan to Urumqi pass through the Tien Shan mountains and closed the northbound side of the highway for an entire day. Fortunately that was the day we were heading south. One explanation: car ownership in China has exploded in the last ten years, but that means most drivers, of any age, haven't been driving that long. This appears to apply to trucks as well, and there are really a lot of them on the freeways.

And we no doubt had one of those new drivers, but we made it back alive—

Love and kisses, Bob

Afterword: The Chinese have much to be proud of, most especially their economic accomplishments since the end of WWII. No country or group of people of any size has ever moved this far, this fast, and with no particular gift of natural resources given to them—no oil, no gold, no diamond mines. Much of what we saw on this trip underlined the magnificence of this success.

They are also possibly the most racist people—and here we are speaking especially of the Han Chinese—with whom I have ever dealt. They don't just think that they are a superior race, they know it deep in their bones and spirits. We saw some of this as we went farther and farther west, and the minorities in the population increased, especially the Uighurs. Given what has been reported about the rounding up of this minority and putting them in camps, I would not make this same trip today. And that is a shame, as it was really wonderful.

[14]

We See Wild Animals Who for Some Reason Decline to Eat Us

November 2013

Dear Aunt Janet,

We just came back from South Africa where we went to see a football game. No, just kidding, to see animals. Wild, untamed, dangerous animals. You're now probably full of thousands of questions about this, which I will preemptively answer for you.

Why in the world would you want to do this?

Going to Africa to see fierce animals up close and, if possible, to avoid being eaten by them, had never been high on my list of potential entertainments. But L said that this was what she wanted as a birthday present, and not more stuff. "I am an American," she declared, "and as such I have spent a lot of time accumulating stuff, such that I now have so much stuff that I cannot find a place for all of it."

I was careful neither to agree nor to disagree with this statement, as

I couldn't see a helpful comment to be made here. Instead, I reprised the old joke of Steven Wright, "You can't have it all. Where would you put it?"

Was there any way to see if you liked this before flying off to the ends of the earth at great expense and personal risk?

Yes. Before lurching off on an African adventure, I thought maybe we should practice. So on one fine Sunday morning, armed with coffee and several cake doughnuts with chocolate icing, we went off to the San Diego Zoo Safari Park. We drove there by ourselves, not in a Land Rover with a cut-out roof, and not accompanied by native guides, but guided only by my smartphone that has slowly begun, under torture, to yield up its secrets. One of its secrets is a map thing that shows you the route to wherever you are going, and then indicates by a throbbing blue dot where you are. You compare the dot with the highlighted route to see if you have just missed a crucial turn and are about to plunge into the river or a McDonald's. This is a little bit after the fact, but if you watch closely you can anticipate when you need to turn. How one simultaneously drives and carefully watches the dot and route on the tiny cell phone screen is not yet clear.

But it's better than nothing, just not as good as the system in the Hertz rental car called, guilelessly, "NeverLost," which gives you both a map and oral prompts in a lilting mechanical accent, usually female. "Right turn in [slight pause] one [slight pause] mile." Or, since even this system is not infallible because the driver is not paying attention or there is no right turn to be made, it frequently says to me "Recalculating route," and "When possible, make a [slight pause] legal U-turn." I think the NeverLost system may itself never be lost, but it's not entirely true for the driver. L thinks that the voice should have more personality, and reward you when you make a correct turn—"Good [slight pause] work on making a [slight pause] right turn." I have a different interpretation, and worry that instead the voice will begin berating me when I screw up: "You are a [slight pause] bad driver. You did not [slight pause] turn when I told you to."

Despite having only this limited and silent aid to navigation, we drove out into eastern San Diego, into the farming part of the county, and after about an hour we were successful in arriving just after the park had opened. The facility spreads over 1,800 acres of hilly and semiarid terrain, although it has been landscaped and hardscaped and built up with the requisite shops and "attractions," which means more than just a bunch of large animals lying around in the sun waiting to eat. The park began as an offshoot of the big San Diego Zoo, which is downtown in Balboa Park and is not as large as this. Originally the overflow from the downtown zoo was housed here, and it also served as a breeding facility, and it was called just Wild Animal Park. Visitors were welcome but it wasn't all that interesting. Then someone did a marketing study and found that they could make money if they added a safari theme. And a zip line. And a balloon ride. And a tram. And an opportunity to sleep overnight in a tent. And stores with monkey hats and rhino T-shirts. And "Jungle Cafés." And nothing at the Safari Park is free. In fact it's really expensive, but it does have lots and lots of animals, roaming about inside large enclosures that you get to drive into once you have paid enough money for your two-hour safari. We had on our safari hats and we had our cameras, so we were ready. No, scratch that, we had our platinum American Express cards, so we were ready.

No walking was required. There were trams, jeeps, trucks, carts, a zip line, and even a balloon, except it was tethered so that it just went up and then came down, as it is not a good idea having the tourists land in the lion enclosure. Although it would have added a certain frisson of terror to the whole experience.

The layout is divided, much like Disneyland, into different areas; in this case Africa, Asia, South America. Antarctica is missing for probably obvious reasons, and so is North America, possibly because your ancestors and mine carefully killed off all the large animals about 150 years ago. The Africans have not yet duplicated this feat, although the poachers are trying hard.

We bought our tickets and met our fellow Safarians, who were three people from Singapore, an unremarkable family from San Francisco, and a young couple from Iowa. The young man from Iowa had a truly remarkable large head of curly, unruly red hair, resembling nothing so much as an escapee from a traveling production of *The Lion King*. I wondered if he feared being recaptured.

We all got in the back of a medium-sized truck with seats and slatted sides and a guide named Bill or Buzz or something. He was wearing khaki

Bermuda shorts and a camp shirt with his name embroidered on it and a sort of cowboy hat in khaki. He was unarmed. This was troublesome.

He imparted many facts to us, some of which might have been true:

Fact #1: Apparently the animals are all well fed. Very well fed, it's a zoo of couch potatoes. As we drove around "Africa" there were lots of animals, really lots, big and small. Rhinos and giraffes and Cape buffalo and plenty of smaller miscellaneous gazelle/deer/antelope creatures, and no one was fighting with anyone else. It should be noted that the carnivores were kept elsewhere or this Eden-like atmosphere might have been somewhat different.

Fact #2: The Safari Park carefully manages each group of animals, so that there is only one male in the group, and a bunch of females. Hence less fighting for dominance and more collegiality—weekly bingo or sewing circles or something.

Fact #3: The place is run like a dating service or maybe Match.com of the jungle. They are very focused on reproduction and are proud of the results they have obtained over the period since the establishment of the facility: 123 white rhinos, 78 giraffes, 57 Cape buffalo, and numberless gazelle/deer/antelopes. So many animal babies that the park trades them off with other zoos, and sometimes the other zoos send new males. The park takes a lot of care with breeding—one male per herd, monitoring of menstrual cycles, isolating pregnant animals if necessary, keeping track of genealogy so that the males don't mate with their own offspring. Maybe better than some human families.

Fact #4: The managers take special care of the endangered species, including breeding more. You do kind of wonder what eventually happens, though. The endangerment is not a function of the animals' ability or non-ability to reproduce; it's a result of habitat destruction or poaching or both, and while this problem may have been more or less fixed in the US, it's not so clear at all in other locations where most of these animals come from. Reintroduction of zoo-bred populations into the wild doesn't make much sense, and the smaller the herd the more the problem with lack of genetic diversity. I decide not to solve this problem on this particular day.

Some interesting learning—you have to have a minimum number of rhino females in a herd before any of them will become fertile—apparently they are able to suppress their cycle if they don't feel the appropriate comfort of numbers.

Fact #5: No safari clothes were worn except the dork hats. And we "learned" that dark colored creatures stand out on the African veldt and so if you are dark, then you're probably a predator—like the Cape buffalos who no one messes with or the black rhinos, ditto. But the lions are beige so how does that work?

All that part is fine, Bill or Biff doesn't say anything really stupid, and as we drive slowly around the enclosure we really do get to see large animals very nearby. There is a mother white rhino with her small baby, small for a rhino although large for a Harley-Davidson, and they both come to within twenty feet of the truck. No one charges us. But I wouldn't want to be walking around next to these folks. They could squash you.

Then the silliness begins. Our guide Chad or Brad says, "Would anyone like to feed the giraffes?" Well, not me, I am a non-interventionist when it comes to wild animals; I have attended the One-Handed Jack School of Wild Animal Feeding, but I am the lone man out in this in our truck. We drive slowly over to where some giraffes are standing awkwardly around, awkwardly being the only way giraffes ever stand around. One giraffe slowly moves over to us. Our guide says, "Oh, look, it's Motambo."

All the animals, at least the big ones, appear to have fake African names like Cho-Cho or Ulama but at least are not wearing name tags. Chip or Chris gets a volunteer to stand at the back of the truck, facing toward the front, and hold up one acacia leaf in her left hand at shoulder level in front of her, and a bunch of other ones in her right hand, down by her side, while Motambo approaches from behind the truck.

"Don't try to pet the giraffes, they don't like that," says Burke or whatever his name is. "Just hold the leaf and she'll take it. Hold the other ones down, only give her one at a time." This does not seem to be a difficult set of instructions, but our fellow truck riders, all of whom take a turn at leaf holding, do not seem to know right from left or one from many, or in some cases up from down, even though Bryan has already demonstrated this technique.

Sure enough, Motambo takes the leaf and eats it, displaying the classic long, black, snaky tongue that giraffes have. And the reason for facing forward finally becomes obvious—it's so your companion or family member inside the truck can take a picture of the feeder with a giraffe over his or her shoulder. Of course.

Acacia trees in Africa have little tiny leaves and very serious thorns on all the branches. Giraffes are specialized at eating these, hence the fur around the mouths, the long eyelashes to detect thorns if they get too close, and the very flexible round, pointed tongues to snake in between the thorns and get the leaves. This is a hard way to have a picnic. Here at the park they feed the giraffes big, non-thorny acacia leaves from an Australian species that doesn't have thorns since kangaroos don't eat the leaves. I guess.

Thankfully we run out of leaves. We proceed slowly over to one of the pens inside the enclosure where we find a large rhinoceros named Buster, which I do not think is African but maybe the name of a colonial hangover. We back the truck up to a small window in the pen, and Buster sticks his head out a little and into the damn truck, and now we get to feed him and pet his nose. Urk. He is solid, firm head and nose, no horn. Everyone in the truck does this but yours truly. He eats apples. How nice. Lots of apple orchards in Africa. And just why is he in the pen, when all the other rhinos are out walking around or, to be more accurate, lying around? Could it be that he had a "behavior problem"? Not charging trucks, we hope.

More driving around, more looking at animals up close, now in the enclosure called Asia that has the black rhinos. Again no one charges us, no animal really seems to give a darn about this green truck puttering around through their territory. I guess it happens every day and so has long since lost its novelty.

The "safari" ends and we have lunch at the Jungle Café, which has typical jungle food: hot dogs, chicken fingers, hamburgers, french fries. And beer and wine, a significant improvement over most family amusement locations.

The elephants have their own special area, and it's different from the "Asia" and "Africa" areas and you don't get to drive around inside it, which is a relief. We hike over there after lunch and watch the elephants do not so much. There's a lot of that here. Except one of them, probably a male, looks like he has five legs. Can this be? Well, no, he has his penis extended and it's almost dragging on the ground as he slowly walks around the pen. None of the lady elephants shows much interest, so eventually it recedes into somewhere. We are fascinated and I am at least a bit daunted. But if an elephant is a very big animal, it makes sense that he wouldn't have a very small apparatus. Nevertheless . . .

I suggest we go see the condors to avoid pondering the five-legged elephant further. I have never seen condors before, but only heard about their size and majesty, riding the thermals of the Sierra Nevadas, etc., and now endangered. Yes, the condor is a North American animal, but at the park they only have injured ones that cannot make it in the world, all clustered in a big aviary at the top of the hill. And here's the unfortunate truth—they're ugly. They're big, but they're large buzzards, with that attractive featherless reddish pink head thing going. Ick, carrion eaters for sure, I don't think they feed these guys apple chunks. Also they just sit in the aviary, doing little, the signature behavior of the park's animals. L remarks that if you are going to be an endangered species, you have a way better chance of someone caring about it if you're cute. No doubt true. Ocelots are cute so if they are endangered it's easier to make a case for them. Cute wins, even in the animal kingdom.

Since we have now maxed out our credit cards, it's time to head home. L is delighted to learn that on a safari you can pet the animals. I am less sure that was the purpose of the expedition. We stop in one of the gift shops on the way out, and it does have a giraffe snow globe, so that's a plus.

How much was this like an African safari, really?

You could easily spend a thousand dollars a person a day here in San Diego, so in that way it's just like being in Africa.

What does "safari" mean? It is the Swahili word meaning "long journey." Which we believe refers to how long it takes to get from San Diego to the Kruger reserve in the northeastern corner of South Africa. Long, as in two-and-a-half-days long. Even in business class this is a long time on several airplanes, and a midnight stop in Dakar is not a positive adder to the experience.

How was Johannesburg? Hard to say, since all we did was fly in, spend the night in a very nice hotel literally across the street from the airport, and fly out the next morning.

On the room service menu in J-burg was a dish listed as "African Fries with Samazulu Spices." We are intrigued, what can this be? Rhino skin with something exotic? It turns out to be slightly limp plain old french fries sprinkled with a red powder that's a cross between chili powder and paprika. The waiter who brings it apologizes that it might be "too spicy" for us (pasty white American people). It is not.

Where did you go exactly? We flew from Johannesburg in a quite small plane to a much smaller town called Nelspruit, and then our lodge people picked us up and drove us past farming and grazing and orchard territory to the area of the reserves. Along the way we saw place names of all kinds: Hazyview, Oakley, Buckingham, Huntington, Skopit, Witrivier, Phalaborwa, Mkhulu, Skukuza. My favorite was a bar called Casa Banana Tavern. Our destination was Kirkman's Kamp, a private reserve of 15,500 acres. It is one of several in the area that contains both the Sabi and the Sand Rivers, and is next to the public game reserve called Kruger. Taken together, the area is an interconnected hunk of real estate the size of Massachusetts—5.5 million acres. And each of the private reserves has its own camp or lodge and its own staff. Some have reciprocal arrangements so that if they've got elephants next door you can drive over and see them. And anyone can go to Kruger but we had so much to see that we never needed to do this.

What were the accommodations like? Did you have to sleep in tents? No tents. This was not roughing it. There was a large main building with a bar and a library and lounging areas and a small gift shop, and a big outdoor dining area in the back. The guests stayed in individual duplex casitas, nicely done with private baths and porches, all very comfortable.

Was there electricity and cell phones and Internet access? Or, as a somewhat naive acquaintance asked, "Do they have Wi-Fi in Africa?" Well, honey, it's a big continent, fifty-plus countries, so yes, I expect so, at least somewhere. In fact there was a Wi-Fi connection, despite the deeply rural, middle-of-nowhere location of the Kamp. And there was warm water and sun-dried towels and cold beer and inside plumbing and flush toilets. And a big generator for the electricity. This is not a hardship tour.

What was the jungle like? It wasn't really jungle and Johnny Weissmuller wasn't there, and this was a surprise. Perhaps we should have read the brochures more carefully. But for seeing animals this was better. It was a rolling sort of savannah but more green than brown, with a number of forestry, bushy parts, officially called "veld." Lots of open areas with grass newly growing as we were there in spring for the southern hemisphere. Lots of medium height shrubby trees and bushes. Some very large trees but none of these were in very thick groves, more like individual large trees dotted here and there. Some flowering shrubs, some recognizable wildflowers (morning glories, lantana, vinca) and some very pretty but not recognizable—sickle bush, for example. A medium-sized river with broad sandy banks meandered down the west side of the property. It was shallow enough to allow the vehicles to cross it at a number of places, and the animals as well. The lodge sat on an area of several thousand hectares, but it was not fenced, nor are any of the areas. The animals wandered around on it and the several other neighboring preserves and also onto the very large state-owned Kruger wildlife preserve. The area was crisscrossed with nothing but dirt roads, probably to keep speeds down and for tracking. We couldn't go off-road except in special cases. The reserve managers do controlled burns from time to time to create areas of new grass.

What was the weather like? Nice, warm but not blistering in the day, cool at night. The cabins all have air-conditioning. It rained one morning while we were out but we put on ponchos and kept going. However, it was the start of the rainy season so we were glad not to have been there any later.

How was the food? Yeah, never mind about a bunch of animals. First, they fed us seven times a day: an 0500 coffee and cake semi-breakfast while you waited for the game trucks to pull up, and a stop at the end of the morning game drive for coffee and cookies, and then a midmorning real breakfast with ham and cheese and omelets and sausage and bacon and hash browns and pancakes and cereal and fruit. Lunch seems like it follows immediately although it's at one o'clock and includes a starter, fresh baked bread, a bunch of salads, a main course, dessert. Followed by a snooze since you had been up since four-thirty. And then "high tea" with tea and cakes at four before the afternoon game drive. And a stop at the end of the second game drive for cocktails and snacks. And then a real dinner at eight, with a decent selection frequently including local game. All accompanied by good South African wines. Whew, it makes me feel stuffed just to think about it.

L ate kudu, warthog, and ostrich, with varying degrees of success. And since none of the animals we saw were successful in eating us, I count the score as three to zero in our favor. I was trying to get points with the animals by not eating any of their buddies.

What should you wear on safari? I suppose it depends on whether you read the guidebooks or not. Our fellow trekkers wore an interesting assortment of clothing items: Day-Glo orange T-shirts; red flip-flops; black gauzy flyaway harem pants; bright lime-green Crocs; halter tops and really short shorts even though you have not the correct-sized hips and thighs for this—so few of us these days are Daisy Duke—and you are ignoring the mosquito warnings; and lots of Giorgio perfume.

On the other hand, you might wear long khaki pants, a long sleeve muted tan or green shirt, hiking boots, and a really ugly brimmed hat, which is what all the books say to wear. We, being the original "read the documents because no one else does" type of people that we are, showed up with exactly this boring outfit, in several redundant copies. A few others did, but most of the guests dressed like they were going to the beach or to the mall and had just dropped by to see a couple of lions on the way. Weird.

What was the average day like? Groundhog Day except the menu changed. Every morning they knocked on your door at precisely five a.m. and by five-thirty you were doing the first of two game drives in the Range Rover truck thing, thundering down the dirt roads looking for animals. Back by nine-thirty for your third breakfast, then really not much to do until lunch and then tea and then a second game drive from four-thirty to six-thirty, then cocktails and bragging in the bar about what you had seen, followed by dinner. It is said that it is best to see the animals at dawn and dusk when they are most active. Maybe. Actually the lions kill things at night and then spend the day sleeping. But I was fine not driving around at night looking for killer lions.

Oh, and sometimes the animals come to you, whether you want them to or not. One evening during happy hour six Cape buffalo had a regular fight, butting heads and serious grunting, on the lawn just off the patio. The guests came out onto the patio to watch although this was finally considered unsafe. Note that the guests were not in green trucks. Note that the nickname of Cape buffalo is "black death."

What is a "game drive"? It's not like John Wayne and Montgomery Clift in *Red River*, trying to get the cattle from Texas to the rail head in Abilene. You get in a specially configured Range Rover right-hand drive 4x4 with three rows of bleacher-like bench seats behind the driver. There is also a funny little seat on the very front left, suspended out over the hood and bumper, where the "tracker" sits. The driver is your "ranger," so he has a rifle in a case laid out over the hood of the truck. There is no roof. There are no "sides." There are no doors except for the driver's access. You climb up on the vehicle and clamber into the seats. The view is unimpeded. Access to your very own tender flesh from outside the vehicle is unimpeded. Some of us notice this right away.

You take off down the many dirt roads of the reserve, looking for animals. Since the resort holds as many as thirty-five guests, there are always four and sometimes five vehicles ricocheting around, and they keep in contact with each other by radio. After a while it comes to me that this is how humans hunt in packs. When one of the rangers finds a desirable animal, usually a lion or a leopard, he lets the other vehicles know and so you get to come and sit six feet away from a lion whose specialty is killing animals very much larger and faster than you. You strongly hope that he has just done so. The ride is jouncy and dusty and confusing as there are no maps. And you have to stay on the roads unless you have found one of the cats. But you surely do see animals. You'd have to be blind not to.

What language do they speak? I presume you mean the people, not the animals. The people in charge speak English with a charming accent. There are apparently many native languages, but these are specific to each tribe and are not even universal among those at the camp.

On our first day out, our ranger says, excitedly, "Look over there, the impalas farting for dominance." We see two antelopes butting heads. Well, OK, there's dung everywhere, and I mean really everywhere, and some of the animals use this for marking their territories, so maybe they also fart for dominance. Later it becomes clear that he was saying "fighting for dominance." Oh.

We are staying at a place called Kirkman's Kamp, which was originally and unsuccessfully a cattle ranch, set up by a Mr. Kirkman. He had, besides the usual problems of disease and how to get the cows to market and what was the price of hamburger, a bit of a difficulty with lions. Said predators, who were used to running after swift things and trying to avoid being gored by slow but mean things suddenly found large and tasty animals that were neither swift nor mean. Yum, yum. It was explained to us that Mr. Kirkman, to protect this herd, went out hunting lions at night with a torch tied to the end of his gun. Wasn't he blinded? Didn't he just illuminate himself? Didn't he occasionally burn himself? Seemed like giving the lions a much better chance than necessary. Then after several days I realized that torch is UK speak for what we call a flashlight. Strapping one of these onto your rifle suddenly made more sense.

How many animals did you see? Geez, I thought you'd never ask. I could simply say, "Many, many, really a lot, a whole bunch" but that doesn't actually address the question. There is also something in Africa safari-land called "the big five" and this means lion, leopard, elephant, rhino, and Cape buffalo. I don't know why hippos were excluded as they are surely big, and giraffes are big in another way, but there you go. We saw at least one of each of these five on the first day out, and then again many times. But I am at heart a data geek and while L was taking close to a thousand pictures, I kept a sort of journal of what we were seeing, how many, what time, how far away, etc. Then, because I couldn't help myself, I entered these observations in an Excel spreadsheet. Here are the results. Spreadsheet available on request.

Species observed and number of sightings during our six and a half days:

Impala, 843

Cape buffalo, 69

Waterbuck, 63

Kudu, 56

Elephant, 38

Lion, 32

Zebra, 28

Warthog, 23

Hippo, 21

Bushbuck, 19

Rhino, 15

Monkey, 14

Leopard, 13

Giraffe, 13

Wildebeest, 10

Duiker, 10

Hyena, 10

Nyala, 8

Wild dog, 8

Four or fewer: jackal, crocodile, steenbok, genet, baboon

Total number of sightings: 1,304 distributed over twenty-four types—and this doesn't count the plentiful birds that included several kinds of eagle, lots of smaller but gloriously feathered birds, and the niftiest stork I have ever seen, called the saddleback stork, with a black and white and red and yellow set of markings that were amazing.

Animal most often seen: the place was lousy with impala. No wonder there are so many lions and leopards. But these were very fast animals, usually found in herds so that one of them could almost always be on the lookout.

Animal least often seen: baboon, thank goodness, as we saw him on the porch of the room next to us. He had big teeth. We made sure to keep our patio door locked.

Mean time between each instance of seeing an animal: this is hard to calculate, as once we found a leopard, for example, we would hang around and watch it for fifteen to twenty-five minutes. That said, the data indicate we rarely on the game drives went more than five minutes without seeing something. After the first day, we no longer stopped when we saw impala. They were all over the place.

Average number of animals seen per hour: 48.3, or one animal on average every 1.24 minutes.

Average distance from animals: well, the reverse of what you would expect. The more dangerous the animal, the closer we got. This was explained to us thusly: we rangers have been driving around in these vehicles and the lions/leopards/elephants/rhinos are used to us and have decided that we're not prey or predators, so they ignore us. So we can drive right up to them and watch them tear a bushbuck limb from limb. They don't mind. Just stay in the truck.

This seemed to be sound advice and we did stay in the truck and no lion jumped on us. I would have preferred, however, to have had a chance to review the document wherein the lions all agreed that they would not eat the slow, tasty unarmed things in the truck so long as the slow tasty things stayed in the truck. Certified by an independent authority if possible. We were also told, authoritatively, by our ranger, "If you're out of the truck and a lion sees you, don't run. If you run, then they will think you're prey. I will get between you and the lion." So, the guide wants us to stand still so the lion will be either so stupid (Lion: "Duh, what is that two-legged thing? A tree?") or so analytical (Lion: "Ah, I see, because all the other prey run away when I stalk them, and this thing does not, then it must not be prey. QED, and thanks, Aristotle.") that you're safe. Seems somehow unlikely. Besides, I had this vision of the ranger saying, "OK, good, stand very still, that's it, keep standing still . . . and I will run away really fast and get help."

Weren't you scared? Hell, I was petrified. As noted incredulously above, the rangers explained that the animals were all used to seeing these nice green trucks roaming around and had decided that they were not dangerous to them, nor were they interesting to eat. Just exactly how they communicated these findings to the humans was not clearly explained.

Lions can run at twenty-two meters per second. We were in open vehicles. We were usually sitting still, once we got close to the predators, with the engine turned off. We were ALWAYS closer than twenty-two meters, usually closer than twenty-two feet. Somehow the vehicle was always positioned so that I was the person closest to the lions. And the game rifle was in its nice little case on the hood, not upright and bracketed like an LA cop shotgun in a patrol car. So, maybe a second for the guide to get the gun case off the hood, a second to get it unzipped, several seconds to load the bolt-action rifle, and by then I am human slider at the Lion Café. Hmmm.

It was explained to us that the hippo is actually the most dangerous animal in that it kills more people than any other animal in Africa. "Why?" you may ask, although as hippos are vegetarians the real question perhaps should be "How?" The hippos leave their nice ponds or rivers or lakes at night to feed, but they have poor eyesight and are also dark in color, so villagers stumble into them. Perhaps the villagers have poor eyesight as well. At this point—what? The hippos sit on the villagers? The hippos bite the villagers with all of their four teeth? It was not clear. Besides why are the villagers roaming around in the hippo feeding areas in the dark? But the lions were there in the daylight and very close and even if they had lion cataracts I was pretty clearly visible, and they are not vegetable-tarians.

In Kruger, the big reserve next door, civilian vehicles are allowed, so people drive their own cars in, see a bunch of lions, and occasionally get out to get a better photo. The gene pool is then upgraded. Ten tourists a year are on average killed in Kruger by lions. And, as was explained to us, that doesn't count the Mozambicans who cross the border at night on foot and try to pass through the Kruger, looking for work in South Africa. Not a good immigration strategy, nor a fair way to count.

What were your five most memorable experiences? On the afternoon of the third day a large herd of elephants was reported moving through the reserve. We ended up maneuvering the truck so that we were right in the middle of a moving herd of eighteen elephants, all but one of whom could crush you to a paste in seconds. And the one who could not, the mischievous baby, was the one playing around by the truck and likely to get her mother, who did not look happy and was doing that ear flapping thing, to make the aforementioned tourists into goo.

The morning of the fourth day we were right beside—yes, ten feet away—from a very large white rhino with romance on this mind, who was crossing horns with another white rhino who was female and was unsure if she too had romance on her program for the day, but was willing to lock horns with rhino #1 and push him around. And these too are very large beasts who would smash the truck and its blameless occupants to pieces if they had a mind to. Fortunately, they did not. Never mind all this "hippos are the most dangerous animals" stuff.

The afternoon of day five we found a mama leopard and cub leopard both up in a tall tree. The cub was determined to play, mama was trying to rest and see if there was anything else around to kill. Then they came down out of the tree, and the cub practiced stalking mama and jumping on her from behind. Mama was tolerant but not entirely amused. We followed them, carefully, for thirty or forty minutes. It really was like in a wildlife movie.

One afternoon we were approaching a pride of three lions, who were doing what lions do, which is mostly eat and sleep. As we crept slowly closer, one of our more clueless truck mates asked that the ranger stop the truck as she had to get out to pee. The ranger said, "No, we can't do that." She said it was OK, there were bushes around.

"The lions will see you and attack you," he said.

"It's OK, I'll just be behind the truck."

"No, you don't understand, the lion can move at twenty-two meters per second. If you get out of the truck I guarantee you will be attacked, and I guarantee that I will not shoot the lion who attacks you." She decided to hold it.

We had just come back from a morning in which we saw a leopard in a tree rip the skin off and wrestle apart bits of a dead impala he had killed and was eating it piece by small piece . But it was heavy work, much pulling with the jaws and neck and holding the rest of the dead animal down with his paws. It hadn't occurred to me, but nobody butchers the animal for you if you're a leopard, you have to rip it up yourself and then eat it, skin and all. A very impressive sight. At lunch L orders ostrich, it arrives, and the "filet" cannot be cut with a knife, despite much effort. It was after all a butter knife. Finally she picks the whole thing up and holding it with her hands, attempts to pull off a bite with her powerful jaws and teeth.

"Very good," I say helpfully, "you're doing your leopard imitation." Then I ask her, once she's torn off a few bites, what it tastes like.

"Teriyaki," she replies. "Really, really tough teriyaki."

Did you get any sense for the politics of the country? We really had little exposure to the tribal people, other than those working at the camp as cooks and waiters and trackers. We did have an odd conversation one evening when we had both our ranger and another local South African Caucasian woman at the table. The subject of relations between the races came up. "The locals are perfectly happy," was the response, which was then amplified by remarks, delivered carelessly, that the natives preferred living in their dirt-floored huts without running water or indoor toilets. "It's a real contented community," was the description. Kind of like the southern parts of the US in the 1950s. My, my.

Whites represent 7% of the population and control 75% of the wealth. It's amazing that Mandela was able to hold the country together and prevent reprisals. Leadership matters, and he will be missed.

Love and kisses, Bob

Afterword: This was so much better than I thought it would be. Even though we only went to one location, we lucked into a good one. It is expensive, but they provide the transportation and guides, the food and drink, the accommodations, and the right location. There is no sleeping on the ground and no eating cheese sandwiches for lunch. The rest of the people there include some who are smart and interesting, most who are nice and interesting, and a few chowderheads, but such is life. There is no assigned seating, so you can avoid the few less good ones. I fear that this experience is vanishing as economies improve, roads are built, land is put to the till, and civilization intrudes. Go see it while you can.

[15]

Why Are These Big Castles
Guarding Such a Puny River?

May 2014

Dear Aunt Janet,

I swore I would never again go to Canada. Or drink Canadian beer (Labatt, Molson, a possible exception for Moosehead just because the name is so wonderful) or watch hockey. Or laugh at *South Park* or watch that cartoon with the squirrel. All this is the result of a bad experience trying to take the solar business public in Toronto last year. Very unsuccessfully, despite the leadership of the two largest Canadian banks. I try to hold a grudge when it's not costly. And when I can remember.

But the best way to get to France was through Toronto. I relented but swore not to buy anything to eat or drink while we were in transit at the airport. Fortunately we stayed in the Air Canada airline club room and it was all free. And just as a reminder of the ways of the world, we were sitting next to a couple from western Canada, both big and very pale and very loud, and a couple from Mexico City, equally loud but smaller and less pasty. They were sharing with each other disappointing experiences of cruises in the Mediterranean. Nobody liked Italy, nobody liked Spain. Goodness, what did they like, Serbia? They liked it that the cruise liner fed them five times a day. And you could get a lot of cheap drinks. I tried not to listen.

Armed with a built-in GPS system in the rental car, and an Apple iPhone with a "blue dot" system, and the written directions downloaded from the Giverny website, and a map from the Hertz rental car place, and four maps ordered from Amazon—France Nord, etc.—we set off gamely on Saturday in the morning, bleary-eyed from our overnight trip from San Diego on a quest to find Giverny—Monet's garden—maybe the best garden in the world. We were successful, although it was cold and raining intermittently. This was the fourth time I have been to this garden, and it remains my all-time favorite. I like a garden that you can find.

Since this was to be a "we can drive ourselves and find things" sort of trip, the next challenge was our lodging. Giverny is northwest of Paris, and the Loire Valley, our ultimate destination, is southwest. So we placed ourselves in the GPS's hands (mind? Program?), and after four hours, we found Amboise and the hotel, Le Vieux Manoir (the old mansion or the old manor house).

Finding is one thing and getting into the parking area is a second thing. An old roman road from the fifth century, a mansion gate from seventeenth century, and a rental car from the twenty-first century are not so compatible. I first tried the standard male headfirst damn-the- torpedoes approach—first just turn off the tiny road and drive through the pretty tiny gate, never mind things like turning radius. I know better, I took geometry; men are supposedly better than women at space relations, I understand how to park a jeep with a trailer attached (another useless Vietnam skill) and the answer to all this narrowness, by the way, is to back in. The predictable result of approach number one occurred: a nice set of scratches on the driver's side back door of the car. It looked like maybe a tiger had attacked us and we were damn lucky to get away, but later I went back with my beaters and nailed the bugger, and that's his skin on the wall of my study, next to the head of the buffalo. Actually now I need to buy a steel-grey magic marker and color over the white marks on the door from the seventeenth-century gate and see if the rental car place notices. The answer will probably be yes. And it was a Mercedes to boot. I probably just achieved €2,000 worth of scratches.

As we progressed on our journey, which was one of visiting châteaux and gardens and eating and drinking, we realized belatedly that the purpose of this trip was more precisely the testing of three or four or five hypotheses about that strange group, the French. L thought that we were going because we had the time and it was the end of May and the Loire Valley is beautiful and I had never been there. This is because she believes in the ephemera called "vacation" when you eat, drink, and see the sites, without a purpose other than sybaritic. Well, really, how, er, "French." No, we were playing scientist, at least one of us was.

Hypothesis number one: Lodging. You can use the Internet now to find comfortable and affordable lodging for your stay in Europe; who needs travel agents or soulless international chain hotels?

Hypothesis number two: Castles. Only the English can do good castles. Maybe they spent all their intellectual energy on castles and not on food. Hard to know.

Hypothesis number three: Gardens. The French cannot make great gardens, at least not routinely (they do get a pass on Giverny), only the English can. We have been to the Jardin Botanique in Paris and it's a waste of time; and the very hard to find rose garden, Roseraie de L'Hay, in the southwest of Paris where we were almost denied admission by the gatekeeper. "You should have come two weeks ago! The roses are not pretty now!" Thus we have amassed some data to support the hypothesis.

Hypothesis number four: Food. There is no bad food in France. Similarly, it is impossible to be served a bad meal in France. Much supportive historic data is available, but it's always wise to continue to test, as things can change over time.

Hypothesis number five: Style. All French people are stylish and elegant, and the women especially are all pencil thin and born knowing how to wear all those scarves. Perhaps the babies use them instead of diapers. They don't look like Americans, for God's sake, which is one reason to come here.

Lodging, Part One

We don't usually stay at B and Bs, which is what Le Vieux Manoir was: six "charming" rooms filled with antiques (this always means a small bed), no Internet in your room (bad), no TV and no phone in your room (good), a gorgeous garden full of roses and lush green grass and rhododendrons (good), a lovely breakfast but you can't get it until eight-thirty, so you'll be late to the opening of the first château, but hey, it's a vacation and scientific expedition, not a scavenger hunt to see who can find the most castles and get his card stamped at each one in the shortest period of time. This is not like the challenging UK race where you have to go to each subway station in the London underground in the shortest possible time. I am not sure how one proves that he or she has done this. And given that it's the UK, it's possible that moderate to heavy drinking is involved.

We are greeted upon arrival at the manor by our hostess who has frizzy white hair, a crutch from a recent operation, and a husband who she calls "old man" and who looks old. "We've been waiting for you," she says. She does not mention hearing any scraping sound. But so much for anonymity, another benefit of large antiseptic business hotels, which you have now traded for very personalized assistance. The place had lovely characteristics, see above, but—no clean towels each day, a room too small to do anything in it other than walk sideways around the bed to get to the bathroom, intermittent Internet, modest to no privacy, lots of "well where did you go" and "where are you going today" sort of polite interest from the owners bordering on intrusiveness whenever you pass by the front desk to go upstairs. Plus you sit with people at breakfast that you don't know and never asked to meet and will never see again. Some of us do better with this than others.

Châteaux en Générale

Let us pause for a moment and discuss, in an analytical sense, just why we are here, other than it's France so the food will be wonderful and the people stylish although occasionally nasty and the wine great. And because it's the end of May, if we have timed this right, the roses should be out—they were at Giverny and we're hopeful.

Fact one: "château" in French means castle. One book says that these were all built in fifteenth century or later, and that this was the age of the cannon and thus as a defensive matter big stone-walled forts were not the right thing to spend defensive money on. Military strategy now no longer favors a "war of position" and instead prefers a "war of maneuver"? Oh, like WWI? In fact, many of the châteaux are strategically or at least tactically located, generally on the top of hills and looking over bends in the river. But the Loire today does not appear to be much of a commercial or recreational artery. We saw no other boats in six days of driving up and down the river to get to the various châteaux. It was more deserted than Myanmar and the Mekong.

It appears that none of these castles were ever actually attacked. This could be attributed to fact two, which was that once built the kings did not spend much time in them, as we were repeatedly told at each castle, except perhaps the one where the tour was in French. In later life several of them served actual military functions—garrison for a brigade at Amboise, a hospital in WWI for Chenonceau—but not headquarters or billeting or armory. So they were not useful military targets. Besides we had moved to the era of large ground armies opposing each other on the, well, ground. And later in the air. While some look imposing from a defensive stand-point, this was not the function.

The river: What's up with it? It seems very shallow although who can tell—we didn't try to wade across it. Mostly there are no boats on it. Not just a few, not just an occasional boat, none. One day we did see two guys in plastic kayaks or maybe girls, we are not sure as it was raining and they did not look happy. We spent six days driving up and down roads that run along the river, with frequent full-scale parking lots by the river for people to pull off and park in, and we didn't see a single real boat, not even canoes, not motorboats, no sunfish, no sailboats, not wave riders, no water-skiers, and no commercial traffic, no barges full of coal or anything. At Chaumont, we did see five funny-looking single sailboats, each no more than fifteen feet or less. All were sitting still at anchor. It was a Monday. Maybe that's a French fishing holiday. And no industrial activity alongside on the banks of the Loire that we could find. No recreational use areas, like boat slips. No refineries, no cement plants, no power plants, *rien*. The river might not have been worth defending, just nice to look at.

Common themes among châteaux—party X builds it, then party Y is given it, then the crown (whoever is reigning at the time) takes it away from party Y and frequently hangs or beheads party Y. And gives it to party Z. And the cycle begins again. There's a message in here somewhere.

Alternatively, the property is handed down, goes vacant, decays, is used as a stable in one or several wars, some rich guy buys it and restores it, the French government buys it in 1905. It becomes a hospital again during WWI and a Nazi battalion headquarters in WWII.

The individual stories have a similar ring to them—some royal person builds a château, usually on the ruins of where a real fort used to be, maybe save some of the real fort, like a tower, but mostly these are no longer defensive installations. They are usually located on the Loire, but not always. They are usually on some sort of river, and the valley has a lot of these—the Vienne and the Cher especially. The houses are always built of tufa/limestone, which is quarried relatively nearby and floated down or possibly up the Loire, and big seventeen-meter wooden timbers as cross-beams. Probably also floated at some point—that's a big log. They generally have steeply canted slate roofs, usually with several round/conical ones for the miscellaneous towers. They all seem to have no basements and no more than three or at most four stories. None were small, since why bother, but some were really enormous. Chambord has 284 "apartments" and almost as many fireplaces.

The builder is frequently the king but sometimes it is an important member of court, not infrequently the treasurer or equivalent, who appears to have become rich by being the treasurer, but has served the king, including going on military campaigns with him. If the house is too nice the king appropriates it. Sometimes the family gets it back, sometimes not.

Sometimes it's the queen who takes it from the owner, on the theory that it was all crown property anyway. The king and or the owner doesn't really live there that much, they just sweep in for a three week stay, which usually includes hunting. The houses frequently become unoccupied; the upkeep cannot have been a trivial expense. They frequently need renovation, and their designs change over the centuries—moats are filled in, gardens redesigned or added, etc. As the centuries pass the houses are at one time or another used as a military lodging or hospitals. Not for fighting.

Eventually the state buys them, frequently in the period of 1900 to 1910. Perhaps it would have been wiser to buy more tanks for the army with this money about then, but never mind. It is hard to say on the margin what is and what is not included as a "château." Some have glorious gardens, some have classic French gardens that we consider to be a whole lot of tightly clipped boxwood arranged in symmetric patterns, with either vegetables (lettuce a big favorite) or flowers in the interstices. Lots of lavender as well. The landscape for the setting is rolling farmland with patches of pretty thick forest. Frequently they came with large grounds as well. The property surrounding Chambord was and still is the largest hunting ground in France. And the king and his entourage did in fact hunt while they were in residence.

It is reasonably clear that these are monuments to one's own glory, rather than "national" monuments. And as king you built these, or at least started them, while you were alive, a more sensible approach if you are monumentalizing yourself. You can make sure that it's done right.

The region of the Loire Valley is on the list of World Heritage sites. It was added in 2000 along with sixty other sites, but was by far the largest "cultural" site—way bigger at 85,394 hectares for example, than the Holy Trinity Column in Olomouc in the Czech Republic, a thirty-five-meter tall column probably taking up fifty square feet. Within this Loire site are located as many as 71 to132 châteaux—sources differed. I was never able to find out just where the definition of a "château" ended and where "old and big country house" took over. We did not see all 132, you will be relieved to know.

Best Châteaux for Architecture and Wow Factor

Amboise—this is an imposing big fort/castle looming over the town of the same name. It has very high ramparts, built on a hill right on the bank of the river, great views of the Loire and of the island in the middle of the river. Only half of it survives but it's a big half. Very dominant site.

Built by Francis I at great expense, sort of defensive but mostly for show and to impress folks. I was impressed.

Chambord—biggest single building that we saw, maybe biggest of all the châteaux, and thus impressive. Three stories inside a significant two-story larger courtyard located in the middle of the biggest forest/game preserve in France. Greatest roof of any château, full of chimneys and round stuff with pointy tops and ornamentation and so on. An entirely square and large three-story design with the double spiral staircase in the middle of it. Remarkable open double helix staircase. White marble everywhere, a king's suite, a chapel, the whole works. And you can ramble through the whole thing. Big rooms, very symmetric design. A really show-offy sort of place.

Many people lived in it including the Polish king in the late 1800s. He was perhaps not a great tenant, complaining of mosquitoes in the summer, freezing in the winter. He finally moved back to Nancy; we do not know if this was better. The tapestries in the castle are a big deal and we finally understand why, and why they're so big.

Blois—built in the heart of the town. If Chambord was a beautiful unity of styles—all designed and built out by the same guy and his imported Italian architects—then Blois is the library of styles. It has four distinct buildings, all connected in an open rectangle around a courtyard, each of the four in completely different styles—medieval, renaissance, baroque, and classical. No apologies for changing style and even the spacing of the floors. It is not entirely clear the buildings even connect. A perfect example of "I'm the king, I'll build what I want." Like sticking together a Howard Johnson and a Red Roof Inn and a Hampton and an Embassy Suites.

Blois as a city needs to buy a vowel, probable an *e*, or change its name to something else entirely that you can pronounce without sounding like you have a speech defect or a mouth full of oyster crackers that you don't want to spit out.

Chaumont-sur-Loire—"outstanding gardens" says the guidebook. Well not really, but a great site overlooking the Loire hence the name, and great history. Smallish building but well executed. Catherine de' Medici (king's wife) let Diane de Poitiers (king's mistress) live here after kicking her out of Chenonceau, see below. We went in part because we saw lots of advertisements for the "International Garden Festival" being held there. The festival turns out to have a great poster and crap for flowers.

Cheverny—another place said to have great gardens, but this was a lie. Pretty but more on the lines of English country house than castle.

Langeais—the site preserves the old wall of the original fort built around 980, right on Loire, with a new bigger building still essentially linear and built to look like a fort but with big square windows. Clearly they had given up on defense. It is a small and wonderful building, but the grounds have a bunch of life-size or bigger photos of previous royals placed around rather like misplaced parade banners. Is this really what Anne of Brittany looked like?

Chenonceau—everybody's favorite château, not as big as some of the others, and built right on the river but not on a big hill overlooking the river. In fact, one of its claims to fame is that its gallery is built over the river Cher, and beautifully so. The second is that it was not built with any rooms for guests to stay over, very odd for the times—go home after the party, please.

The place is impressive, but not in a "size matters" way like Chambord and Amboise. There are two distinct gardens, one of either side of the château, one created by Diane de Poitiers, the first resident, and after she was booted, the second by Catherine de' Medici. Both are the standard French boxwood parterres but at least filled with nice plants and lots of roses along the borders. And you could look out the windows of the château and see the gardens, unlike many of the other places where they were somewhere else more distant.

Villandry—"best gardens of the Loire Valley"—again not even close, who writes this guidebook stuff? The allegedly great gardens are big all right, but mostly boxwood cut microscopically into patterns that might mean something but not to me. Some interplanting in the spaces between but that's lavender (not blooming) and something else (not blooming) and something else (also not blooming). It's May, people, everything blooms now!

The potager is similarly extensive and full of more colors of lettuce than you can imagine, plus occasionally artichokes and cabbage and a couple of squares of chives (in bloom!) but no celery or cukes or anything but long beans. Where are the tomatoes? The pumpkin and the squash and the asparagus and the carrots and radishes? But literally acres of all kinds of lettuce. No idea that salads were so important in medieval France. I thought they just ate elk.

Chevigny—small (well, comparatively small), elegant, sitting in the middle of a huge expanse of lawn and gravel—shouldn't this have been a garden?

Azay-le-Rideau—a good example of a drive-by château candidate, although we didn't. Few details stand out, except the real tourist shop with aprons.

Lisses—nice, and sort of a sister to Azay-le-Rideau—good water setting, and inside the house you got to see the modernization that had been done, as the owners are now living in it. Unfortunately all in French. Former moat, now partly filled in. Unfortunately the tour was all in French and long.

Lodging, Part Two—Would You Like Toilet Paper with That?

After three days at Le Vieux Manoir, we changed locations to Richelieu and a three-star spa named Relais du Plessis, which had a nice website and good recommendations. Which only goes to show you: websites lie, there has been tremendous grade inflation in stars, and you can't really trust the Internet. (But then what can you trust, the government? Wait, they administer the stars. . . .)

We decided we had blundered into YMCA camp. Nice enough buildings although Spartan on the furnishings, no TV, no Internet, and decorated in a nasty combination of chocolate brown and orange. An outside deck where the only table for eating was (green plastic) but the best part:

» no soap or shampoo
» one towel
» terrible breakfast with bad coffee. Yes, France, bad coffee. "You can't get a bad cup of coffee in France . . ." The coffee actually gave one of our party diarrhea.

» no maid service; in fact when you checked out, you had to strip your bed and put the sheets and linens—if it's only one towel is it "linen" singular?—in a bright orange bag and take them out to the sidewalk. And also empty your trash. And keep the recycled bottles in one can, the other trash in another. And it was FULL, mostly younger families with children. It wasn't clear when the prayer service was.

The fancy B and B we first stayed at had no laundry facilities, and we are assured there were none in the whole town. So we washed our delicate things in the sink. At $250 per night, this seemed strange, but we're good sports. L worried that she had turned on the heater in the bathroom and was melting her dainty underwear. I am an expert in this I assure her. I do wonder why I didn't bring a small container of Woolite—I assumed that France was a civilized country and actually had laundry facilities.

At the YMCA there is a separate laundry room with three washing machines (one broken), a dryer, and a machine from which one can buy one helping of soap for €2—but it is broken as well. There is also a sixth magic machine that communicates with the others (wirelessly? Wired? Pneumatically? By Ouija board?) and you put all the money into this machine and push a button (one button for washer #3 is missing, and #3 is one of the working washers) and then it washes or dries or gives you soap. Note to French designers: always use six machines when five would do.

And this is three stars and they're charging you two hundred euros per day? One wine glass in the cupboards. No dishwashing soap, no sponge. Unpredictably weak Internet, available only in the lobby. We say again, three stars??

Food—You Can't Go to France and Not Talk about Food

The food ranged from spectacular to very good to awful, disproving the "you cannot get a bad meal in France" hypothesis.

We had dinner the first night at the "Le Poids something" in Richelieu, a random choice as not a lot was open. This was very helpful in a scientific way as it helped to prove conclusively: yes, you can get a bad meal in France.

An initial conversation with our tall teenage waiter, who had reluctantly brought us several pieces of bread: *"Est-ce que vous avez le beurre?"*

"Comment?"

"Le beurre, pour le pain."

"Comment?"

"Beurre, butter, you clod-like copy of Liberace."

It went downhill from that.

Or the Lion d'Or, strongly recommended by our keepers at the first location, where they won't serve you at all, *beurre* or no *beurre*. After twenty-five minutes of sitting there with menus and no water, no drinks ordered, no wine ordered, and the entire menu actually memorized, we left. L threatens to blast them on Yelp as soon as she can get enough connectivity. That will fix their butts.

The following day we were going to go to the *hypermarché* when we got done with elegant country houses and just get some bread and cheese for dinner. Well, also a bottle of €4 wine. But it was Ascension Day. All was *ferme*, even the Quickie Mart. So we ate the leftover bread and cheese in our room from the day before, and the potato chips had held up rather well also, but elegant it was not.

On the way to Villandry, a guidebook recommended a stop at L'Étape Gourmande, just out of town. We had lovely and delicious lunch in the gravel-paved patio among budding trees. Also found a very funny sign: an arrow pointing to *toilettes* on the first line and *cheverie* on the second. Used to be a cheese farm but more fun herding tourists than goats it appears.

We also stopped randomly for lunch at L'Aigle d'Or (golden eagle) because we liked its sign. An example of drive-by eating, on the way to Azay-le-Rideau from Chatonnière. Excellent, and complete luck.

Best dishes: the small coated cherry tomatoes at La Fourchette in Amboise (thin, crisp sugar coating, then dipped in *graines de pavot bleu* so the bottom half is covered in this blue/ black granular coating); goat cheese beignets with the salad at Le Patio in Amboise, dessert at L'Étape Gourmande outside of Villandry. Which was three layers—crumbles on top, white cheese in middle, mixed summer berries (currents red and black, raspberries) on the bottom.

And one more area where the French are ahead of us on food: potato chips. Of all things. Lays potato chips in France are available in the following ten, yes ten, flavors: nature, barbecue, bolognaise, spicy, *poulet rôti & thym*, *moutarde* pickles, *fromage*, *maxi craquantes nature* (most natural crunch), salt and vinegar, and (OMG!) cheeseburger. And who do you think invented the cheeseburger? Not the French, for sure. I am flabbergasted.

Roses and Iris and Centranthus, Oh My

Our Giverny visit is fabulous as usual. And it is always consistent. It was cold and slightly rainy but still had roses, clematis, and iris everywhere.

Chédigny—we left time on the plan for side trips and surprising discoveries, and this was one. This is "the village of roses," recommended to us by the host at the Vieux Manoir. It was a small village literally drowning in roses all in bloom, with no one home. All the mailboxes have a note "nonpublic SVP," as in don't just wander into my yard you stupid tourist. Well, then, don't grow such nice roses. There was to be a festival there in several days, but on the day we went, it was a ghost town.

La Chatonnière—we got there at ten exactly when it opened. The one guy keeping the gate had to unlock the parking area. This site was not listed in two of the three guidebooks. The small château is not open to visit at all, just the gardens—but five thousand roses, mostly blooming, many climbing over the pergolas and tuteurs on the edges of the garden sections. And fields of wildflowers at the garden borders, four gardeners actually at work, good plant labels, and sure, lots of boxwood but the profusion of roses was breathtaking. Very lightly visited—we were there for two hours and saw maybe three other people not counting the gardeners.

Château du Rivau—again not highly recommended. A medium-sized château, some very nice towers, the bottom two floors open although tarted up with goofy modern art. But the gardens were wonderful, not nearly so much boxwood, more "English cottage garden" design sensibility, and numerous roses. The castle moat had been filled and turned into grass, and all along the edges cascades of rambling roses, all in pretty much full bloom. Centranthus everywhere. And lots of everything everywhere, including more clematis than in other gardens. Best garden except for Giverney—wonderful stop.

Style? What Style?

Where have all the pencil-thin French women gone? I don't think we saw any. We saw lots of size twelves and occasionally really blimpy women, even young ones. What a change from the days of yore. Sadly, French fashion sense has degraded at the same time. Lots of casual clothes, including jeans and T-shirts and sneakers on person after person, male and female.

We saw one stylish couple the whole time, and they were Brits. Lots of $150 jeans. Lots of scarves, but poorly worn. At least there weren't any baseball caps, and certainly none worn backward—at least not yet. We did not feel underdressed, just surprised.

More surprises—they seem to like Americans. The gendarme in one of the small towns who has a Camaro and whose "dream" is to go to the US, and the waiter at the Hyatt—"Please speak English to me."

Not good surprise—the creeping insidiousness of the *supermarchés*—even in Richelieu. Soon the local *boulangeries* and *pâtisseries* and *boucheries* will be gone. But even these paragons of commercialism were closed on Ascension Day.

Very little smoking, and none in the nice restaurants.

Do as I Say

Don't rent a big Mercedes, it's just a car and it's too big for all the roads and parking areas. Smaller is better, besides we couldn't figure out how to work some parts of it, like adjusting the seats. Fortunately the GPS worked close to perfectly, which was very useful in finding where we were going.

Parking at the châteaux was never a problem. Probably someone figured early on that if each of these small villages was overrun with cars of tourists parking along the very narrow roads, it would not be good. It was also usually free. But the admission to the châteaux was expensive—never less than nine euros and sometimes as much as sixteen. And nobody takes

Amex and you really do need a credit card with a chip in it.

Our timing was good although the weather was spotty—four days of drizzly rain, then four days of not rain but cold and only bright and sunny the last two days. It was good to have packed raincoats and warmer clothes. Us Californians are so spoiled. But crowds there were not, limited tour groups, and limited groups of students getting in the way. We only felt crowded in one château and frequently had whole rooms to ourselves. And then there were the roses. . . .

Why a flea market in the middle of the Richelieu square on Ascension Day, and why were people there, with no food or drink near at hand, and the stuff was crap? Because they couldn't go shopping anywhere else since everything was closed?

How times change. The old days: prevalent use of cash, bathrooms were nasty, lots of French language, and lots of attitude. Today: credit cards everywhere, in some cases they would not take cash, plenty of English everywhere, really nice and clean bathrooms, and very little attitude. Let's hear it for the international financial crisis.

Interesting but Strange—All Our Trips Seem to Have a Fair Helping of This

Leaving the Blois château by the front gate, across the square is the Museum of Magic (Maison de la Magie). This is where the eight-foot-tall puppet heads of big golden salamanders come out of the four second- and third-floor windows, and move around in puppet-like moves, then go back in and all the windows close up. What?

So when you can't take one more château, think mechanized warfare and, aha—the Musée des Blindés. This is probably the world's largest tank museum—more tanks and armored artillery and mechanized personnel carriers than you would ever see anywhere else except maybe WWIII, but located curiously at the top of a hill in the small town of Saumur. Why exactly you would want to visit was not clear to one of us, but she was a good sport. Elegant and sexy gives way to brutal. It was mostly men taking pics and wandering about the tanks, the women mostly sitting outside. Strangely missing was an Abrams tank from US, but they surely had everything else, nicely displayed in a series of big warehouse rooms. And no place to eat. After enough tanks, we drove to a small *brasserie* overlooking the big fortress/castle at Saumur and ate a medium-quality lunch with less than medium-quality wine. We didn't feel it was necessary to go in the castle. We didn't even finish the wine. Time to go home.

Love and kisses, Bob

Afterword: I have been going to visit gardens, mostly in the US and Europe, for twenty-plus years now. It is an inoffensive pastime. The gardens are generally where they are supposed to be, so you don't have to chase them down. Their designs generally don't change in terms of garden architecture, so you'll see what the guidebooks, at least the garden guidebooks, say that you'll see.

The one variable is season. I don't know why it took me so long to realize this. But I finally did, and we picked the exact right time of year for these gardens in this part of France. The châteaux by themselves would have been fine, but seeing many of them with their gardens going full tilt was really amazing.

[16]

Wherein Our Hero Narrowly Misses Imitating Tom Hanks in Cast Away

September 2014

Dear Aunt Janet,

Summer has come in Leucadia and not gone. The beach is still lovely and the weather is uncharacteristically hot and even a little muggy. San Diegans are complaining bitterly about this. We have had one real rainstorm for one day since April. We complained about that as well—we don't expect rain in the summer, or any time really, and then we want it to fall where it will go into the reservoirs, not on us where it just goes into the ocean.

We also lost our good judgment and went to Hawaii, to the island of Kauai for a week in July. The smarter one of us remarked, "You know, we're leaving a house we could rent for two thousand dollars a week, at a beach well known as among the best in the world, where we have a fully stocked kitchen, plenty of towels, beach chairs, access to excellent fresh vegetables, and a full wine refrigerator with wine we selected and have already paid for. We're going to Hawaii where we will find essentially the same things, except all of that will have to be paid for again, but at higher prices."

"Oh yeah, well what about the Na Pali Coast?" I countered foolishly. But we had a nice package deal so off we went to Kauai and stayed at the St. Regis for five days, on three of which it rained, hard. This was not in the brochure. No rain pictures at all in the brochure.

Kauai is known as the "Garden Island," and it was indeed green as befits a garden, and the rain helps explain the green part. And it was overrun with chickens, which is not explained by either the rain or the moniker. Nor are there chicken pictures in the brochure. Kauai could be the "Garden and Rain and Chicken Island." What is not clear is why the locals, who do not seem overly wealthy or particularly opposed to eating meat, haven't simply captured the chickens, who do not appear crafty, in the way of all chickens. They could then wring their necks and stuff them in pots, pans, and rice cookers. It is said that the chickens all used to live in coops but Hurricane Iniki, which did knock the island around a bit in 1992, smashed all these not-hurricane-proof small chicken tenements, and ever since you have chickens everywhere. I am not sure if Iniki means "chicken liberator" in Hawaiian. I do not believe this is a good chicken origin story, but I have no better suggestions to explain the chicken mystery. There are no foxes or coyotes to right this imbalance of nature. The chickens at first appear quaint and colorful, but eventually look out of place and even a bit belligerent. Perhaps they want their cages and their regular food back.

Since we were there for this in particular, we toured the Na Pali Coast. It is steep, rugged, beautiful, and inaccessible by land unless you do a death-defying hike along knife-edge ridges of eleven miles each way, not a good idea in rain, perhaps not a good idea anytime. This particular coast stretches along the northwest corner of the island and is essentially a bunch of small beaches defined and isolated by very high and very steep bluffs. If you don't choose the hike, you can take a lovely eighty-five-foot catamaran and sail along the coast and admire things, including the gentle rocking of the boat in the white-capped sea. Or you can take a much smaller inflatable raft/speedboat thing called a Zodiac, propelled by two large outboard motors, and have your butt slammed into the seats with the traverse of each wave, and the rest of you doused with salt spray. For hours. Maybe the sea was rougher than usual because of the imminent approach of two hurricanes, which also was the source of the generous rain. At any rate, in a moment of abandon we made the bad second choice, mostly because the boat left from a site closer to the hotel. And a boat is a boat, right?

There are no seats on a Zodiac, so you sit on the round inflated sides of the boat and stuff your feet under tight little ropes strung along the floor, in place of real safety belts. And then you hold on for dear life to the other safety ropes running along the "seat." This is important to avoid getting bounced out of the boat, and served as a real test of one's ability to make and maintain a strong grip on a rope without having your hands cramp. No safety ropes on a catamaran, and you can stand up and look around. "Best weather we've had in eight days!" said our jovial captain through clenched teeth. He was a young Hawaiian named Jason whose trunks were worn so low on his hips while still managing to stay up that I wondered if he had been surgically altered.

Four bottom-numbing hours later having cheated death, we returned. "No more small boats ever again!" we pledged to each other, as we at last stumbled gratefully into the mud of the dock area. Jason graciously suggested five Advils and three mai tai's (not included in the fee) as a good follow-up to the trip. We took this advice and a two-hour nap that we deemed a part of the ceremony of thanks to the Hawaiian gods, whoever they are, for our safe return. This seemed to blur the memory and alleviate the lower back pain and modest spinal contusions. I don't think they have these opportunities in Nebraska—the sea and the cliffs thing, that is. You are fortunate in that regard.

Besides the mystery of why anyone thinks that a Zodiac is the right transport vessel for a pleasure cruise along the dangerous and stormy Na Pali Coast, there are the mysteries of the Hawaiian language.

It is said in the tourist material that *aloha* means "hello" and "goodbye," although perhaps not simultaneously. It is thus one of the eight parts of speech called (unsatisfactorily) an "interjection." But it is used profligately in Hawaii. There are frequent references to "the aloha spirit," which means what exactly? The spirit of hello and goodbye? The spirit of the islands? What is that? One of the people with whom we arranged our Zodiac "travel adventure" signed her letter "with much aloha," which meant in her case that they were going to kill us. A San Diego weather person is named Aloha Taylor and is said to be "one of SD's hottest TV chicks," which may or may not be true, but she has trouble staying in the camera's frame as she does the weather report and forecast. This leads to a somewhat disembodied performance. Could this be the aloha spirit, reporting from beyond the frame of your TV set's picture? The ghost of weather future?

And the Hawaiian language has another secret that they don't tell us *haoles*, allegedly a name for white persons meaning originally "no breath." This is because foreigners did not rub noses as a greeting and thus were not sharing the other party's breath. Wait, I thought you were supposed to say aloha as a greeting? I have never seen anyone in Hawaii doing this nose thing, so the no breaths appear to have taken over the field. Anyway, the word is *mahalo*, which you see and hear frequently in Hawaii and is supposed to mean "thank you." But in fact it does not. My friend Holly Hemphill discovered this on a trip to Oahu. She says it's a little Hawaiian joke on all of us, because what *mahalo* really means in Hawaiian is "asshole." Just look at these recently collected examples, and substitute the new and accurate translation, and I think you'll agree:

 » United Airlines flight attendants: "Please keep your seat belts buckled until the plane comes to a complete stop, mahalo."
 » Sign at Hawaiian Trading Post, Koloa: "Wipe Shoes Before Entering, Mahalo"
 » Sign at the Kokua Pizzeria: "Aloha Please Seat Yourself Mahalo"
 » Sign at the Kokee Museum in Waimea Canyon: "Suggested Donation $1.00 Per Person Mahalo"
 » Posted at the bottom of the menu at the Tiki Iniki restaurant in Hanalei: "No Substitution Kitchen Too Small Mahalo"

Besides traveling around to various places, back in Leucadia we have rebuilt a large concrete block garden wall that the trees had pushed over, and we are now planting the garden anew. The offending trees, who may not have been radical Islamists but caused trouble nonetheless, were carted away as punishment for their unprovoked wall attack, although not to Guantanamo. The whole process is great fun; one doesn't often get the chance to watch a large backhoe thudding around in your own small yard, or have a contractor who also has a country and western band and who calls himself the Catholic Cowboy. Or the chance to start a garden from scratch. It's a trifle expensive, however; the trip up the Na Pali Coast was cheaper.

I have also joined the local angel group, called the Tech Coast Angels. These are brave folks who invest in start-up ventures, so now I go to meetings and hear entrepreneurs describe fuzzily their new and wonderful ideas for improving or revolutionizing or doing away with various businesses or business practices, or for curing assorted diseases I have never heard of and do not wish to contract. The angel investors are smart, and the entrepreneurs are earnest and of wildly varying quality. Mostly the money-seekers don't tell their stories well. I went to the most recent investment meeting. The entrepreneur said, "Our advantage is that we have the first SDK for the IOT." I raised my hand and said, "WTF?" Ideas ten, communication zero.

There is progress on becoming a famous author. Slow progress. Nope, Oprah hasn't invited me on her show yet since she doesn't have one anymore, nor has Stephen Colbert. What you have to have first is an actual book, it appears. And now I have a book. It was printed at the end of June and has been sent out to traditional reviewers, and to Internet bloggers, who also review books. So far there have been two blog reviews published, both favorable. Done by people I do not know! And they say nice things!

There is now a website featuring the book, and it includes a blog where clever/interesting things (I hope) are written and published weekly, more or less, by me. And while we are speaking of shameless self-promotion, my marketing guy has made me set up a Twitter account, and even write things in it (@globeroamingceo). And a Facebook account (R. F. Hemphill or Robert Hemphill) where I now have three friends, up 200% from yesterday. Feel free to follow me (in the Twitter sense of the word, not in the stalker sense of the word, although I might find both flattering) or "friend" me or "like" the page on Facebook. I do wish that "friend" were not used as a verb, but it's too late. . . .

What there is not, yet, is the ability for normal people with good intentions and most importantly money to actually buy the damn book. It's on Amazon for presale and will be published as opposed to printed on 1 October, when it can actually be purchased. Kind of like the release date for a movie. If you peruse the Amazon page carefully, you will find that the book— *Dust Tea, Dingoes and Dragons*—is ranked number 4,605,507 of all Amazon books. Although there is no official number from Amazon, it is rumored that there are about seven million books available on their website. I am surprised that a book you cannot even buy is ranked as high as it is. I am assured that once a couple of copies are actually sold, this ranking will increase. My goal is to get into the three millions. If you scroll down further on this same Amazon page, you will find that my name has mysteriously changed to Renaldo. I pulled out my birth certificate to check, but it's got the same old name on it. Publishing is strange.

I will be back in Washington for an AES-sponsored book launch on 7 October, and around DC for a couple of more days that week. Then we are off in November for a Cornell-sponsored trip to Vietnam. I think the Vietnamese are our friends now. Or maybe they just hate the Chinese more.

Best wishes and much aloha (say, you don't suppose that aloha actually means dog poop, do you? Those Hawaiians, they're always kidding around, I wouldn't put it past them)—

Bob

Afterword: The AES CEO, Andres Gluski, not only offered to have a "book signing" for me at the company headquarters, he also had AES buy three hundred copies of the book to hand out to all the employees there. This was incredibly generous and gracious of him.

The event itself was a big success. I got to see lots of old friends who I had not seen in some time, and I got to tell stories that the newer ones had never heard. It was a real delight.

[17]

It's Better Without the Shooting

November 2014

Dear Aunt Janet,

Part One—Hanoi

There are a couple of classic Vietnam War T-shirts. The first has some variation of the outline of a map of Vietnam with the legend superimposed: "Participant, Southeast Asia War Games, 1961–1975: Second Place." The second has a similar background and the text is: "We were winning when I left." Although there are lots and lots of T-shirts available in the markets, we could not find either of these. Perhaps no one cares that much anymore, which is just as well.

I had always wanted to go back on a real trip (not on business) since being here before as an infantry officer and platoon leader with the 1st Cavalry. Hence we are in Vietnam touring about and seeing stuff. Or in some cases not seeing stuff. We went to Ho Chi Minh's mausoleum in Hanoi but he wasn't there, he was out on vacation. I didn't know you got vacations when you were dead, but socialism in general is hard to under-stand. Jane Fonda was not there either. The war does seem to be over, in case you were wondering.

This is a tour whose itinerary is a kind of a Whitman's sampler of Vietnam—some historical stuff, some war stuff, some "life in the villages" stuff, some natural beauty stuff, some forced shopping. Like seeing the US by going to a play in NYC, visiting the Washington Monument, eating barbecue in Memphis, seeing the Grand Canyon, and going surfing in Hawaii. It's a picture but not a complete one, and unless you do a lot of your own research and reading, you're captured by your guide and his view on what you're seeing. Fortunately our guy is OK—knowledgeable, candid, excellent attitude, and great English. And our group of fourteen Americans has no children in it, mostly retired professional folks who are decently educated and game. Four of the men are veterans, three of them including me with Vietnam service. But no one is annoying and no one routinely shows up late for the bus.

A few background facts and observations:

» The country is geographically the size of California, but with 95 million people, half under the age of thirty-seven. California has half that many. There are three large cities: Da Nang, Hanoi, Saigon—with other urban centers much smaller and 85% of the population still rural. This makes it the fourteenth largest country in the world by population.

» The economy has only been "liberalized" since 1991, which in this case means reversing the disastrous collective farm decree and allowing subsequent "openings" of various sectors. Capitalism down on the farm: in the seven years after private ownership returned from its vacation, the country went from a net importer of rice to the world's second largest exporter. GDP per capita in 2000 was around $200, it's now approaching $2,000. They're still fifteen or twenty years behind China, but closing.

» The infrastructure needs much work, especially the roads. There are only two short freeways, one near Hanoi and one near Saigon. The rest of the major roads are the same as forty years ago but without the ambushes. QL-1, the Highway 101/coast road and most important commercial artery, runs from north of Hanoi all the way to the tip of the Cà Mau Peninsula in the far south. Until four years ago when two bridges went into service, the Mekong Delta stretch of this road was still interrupted by two ferry crossings, with associated waits for traffic from one to nine or ten hours. When cars really begin to penetrate the market, the roads will be a huge problem.

» Everyone remarks on the motorbikes, and for good reason. Bicycles are largely gone from the traffic mix, even in rural areas, and the private car is still very rare and heavily taxed. But motorbikes are everywhere. They are driven with an attitude ranging from crazily aggressive at the low end to homicidally suicidal at the high end. It makes crossing streets an exercise in fatalism.

» The history of the country for the last two thousand years reads a bit like this: conquer some local people who are not Vietnamese, be conquered by China, resist, local uprisings, throw out the Chinese, repeat, repeat, repeat, repeat. For China, substitute France and the US, but only in the 1850 to 1975 period. Our tour group asked the guide the inevitable questions about Vietnamese attitudes toward the US. "Very friendly," he said politely. "You were just one more war." There was some grumbling in the group later along the lines of "Well, weren't we the *best* war?"

» The government has changed the second language taught in the schools from Chinese to Russian to English. They are very worried about China. The US Congress has very recently passed a law with substantial bipartisan support that allows the US to sell military weapons to Vietnam. The enemy of my enemy is my friend.

» The food was good to very good. You could eat the salads and raw vegetables in the better hotels and restaurants. The best meal we had was at a beachside seafood restaurant in Da Nang called My Kanh. It was steamed clams and mussels with ginger and

Thai basil—fabulous! We also attended a cooking class in Hoi An that was quite good. The spring rolls were good everywhere. And they serve pho, the national noodle soup, for breakfast! This is an advance over scrambled eggs.

» We did receive two guidelines on drinks: 1) Don't drink the tap water, anywhere; even the Vietnamese drink bottled water, and 2) Don't drink the wine, it's lousy. Fortunately lots of imported wine is available, and the local beers are quite good. We researched them carefully. Hey, it was hot there.

We started in Hanoi with the obligatory tour of the Ho Chi Minh Complex, to include his tomb and the small houses where he lived during his last ten years. The mausoleum of Uncle Ho is possibly the ugliest piece of Stalinist architecture I have seen lately. Maybe the big awful Palace of Culture and Science in Warsaw is worse; it's a close call. And Ho was not at home, he was out getting a facelift or something. It is said that he was embalmed rather than having the government honor his personal wish, which was to be cremated. He made this wish when he saw the plans for the building.

The square on which the mausoleum sits is maybe one-tenth the size of Tiananmen Square in Beijing. There are a series of mustard-hued, French-built classical/colonial buildings in the area; these are attractive but for the color. The Vietnamese government favors this color and all the government buildings we had pointed out to us in Hanoi were this same dank mustard. They probably got the paint from the Russians. In Saigon it was usually a cream/mustard color. The site is said to receive fifteen million visitors a year, but when we were there it had maybe a hundred.

We went to the Hanoi Hilton, not as you no doubt remember a hotel, but the rueful nickname for one of the several prisons where downed US airmen were kept, some for as long as seven years. John McCain is the most famous prisoner, but there were many others, including some of my Air Force Academy classmates. It is called the Hoa Loa Prison and still has an inscribed legend over the door saying "Maison Centrale," a French euphuism for prisons. Touring the prison is not pleasant. The facility was built in the 1885–1900 period, and the remaining museum portion is divided. One side is where the French held Vietnamese prisoners since their gentle colonial rule kept generating lots of revolutionaries and troublemakers. Frequently these prisoners were in leg irons. The other half shows small cells as well as several videos of US planes being shot down, and pictures of the US prisoners in happy activities. Like playing volleyball. Right, lots of fighter pilots love volleyball.

From the exhibits in the prison we conclude several things:

» Jails are bad regardless of who runs them.
» The French were especially bad jailors.
» The US bombing of the north was bad.
» The US prisoners were sorry and had a nice time while in jail.

Most of the original prison has been torn down and in its place is the first high-rise building in Hanoi, the "Hanoi Towers," which is half condominiums and half office space. It appears to have a high occupancy rate. I assume that the Vietnamese didn't have a strong enough sense of irony to build a hotel there.

The next day we drive to Ha Long Bay, several hours outside of Hanoi, and embark on a boat at the boat center. There are a lot of boats, big ferry-sized ones and just slightly bigger than sailboat-sized small ones that unpleasantly resemble WWII landing craft and where all the passengers wear orange life preservers. We were on a big one, thank goodness. Most of the boats have no passengers and are just anchored there, maybe twenty of them. They float alongside the stalled real estate condo development of the "Ha Long Bay Resort and Condominiums" project whose administration building is decorated on either side of the front doors by giant sphinx heads. I don't recall the riddle of the sphinx being "Who will buy all this real estate?" or perhaps "Where will we find the money to finish this construction?" but maybe it has been updated.

Ha Long Bay is a big UNESCO World Heritage site, composed of 600 square miles of bay and 1,900 small islands, of the "sticking straight up picturesquely out of the ocean with really steep sides and oriental-looking pine trees on the top" type. You motor out to see them and then cruise around among them standing on the deck and going, "Wow this is pretty cool," and it is. Then you go down below to get warm and have a beer and good Vietnamese food for lunch. The water is calm and the Dramamine works and you get back to port and get on the bus and fall asleep as you ride back to Hanoi for three hours.

In the morning we walk about the "old quarter" in Hanoi. It's old all right, and very commercial and full of folks selling stuff on the sidewalks and inside their little shops and women carrying around baskets of produce on the carrying sticks, called *thuc hien thanh* in Vietnamese but always referred to by GIs as "choggy sticks." I guess this is an efficient way to carry things, I haven't tried. And I don't see any men doing this. We also creep down one of the alleys and "visit" a local apartment. Not attractive. Then we fly to Da Nang to stay at an elegant beach resort.

Part Two: When I Was There Before—Guard Duty

Quan Loi Fire Base, home of the 3rd Brigade of the 1st Cav to which I was assigned as an infantry first lieutenant, was pretty far out into Indian country. It was near places with names that now mean little—the Parrot's Beak, the Angel's Wing, War Zone D—but were then recognized as quite hostile locations, full VC control, NVA staging areas, etc. The base had a perimeter surrounding it, with bunkers every fifty meters or so, and three big observation towers, their small boxy tops supported by metal skeletons, and accessed by climbing up exposed ladders. They were just like the ones you see forest rangers looking for fires out of, or Nazi prison guards manning to keep resourceful GIs from escaping from gruesome POW camps. The towers were probably not more than ten meters off the ground, and had been built by the 1st Division, the US unit who had built the base and initially garrisoned it. Quan Loi was really a headquarters and support base; all the infantry fighting troops who were assigned to the 3rd Brigade were out in the field, chasing the bad guys. But every night, someone had to man the perimeter, which for some reason I never could discover, was called the "green line."

Sitting inside a hot bunker all night, waiting for VCs to attack, was not good duty. Thus it rotated among the enlisted personnel at the base, with the forty-plus bunkers manned each night by two EMs and the perimeter divided into three sections, each commanded by a lieutenant, again drawn from a duty roster. Your job, when your turn came up, was to drive or walk between each of your assigned arc of bunkers every hour or so and make sure they guys manning them were there and awake and not smoking dope. You also had to call the TOC (tactical operations center, the headquarters for the base) every hour and let them know what was going on. What you inevitably said, after you identified yourself, was "Stirep: negative change." In English this meant: "There is no change in the situation here since last I reported." I always wondered who made the first report to establish the situation from which subsequent change was calibrated, but there was no answer to this question. The rest of the time you were supposed to be up in the observation tower, observing. There wasn't a heck of a lot to see, since it was black as pitch outside the perimeter. This was explained by: a) we were in the middle of a plantation of rubber trees, and the nearest village was some number of clicks (kilometers) away; b) Vietnam was an underdeveloped country with not many electric lights around out in the provinces anyway; and c) there was a war, and the other side usually didn't attack you while carrying flashlights or torches to light the way.

The observation towers were pretty classic construction—a metal scaffold, a wooden box with partial sides, and a roof sitting on top. Sandbags lined the outside edge of the box, and the inside as well, to provide protection. You climbed up an exposed metal ladder to get in, lifted a trap door in the wooden floor, and there you were. You had a radio and several other enlisted troops with you, also selected from a roster. In short, you had no idea who any of these people were whom you were Queen for a Day of, whether they knew how to fire their M16s or not, nothing.

You had a radio so you could send your hourly reports to the TOC, and any special reports required when the local VCs got drunk and decided to attack while wearing miners' helmets with lamps blazing. It was like so much else in the war: tedious, tiring, and tactically questionable. Also boring and usually not particularly dangerous, except when it was. We were an unattractive target, probably not because of these highly trained guards dozing in the bunkers and three lieutenants peering pointlessly into the darkness, but because of all the minefields and flares and barbed wire that surrounded the place. It was occasionally scary, though, because each of the guys in the bunkers had several hand poppers—handheld rocket-propelled parachute flares that could be fired off if he thought he heard something— or someone—in the wire. You could be sitting there peacefully at three in the morning, dutifully peering into the blackness from your tower, and suddenly be scared out of your wits by somebody lighting off one of these miniature rockets. I drew this duty three or four times at Quan Loi, and never saw a soul to shoot at, although I did get regularly startled by the troopers in the bunkers.

About the third time I pulled green line duty, however, I had the bad luck to be in charge during an attack. We never got attacked in the standard Korean War-style of a mass of crazed communists running at us in an orderly human wave-style line. Mostly we got rocketed and mortared. This made a fair amount of sense, viewed from the perspective of the other side. The best thing we had at Quan Loi was all our helicopters, and there they were in the middle of the firebase, sitting alongside the runway. The easiest way to destroy them was to fire rockers or mortars at them—forget this tedious storming through the barbed wire and getting blown up by mines, shot at by cooks and mechanics, and at least having your best uniform snagged by barbs on the wire. Even if you got safely past the bunkers, there were still lots of tents and hooches to maneuver through, which by that point would have armed GIs in their underwear pouring out of them, ready to shoot anything they saw, including probably other GIs. And you still had to carry explosives with you to blow up the helicopters, then you had to go back through all this same mess and confusion to escape. Bad idea.

As an alternative, you could set up mortar tube, drop in a dozen rounds very quickly, take it down, and leave before we really had figured out where you were, lined up a fire mission or launched a helicopter gunship, and came around to try and shoot you. Rockets were even better in some ways—just poke a couple of sticks lashed together in an X into the ground, generally aim the rockets toward the airfield, light all the fuses, and walk away. Of course, neither of these methods would rank high on any military list for accuracy since you had no forward observers with radios watching where the shells hit and radioing back corrections. You didn't want to stick around that long anyhow. But every ten or fifteen days, you and your VC buddies could decide to go screw up the Americans a bit by sneaking near the base and lobbing a few rockets into Quan Loi. Somebody had carried the damn things all the way down from the north, might as well shoot them at something. You could always get lucky.

Being on the other end of such an attack was disconcerting. The noise was the most remarkable and distinctive part of it. In the war movies, incoming rounds sound pretty much the same as outgoing rounds—but then that's all just stage explosives, so why wouldn't they? In a real war, there are all kinds of explosive sounds, and you quickly learned to discriminate the friendly ones from the others. In the field, AK-47s sound boomier than M16s. At a firebase, there's always some sort of random artillery firing going on. At Quan Loi, we had assigned to the brigade a battery of 175 mm guns, called "Long Toms." They fired a big shell for a distance of more than twenty miles. They were used almost exclusively at night for "H and I" fire—harassment and interdiction. Because their rate of fire was less than one round per minute, they weren't much good as fire support if you had a company in contact, but they had a very long reach. Every night the S-2 section would pick out road junctions or supposed assembly areas and send a list of targets to the battery, and every night, on a sporadic basis, the big guns would go off. It was unclear to me, given the inadequate intelligence and thus the essentially random nature of where they were shooting, whether any of this ever did the slightest bit of damage to the NVA. It did harass those of us on the base. Except that after a while you learned actually to sleep through it.

Incoming rounds were a different story. They made an unforgettable high-pitched screaming noise, very loud and very scary—much louder and more menacing than anything you could imagine. You heard it the first time and turned to ask someone what in the world that was, except that all the someone's you could ask were busy scrambling for bunkers to jump into. So you learned. You could be in a sound sleep and suddenly find yourself scrambling into a bunker twenty meters away from your hooch with no memory of exactly how you got there, except that it was clear that there was a rocket or mortar attack going on. It was best if this didn't happen while you were in the shower, because the "bunkers" inside the base were just holes in the ground, with a lid of PSP (pierced steel planking, usually used for making quick airstrips but with many other evolved uses) and a layer of sandbags on top. These weren't fighting positions like the ones on the green line, they were just crude bomb shelters. And if you jumped into one while wet, you ended up covered with red mud. This was still preferable to being blown up. You just had to hope that your shower hadn't run out of water while you were being attacked.

The night in question was probably sometime in April. We hadn't been mortared or rocketed for a week or so. It was about one-thirty in the morning. I had already made the rounds of all my unknown troops three or four times. They were all about as alert as one could ask for, and I didn't smell marijuana anywhere. I was up in the observation tower with two black Spec- 4s, enlisted guys who turned out both to be from the brigade maintenance company. The usual pleasantries had been exchanged—how long you been in country, when do you go back to the World, what unit you with—and we were all standing there, looking out over the edge of the tower at the blackness, listening to the continuous nighttime noises of a jungle and the occasional bangs and crashes of outgoing artillery. I was eating a C ration can of ham and lima beans, one of the twelve "menus" that came in a case of C rations, and one of the most despised. For some reason I liked it, but this particular item was referred to by grunts generally as "ham and motherfuckers." This was not a flattering designation, although its etymology was obscure.

Sure enough—*screeeeeeeeeeeeeeWHAM!*—an incoming rocket rounds lands somewhere in our general one-third of the base, near the edge of the perimeter. We all automatically drop to the floor of the tower.

Let's pause on this point for a minute. We are in, as noted above, an "observation" tower. Our mission is, not surprisingly, to observe things. Hard to do from flat on the floor, looking at the sandbags along the side walls of our wooden booth. Several more rockets come in, same noise, same posture on the part of sector commander and his two assistant observers. I was also by this time aware that I was lying in a smashed puddle of ham and beans.

The rockets stopped, so after a while we got up. I radioed the TOC that we had incoming and were checking to see that everybody along our sector of the green line was OK and that we weren't being attacked by screaming hordes. They duty officer on the other end of the radio said, "Roger that," and politely asked if we had a location on where the rockets were coming from so they could call in some red leg (artillery fire). Of course we didn't since we hadn't been in prime observing posture during the attack.

As I was walking around checking on everybody I thought some about this, then climbed back up into the tower. About an hour later, another attack came screaming in—five rockets each separated by about ten seconds. My two guys immediately hit the dirt, or rather the floor, again, but by this time I had concluded that these rockets were a) not capable of being aimed; b) if aimed, would be trying to hit the helicopters, and c) if they hit the tower by mistake, lying down behind the sandbags would not do one single tiny bit of good. So I just stood up and watched. I wasn't being especially brave, I was mostly curious to see if I actually could see where they were coming from, and what they looked like when they landed and exploded. It was fascinating and exhilarating—the explosions looked very much like a traditional fireworks display. There was an orangish burst of fire, with trails of sparks shooting off in all directions, then slowly dying out. The entire size of the fireball and sparks probably wasn't twelve feet in diameter, a lot smaller than I would have thought. But because the guys setting them off weren't total idiots, and because these were high angle of fire munitions, and because we were surrounded by forest, I couldn't see where they were coming from at all.

I looked at my two EMs lying on the floor of the observation platform. "You know," I said, "I've been thinking about this. These rockets are mostly hitting the ground and exploding, so all the shrapnel is either going outward at ground level, where we are not, or going up, where we are. All of this platform has sandbags, even the roof, but not the floor. And that's the most likely place the fragments are going to come from. Right below us from a rocket explosion on the ground. You know what would be the best thing to do during the next attack to minimize your chances of getting hit?"

They both peered up at me curiously. "What's that, loo-tenant?" said one.

"Well, I've been thinking about this," I repeated helpfully, "and what you really should do up here is just stand up as straight as you can, then you'll present a much smaller potential target for any fragments that come up from below and penetrate through these crumby floorboards. That's were the most danger is."

They both stood up slowly—the attack seemed to be over for the moment—and then one said, with a certain weary air of explaining the obvious to the FNG ("fucking new guy," GI slang term for someone just arrived in-country), "Loo-tenant, I don't care what you been thinkin', we ain't standin' at no fuckin' attention while those VCs shoots rockets at us."

Part Three: Da Nang and Hue

The morning of our first full day in Da Nang, the group is suddenly overcome with an outbreak of the dreaded lacquer factory syndrome (LFS), a troublesome medical condition that is insufficiently monitored by the World Health Organization. When it strikes, your tour guide adds to the agenda a visit to a commercial establishment usually owned by his uncle. The establishment is always said to employ handicapped people or young children who otherwise would be sold into prostitution. The visit invariably includes a short tour of the workspace to prove that the products on offer are in fact not being made by some machines in Shenzhen. And then bevies of salespeople latch onto the group, explaining how cheap the (rugs/lacquer ware/herbal remedies/jade jewelry/cultured pearls/coconut fiber kitchen items including chopsticks) are and how the factory can ship to any place in the world. In our case it was a visit to what is introduced as a marble factory although it doesn't make marble, since it is a natural substance created through geological processes. Nor does it make marbles since the demand for this child's plaything has been subsumed by video games. Try finding marbles at a toy store. Even better, try asking a child whether he or she knows how to play "marbles." It's no wonder that young people don't want to talk to you.

What this factory cum showroom/sales floor/display area does is take large chunks of marble that come from somewhere around Da

Nang—where we are not told—which are then sawed and carved and polished into many different figures, all with varying degrees of unattractiveness. And in varying size, ranging from too big to put in your pocket to too big to put in Yankee Stadium. A short list of the subjects of the marble carvers' art follows: dragons, toads with Chinese coins on their backs, toads with Chinese coins in their mouths, Buddhas fat and Buddhas ascetic, Kwan Yin figures, foo dogs (usually in pairs), elephants, jumping dolphins, leaping lions, a boy riding on the back of a water buffalo, small crucifixes (nothing life size), urns, big vases, round tables, stools to go with the round tables, round tables with carved tops so you can't really use them as tables, strange abstract swirly things, and partially clothed women. We pause to announce that the part that is unclothed is always the top half of the woman in question, she is always carefully draped from the waist down.

What you don't get: partially clothed men, St. Francis of Assisi holding a bird in his hand, sleeping Mexicans wearing big sombreros, coyotes howling at the moon, the Statue of Liberty, darling little kittens, Winston Churchill, Babe Ruth, sea otters swimming on their backs, or reproductions of any of the wonderful and generally ominous Aztec stonework, mostly coiled snakes.

Who buys this stuff? Who has room in his or her house for a seventeen-foot-long marble reclining Buddha? The salesperson helpfully notes that for the heavier pieces they ship them only to a port of entry, you have to go there and pick them up, presumably with a crane and a tractor trailer. Yes, I can see showing up at the Port of Los Angeles and asking about picking up my polished brown marble twelve-foot-tall figure of the Virgin Mary.

And the place we visit is only one of a whole string of these "factories," all running along the beach road. Probably at least five large ones and several smaller ones. Same images. Why and why here?

Somewhat marbled out, we proceed to visit Hoi An, another World Heritage site. It is known for being a cute little well-preserved town of modest size. The well-preserved part is bounded by a small river and consists of three major streets, each running for five blocks or so. No cars are allowed, but motorbikes with bad intent are permitted. There are lots of small shops and "art galleries" and small restaurants and temples, all of human scale. There appears to be a height limitation on the buildings. Some Western tourists but not a lot. One group is all wearing the conical hats called *nón lá* or "leaf hat." The tourists perhaps do not realize how completely silly they look, but World Heritage sites do not include a limitation on dumb tourist behavior. Which is unfortunate.

We take a walking tour with the admonition to keep together and "no shopping." We generally comply, and it's marginally interesting. We start at the central food market because it's photogenic and because all us tourists like to *oooh* and *ahh* and sometimes throw up at the stuff there. Hiep, our guide, explains to us what all the odd fruits and vegetables are. The silkworms are local, the apples are imported. Cheers for you, international trade. Then we are released for "free time" which is really "shopping time." The marble factory obviously wasn't enough, we need more souvenir keychains and clever T-shirts. It's bright, sunny, and downright hot, although Hiep confesses that this is the worst possible month to visit Da Nang, as it is the height of the rainy season. So we're staying at a beach resort? Love beaches in the rain.

We finally have first-class Vietnamese food for lunch at the Cargo Café, starting with three kinds of spring rolls, along with Biere Larue, another Vietnamese beer, also quite good. The roster of good local beer now includes Hanoi Beer, Saigon Beer, Biere Larue, and 333 Beer. The latter is odd as to its name. "When I was here before" the only local beer was something called "33 Beer," which was also referred to as *ba muy ba*, which is Vietnamese for, of course, thirty-three. It's the same beer but it was sold to Fosters and the new owners decided to add another three to make it clear that something had occurred. I do not understand marketing.

The state of real estate development in Da Nang is odd—about half of the beachfront property on the beautiful wide beach on which stands our resort is either vacant with decrepit fences announcing fancy new projects but protecting vacant land, or it's half-built stuff. Buildings with floors and roofs and support columns but no walls or windows or paint. Ghostly, really. And then next door is a real resort with landscaping and bellmen and nice rooms and pool boys and all that goes with a beach resort. Across the "beach road" from the beach resorts, on what must surely be almost as valuable property, is generally nothing—some agriculture, small plots of lettuce and other vegetables, or very small stores, but mostly nothing. Odd indeed. This is not the only place we see frozen development, but it's by far the grandest.

We visit a small village outside of Da Nang and run into the old folks getting their pictures taken at the community center. They are happy to see us. Not much to do in a village. It starts raining and stops raining and starts raining. We go back to the hotel, where it stops. I take a walk on the beach in the on/off rain and a guy riding a horse comes out from somewhere and rides down the beach and another guy fails to get his kayak launched. The waves are pretty serious and the red flags are up.

We go back to Hoi An in the late afternoon for a cooking lesson and to walk around with all the lanterns lit. It is really quite nice and very festive and there are lots of people out doing the same thing, mostly Vietnamese and Euro tourists. The cooking lesson is fun and we eat the spring rolls and the crispy pancakes that we make. They serve us lemongrass ice cream and it's remarkably good and just weird enough that you realize again that you're in Vietnam. "Nuoc mam" goes into everything, well probably not the ice cream, and while you may think that it is just fermented fish sauce, it is—but which fish get fermented is important. The best kind to use, we are instructed, is based on anchovies, but there are also varieties whose operative fish is tuna, salmon, and perch. I did not know this. I wonder what the tuna one tastes like.

Then on to Hue—we drive up in the bus, including a hair-raising portion of QL-1 leaving Da Nang and going through the Hai Van ("ocean clouds") Pass. It's a very narrow two-lane road, occasional guardrails, steep drop-offs, and beautiful views of Da Nang and the bay and the beaches. This is the major and only road running to Hue and on to Hanoi from Da Nang. Note that Da Nang is the third largest city, Hanoi second largest. There's also a railroad and you can take a train from Hanoi to Saigon in a mere thirty-two hours for the 1,000 kms for an average speed of 33 mph.

Probably you can do better on the road, but this part is scary. And it is unchanged since the sixties.

Hiep says that the Ho Chi Minh Trail is now a paved two-lane highway, and he and a friend have driven it, but no one uses it because it adds too many miles to the trip, as you have to cross the country from the Laos border where the trail is to get to the coast, which is where all the action is. Only about a third of it is complete, however.

After a lunch that includes Hue Beer and that thus raises the approved local beer list to five, we tour the Citadel, a major feature of Hue. It sits on a ninety-degree bend in the Perfume River and overlooks the commercial part of Hue. This is a sort of Imperial City of Vietnam, except there's no Tiananmen Square in front of it and it was only built in 1802, although it looks older. A twenty-foot brick wall surrounds the whole complex. And inside there is the "purple imperial city" that does not seem to be purple. It also does not seem to be there. This area was largely destroyed during the Tet Offensive of January 1968, first by the VC who took it by surprise and dropped the one major bridge across the river, thus making it way more difficult to attack. It was, after all, designed as a fortress. Eventually the marines rooted out the occupiers, but not before the VC had rounded up and executed about one thousand Vietnamese government folks and probably just middle-class people who had the bad luck to live in the neighborhood.

About 90% of the buildings were destroyed during the fighting. These were one- to two-story temples and audience halls and passages and living quarters, all wooden buildings with tile roofs. Air strikes and artillery apparently made short work of them. It would have been a mess to fight through. The entire outer wall is bricks and mortar and has not been destroyed, so the pictures of the engagement show marines clambering over it, but that wasn't so difficult. There are still shell and rifle holes, gouges really, in many parts of the wall, inside and out.

What you have inside now is mostly open grassy field, with three or four major buildings—the moon gate, the emperor's hall, an ancestor temple— still standing and/or refurbished. And some rebuilding is underway. The plan is to fill the site again with what was there before.

The site is big and monumental and dramatic, and that's nice, and it's a UNESCO World Heritage site. But one wonders whether any money available shouldn't be used for some of the other more consequential sites in the country. Note the first: this one dates only from 1802, which is not very old in Asian terms. There are lots and lots of significant sites in Vietnam older than this by a lot. Note the second: this whole thing was built by and lived in by the Nguyen dynasty, the emperors who are generally credited with losing the country to the French. If it were me, I would rebuild a couple of the Cham sites, where the stonework rivals Angkor Wat, and leave this one as it stands. But that's just me.

I have never, ever, ever wanted to ride in a rickshaw. Ever. I think you look silly and you feel conspicuous and it seems incredibly exploitive and the apotheosis of "round-eye tourist in Asia." At the end of the walking tour of the Citadel, which ends nowhere near our hotel, we are all hustled into prearranged rickshaws for "a tour of the neighborhoods" that involves going slowly along the streets and looking at the storefronts and having small children wave at us and shout hello. Fortunately these are bicycle rickshaws, not the classic kind pulled by a guy running between two poles like a horse pulling a cart. Ugh. I am slightly mollified when the lowly coolie in the conical hat peddling in the rickshaw in front of me pulls out his cell phone and has a conversation.

We are taken to a "French" restaurant, said to be the best in Hue, called Le Jardin, for a treat—a Western dinner. The food is so-so; Caesar salad is not made with iceberg lettuce and besides Caesar salad is a classically American dish. There is a six-piece Vietnamese musical group who serenades us before dinner by playing way too many songs, way too many being more than one. Whiney, nasal, arrhythmic. They do intersperse "Auld Lang Syne" and the theme from *The Godfather* with the more traditional pieces. They pick up and leave before I can request "Foggy Mountain Breakdown."

The next day we go for a "dragon boat" ride which is nice, as I am out of Dramamine but the Perfume River is calm and the weather is warm and pleasant. Cruising along in the boat gives the crew a chance to sell the Americans more Chinese pajamas and metal replicas of Buddha and embroidered pictures of slim girls in ao dais and conical hats and so on.

There are several takers. We then visit the seven-level pagoda that is a functioning Buddhist monastery and religious center, the same one whose head monk drove to Saigon in 1963 and set himself alight, starting a chain of events that led to the downfall of the president, Ngo Dinh Diem. And perhaps the ultimate American commitment of ground troops in a civil war in which we had little or no strategic interest. George Santayana, where are you when we need you?

Then we visit the tomb of Minh Mang, second emperor of the Nguyen dynasty. He ruled from 1820 to 1841 and spent many of his last years building himself a nice burial area, twenty-eight acres including several large ponds and four temples, each on a significant platform with steps leading up to it. The plan was for him to use this as a recreation site before death, and then to be entombed afterward. After all, the only place he had was the 1,700 acres of the Imperial City sitting on the Perfume River. And courtiers and eunuchs and concubines and servants and slaves to take care of him there. You can see why he would need a country place to which to escape.

I am now maybe becoming a communist as well as a snob with regard to history. I couldn't keep from thinking about the resources used to build this place and thus diverted from other purposes, perhaps like building an army so his descendants wouldn't shortly have to turn the country over to the French. Or building some roads better than the ones they have now. Or educating a few more of the people. I also kept thinking that this place was newer than Mount Vernon. It's rare that I get to think that about some historic facility we're visiting. At least the day is pleasant and the site is pretty and it doesn't start raining until we get in the bus.

At the hotel the four of us who are veterans go to the rooftop bar and have several drinks to celebrate Veterans Day. When I was here with the 1st Cav, I am sure I did not think that forty years later I would be sitting in a bar in Hue overlooking the Citadel in a country not only at peace, but one rapidly developing and making sounds about buying arms from the US. I suppose they have to replace the ones they seized from the ARVNs when everything fell apart in 1975. M16s only last so long.

Part Four: When I Was Here Before—Trip to Saigon

When you run a PX in a war zone, which for some curious reason I was assigned to do at Quan Loi after I came out of the field, it's an all-cash business. No checks, certainly no credit cards, nobody buying on "an account" (they might be dead the next day and then what would you do). This makes some of the accounting easier—no depreciation, no amortization, none of that confusing noncash stuff that always gums up income statements. And as best I can remember, we sold all our goods at cost, so we could never have any profit. Of course, our space and electricity were free, as were the GIs who ran the store with me. We did have some civilian help, and they got paid, but basically the model was "inventory in, inventory out." Good thing, because we weren't long on CPAs out in the middle of the jungle.

What this did mean was that cash piled up. The PX was the only "commercial" installation on the firebase. Anything else you needed either the army gave to you, you scrounged from the local economy, or your wife or girlfriend sent it to you in a care package. No banks, no post offices, nothing like that. And everybody in Vietnam got $50 a month to spend from their paychecks—the rest was sent home or put in a savings account—so they had some cash and literally nowhere to spend it, except this PX. Every so often, you had to open the safe, scoop up all the money into a duffel bag, and have somebody take it back to Saigon. Physically. Actually two somebodies, one with a gun.

For a while I just made one of the sergeants working at the PX do it, since being a courier didn't really meet my concept of what the army wanted out of its first lieutenants. Of course, I wasn't entirely sure the army had planned for me to run a PX in the middle of a war, either.

One day in February, I was telling my hooch mate, Chad Ragland, about what a pain it was to have to send all this cash back to Saigon every so often. Chad had been in the field as a platoon leader, same as I had. He was a very handsome, well-educated guy with a sort of an English look—light complexion, wavy dark hair. He was serving as assistant brigade S-3, but he was one of many, and didn't have a lot to do other than man the

TOC during one of the evening shifts. And because there wasn't much going on in our AO (area of operations) and there were lots of assistants, even this wasn't a real burden.

In the middle of my grousing about the cash run Chad says, "Wait. Perhaps you're thinking about this wrong."

"Huh?" I respond intelligently.

"Have you ever been to Saigon?" he asked. I think he knew that I hadn't. "Well, think about it for a minute. They send a special plane for the PX money?" I told him that of course they didn't, we didn't even have a regular schedule, we just sent the money down when there got to be too much to fit into the safe.

"So you have to catch a hop down, and then you have to catch a hop back?" he asks. "And is all this a precise, carefully scripted, timed performance?"

"No," I say, "of course not, we're going Space A and there's always people DEROS-ing [leaving because their tour was up] and bumping our guys off, or the plane doesn't come because they need if for an operation, and shit like that."

"Well, I believe," says Ragland, "that you are turning down a three-day leave in beautiful Saigon, and instead giving this important mission to several of those worthy E-7s who work for you. Do they ever come right back the next day from one of these cash runs?"

I couldn't remember that they had, although they were generally so adept at being hard to keep track of that I had long since given up on that anyway. The PX had turned out to be a nice place for the S-1 to stick people with profiles, physical limitations that kept them out of the field.

"Any rule against an officer taking the cash to Saigon?" he asked.

I said, no, this was entirely a PX sort of thing that nobody else on the base either knew or cared about.

"OK," said Chad, "the next time that it's time to do this, let me know a couple of days ahead, and you and I will go off to Saigon, couriers extraordinaire!"

I thought about it, overcame my scruples—the PX would run just fine without me for a day or two, without question—and decided that sure enough, we really ought to go to Saigon. No sense spending a year in Vietnam, including mostly in the worst parts, and never see the capital.

"Fine" I said, "but you have to be the guard and carry the gun."

"Deal," said my hooch mate.

About three weeks later, first thing in the morning, two young first lieutenants are waiting at base ops at the airfield, a fancy name for a small tent with a desk and a bored Spec-4 inside. We're on the manifest for the next flight heading east toward Saigon. There was a daily courier flight on a Caribou that went to Binh Loc, where the Division HQ was, and that seemed a likely place to start. We made that flight, and then luckily caught another from Binh Loc to Long Binh, the army's main base just on the outside of Saigon. We took our duffel bag of cash, hitched a ride on a passing jeep, and deposited the money in the PX main headquarters. We had done everything we were supposed to, and it was only about noon.

"OK, we're going into town!" said Ragland.

"Wait, shouldn't we check into the BOQ [bachelor officers quarters]?" I asked.

"Hemphill, we are in one of the most famous and luxurious and beautiful and storied cities of the Orient, and we damn sure aren't checking into any BOQ on any army base! We are going to the Caravelle Hotel."

"What's that?"

"It's the famous old French hotel on Tu Do Street, the heart of the city—it's where Graham Greene stayed, where Somerset Maugham stayed, where Papa Hemingway would have stayed if he hadn't blown his head off with a shotgun in Idaho instead. Come on!" Ragland had a romantic streak that was pretty appealing at times.

"Do we need a reservation" I asked timidly, still unsure as to whether this was such a good idea.

"We are the mighty American military, this is a war, and who in the world would turn such as we away if we be in need of lodging?"

That gave me pause. It's important to take a minute to explain how we looked. How we looked was dirty. Quan Loi was a firebase smack in the middle of the rubber plantation area of Vietnam, near the Cambodian border. The rubber plantations were there because the soil was particularly suited to growing rubber trees. That seems to follow. The characteristic of the soil that was most important was its laterite content. Soil with a high laterite level is a rich magenta red; it also seems to have special properties that makes the dust not only stick to clothing, but stain it, and this color adheres through multiple washing cycles. Bear in mind that the firebase was nothing but a modest unpaved (red dirt) runway, surrounded by tents and equipment parks, maintenance areas, fuel dumps, ammunition bunkers, and the like, all of which was in turn surrounded by a chain of sandbag-clad bunkers, fronted by triple concertina and minefields. It was a big oval and sitting on the edges of the airfield in its center were probably 150 helicopters, which were always taking off and landing.

And because it wasn't the monsoon, it never rained, so the soil turned into pernicious red dust, and the red dust was everywhere, into everything. Every time a helicopter landed, it generated a hundred-foot column of dust that wafted over the firebase, adding yet another layer to the hundreds of layers of red dust already present. It wasn't quite like a sandstorm, but it was inescapable. Every tent and every piece of gear was tinted red or coated with red dust. And because it wasn't the monsoon, and because we were out in the field, and living in tents, there wasn't any air-conditioning. And because it was the tropics, everyone sweated a lot every day, from the moment you got up in the morning. So your uniform got sweaty in about fifteen minutes. And every morning, after the first fifteen minutes, every uniform on every soldier had cakings of red dust. It was just routine and ordinary, from the colonels down to the privates. Except when you got to Long Binh, where everyone seemed to have access to a laundry service that was doing more than just using the local river. They had fatigues that actually were still green rather than reddish green. And they were even pressed and starched!

And let's not forget headgear. There was an ongoing debate in Vietnam about headgear. Concisely, it was the helmets vs. the boonie hats. A boonie hat was a round cloth hat, soft, brim all around, low crown, and of course olive drab. It actually looked pretty cool and tough. The helmet was a steel helmet. The arguments went thus: helmets are heavy and hot and make noise when you bang into things like tree branches when you're trying to sneak quietly through the jungle. Boonie hats are not heavy and not hot and don't make noise. They also don't stop bullets or shrapnel. There were no points awarded for looking cool, which helmets did not. Since this was the army, the helmet/boonie hat decision was usually made by the division commander, or equivalent person of rank. Of course in the rear areas like Saigon, it was 100% boonie hats, since little shrapnel was expected as a daily matter. The 1st Cav had always been a "helmet" division, with no boonie hats allowed anywhere, for anyone—not in the rear, not off duty, not allowed. You get the picture.

So here we are in Saigon, wearing curiously red-tinged fatigues and clunky metal helmets, with Chad carrying his M16 in case Jesse James ambushes us. It is clear that we do not fit in, that we are in fact JUST OUT OF THE FIELD. Humans being what they are, if you can't fit in— and we couldn't—then you make a virtue out of necessity. We were proud that we were field troops, rather than fat-assed headquarters weenies who'd never been shot at or eaten a meal in the rain or slept on the ground their whole time in Vietnam. We adopted "attitude" as our credo long before it was popular. We were sure we deserved respect and admiration, although we expected bad treatment. We knew secrets that the Saigon commandos didn't know, and we knew that they knew it. It made looking like dirt-colored guys with funny helmets almost all right. Armed with attitude, we caught a cab into town. And they let us into the hotel with alacrity and graciousness. I began to relax.

"What do you want to do now?" asked Chad. "It's probably too early to start drinking and chasing women."

"What I'd really like," I said, "is a decent souvenir of Vietnam. Not some poor VC's ears, not an AK-47 that I'd have to mail home in pieces, not a poncho liner, I want an example of the folk art of the country. And what I want is a dragon mask. Probably we can find one here in Saigon."

"You want what?" he asked, more than a little incredulously.

"You know, a dragon mask, like they use during New Year's for the dragon dances. It's a big papier-mâché thing and a guy sticks his head inside it and holds on to it with his hands, and then dances along the street. The head has a long cloth tail, and other guys are in line behind him underneath the tail, forming his body."

Chad hated to seem unknowledgeable about anything, so he just said "Of course." We got in a cab, after first asking the driver if he spoke English. "Yes, GI" he said, so that proved it. Then it got harder.

"OK, I said, "we want to go to a store where we can buy a dragon mask. Like they use on Chinese New Year."

No reaction, other than agreeable puzzlement. "You want girls?" the cab driver asked.

When in doubt, act out, I thought. "No girls. We want to find a dragon mask, like this." I scrunched up my eyes, stuck out my tongue, held my hands up to my ears, and bobbed by head around, going "*yaa, yaa, yaa*" in a sort of guttural growl. I thought it was a pretty good imitation of a dragon mask, and Chad got into the spirit of things. He scrunched up his eyes, stuck out his tongue, and made the same bobbing head face at the driver, only going "*grahh, grahh*" rather than "*yaa, yaa,*" which I had to admit was a nice touch.

"OK GI, OK," said the driver, and we took off like a shot.

After a while, though, it became clear to us that we were merely driving aimlessly through Saigon, especially after we passed the same heroic statute three times.

Chad said, "You know, this poor guy thinks that he's got two crazy Americans in his cab, just out of the field, and armed to boot, making weird faces at him and growling. I suspect that what we've done is scare him out of his wits, and he's trying to look compliant, but he hasn't got a clue as to what we want. Probably thinks that if he drives around long enough we'll forget it or see it. Or decide we'd rather have some girls after all."

"We need a dictionary or some American that speaks Vietnamese so we can get a translation of the word, then he'd know what we wanted," I said. We both thought.

"I know," said Ragland, "we'll go to the American embassy. They'll surely help us."

This time the cab driver knew where to go, even without animated facial gestures, which is probably a good thing since acting out "American embassy" would have been even harder than "dragon mask." We pulled up in front of the American embassy, on a curiously empty street—no cars parked at the curb or anything. Suddenly, about six large MPs surround the cab.

"Oh shit," I think, "here we are in Saigon, two grungy infantry lieutenants, we got no orders authorizing us to be here, and if all we're doing is delivering PX money, why are we doing it at the American embassy? We're screwed."

But the MPs, after seeing that the cab has American officers in it, very politely point out that no one can stop in front of the embassy because they might have a bomb in their car, so if we could just move down the block, they would appreciate it.

"OK, yes, sure, we're very sorry, Sergeant, we didn't know . . ."

So two field troops stalk into the embassy annex, expecting the worst. Ready for bureaucracy and rejection, we approach the receptionist. She politely asks us what we want, we explain that we need someone who speaks Vietnamese. With no further ado, she calls someone, asks if he can help two lieutenants with a problem. Nice looking middle-aged guy comes out, takes us into his office. We tell him we need to know the Vietnamese word for dragon mask. He doesn't ask why, he doesn't ask who we are or why we're here or how come we're so far from the Cav's AO, he just rummages around in several dictionaries, finds the word—*long mianju* or something like that, and even writes it down for us. We are incredibly pleased and surprised—it's almost like we're disappointed not to have been treated badly, especially because after all, we're field troops, and everybody in Saigon is headquarters weenies, and the embassy most of all. Remarkable.

We get back in the cab and say to the driver, "*Long mianju.*" He looks blank for a minute, then says, "Oh, *long mianju*" and sticks out his tongue, squinches up his eyes, holds his hands up behind his ears, bobs his head from side to side, and goes "*rargh, rargh.*" Everybody laughs—it's like "Why didn't you just say so in the first place?" Off we go.

We wander our way deeper and deeper into non-colonial Saigon. The streets become narrower, more crowded, the shops smaller, but somehow they have more merchandise, much of it hanging out into the street from awnings, poles, and whatnot. Vendors are selling food from carts, cooking it over little stoves made from old five-gallon water cans. Lots of people on foot and on bicycle and on motorbike, not so many cars. I am in heaven—I've always liked Asian cities—Tokyo, Hong Kong, Singapore, even Bombay and Delhi—and this is sure enough one—same sort of sights, sounds, even smells.

Ragland appears not to be in heaven. As we progress, he slouches deeper and deeper into the seat, and seems to be curling up into his helmet. I ask him, enthusiastically, if this isn't great.

"Do you know where we are?" he asks.

I'm confused by the question—we're in Saigon, of course.

"No," he says, "we're in Cholon." Cholon is the Chinese part of Saigon, and it was basically taken over by the VC during the Tet attacks.

"Looks safe to me," I say.

"Bob, this is a guerrilla war, it always looks safe until they drop a grenade into your truck!" Ragland sinks even lower into his seat, muttering something like, "Nine months in the field without a scratch, now I'm going to get killed in a taxicab in Cholon, looking for a fucking dragon mask . . ."

We find one, we buy it, we don't get blown up, we even figure out how to find the army post office and ship it home—not a great item to carry around with you for four more months. Back at the Caravelle we shower, taking lots of pleasure in a real bathroom and real hot water coming out of the shower. Then we eat dinner at the rooftop restaurant of the American hotel down the street—real steak and french fries and salad—real American food. Amazing! From the roof you can see all the way to the outskirts of Saigon, where the occasional flares and the flashes of outgoing artillery leap out against the general background of black. The night is not quiet, but sitting at a white tablecloth restaurant with a nice bottle of wine, it all looks more like fireworks than war.

"Time for the bar girls!" says Chad. Our hotel is on Tu Do Street, the concentrated location of the bars frequented by American servicemen. And thus the location of the bar girls. It worked like this: lots of reasonably nice-looking young Vietnamese women, dressed in Chinese style dresses, are lounging around the bar. You walk in, and one, or even several, come up to you—depends on how much else is going on—takes your arm, says hello or something and always, "You buy me one Saigon tea?"

And the answer is yes, you buy her one and you buy yourself a beer and then you talk. Sure, she touches your arm, tells you how good looking you are, asks where you from, you like Vietnam girls, all sorts of flirty questions. And if you really look like a player, then she asks, "You buy me oo-ees-soo-key [whiskey]?" Of course, each of these beverages is costly to purchase, and no doubt merely colored water. But that's OK. It seems a bit strange, but that's just because there's really no Western analog. It's the geisha in Japan, or the bar girls in modern Tokyo. It's flirtatious companionship; it's the hint of sex without the sex. On the other hand, we're just out of the field, we maybe don't know the rules and rituals quite as well as the others.

Chad is particularly taken with one attractive girl. We come back to her bar a second time, then a third. Each time she is more glad to see him. Each time he buys her more oo-ees-soo-key. Finally he asks her to come to his room at curfew, and gives her his room key. She agrees gladly, tells him she never sees real soldiers, guys who kill many VC, the enemy of my country, etc.

At 10:00, we go back to the hotel—it's the curfew for all Americans in Saigon; we have to be off the streets, mainly for security reasons. We sit in the lobby and have a couple more beers. The curfew for the Vietnamese is not 10:00, it's 11:00. Chad is eager with anticipation, I'm pretty curious myself. At about ten minutes before eleven, there is a low but distinct motorized roar in Tu Do Street. We step out onto the porch of the hotel. All the bar girls from all the bars are out on the sidewalk, standing in little groups in front of their respective bars. Coming along the street is a veritable army of young Vietnamese guys on motorbikes. Each guy stops at the appropriate bar, picks up his girlfriend, she hops on the back of his bike, and off they go. Amazing sight—like some sort of odd harvest or choreographed modern dance routine. In ten minutes the street is completely empty. Chad is minus both girl and hotel room key.

I at least have my dragon mask.

Part Five: The Mekong Delta and Saigon

We fly to Saigon then get in a bus and drive the three hours to Can Tho, largest city in the Mekong Delta. This is one of the things I have been looking forward to, as I have never been to this part of Vietnam, war or peace. The land is supposed to be flat and watery since it is, after all, a river delta for the tenth longest river in the world, home to twenty-five million Vietnamese mostly doing rice farming and fish farming and informal but intense motorbike racing. Sure enough, we see lots of rice fields and lots of flooded fields that may hold fish or something else. In fact, that's all we see in the fields except for an occasional small clump of banana trees or mango trees. It is also said to be "laced with canals" but I am a skeptic. I start to count to see just how many canals there really are. In an hour on the road, we cross twenty-four canals and the two branches of the Mekong, which the river splits into when it leaves Cambodia. Progress in the bus is slow along a narrow four-lane highway running through every town that there is between Saigon and Can Tho. I assume we are averaging twenty-five miles per hour, but that could be generous. So that means that we cross a canal every mile, give or take. And that's only the ones flowing east, since we are heading south. I concede that this meets any reasonable definition of "laced." The short answer to the question "So what's the Mekong Delta like?" is: flat, green, and watery.

There's not so much to see, after the water. Can Tho is a modest 1.2 million-person city of low-rise buildings and wide enough streets and lots of commercial street life and not much else. We take a boat trip to see the floating market, recommended in the guidebook as a must-see item for Can Tho. Actually this is the only item at all recommended for Can Tho; no temples, pagodas, war memorials, dramatic pieces of landscape, just the floating market. So we see it. It is men and women in medium-sized boats selling fruits and vegetables to men and women in slightly smaller boats. It's a wholesale market, we aren't expected to buy anything. Besides, I don't at the moment need twelve pumpkins or a sixty-pound bag of sweet potatoes.

The next day we take another boat trip and see more riverside and more canal side. We go through a large canal that cuts in half a populous island called something Vietnamese. I am still in data-collection mode so I start counting how many boats I see. In ten minutes we pass seventy-three boats of various sizes, and none of them are tourist boats. That's a lot of boats for a small channel.

We then visit a candy factory that is a very small business employing seven total persons, and is being viewed by roughly eighty-five tourists, us and a bunch of Europeans. There's not so much that is interesting about watching someone boil sugar in a pot to make taffy, or cutting the taffy into pieces and wrapping each piece by hand. It does make you glad that you went to college. And now I know where all the tourist boats went. We are served samples of the taffy, small squares hand wrapped in cellophane. Two of our number try and eat the entire thing, wrapping and all. Not completely successfully.

Our last three days are in Saigon. It is everything that the books say it is—big, bustling, more traffic, more tall buildings, very commercial, full of hustlers and street commerce and crowded knockoff markets where a Montblanc pen is only ten dollars. And this side by side with very nice hotels and quite elegant shops. Riding in we travel along the Saigon River. As we get to the downtown area there are eight identical and very large billboards on the other side of the now pretty small river, clearly designed to be seen together. The four on the left have an image of Uncle Ho and political exhortations to good citizenship, loyalty, respect for the communist party of Vietnam, don't throw paper in the toilet bowls, etc. The four on the right are one big advertisement for Heinekens. We lost the war but we won the peace?

In the morning we visit the Presidential Palace, now the Reunification Palace, left intact except for the gates since 1975 when then president Thieu *"di-di-ed"* (slang for took off or left) to the US along with Nguyen Cao Ky and the other vice president. The building is big and square with very sixties architecture. This is the place where one of the iconic photos of the Vietnam war was taken, the one of the two NVA tanks breaking through the twin wrought iron gates of the palace. With smiling NVA infantry riding on top of the tanks. This is a bit of a giveaway. The infantry doesn't ride on top of the outside of tanks because it's dangerous and it blocks the driver's vision and if you have to traverse the turret rapidly you whop the infantry guys in the head with the gun barrel and they fall off and are run over. So clearly no one is really shooting at them or putting up any resistance. The president has flown the coop and all the ARVNs long since knew that the game was up and have thrown away their rifles and taken off their uniforms and are running home in their skivvies. The tankers could have stopped and simply pushed opened the gates and driven in.

The building has been left as it was, with the president's briefing room and the bunker with the maps of all four corps areas and the old Bakelite phones and the old radios still in place. Two tanks, #844 and #390, big white numbers freshly painted on their sides, sit near the gates on little concrete pads. In the gift shop you can buy a replica of tank 390, $4.00 US. But if you go back and look at the photos, the gate crashers were #6 and #843. It's important to read the documents.

We went to a lacquer factory next. I amused myself thusly:

"Of commercial things there's nothing tackier

Than visiting a shop where they sell you lacquier."

Before we go into the restaurant for lunch, our guide says, "I recommend you the seafood noodle soup. It's very good."

"What's in it?" asks one of our number. "Beef," says our guide with a straight face. He's probably always wanted to do that.

On our last organized morning in Saigon we made the obligatory trip to the Cu Chi Tunnels. It was a hot, long, bumpy ride, like rural Vietnam in III Corps always used to be. We walked around in a forest and looked at replicas of punji stakes and spider holes and bunkers and tunnels and manikins of NVA and VC sitting around peacefully, well clothed and armed. At least there weren't any pictures of American POWs or atrocities. It's hard to dramatize a lot of small connected tunnels that are also dark and hot and made of dirt or technically the absence of dirt and so are dirty. Several group members climbed through a small section and came out the other end. Their knees were dirty. Seemed fitting.

In the afternoon, L and I walked to the cathedral and the old and nicely restored post office and then down Tu Do Street to the Caravelle Hotel. This main Saigon street was originally named Rue Catinat by the sensitive French. "Catinat" was the name of one of the warships that said party used to conquer Vietnam. It was renamed Tu Do, or "Liberty" Street, by the South Vietnamese in 1954. But that wouldn't do, and when the northerners took over Saigon in 1975 they renamed it Dong Khoi, which means "General Uprising." It is now lined with very upscale stores—Versace, Chanel, Hugo Boss, Hermès, Gucci—and no cheap bars. Oh, there's also a very large HSBC building.

We went to the bar on the roof of the hotel and looked out over the city. This used to be the highest place in town, but no longer. We had a glass of Dom Pérignon to celebrate the strangeness of life and our intense appreciation for being alive in a country where so many people died. A small ceremonial moment, but an important one.

We walked sweatily back to the Sofitel, took a shower and a bus to the airport, and went home.

Love and kisses, Bob

Afterword: When I found out that I was going into the army and thus to Vietnam, I was in graduate school. I didn't particularly like graduate school. I had figured out that the only thing that a PhD in political science would qualify you for was teaching in graduate school so you could make more PhDs in political science. Hence I was not overly troubled by my upcoming change in occupation and venue.

My favorite professor, with whom I shared this information, said, "You will have a unique experience in Vietnam that many of your fellow citizens will not have. You should write it down. And the easiest way to do this is in letters to your wife or friends. Make sure that they keep these for you to have when you return."

I followed this advice on the writing side as well as I could. In truth, there is plenty of time in a war when nothing is happening. But you have to stay where you are and look alert. Perfect setting for writing home. I asked my then-current wife to save all the letters, and she did the best she could, but when I finally got around to reading them, about half were missing.

My thought had been to take my dad's letters from WWII, which my mother had carefully saved, and write a book interspersing our two sets of letters. But then I read my dad's letters, and they were, well, awful. "Tonight we had canned peaches for dinner at the mess tent." All of them were like that, nothing about flying or dropping bombs or shooting down Japanese planes or losing squadron mates or narrowly escaping death. My father was a smart and educated man, so I was mystified. Finally I came to the answer—all his letters home to my mom were censored before they could be sent. Any mention of interesting military stuff was edited out. Mention of which island they were flying out of—censored. Details on how well the squadron was doing—censored. Information on the squadron's losses—censored. I am sure that after a bit of this the rules became clear so my dad simply stopped putting anything censorable into the letters. This made the job of the censor less difficult, and the letters really boring.

So there you go—the letter above is as close as I have ever come to writing up some of my experience. Norman Mailer and The Naked and the Dead *are safe.*

[18]

For God's Sake, Don't Order the Salt Cod

May 2015

Dear Aunt Janet,

It had been a year since we'd traveled to the Loire region of France, relying on our own resources to figure out where to stay and what châteaux to visit. So we had naturally forgotten all the bad parts and only remembered the good parts, of which there were many. Well, heck, let's do it again, only this time in Portugal, we said to ourselves. Neither of us had spent any time there and it continues to get good reviews. It's always "the next Spain" or "the next southern Italy" but not usually "the next small crumby country with bad food," which would have been more accurate, at least some parts.

We bought a couple of guidebooks on Amazon, did a couple days' worth of making reservations, told American Express to get us tickets, and off we went.

Portugal is long and thin and rectangular; Lisbon and Porto are the only real cities. It has France on the north, Spain on the east, the ocean on the south and the west. Lisbon is on the west coast in the middle, and Porto on the coast in the north. The "Algarve" is the southern end of the country and is famous among Euros who don't have a lot of money as a great beach area. Nobody who has ever been to Hawaii or Florida or even the outer banks of North Carolina says that, but we weren't going to the beaches so that didn't matter.

Lisbon

We started in Lisbon at the Hotel Avenida Palace, a reportedly five-star place, with big tall windows and two balconies both looking out over the Rossio Square, one of the main ones in Lisbon with grass and statues and such. It seemed lovely until that evening at eleven when the soccer game let out and all the fans, all wearing the same type of red jersey, came down the street and drunkenly marched around the square, shouting and singing and blowing horns, for approximately six hours. Or so it seemed. Someone had just beaten someone else, one presumed. I knew that the English were big soccer fans but hadn't expected it from the Portuguese. And big old elegant colonial hotels with tall windows and balconies are not good about sound proofing. It wasn't a great start.

The next day we went to the biggest site in Lisbon, the Jeronimo Monastery, which is misleading because it's got a pretty darn big cathedral with the two-story square monastic building, and another very long hall with "apartments" or just a lot of rooms. It is on the Tagus River in the southwest quadrant of Lisbon. And a World Heritage site to boot.

Note that this is one of the best examples of the "Manuelite" style, named after King Manuel, who presided over Portugal when they discovered and then owned roughly half the world. The style's maxim appears to be: "Leave no stone uncarved!" It's gothic if gothic were suddenly out of control and any item—animal, vegetable, or mineral—was fair game to become carved decorations. Inside the monastery we saw gargoyles of a bishop, a lion, a horse, a sheep, a dragon, Jiminy Cricket—but no snake or dragon or the Chinese zodiac would have been complete. One sarcophagus inside the cathedral is a sculpted figure of a woman lying on top of her coffin reading a book. Next sarcophagus: man lying on top of his coffin, holding a sword.

The entry to the cathedral clearly posted this sign in English and several other languages: "No Shorts, No Tank Tops." The dress of 58% of the tourists entering the cathedral: shorts and tank tops. The dress of 40% of tourists: shorts and T-shirts. Remaining 2%: cannot be described accurately.

Entry into the church was free, but to go into the monastery cost five euros. But there was no posted dress code.

We stopped for lunch at a small restaurant that proudly advertised, on its menu no less, that it had free Wi-Fi in the bathrooms. Multitasking a big demand in Portugal? After lunch we wandered over to a big white marble statue of Stalinist design, sited at the river's edge. It paid tribute to the "discoverers" from Portugal during the age of exploration. There were twenty-eight of them, individual large marble figures who were all moving purposely up a ramp as if getting ready to jump into the river and get on with discovering although they were missing a boat. There were twenty-seven men and one woman; she's kneeling, toward the back. Salazar, former dictator of Portugal, built it in 1960—no explanation of why he waited this long.

We headed back toward town and passed but unfortunately did stop and go into the Tower of Belem, not recognizing that we haven't gotten enough ornamentation in the monastery and cathedral. Another Manuelite masterpiece, also crowded, dangerous (open stairs, no railings) and hot. Only two stories, which does not make it a tower in my book. At least it would have been hard to fall to your death.

In a testament to "wandering around," we also passed the National Museum of Ethnology, which wasn't in any of our guidebooks. We figured this out because it had a two-story banner on the front with a picture of a large African mask. It was uncrowded and wonderful, although there was a seven-piece touristic band playing in the foreyard.

We went to the Tile Museum, which was full of tiles, mostly blue. Then we climbed up one of the seven hills that the city is known for, although not by me as I could only find this one. It had bits of a fort on top, nice views of red tiles on the roofs of the buildings, and lots of blue tiles decorating vertical surfaces. This latter phrase or some variant including the words "lots of blue tiles" could be repeated every other paragraph, but we won't.

We had dinner at a fish place where L ate a lobster while we were sitting next to the large lobster tank; they watched us. I had the first of many bad versions of salt cod, the national dish. This is the second sentence that could be repeated every other paragraph.

Sintra

Sintra is one of seventeen World Heritage sites in Portugal. It is an easy train ride from Lisbon. There are various castles/palaces there, two on top of the two town hills. There's one old and sort of famous and broken-down one but looks like it could have meant business. It is called the Castle of the Moors, built of stone around AD 1000 when the Moors still owned all of Portugal as well as Spain. The other is much newer, in good repair, and appears to have been designed by Walt Disney on acid and painted by Joan Miro in his sleep. Lots to wander around and ask yourself, "Why, really, did they build this?" and then get on the train and go back to Lisbon and more cod.

Sagres

We wanted to see the "easternmost point in Europe" so we drove down to Sagres, on the far southwestern corner of Portugal. It was windy and cold when we checked in to the Days Inn equivalent. It had a small pool and there were some hardy Brits "sunbathing." When you have the UK climate, you're willing to settle.

It turns out there are competing "easternmost points." One in Sagres with the remains of a fort and some flowers and a very small chapel of no importance. Henry the Navigator was said to have launched one of his voyages of discovery from here, except that there's really no harbor, just cliffs. The next day we went up the coast about four miles and found Fortaleza and its lighthouse, the other claimant. It also had a small fort/castle, slightly more interesting, and equally cold and windy.

That evening we went to a local restaurant called The Hangout that advertised "American food." Sadly, no cod; we had a hamburger and Roquefort pasta (American Roquefort?) and found that the waitresses were from Vancouver and Boston. They were both wearing warm sweaters.

The local square in Sagres had a modest statue of Henry the Navigator. The trunks of the trees in the center of the square were covered with brightly colored crochet tubes. We didn't see this anywhere else and there was no explanatory sign.

We went back to the *pousada* (inn) where despite Sagres fame as the location for kicking off the age of discovery, there was nary a picture of Henry or Vasco da Gama. It is interesting to note that the Portuguese focused on voyaging down the coast of Africa, then around the Cape of Good Hope. Vasco da Gama led the crew who were the first Europeans in India. Other Portuguese "discoverers" moved on to southeast Asia, then to China and ultimately Japan, setting up trading outposts as they went. But when Magellan (who was actually Portuguese, real name Magalhaes) came to the king of Portugal requesting funding to head west, he was rejected, as had been Columbus before him. The 1492 deal where the pope divided up the world between Spain and Portugal at least gave Brazil to the Portuguese. Seeing the country today it is hard to imagine how they mounted such an ambitious and largely successful campaign of discovery— but they did. Talk about punching above your weight! Probably they were just looking for somewhere warmer.

We washed our underwear and it dried quickly on the windy balcony and did not blow into the swimming pool. We did not know at the time that this was a Portuguese tradition.

Evora

The drive up the coast and into the middle of the country to Evora was easy—good road signs, good roads, little traffic. Evora is a classic walled city, and the whole place is a World Heritage site. You find the classic narrow twisty streets, overcome by the classic too many cars parked everywhere. And no street signs.

Unfortunately we finally found our hotel. The Residencial OS Manueis was said to have good English from the jolly host, a good location, breakfast on the terrace with a view of the city. It actually had no elevator and very long and very steep and very slippery stairs going from the street up to the place. We decided that it should have been named the Hotel of the Alpine Steps. No one was available who spoke any English, jolly or otherwise; there was no breakfast on the terrace, and no noise insulation at all. The rooms were nun size if you were smaller than even Sally Field; the room so small it had no chairs in it which was a good thing as the chair would have had to sit on the bed and we were already sitting there as was our luggage. The bathroom was so small it looked like it had been rescued from a failing cruise liner—maybe that Italian one that ran aground. Except probably the liner had bigger bathrooms. For a while after we got there the room had no water at all. No noise insulation, and raging soccer celebrations in the late evening, of which we could hear every word even with the window closed and bolted. Sometimes €60 is not a good deal.

We were close to the city square, where, as no one mentions much, most of the Portuguese portion of the Inquisition took place. There is one really great site, the Palace of the Dukes of Cadaval. Blue tiles inside compete with lots of gilded wood and real gold everywhere, and the tiles lose. You could go up on the roof and walk around. We also liked the very nice Roman ruin of a temple of Diana, with lots of columns still standing.

And then there's the Church of São Francisco, with walls all inlaid with human skulls and bones. Unpleasant and somehow disrespectful—I fail to understand the allure.

We took an excellent megalith tour with a smart guy named Marius. His English was very good, he had started and ran his own company, and had good archaeological knowledge. It was interesting to see the calendar circles and the dolmen—sixth to fourth century BC. The site is very poorly maintained and signed. It is all in private ownership, so Marius and his tours arrive on suffrage. We were urged to write the Evora city council suggesting more resources would be appropriate, so we did. They didn't write us back.

The most interesting original bit was a funerary site with fifteen skeletons and associated funerary goods. It was located in an artificially constructed rock crypt with six large stones five-by-eight-feet wide making an oval, capped by a very large capstone, and then the whole thing covered with rocks and dirt to resemble a small hill.

When the first archaeologist had finished getting all of the rocks and dirt off, to open the place up he used dynamite—a well-known and precise excavating instrument. This blew the capstone into four or five pieces, and since this was essential to the site, it all collapsed. At least the skeletons and artifacts had been removed first. We think.

Nazaré

A beach town on a cliff sloping gently to the beach, hence a very steep place, but hard to get lost—just head downhill. There is a long beach of nice sand except for the broken glass and the dog shit. We arrived around eleven, and some people were there already on the beach, although it was windy and a little cold. Yes, as before. Probably Brits.

A funicular (*ascensor*) runs you to the top of the cliffs where there were more houses and predictably another church, and lots of souvenir stands selling rooster things (corkscrews, bottle openers, magnets, T-shirts, coffee mugs, snow globes, etc.) and warm wool ponchos. And a great view of the long and not especially crowded beach, and the equally uncrowded harbor.

The local women in Nazaré wore seven-petticoat skirts which made them look like they were wearing barrels covered in cloth. They also wear odd turban hats. This "native dress" was no doubt subsidized by the tourist board. A few even went for the all black, little old widow look, which qualified them for a double subsidy.

We are told that Nazaré was a fishing village until a few years ago when tourists discovered it. But why did they build a funicular here 125 years ago, roughly coincident with the construction of the Eiffel Tower? I don't think the fish used it.

We saw lots of colorful and photogenic instances of clothes drying on balconies. We suspect there could also be a subsidy for hanging out your clothes on your balcony. Dryers have been around a long time and don't cost much. I am also uncertain of how really interesting it is to take pictures of someone else's underwear when it is not on them.

Fátima

We took a leisurely journey from Nazaré to Coimbra, the weather had gotten a little warmer and it was only fifty miles. Our first goal was the Monastery of Batalha, a religious building said to be "the country's most glorious gothic church." And one of the few places to get three stars. It was built by some king or other to commemorate the Battle of Aljubarrota, the 1385 encounter that nailed down Portuguese independence from Spain. No, we hadn't heard of it either. But no matter, despite significant effort, we could not find either parking in the town or the monastery itself. We left it in God's hands and headed for our second choice, Fátima.

Technically this is the Basilica of Our Lady of the Rosary of Fátima. It has grown from a rocky outcrop where three shepherd children in 1917 saw a vision of the Virgin to a big deal—a huge square, two big churches, and many pilgrims, 9.4 million in 2012. On the way, we passed many people walking alongside the road, heading toward the site. Most of them were wearing Day-Glo safety vests, which was good as the roads aren't much for sidewalks. At the edge of the site is a clearly marked and roped-off path through the plaza and on into the sanctuary. At that point most pilgrims kneel and form almost a half mile long queue of devotees proceeding slowly forward on their knees. Even if you're wearing knee pads, as some were, this is an impressive expression of belief. One woman was crawling forward on her stomach. Most of the people on the square, kneeling or not, were not tourists. There was, however, ample parking, so maybe you didn't have to walk all the way.

We went on to our last stop, Conímbriga, a former Roman settlement, back when they owned Portugal. I was surprised by this but shouldn't have been, since the Romans at one point owned all of Europe. Nothing but foundations and bits of walls left, and terrific mosaics. Very few people, given what an interesting site this is.

Coimbra

Another World Heritage site, especially known for the university there. But first we roll snake eyes on hotel choices.

The Hotel Astória is on the river, and right at the end of an extensive pedestrian mall, and close to the university. But despite its name, it's a down-on-its-luck art deco hotel with no parking, no clear idea about parking (only after intense questioning is it revealed that there is an underground garage a block away that always has space), shabby carpet with stains and holes in the treads on the stairway, one slow elevator, no Wi-Fi in the rooms, a room that smells bad, no laundry service, squeaky beds, no screens on the windows. Not a good place, but it must have been lovely at one time, perhaps before cars were invented.

The university is the World Heritage site here. It sits at the top of a steep hill you can only walk up. There is a large and beautiful church at the top—two, actually, but only one is open. However, the key is the plaza where one finds the Royal Palace with an open-air view from way up on its tower. Second is a very impressive church with lots of tiles and a wonderful large organ, and the usual altar of three stories, all gilded and all heavily ornamented and worked, lovely and completely gold covered. At the south edge of the plaza overlooking the river stands a big statue of King João (John) looking a bit like Orson Welles playing Falstaff.

The Library of King John is the real centerpiece of the site. A long two-story rectangle divided into three large rooms of two stories, each lined completely with books to the ceiling. And gold work over the central passageway at each of the three rooms. And gold coming down the walls. And gold covering the bookcases and the tables and the chairs. And gorgeous painted ceilings. It's literally breathtaking to see this much wealth devoted to the preservation of books. Access is limited so it's not crowded, but you do have an assigned time to go in, and a bell rings after your twenty minutes are up. Magnificent.

Leaving Coimbra we stop at the Convent of Saint Queen Isabella (Convento da Rainha Santa Isabel), the woman/Spanish queen who financed Columbus. This in itself was perhaps miracle enough to grant her beatitude. And then he found something. It is not clear why the convent is here and not in Spain. And by the way it is far better than its one-star guidebook rating, especially the chapel, which again is nothing but gold everywhere. Who needs a bunch of blue tiles if you have discovered America and all that gold?

Porto

As usual, very, very difficult to find the hotel given one way or closed or streets so narrow no one could drive one car down them, except they were two-way streets. I would like to say that we were by now used to this, but we were not.

We open with dinner along the Douro River at a restaurant with a great view, but the worst meal of the entire trip. This isn't easy. Cod with bones, cod mushed up with bread and without the garlic. Cold red wine with carbonation—grape Kool-Aid made fizzy. Indifferent waiter. Sausage made of gristle. Black sausage—did they add food coloring? It was only black outside. Tasteless cheese—this is really hard to do.

Church of Sãu Francisco—this is the only thing for Porto listed in any of our guidebooks that receives three stars, and it deserves it. It is sometimes called the "golden church" and that's pretty accurate. We thought we had by that point seen lots of churches and palaces (and one library) with a lot of gold, but this surpassed any of them. You almost had to put on your sunglasses to see it.

We did the obligatory port wine tastings in several of the "lodges," but it was generally too sweet for us. We're California spoiled, I concluded.

Because it was there, we took a short boat trip of two hours, up the Douro River, in a slow-moving tourist boat. We were assured that if you go further up the river, it gets really interesting. Maybe.

General

It was very hard to park or find parking in every city we visited but Lisbon, and we didn't have a car there. Too bad they haven't discovered valet parking. On the other hand, the roads were very good, very little traffic, well signed and easy to navigate. Very, very little traffic.

The cities are a little shabby and not ready for prime time for tourists. Accommodations, even five-star ones, were generally not great, the food only so-so despite lots of fish available. The wine surprisingly good and cheap, ditto the local beer. White wine in the south—Vinho Verde ("green wine") was especially nice, the Albariño also.

You could get by on English most of the time but sometimes not in the places where it was most needed, i.e., the hotels.

If you are thinking of going into the colonies business, you have to ponder your business plan. The choice of generating wealth by extraction vs. agricultural or industrial production is a difficult one, even if there are lots of locals who you can enslave at little or no cost. Maybe you should just find all the gold, steal it, and leave. Organizing agriculture or industry is time-consuming and labor intensive, never mind the capital.

There is a famous budget hearing where the then secretary of defense Caspar Weinberger is defending his stewardship of a significantly increased Department of Defense budget. After much back and forth that was remarkably short on facts or concrete answers, one senator finally got fed up. He posed the now famous question: "What did you do with the money, Cap?"

In Portugal, the question is: What did they do with the gold? The answer appears to be they built churches and convents and monasteries. Lovely ones indeed, and many. In every town we visited, there was always more than one church listed in the Places to Visit section of the guidebooks, and we saw many more by just stumbling around. And they were of all sizes, but in every case, full of gilded and elaborately carved altars, golden candelabra and goblets, chalices and side chapels and organs, and on and on. And they used the Manuelite standard: every surface must be decorated, preferably with gold.

It is interesting to speculate on what would have happened if all this gold had been invested productive enterprise—agriculture, science, industry, trade—rather than in religion. Portugal had a huge head start over the UK and France in amassing colonies and trade routes, but by 1800 they were done and others in Europe, notably the English and the French, were dominant. And remained dominant for a century and a half.

The all-cod-all-the-time experiment concluded with substantial data. When we were next in Paris, I ordered steak frites eight straight times.

Love and kisses, Bob

Afterword: I had only been to Portugal once before, on a one-day in-and-out stint trying to track down an elusive business development opportunity. It proved to be so elusive as to be illusory, so I never went back until the trip recounted above. Perhaps I should have looked harder.

[19]

Yes, It's As Bad As You Think It Could Be

November 2015

Dear Aunt Janet,

Havana—shabby, shabby, shabby. Not India decrepit—no long, black rain/mold stains streaking down the buildings, even the new ones. And lots of bright and pastel paint—blues, yellows, lime green, pink, some white—but much of it faded. Lots of disarray in the buildings, even the obviously nice ones near the waterfront, near the Malecon, the boulevard along the seaside, which is really just a big road with cars whizzing along it. It is famous but in bad repair. The concrete of the sidewalk is disintegrating, in some places down to the underlying rock. This makes walking along it for an evening stroll a bit unpleasant. But that's OK because there is a small concrete wall and then the sea. No beach, just some odd chunks of coral. No shops, not so many people except at night, few vendors. Windy and hot.

Height not much. Few tall buildings. The Hotel Nacional sits on the ocean, but across the street from the ocean, and cannot be entered except from the rear. The front is coral, with several gun emplacements. We stop and sit on one of the several terraces and have a Cuban beer. It tastes very beer-like, which is good news.

There are indeed old US cars here, maybe half the cars. But also newer small Euro cars of indiscriminate provenance, Yugos or Ladas? Maybe Anglias like I had in high school? And very, very little traffic for the downtown area of a 2.5 million-person capital city.

Informal dress code; well, it's hot and humid and air-conditioning is still a window-installed thing, even in the tall buildings, dotted in almost every window with small rectangular protrusions. T-shirts, tank tops, polo shirts, a couple of long sleeve shirts on the men, long pants, shorts, short skirts, and they all look pretty young. Sandals and running shoes.

Some big propaganda billboards on the way in from the airport: "Our dear friend President Chavez [now a dead guy] from Venezuela stands with us." "The embargo is the genocide of the 20th century." "Socialism or die." Some of us quibble if the second slogan is correct, then the third slogan should be "Socialism and die." But not much of this stuff in town.

Everything shuts down at four-thirty and everyone gets on the busses to go home. Or hangs around in the street waiting to get on the busses. The busses are relatively new and come from China, who has no problem with the US embargo. Of course, the transaction still requires that Cuba provide China with money to pay for the busses. So that's a problem.

Because this is a horticulture tour, we visit the major Havana botanic garden that is naturally enough called "Jardín Botánico Nacional." Carlos Alvarez, a deputy something at the garden and a researcher who has been at the garden since its founding in 1968, shows us around the glass houses first. Tropical dry (all cactus all the time) then semitropical wet with bromeliads galore, then tropical wet with vines and other stuff trying to escape. Vanilla orchids growing to the top of the peaked support structure—no flowers or vanilla bean pods, however. Some lovely flowering plants no one can identify including Carlos, who specialty incidentally is ferns, my least favorite plant class. "Maybe it's a clerodendrum" Or maybe not.

Then a drive in the bus around the remaining 1,590 acres, the greenhouses having taken up ten acres and most of the morning. The rest is basically an arboretum, with special soil in some sections, organized by tropical regions of the world. Trees of Africa, trees of Asia, trees of the tropical Americas, trees of Cuba. There is a brief and sad stop at the "Japanese Garden," which hasn't much about it that's Japanese, no raked gravel, no irregular and pitted boulders, no plant material from Japan (Japanese iris? Chrysanthemum? Wisteria?) We walk over a small causeway to a wooden pavilion that is for meditation and sits about a quarter of the way out in a small lake. A race is being run to see whether the water feature fills with trash first or the encroaching water plants/weeds fill it up. I count four Coke cans, one cinder block, and two newspapers, and that's just from the pavilion. About 25% of the water has green spikey goo growing on it, moving from the shoreline out. It kind of looks like crab grass with attitude, and is definitely not ornamental.

While we are sitting there meditating on either this or what's for lunch, the only member of our tour group younger than fifty shows up. She is a nice, slightly spacy twenty-five-year-old with curly red hair in two long pigtails, and a Pancho Villa straw cowboy hat. She is there to take care of her grandmother in case she wanders off. In this case her grandmother having made a valiant effort on all the cobblestone paths has reasonably wandered off back to the bus. Space girl shows up in the distance, poking at some flower bushes. "Dorothy of Oz lost in the Japanese Garden" says L. As we leave the meditation platform after having a group picture taken (tourist meditation I presume), Carlos says the garden is working on repairing the Japanese Garden, but there is no obvious work in progress that one can see. He also says that money is a problem.

Our second guide in two days is a loud and chubby woman who is very charmed with her own wit and insights. She replaces Ivan, our first guide, who is now sick, although we don't think he's sick of us as we as a group have been very docile. After the garden, she takes us on a walk through old Havana including a mandatory shopping stop at a cigar factory. I have over time become allergic to mandatory shopping. And I hate cigars, so I stay in the bus. Old Havana is fine, with a statue of José Martí about every block, but that's how they do it here. I had no idea he was such a big deal, and he wasn't even in the Sierra Maestre mountains with Fidel and Che. In one of the plazas there's even a statue of him disguised as a bald naked woman wearing only high heels and riding a rooster. I can't remember which plaza it was, but it had a couple of cafés so we had a beer, the local Bucanero Fuerte, which means of course "Strong Pirate," so I liked it immediately. So far no one serving it has said "*Arrgh*" although maybe that's not Spanish.

Because we are here on an "educational, people-to-people" trip, we are supposed to make an effort to talk to the Cuban people, and the rules require that we keep a sort of a diary of those with whom we have spoken, including their names. So, right, you as an American and thus lifelong sworn enemy of the Cuban revolution and illegal possessor of the best harbor on the island at Guantanamo go up to a Cuban and, notebook in hand, ask him his name, which you write down. Then you make conversation with him. "Well, how do you like the Dodgers?" All Cubans like baseball, so this should be good. Said Cuban looks stricken and turns and hurries away.

A more successful encounter:

Tour group member to our bus driver at the stop to buy cigars: "Do you like cigars?"

Bus driver who cannot run away as he is getting paid to drive the bus full of Americans after all: "No."

TGM: "So you don't smoke?"

Bus driver: "No."

Or this encounter with yours truly:

YT: "Do you have *cerveza*?" A silly question because on the menu at the café in the plaza of the cross-dressing Martí it says *cerveza* as well as white wine, mojitos, etc.

Young waitress: "Yes."

YT: "I would like to order one *cerveza* Bucanero and one glass of white wine."

YW: "OK."

I am developing a warm feeling for the gracious Cuban people already based on these uplifting person-to-person exchanges.

What we have learned so far as a result of our botanic garden visits:

Best spice: Cuban oregano, *Plectranthus amboinicus*, widely used in Cuban cuisine; also called Spanish thyme, Indian borage, and Mexican mint. I resolve to plant some as soon as I get home.

Best Cuban tree, endorsed by Fidel Castro, is the moringa tree. You can eat the leaves, which taste a little like arugula, the seed is a good oil source and the oil tastes better than olive oil. The seed if swallowed enhances your fertility but you should not eat it as it is bitter, the root can be ground up and eaten like cassava, the bark makes a tea that prevents diarrhea, etc. Possibly also cures cancer, it was not clear.

Another day another botanic garden: Organopónico Vivero Alamar garden just outside Havana. This is really a truck farm, run by an enormously talented and energetic woman, Isis Salcines Milla. She is the director and is well spoken, funny, and capable. The eleven-acre farm grows vegetables, herbs, and medicinal aromatics. We saw rows of lettuce, bok choy, carrots, cauliflower, sunflowers, eggplant, basil, mint, and cucumbers. She sells at her local roadside stand and to the *paladares* (privatized restaurants vs. the state-owned and run ones—guess which kind is better?) where the chefs appreciate fresh produce.

She gives a very good explanation of how they run an organic garden/ farm. There are 150 workers, no tractors, three oxen to pull the plow, several horses to pull the cart. They'd like to have a tractor but cannot afford it, and then there's the embargo. They have a hard time as most Cubans don't eat vegetables very much. Interesting factoids that could even be true:

80% of Cuban food is imported. This seems odd, given that they live on a generously endowed piece of real estate in a primo tropical location.

Cubans eat more rice per capita than Chinese. But they raise only token amounts of rice. This seems odd (see above) and we raise rice in the US around Sacramento, where there is way less water than in Cuba.

Ms. Salcines Milla is also the most serious capitalist we have met in Cuba so far. She has set up a profit-sharing program with her workers, based on seniority. She posts the numbers every week as to how the annual share is accumulating. But she doesn't own her land, she only gets it from the government. The nature of the allocation is not clear, certainly she or her company doesn't own it or lease it in the traditional Western sense. The government charges her no property tax but taxes her sales at 5%. But if you don't own your land and the government can take it away any time; there's little incentive for capital investment that will be amortized over more than a year or two. This may explain the "no tractor." She's worried that when US/Cuba relations are normalized, someone like Monsanto will come in and compete with her. I'd worry more that the government will force her to start raising yields by using pesticides and herbicides. It's a dicey position, but what should she do? Write a letter to her congressman? In the meantime she does her part to increase the consumption of vegetables by paying each of her two boys twenty cents each night if they eat all the vegetables on their plates.

At the end of a really interesting discussion, one of our group, no doubt thinking of some organic seeds or a trowel, asked what the one thing was she could use most to improve her garden. Her answer was quick: "A Home Depot."

The next day we visit Quinta de Los Molines, said to be the oldest botanic garden in Cuba. We are to "learn about their educational outreach" of which there is essentially none. Salient points:

> » November Bravo Tango—nothing but trees, occasionally with faded labels.

> » Four guards standing around watching us, but of the four restrooms, three are "broken" and locked, and one, for men, has no running water, no toilet seat, and the toilet won't flush.

> » They have a "greenhouse" made of netting where they grow seedlings for planting in the garden and elsewhere in the city. They don't say of what. They use "modern technology" by which they mean a series of plastic irrigation tubes and water emitters, just like ones that can be ordered from any garden supply catalog. This "technology" is probably fifty years old.

> » Yes, they have a murky lily pond with too little sun and water lilies not blooming because of this, and so does every tropical botanic garden we've seen.

> » Yes, they have a cannonball tree (*Couroupita guianensis*) and so does every tropical botanic garden we've seen. Said to have

beautiful flowers but it's not blooming

» No, they don't really have any flowers to speak of, nor does most every tropical botanic garden we've seen, although it cannot be explained why.

» Yes, they have an "educational room" with faded charts and pictures from 1985, and so does—you get the picture.

We are shown a large netted enclosure of maybe a quarter of an acre, a "butterfly garden" with nothing growing in it and three butterflies in the generous space, all flying near the net ceiling, desperately looking for escape. By this point, me too.

We take a field trip west of Havana, to the "sustainable community and ecotourism center" of Las Terrazas. This is a real showplace according to Oriole, our new and very energetic guide. The area was deforested to make charcoal in the bad old days, but now it has been reforested. The new trees don't look happy and are well short of a forest. It has also been reterraced, rebuilt, and a big pond was added for good measure. The money came from Russia back when they had money. Twenty sites across Cuba were picked for development. Perhaps by throwing darts.

The village (?) has 1,050 residents. All water and electricity and gas come from the grid. All food is brought in but they have some pigs and chickens. There is one PV panel on one house. Everybody works in tourism but God knows where—there is nothing here worth seeing. If this is sustainable then I am Castro's uncle.

We are fed lunch at a tourist house, very good but the standard menu—beans, rice, plantain chips, canned vegetables, shredded beef, a nice chicken dish. I asked what it was called and the guide said, "*Pollo asado*," which means "roasted chicken." So much for the secret ingredients. I add this to my log of "getting to know the people" conversations.

On to the orchid garden, Orquideario de Soroa. We are slowly led up a very steep hill by a pleasantly knowledgeable woman who had worked there fifteen years. We don't see many orchids as most of them are kept in a small orchid house at the base of the hill. Ha, fooled you. But lots of trees and green plants and some birds and much pointing and asking, "Do you see it? Right over there." This is not a helpful comment to make but seems to be how bird people operate. The birds are small and flying around rather than posing obediently for the tourists. Creating this area on a steep limestone hill must have required a lot of very expensive civil work—paths, steps, clearing terraces, etc. It was owned and created by a local businessman, seized by the revolution.

Off into the hinterland: we get in the bus and drive for three hours, across broad expanses of what is essentially tropical savannah, on a nice if poorly maintained four-lane divided highway. There is very little traffic. One thinks on how the transportation system develops. And one notices, especially as we get farther from Havana, a serious number of horse-drawn carts. Data intrudes: during this three-hour trip, we count seventeen horse carts and four motorbikes, counting all four lanes. In Havana, there are almost no bicycles, almost no motorbikes, very few cars of which half are probably taxis, and probably for the tourists, and a reasonable number of busses. Public transportation is virtually the only way for a citizen to get around. I think about all my trips to China starting in 1990 when Beijing had one ring road, almost no motorbikes, and half the few cars were taxis. But there were literally hordes of people on bikes, that's how you got around. And no horse carts. Beijing rapidly went through the cycle of bikes to motorbikes to cars to way too many cars and six ring roads. Hanoi is in the motorbike stage, moving toward the enough/too many cars stage. I keep reminding myself, "This is a poor country."

Best meal of the trip so far: we come to Playa Larga after passing a number of billboards denouncing the American-sponsored invasion and memorializing the triumph led by Fidel. This is because this is also the Bahía de Cochinos (Bay of Pigs), with a small beach town with a nice bay and a thin beach. We stop at Hostal Enrique and have a really great meal. Beans, rice, plantain chips, canned vegetables, then pork and shredded beef and roasted chicken and crab and lobster. And Tabasco!—first time on the trip. It's all good so we fill our plates. "Eating like pigs on the Bay of Pigs" I remark to no one in particular. And of course, says the capitalist, this is a privately owned facility.

About five, we finally reach the turn off to go up into the mountains to our hotel. But problem: the road is under construction and the big bus cannot go up the hill. So we have to transfer into Russian trucks, the equivalent of an army "deuce and a half" with rows of seats in the truck bed. This takes a while to organize, since there are several other stranded tour busses ahead of us. But we retreat to the little shop across the road where they have cold beer, so all is not lost. The trip up the hill is bouncy and twisty and made in fading light. Probably would have been hard for the bus to navigate this safely. Going up it in the dark in the back of a Soviet truck with no springs is a bit of an adventure.

The rates at the Los Helechos—"The Ferns"— hotel where we are staying, if you just show up and get a room, is thirty-eight dollars per night, with breakfast. Probably less for a tour group. As a result we have a lot of remarkably classless Euros at the hotel, smoking and running around in tank tops, all pretty bulky including the women. Maybe they are all East Germans and Poles and Czechs hungry to experience the old times again before the wall came down. It is a pretty Bolshevik place in terms of architecture and transportation, as noted. There are no ferns.

Next day, another truck adventure, this time a fifteen-kilometer drive to Codina where there is a 1.5-kilometer hike in a nature area said to have flowers and birds. It turns into a long walk looking mostly at birds. Which isn't really what we came for. Then after lunch we visit the local Museum of Cuban Modern Art, which is small, maybe six rooms, and not much visited. And has art by no one anyone would recognize since the artists are all Cubans who painted in the eighties and nineties, which I believe was a long time ago as modern art goes. The modern metal statues (David Smith is safe) are all rusting away. The remaining items are all paintings, not so good. As we leave this really fascinating venue, another tour bus is pulling up.

I am beginning to formulate my theory of Cuban tourism. We have not yet been to a single place where there are no other tourists already there or coming just behind us. There is the exception of the dreadful garden of the few flowers and fewer butterflies. However, I posit that there are perhaps six tourist attractions in Cuba, and we have twelve days to visit them. So does everyone else: the National Hotel overlooking the Malecon, to include the nine o'clock cannon shot at Moro Fort and the Plaza of the

Revolution, a walk in Old Havana where one finds the "artist's market" that should be called the Usual and Customary Tourist Crap Market, the "ecotourist park" at Las Terrazas and the orchid garden in the same vicinity, the Topes de Collantes "mountain resort" with the Russian truck experience, Trinidad (World Heritage site), the Bay of Pigs, and that's about it. We have dropped in a couple of botanic gardens but other than that we're making the same circuit as everyone else. Six days' worth of things to see crammed into twelve days.

A ride back down from the top of the mountain to where we had to leave our bus, again on a Russian truck, but this time the logistics got confused and there was not a second truck to carry our luggage so we piled it all up on the same truck, without complaint, and careened down the mountain to much down shifting, jouncing, and screeching of brakes. The fact that there was a spare set of brake shoes in the back of the truck under the last row of seats was either comforting or disturbing, you choose.

On to Trinidad, founded five hundred years ago as an important port city and now a World Heritage site. So what have we got? About ten or twelve city blocks with a couple of churches (no stained glass), a plaza with some hedges, a lot of shops all selling pretty much the same things, a series of *paladares*, and some guys on the street playing (*gasp!*) Cuban music. You can tip them or buy their CD. It's also a car-free area, which is nice, and it's hotter than blue blazes, which is not as nice. No gardens.

Having been fed (black beans and rice and meat) and encouraged to walk around the city until heat stroke intervenes, we get back to our bus and go off to the Hotel Faro Luna, which has a seafront setting (no beach) but a spacious and lovely saltwater pool. Half the group convenes there and floats around for an hour or some, with a few of the ambitious ones actually swimming laps. The rest of us discuss whether GMO-modified food is a good idea or not. At least we stay away from the subject of Donald Trump.

Off from the hotel we go to the best botanic garden of the trip, one at Soledad—Jardin Botanico Soledad. We have a really good guide, a career botanist woman with great English and great knowledge. It's yet again largely an arboretum, but they have had the good sense to plant lots of flowering bushes, and to tolerate the vines and other colorful stuff. There are precious few birds around to distract our easily distractible group. We see many things that I have never seen before, many of them flowering, and then something that is brand new to me, a truly giant tree, about sixty feet tall and as easily that in diameter. It has large pink flowers bigger than your hand, some in bloom and some that have fallen to the forest floor. It's the largest variety of hibiscus in the world, we are told. Well, I'll say! It's the largest by about a hundred times. I am completely enthralled and try to figure out how to plant it in our garden that is in total area less than half the size of this single tree. Perhaps that is not a sensible idea but it's really marvelous.

Why haven't I heard of this before? Why didn't I do my homework and read the botanical stuff about Cuba that we got before the trip? Why doesn't everyone in America lose twenty pounds? And, by the way, everyone in Cuba?

Lunch in Cienfuegos at what was at one time the Yacht Club and is now a government-run restaurant. Beautiful and well restored three-story elegant building on the impressive Cienfuegos harbor, and typical Cuban menu food. Then for some reason we go into the center of town and attend a performance of the Cienfuegos Choir, an a capella group of nine men and twelve women, who perform both classical and Cuban songs, then hustle us to buy their CDs. Lovely voices but why this, exactly? Horticultural significance? We are turned loose to wander among the shops, find ATC as we now call it (average tourist crap) but several markets or food stores, which resemble poorly stocked 7-Elevens. It really would be difficult to live here.

On the way to our next treat, we make the obligatory stop at the Bay of Pigs Museum. I only feel sorry that the invading Cubans lost.

And now, a real treat, a beach hotel that was restricted to Russian military officers before they all went home. It's officially the Playa Larga Hotel.

Wow, the Famous Beach Resort of the Russian Officers! With cold-water showers for health! With narrow sandy beach covered with cigarette butts and no showers and no towels for health! With very shallow water that you cannot swim in unless you go out a mile into the bay, for health!

With trash everywhere for health! With only one air-conditioner working, maybe, forget the other one, for health! With one comfortable chair on the porch with an actual seat so you can sit in, and the other one with a hole where the seat should be, to play funny joke on friends, for health! With TV with no controller so you cannot turn it on, because you should be out swimming a mile off the shore and not sitting on your fat Russian ass watching bad Western soft porn like *Baywatch* with lots of static, for health! With small frog in door wedge, for health! (Do not eat this.) With only one closet door that opens, so you can push on other door as form of exercise, for health! Unfortunately we have to eat dinner here as well, but no one has hot water, even the kitchen, so the dishes are not very clean and half the group gets diarrhea. Who thought this was a good idea?

We are released from the Soviet prison camp with the condition being that we drive for four hours through a swamp and see flamingoes, several; and ibis, a couple; and egrets, also a couple; and some flying black birds that could be some kind of teals, or warblers, or American coots (at this point in the trip I myself am turning into an American coot) or killdeer (strange name for a bird, there's probably a story here) etc. We drive and drive on a one-lane road through the Zapata Swamp that has all the charm of a, um, swamp. Initially I worry that we will run into someone as there really is no shoulder, but it turns out that really no sane person, Cuban or tourist, is interested in what goes on in the middle of the Zapata Swamp, the largest wetland in the Caribbean/Americas/world/solar system. So no head-on collisions on this sandy, bumpy road.

The guide, when introducing himself, is asked by one of our party if we didn't see him at the museum in Topos de Collantes: "You look familiar." He says, "Probably you were looking at the statue of a Greek god." But unfortunately he knows a lot about birds and is eager to share all of this knowledge with us. "First flock of something teals I have seen this season" he announces with excitement, as a distant bunch of dots move across the horizon. Could be ducks, could be commas and apostrophes, hard to tell.

We get to the end of the road, at last, get out, climb an extremely rickety wooden tower stolen from a WWII prison camp movie, climb back down quickly, and wander around looking at mangroves and slimy water and not so much birds. And no flowers whatsoever, what were you thinking? This is really fun, if you are a low-expectations birder and a self-flagellant. Combined.

But there are no other tourist busses here! For the very first time, not even the crazy Euros want to engage in this activity. Besides, it's now ten o'clock in the morning and close to ninety degrees, so they're all in the bar drinking and getting ready for lunch.

We return gratefully to our original hotel in Havana. To welcome us back the hotel informs us that there is a water problem. Great, I think, yet another morning with a cold shower. Some fancy vacation this is. Then I find that there is one thing worse than being restricted to cold water only, and that is having no water at all.

Love and kisses, Bob

Afterword: It is very difficult to understand how presidential candidate Bernie Sanders, if he had exercised even a minute amount of fact finding and due diligence, could have come to the conclusion that Fidel Castro was a genius and Cuba a society and model worth emulating. He was not and it is not.

[20]

Swimming with Baboons, or
Can You Still See Elephants in Africa?

July 2017

Dear Aunt Janet,

It's always good to start with something boring, then come back with the more interesting stuff. Short summary: southern Africa is a very long way away from San Diego. Map research will validate this, if you don't believe me.

One and a half hours from San Diego to San Francisco. Four hours on the ground in San Francisco. Fourteen and a half hours on the Emirates flight in the air from SFO to Dubai. Five hours on the ground in Dubai. Seven hours on the Emirates flight in the air from Dubai to Johannesburg. Total elapsed time: thirty-two hours. This seeing animal stuff better damn well be worth it.

Interesting notes: the Emirates airplane had a fancy screen in the back of each seat, which trumpeted that the entertainment system was now offering 2,500 channels of entertainment—movies, TV shows, music, news, cartoons, documentaries, video games, back rubs, you name it. Because I can't help myself, I calculated that I could spend 20.4 seconds on each channel and get through all of them during the longest flight segment. I did spend 20.4 seconds on the new "hot" movie, *La La Land*, and that was enough.

The airplane drinks menu offered a new breakthrough in alcoholic creativity: the breakfast martini. I quote: "Gin shaken over ice with marmalade, Cointreau, and orange." The editor sitting on my right shoulder points out that this probably should have read: "Gin, marmalade, Cointreau, and orange juice shaken with ice, poured into a chilled martini glass" or something like that. I was tempted but since I don't like martinis of any description, and especially not for breakfast, and even more especially not made by flight attendants who are from Abu Dhabi, not a martini sort of town, I deferred.

Unexplainable mysteries: Zambia has lots of copper as well as wildlife. But no secondary manufacturing capability, so all the refined ore has to go to South Africa, the powerhouse economically of the region. It is smelted into ingots—large, thick rectangular pieces of metal as big as four phone books laid in a square, and placed on big modern semitrucks. There is a decent road from Zambia to Johannesburg. There is one major river to cross. Yes, the Zambezi. I am pretty sure the river has been there for some time. The river at this point is wide and placid. There is no bridge. If I had a company of army engineers we could bridge it in a day.

There are four "ferries" that are really barges with outboard motors on the back for power, and they can take one truck at a time across the river. Several of the ferries seem to be broken, always. Trucks have to wait as long as a week to cross the river. What? Is it a surprise that there's a river here? We tourists cross on a "private ferry," which turns out to be a glorified metal motorboat. No white tablecloths. We are told that there is also a railroad but it doesn't work.

Politics

First we spent a useless day in Johannesburg visiting the Apartheid Museum, South Africa's answer to the Hanoi Hilton Museum in Hanoi and the Bay of Pigs Museum in Cuba, all with the subtheme of "see how much we have suffered, you bad Western people." The museum was quite high on Nelson Mandela, deservedly so, and not so much else. Not much on Jacob Zuma, the current president, thought to be corrupt and autocratic. We then drove around Soweto to see Mandela's house and another museum commemorating the massacre of some schoolkids who were protesting one of the many foolish apartheid mandates—this one from 1976 when the government decreed that all black students are to be taught in Afrikaans, not English. But we couldn't go in the museum, a large, two-story, institutional-looking brick building, because the roof had collapsed. So we stood around outside and had a local Soweto person who had been there describe how awful it was. Then we drove around Soweto some more and had our guide point out Desmond Tutu's house, only he doesn't live there now.

The 1994 elections were a turning point in South Africa, the first in the country with universal suffrage, held after the deal Mandela and De Klerk made to end apartheid, convert to a liberal democracy, and let everyone vote. But according to one of the plaques in the museum, there were 25,000 people killed in various election-related disturbances. This was more than the total estimated number of people killed during the entire apartheid period. No one, black or white, made us feel like this was a country where they felt comfortable and safe.

Other miscellaneous factoids: since the 1948 official beginning of apartheid to now, there has been much out-migration of the white citizens, many of whom had not only South African but also Dutch or UK passports. And when you look at the seventy years of turmoil and violence since that date, it's a wonder that anyone is left in the country, black or white. Not that it's been much of a picnic since independence, either.

One other note while we're on the subject of guilt: the US policy toward apartheid was strongly opposed and became tougher as time passed, to include a serious, enforced embargo on South African products. We were probably the most focused of all the countries exerting this political pressure. Although I cannot prove this, there were never any mainline US politicians who tried to explain away South Africa's racist policies, or excuse them. Good for us.

So much for history and politics and guilt, on to the waterfalls and rhinos.

Wildlife

Which is, after all, why we're here, we aren't going to try and lead the charge against President Jacob Zuma, corrupt fellow that he may be. That's now the job of the voters of South Africa.

If you decide that you want to see the Grand Canyon, then you fly to Las Vegas, rent a car, drive to the Grand Canyon, look over the edge, and there it is. If you want to see the rose windows in Notre-Dame, you fly to Paris, go to Notre-Dame, go inside, look up, and there they are. But seeing wildlife is more akin to fishing. You need to go to where the wildlife is likely to be, and having a good guide is useful, but there are no guarantees. Well, perhaps impalas can be guaranteed. The animal not the Chevrolet.

Driving around the park in Zimbabwe, our first stop, we saw impala, kudu, sable, warthogs, Cape buffalo, zebra, and finally a mother and baby black rhino. We allegedly see where three lions are lying in wait to attack some impala, but we can't really see them in the grass. Lions are sneaky that way. We also see lots of birds, none of which are found in San Diego.

That first evening we drive from the lodge to a point on the Zambezi River above the falls for a "sunset dinner cruise." I am apprehensive, as my experience with dinner cruises has been mixed to bad, notably the stupid *bateau-mouche* in Paris, don't be suckered in by that one.

But this cruise was wonderful. Virtually as soon as we get on the boat I spot four hippos in the distance, we cruise over to them and it's more like eight, all floating hippo-like in the river, snorting and blowing and wiggling their ears just like on the Jungle Boat ride in Disneyland. We cruise around some more, enjoying the scenery and not going over the falls by mistake, then come to one of the islands in the middle of the channel where a couple of elephants are calmly eating the vegetation and trampling on whatever they haven't eaten. We putter around further and find a crocodile looking at us with beady crocodile eyes from a submerged location by the bank. Then we all sit down, watch a really glorious sunset, and are served a terrific dinner of roasted bream on the boat.

On the drive back to the camp we are stopped by three elephants in the middle of the road. Three elephants, side by side as these are, actually should be described as being in all of the road, not just the middle. They finally decide to crunch off into the bush so we can proceed. We do not flash our lights at them, we do not toot our horn, we do not stick our arms out of the window and make rude gestures at them. For they are big and we are small, even if we are in a twenty-five-person van.

We're sitting at the pool of the hotel after another game drive. I am reading a James Patterson thriller because I am an intellectual and L is swimming, even though the water is a touch cold. But it's warm and the sun is shining and I am thinking about having a local Mosi beer.

The resort is situated along the crest of a small ridgeline and is laid out in a linear fashion, fourteen generous suites, and a central lodge/bar/library/dining area and patio. About halfway down the hill is a brick wall with a four-strand, serious electric fence on top of it, to discourage the elephants from coming any closer. And the lions and anyone else who could cause trouble by wandering into the manicured part of the property where us tourists stay. We're sitting here because we only do game drives at 0530 in the morning, and just before dusk. Everyone knows that this is the only time you can see animals. One of the more diligent of our group is by the edge of the human's part of the resort, looking out over the fence at where the animals would be if only it was the right time. There is a small river resembling a bunch of watering holes at the bottom of the small valley, and it's all grassy from our brick barrier to about halfway up the ridge across the water.

"Hey," she calls, "the buffalo have come down to graze by the water." Sure enough there are eight Cape buffalo slowly emerging from the tree line across the valley and meandering down to the patches of water, eating the grass as they go. Then ten, then fifteen, and eventually a whole herd of twenty coal-black, large, bad-tempered Cape buffalo are right there, very much like a normal herd of cattle. Which they are not. And clearly they cannot tell time. Not even L has the urge to pet them.

In Chobe, Botswana, we went on three game drives, two in the morning and one in the afternoon; and three "river cruises," in small metal boats that comfortably held twenty-five to thirty people—not Zodiacs, thank God—and puttered along the river so we could stop and see whatever there was to see. Here's a summary:

> What we did not see here that we saw in Zimbabwe: white rhinos, sable. What we saw here that we did not see in Zimbabwe: lions, giraffe, hyena, a family of mongoose.

> What we saw in South Africa two years ago that we did not see here: leopards.

> What we saw in both places (Zimbabwe and Botswana):

> Lots of elephants—Botswana is said to have the most elephants of any country in the world, about 150,000, which does seem a lot. Sri Lanka boasts of its wild elephants and has about 5,000.

> Lots and lots of impalas—a beautiful little antelope and obviously very fecund. We came across small herds about every fifteen minutes. Also, known in the game drive business as the McDonald's of the forest, as they supply food to all the large predators. When the world catastrophe comes and all the humans are wiped out, the impala will inherit.

> Warthogs, a goodly number. Including some hanging around the immigration shack between Zimbabwe and Botswana. Perhaps they couldn't get a visa.

> Cape buffalo, large numbers. Hippo, mostly on the three river cruises. Well, of course, it lives in the river.

> Kudu, a large antelope—mostly solitary and few. Baboons, lots, in packs and also trying to get into the resorts. Unpleasant fellows really.

> Crocodiles, mostly on the river cruises, single members including one hanging out at the Chobe Hotel just below the swimming pool. This gave us pause. But it wasn't a heated pool so we weren't swimming in it anyway. Standards are important.

We spent more time than one would have thought on birds. We had as part of our group a serious but pleasant woman of the birding persuasion. We fell under her evil spell and spent at least half of each "game drive" peering up at dead trees or down at the ground or out at the nearby bushes trying to identify indistinct medium-sized, brown, birdlike things before they flew away, which they did routinely 85% of the time. But the remaining 15% was pretty rewarding. We saw in no particular order:

» Red-headed partridge: it does in fact have a bright red head. So there. Not easy to find online or in bird books.

» Yellow sparrow weaver: one of the trees at the lodge in Zimbabwe had probably thirty individual nests hanging all over it, made by these birds. Industrious. Don't stand under the tree, however.

» White-backed vulture: lots of these in Zimbabwe, slightly but only slightly better looking than the US turkey vulture. This is not a high standard for attractiveness.

» Cattle egret: many, hanging around the Cape buffaloes. Nice looking white member of the heron family.

» Oxpeckers: these live on the bugs found on larger animals, and so sit on their backs and eat ticks, etc. Mostly we saw these on antelopes and Cape buffalo. Hard way to have lunch.

» Wattled lapwings, magpie lapwings, blacksmith lapwings (all formerly "plovers"—apparently, there is as much revisionism in bird taxonomy as there is in horticulture)—great looking medium-sized black-and-white bird, easy to identify by its distinctive marking. Also, not concerned to find itself by the side of the road with vehicles grinding by. We like self-confidence in a bird.

» Fish eagle: looks a lot like the American eagle, lustrous white head, large black/brown body, and the pleasant habit of perching at the top of dead trees so you can see it. Apparently the fish cannot. National bird of Zambia.

» Lilac-breasted roller: dramatically colored bird with nothing but bright colors making up for its relatively small size.

» Kori bustard: largest flying bird in the inventory, but not a predator. Anything bigger than a Canadian goose—and this is— is impressive in flight. National bird of Botswana.

» Glossy starling: if a crow were smaller, quieter, had shiny feathers to include a shiny dark blue, almost iridescent head and a bright yellow eye, it would be this interesting bird.—Sombre greenbul: seen eating a moth, tediously, while sitting on an outdoor lighting fixture at the camp in Zimbabwe. This would make anyone somber.

» Hornbills: several kinds, easy to identify due to long tail and curved bill. Like a junior varsity toucan.

» Bee-eaters: another family of small but flashy birds who do eat bees, God knows why. Maybe they got to the food line late and this was all that was left.

» Pied wagtail: in fact did walk around wagging his tail. Strange.

» Red-backed shrike: with orangish back, not really red. But who would want to be called "orangish-not-quite-red-backed shrike?"

» Tawny eagle: smaller than fish eagle but no less impressive.

» Drongo: your basic blackbird, broad range, forked tail, cool name.

» Pearl-winged goose/Egyptian goose: hard for me to get past the "goose" part on these.

» Waxbills: very small bird but colored baby blue. Quite nice. Hard to see. These last two characterizations seem to go together.

» Guineafowl: ground dweller with odd black feathers spotted with white, and brilliant blue head too small for its body.

» Long-tailed paradise whydah: fabulous-looking bird with style and presence—basically black with a brilliant red bib and yellow breast. And a very, very long tail, maybe two feet long. Also an odd flight pattern, it makes J shapes in the sky.

By the time we get to Zambia, our last destination, we have broken down into the people more interested in birds and the people more interested in cats, e.g., lions and leopards. But we haven't seen a leopard on the whole trip, and only two lions once. Everyone is really eager for a leopard, except me and the most committed bird person. Large predators make me nervous. On the second morning there, we divide into two trucks and the "bird nerds" go in one and the "cat people" go in the other.

Because the universe is not always fair, we bird fanciers come upon a leopard within fifteen minutes of getting into the park, follow it, get pictures of it, and so forth. We are decent human beings so we send a radio message to the other truck saying where we are. They hurry over, by which time the leopard has disappeared into the bush, we go on watching birds, and the cat people spend five bouncy and frustrating hours with no cat siting. Ah, life.

Interesting Geographic Features

I confess to not really being a big fan of geography, or of dramatic bits of geography like waterfalls. They're fine, I suppose, but once you've looked at one for a while (for me, fifteen minutes) then I am ready for something else—a cheeseburger, a bus ride to the souvenir shop, a cool drink, whatever is next on the program. I suppose I simply find human accomplishment more interesting. Although whether a cheeseburger is the apogee of man's endeavor is more arguable. Depends on the cheeseburger. But Victoria Falls was on the program, so go there we did.

To get to Victoria Falls, should one be so inclined, it's useful to know that it's in the middle of the southern part of Africa, and the Zambezi River, which nourishes it, is the border between Zimbabwe and Zambia. It might be the only place in the world with this confluence of the letter Z. We are staying on the Zimbabwe side, but have to land at Livingstone, where the airport is, in Zambia. We get to stand in line a long time while individual visas are filled out and eighty US dollars are collected, then we drive over the famous Vic Falls iron bridge built 110 years ago. The legendary and now much reviled Cecil Rhodes was its sponsor although he died before he ever got to cross it. So much for fame.

The bridge, fortunately, does not fall down as we pass over it, but only one truck at a time is allowed across the one-way, one-lane structure. And trucks there are, mostly loaded with ingots of copper, headed from the mines in Zambia to the factories in South Africa. This is a longer route, but at least there's a bridge and not a faux ferry.

We get off the bus on the Zimbabwe side and walk along a trail along the edge of the falls. One cannot really see much because all this crashing water makes huge clouds of mist, which obscure the falls. You can hear them. You can get wet from the mist while you're walking along the trail, trying to peer through the mist and see one of the wonders of the world. You can take pictures of your friends standing in front of the large cloud of mist. You can wear a poncho and keep dry from the mist but get wet instead from sweating inside the poncho. No end of interesting activities awaits you.

OK, check, did that. The other interesting feature is the Zambezi River itself. Although since it falls down into a gorge right there, you cannot see it either through the mist. But later we are told that the Zambezi is the fourth largest river in Africa, after the Nile, the Congo, and the Niger. I studied African politics some time ago, and I don't recall the Niger even being a river. But it apparently is, and runs thorough West Africa and (hey, this is cool) through the country of Niger, not to be confused with the country of Nigeria, which is next to it on the south. Little else is known of Niger, at least by me, or of the river. According to the website "Ask me something stupid.com," when you ask, "Is Niger a country?" the answer is "Yes." The answer should of course be "Yes, and also a river." But we digress.

We spend a lot of time on the Zambezi, at each of our three lodge sites. It is always time well spent, as the Zambezi is shallow, dammed only once much lower down at the Kariba Damn, and not dredged or channeled or anything like that. It is full of wildlife, mostly hippos and crocodiles who seem to get along. The Zambezi that we experience is shallow, slow moving, and clogged with many islands. All the better for the hippos and crocs. We do not see, in ten days, a single "commercial" boat hauling stuff up or down river.

Lodging and Lodges

We are not Boy Scouts, or army rangers, or hippies traveling in a van with sleeping bags. We are mostly over fifty Cornell graduates. If we ever knew how to pitch a tent, we have forgotten. We do not cook over camp-fires. We stay in lodges that have walls (mostly), roofs (uniformly), screens on the windows, hot water, buffet dinners, and intermittent Internet. These places are sometimes called lodges and sometimes called camps, but it's the same.

The purpose of the lodges is first, food and shelter, and second, they are close to or even in a game preserve or park. And they all provide trucks and guides so you can go on these game drives in said preserve/park.

Our first lodge, the Stanley & Livingstone Hotel, is in Zimbabwe about ten kilometers from the falls, down a dirt road, and situated on its own 15,000-acre game preserve. We get up at five-thirty and are in the open Land Rovers by six-thirty, roaring off into the preserve. It's very green and thick as there has been a lot of rain here, but there are also many open stretches and a nice little fordable river running down the middle of the park. We drive around for three hours and yes, there are animals.

This pattern is repeated with a water variant at the other two lodges: the Chobe Marina Lodge and the Royal Zambezi Lodge. Good, that's why we're here.

On to Botswana, by bus, a two-hour trip to the Chobe Marina Lodge, a big riverside property of mixed style: "old colonial" with "faux African village" with Travelodge. Big suites with small furniture, mosquito nets, spotty Internet, a "riverside" bar overlooking, yes, the riverside. And the Chobe River, which is a tributary of the Zambezi. Native touristic dancers are performing in the bar whether you want them to or not. I asked if they knew "Down by the Riverside" and offered to hum a few bars, but this offer was not accepted. The focus here as in Zimbabwe is game drives, in this case in the Chobe National Park, a 20,000-acre preserve very nearby, with lots of game animals and no fences so the animals can come and go. And the tourists. It was previously a teak plantation, but one year after Botswana's independence from the UK, the president, Seretse Khama, had the presence of mind to buy the land up. Diamonds are Botswana's largest export but the country's leaders have figured out that diamonds are not in fact forever, and when they're gone they'll need something else to keep everyone busy and employed. And that else is game tourism.

They have also figured out that having poachers shoot out all the rhino and elephants will put a serious dent in their tourism future. So they have passed a "shoot to kill" law on poachers and stationed army troops in the park. Since the poachers were shooting the antipoaching police, the new law seemed reasonable and even-handed. We will set aside here discussions of notice, probable cause, willful blindness, and due process. The law and the trigger-happy soldiers have pretty much stopped poaching in the park, which is a good thing. We actually ran into a small cadre of soldiers, in olive drab, carrying backpacks and bedrolls and AK-47s. Bit scary.

Our final lodge was the Royal Zambezi on the far east side of Zambia. The lodge is on the Zambezi River, which everyone has now told us roughly seventy-four times, is the fourth longest river in Africa. See Geographic Features, above. It is also at this point the border with Zimbabwe where lives Robert Mugabe, president for life, and who has unfortunately lived ninety-four years and basically ruined his country. This is an interesting example which can be used to prove the following rule of political science: good political leadership does not guarantee a successful country, but bad leadership guarantees an unsuccessful one. See also Venezuela for further proof.

The lodge is right along the river, beside the Lower Zambezi National Park of just over a million acres and really poor dirt roads. This is pretty big; the largest national park in the lower forty-eight is Death Valley at 3.3 million acres. The lodge has tents with roofs and wooden floors, each one a separate cabana, and the area is not fenced. Hence the animals can come right through the compound to get to the river. And they do. Also, the hippos come up on the shore to feed every night around two, and they make coughing, grunting, chomping noises. We are told that elephants sometimes come through, and lions. You are encouraged to stay in your cabana after dinner. Hey, no problem. After dark, you are also encouraged to have one of the staff, armed disconcertingly with only a large, bright flashlight, come and escort you to or from the lodge. We didn't need a lot of encouragement to adopt this practice.

Fortunately, the food is really good, the staff is responsive, and the guides are terrific. And the park is full of, well, wildlife. Up until 1983 it was the private game preserve of the president. It is enormous, as noted above. It is very hard to get to, no paved roads in or out, a trackless mountain range along the western border, the Zambezi on the eastern border. We take a private charter flight to go and then later to return. There are few other lodges around so we have the park to ourselves. How they keep the lodge running when they are near nothing and there are no roads anywhere and guests arrive on a charter plane at the small landing strip a quarter mile away, is beyond me. How do they get fuel? How do they get mail? How do they get fresh lettuce? How to they get beer and South African wines? How do they watch President Trump say something stupid? This is a hard business, it seems to me.

The third night we are there, a grazing and very noisy hippo comes out of the river and grazes noisily right beside our cabana/tent. Hippos weigh from one to two tons and just trample things in their way. L lies there worrying and hoping that he or she won't decide to come through the tent wall/screen in a quest for more grass. I am sure that this was disquieting, but I don't really know since I slept through the adventure.

We had baboons using our small outdoor swimming pool during the day, which we did not discourage since there were four or five of them. They ran off with the towels.

Miscellaneous Cultural Experiences or Dumb Things We Did Because It Was on the Schedule

On our second morning in Zimbabwe, we make a scheduled visit to a primary school. We don't know why. Yes, the kids are cute, shy, and yet curious and energetic. I do not believe they are considered "wildlife." Yes, the school is not in great physical shape, but somehow, they have a computer room with forty modern desktop computers. And the room where we are briefed has six light fixtures and two light bulbs. It's hard to get a good education in Zimbabwe as the country is broke and exceptionally poorly served by its political leadership.

We have been directed in our trip material that we should bring school items to leave, so our group gives the administrator Costco pencils and copy books and an edition of *Yertle the Turtle* by Dr. Seuss, printed on renewable paper. We were impressed that the kids speak better English than some US schoolkids we have seen, and the country does seem to be committed to education.

While we're on the subject, let's stipulate that all third world schools are difficult, facilities are not first rate, teachers are not particularly well qualified and certainly not well paid, there are not enough books, and computer access and training is limited. And the kids are bright and eager and full of energy. We're sorry about this situation, although you could apply this description to more schools in the US than one would like. However, one visit to an African school by a bunch of middle-aged mostly white people bearing inexpensive gifts is not going to change this.

We had not one, not two, but five instances of native touristic dancing pressed upon us—once at the school, once at the goodbye dinner in Zimbabwe, once on getting into the boat on the Zambezi, once in getting off said boat three hours later, by the same group, and once at the riverside bar in Botswana. Number three and four should perhaps be counted as one instance, since it was the same dancers who had just taken a three-hour intermission. It was all the same stuff: costumes that looked like they came from the original *King Kong* movie, drumming and much chanting that sounded suspiciously like the Kingston Trio playing "The Lion Sleeps Tonight" on acid. Low quality acid. If you have ever seen real documentary footage of dancers in tribal villages, there is not so much chanting, there is not so much skin, and there is certainly not so much jumping about. Perhaps globalization will finally reduce all such performances to the same thing. I believe based on my extensive and generally unwilling observation of many cases of touristic dancing that there is already progress in this direction.

The Romance of Africa

Since this is the tropics or at least one of the warm, humid parts of the world, we are concerned about mosquitoes since they carry malaria, dengue fever, Chikungunya, and perhaps the gene for obesity. Hence we are implored/directed by our tour director to wear insect repellent with a high percentage, i.e., 100%, of DEET, which is diethyltoluamide, which means it has one too many *e*'s. It is effective but carries an unattractive odor and is kind of greasy. Its sustained use is also associated with seizures, insomnia, impaired cognitive function, and mood disturbance. I suppose this is part of its effectiveness. From time to time we put it on exposed parts of the body like neck and ears and hands before going out on a game drive or river cruise. We came back from one of these, went up to our room, and L, being the lovely person that she is, proceeded to kiss me on the back of the neck. "Ugh, crap, DEET!" she said, making a spitting noise and an unattractive face. "I guess I'll have to go back to Old Spice," I replied. It appears they were right about the mood disturbance side effect.

Great Tourist Moments

We for some reason were all discussing our malaria medicine, Malarone, which almost all of us are taking as malaria is a not good thing to have. One of our tour companions said, "Oh, I don't take it, I don't want to become addicted." Pause, while the rest of us politely tried to figure out how one would become malaria-preventive dependent, even if one did live in Manhattan. "Instead I take Aleve PM," she added. Not much of a substitute but to each his own choice of medications. The guide offers: "Oh, well, malaria is treatable."

More: outside the modern clinic on the main street in Chobe is a small poster that promises to use traditional medicine to cure STDs, unwanted pregnancy, impotence, financial problems, and witchcraft. The URL for the proponent's website and his or her WhatsApp number are then added as contact information. Marketing is so important, especially for witchcraft.

Things our guides told us, but may not be true, #1: Johannesburg as a city has more trees per acre than any other city in the world. However, none of these trees is native to South Africa. Fact check: Sacramento, CA, appears to have the most trees per capita, but Johannesburg may have the most trees by absolute number. No way to check on the nonendemic claim. Toronto has a lot of trees as well, in case you were wondering.

Can this be true, #2: crocodiles live to be 120 years old. Fact check: nope, sixty to seventy years old.

Can this be true, #3: hippos live in the water because they're subject about sunburn. Fact check: no, they secrete a red oily substance that protects their skin from sunburn. Whales, however, can get sunburned, not that you asked.

Best Moments in Each Park (Excluding the Birds Because That's an Acquired Taste)

We took the Victoria Falls helicopter flight. It was expensive and short, but a dramatic way to see and marvel at this amazing natural wonder. Plus, you could actually see something not masked by all the mist.

Zimbabwe—a mom and baby rhino emerging from the bush and crossing the road at a leisurely pace behind our stopped truck, but quite close—maybe ten feet. No rhinos in Zambia or Botswana.

Chobe—river cruise with twenty-three elephants emerging from the bush and coming down to the water to drink and bathe and screw around; two female lions lying in the sand, raising their heads simultaneously and looking around disdainfully at the eleven game drive trucks surveying them, from a respectful distance of course; then at the end of the day game drive, when we are almost to the park gate, eight giraffes come out of nowhere and graze very close to the road.

Zambezi—we come across a herd of fifty-five Cape buffalo who all initially ignore us, then stare at us unhappily, then stampede away. Thank goodness.

A Rare Moment of Good Judgment

On a canoe outing on a tributary of the Zambezi on one of the last days of the trip, several of our trip members had come across a dead hippo caught in a snag. They encouraged us to take the canoe trip the next day and see what had happened to it. We demurred, but several others did not. They got close to the hippo but it was being eaten by eleven crocodiles. They decided to portage their canoes around it and continue their trip up the tributary. Goodness. I am not getting out of my canoe in the presence ("presence" defined as close enough to see them) of eleven crocs in high feast day mode. I am turning around and going back to look for more birds.

Instead of the canoe, we selected an afternoon boat cruise on the lower Zambezi. Most all of the others wanted to go off for more kidney-jarring hours of bouncing through the park in search of the elusive leopard, and maybe some lions as well. We decided that we'd seen the leopard. For two and half hours we cruised slowly down river in an aluminum boat with an outboard, a guide, and a helmsman, for maybe three miles. We saw an elephant at the riverbank and were able to get to within fifteen feet of him. Head on. And he was even in musth. We saw a beautiful fish eagle on a tree beside the river and a really lovely malachite kingfisher, small and a jewel-like blue. We came right up to the edge of an island where herons had nested, three or four types. We probably disturbed fifty birds by this, who all went flapping away in various frames of mind. And we saw, honest to goodness, thirty-five hippos, all in the river, in groups of three or four.

We managed not to hit any, which was good given that the crocs were waiting for just such an opportunity. If you live to be 120, you probably get good at waiting.

Love and kisses, Bob

Afterword: The Zambezi River is now in the process of being bridged at the choke point where we had to cross on a small boat. This is a very good thing for the economies of Zambia and Zimbabwe, the latter still struggling to overcome the legacy of former president Mugabe. North/south commerce will be enhanced, economic growth will be higher than it would have been, local citizens will be somewhat better off. I am not at all sure the local wildlife will be better off.

As more roads are built and more people have access to more land, reserves will shrink and poaching will grow. I hope that I am wrong, but I doubt it. If you want to see wild animals in their more or less natural habitat, go now or soon or again. I plan to.

One: India, Mystical and Otherwise

December 2017

Dear Aunt Janet,

Introduction

We landed in Delhi, India's capital, on the third of December. It is foggy/smoggy and there is more traffic than I remembered. Of course, you could probably say that about every major Asian city. And you could say that it sure does take a long frigging time to get here even flying through Vancouver on the way (why?) but we already knew that.

We are on a two-week-plus India trip, fetchingly labeled "Mystical India" by the travel agency, although so far the only mystical part is why it takes an hour to get the luggage off the plane. All life is suffering? Also, why in a largely Hindu and minority Muslim country there are so many Christmas decorations? I counted four large images of Santa Claus in the airport alone. But since I have not finished my reading program on Buddhism and Hinduism, I will not suggest that he (S. Claus) might be a bodhisattva somewhere in the Buddhist canon, or some reincarnation of Vishnu or Brahma for those of the Hindu faith. I don't think he's an analogue of Shiva the Destroyer, however, as there are sex identification problems and all the images of Santa that I have seen does not have him wearing the traditional necklace of skulls. I will stay alert for additional mystical encounters and keep you posted.

We were pretty starved after a fourteen-and-a-half-hour airplane ride, and the hotel provided us with good Chinese food at their restaurant called the Spicy Duck. I always come to Delhi for good Chinese food since we don't have it in Encinitas. We do have good Indian food, however. Not sure if people come from Beijing to eat at our local Indian restaurant.

World Heritage sites—you know I am a bit of an ancient site/archaeology fan, using the World Heritage site system as an indicator and a guide to a country is a useful shorthand to more disciplined research. It's not perfect, and the fact that UNESCO, who manages the system, keeps adding sites means inevitably that the quality will decline over time as more sites receive this status. Or maybe the Taliban will keep blowing up images as they did to the giant standing Buddhas of Bamyan in Afghanistan, and things will even out. Let's hope not.

There are thirty-six World Heritage sites in India, although they count six Rajasthan forts as one site. When I read through the descriptions, I get forty-one. The USA in comparison is home to twenty-two of the 981 sites worldwide. But we are a much younger country than India. The Indian sites can be categorized, roughly, as eight forests/parks/reserves, eight temples, eight forts, four tombs/monuments, four rock shelters/caves, and then single examples of cities, observatories, step wells, etc. Of these, our plans are to see only five. So it goes.

Itinerary

We visit four major cities—Delhi and Jaipur in Rajasthan, Agra and Varanasi in Uttar Pradesh, and the Ranthambore tiger preserve in Rajasthan—all in the north central and northwest part of the country. Mostly we drove between locations in a large bus labeled "Tourist" across the front, as if anyone who saw us might have thought we were traveling vacuum salesman or the national senior lacrosse team. The other giveaway was that most of us wore our red "Cornell" baseball caps, which the tour organizers had given us. Not very many people in India wear red Cornell baseball caps, not even Rajan Tata who is the most famous Cornell alum in the country.

Gandhi

Background—most of us know vaguely that Gandhi stood for nonviolence and was important, even instrumental, in getting India its independence from the UK after the Second World War. He dressed in funny white clothes and walked around barefoot. However, it is hard to overestimate his importance in India, or the reverence in which he is held, even seventy years after his death. For example, his picture is on every piece of Indian paper currency. George Washington only makes it onto the US twenty. Gandhi's persona or his policies are routinely invoked by every major political party, even the Hindu nationalist BJP.

Cremation site—we visit two Gandhi sites in Delhi. The cremation site is along the Yamuna River, except it's really in a big wide park that follows the river. In fact, it's not at all clear where the river is, so we take its presence on faith. Many high government officials and prime ministers have also been cremated at points in the park, and their ashes put into the river. You may visit them if you take a liking for cremation sites. The Gandhi bit itself is a simple marble slab and an eternal flame in a lantern-like enclosure. It is in the center of a big expanse of grass, laid out in a square with intersecting gravel pathways and a couple of plumeria trees not blooming. A one-story walkway surrounds the cremation site/garden of maybe two acres. This is said to be the second-most visited site in India after the Taj Mahal. The Gandhi story has an interesting parallel with that of Abraham Lincoln, especially the assassination after the success of an important political achievement—independence for Gandhi, holding the country together for Lincoln. But honestly, I like the Lincoln Memorial better. I may not be a "simple is better" sort of person.

Museum—and there's the Gandhi museum/assassination site. It was the home of a wealthy patron and Gandhi stayed there when he came to Delhi from Gujarat where he mostly lived. One odd thing—a set of concrete footprints are set in the ground, tracing each step Gandhi took the morning of his assassination, from his bedroom to the portico in the garden where he was meditating when his assailant shot him three times. The concrete footsteps look a lot like shoe inserts, but you can't walk on them, you can just walk beside them. The rest of the building is filled with large blowups of Gandhi comments—mostly along the line of humility and how everyone should love one another, and animals too, and don't eat either one. Plus twenty-some wooden diorama cases looking like old Philco TV sets, but instead they have small doll-sized figures inside, depicting events in Gandhi's life. If you read the descriptions of each event you rapidly come to the conclusion that it was way easier to get the country independent than it was to stop the religious and caste and tribal violence. This might be a depressing conclusion for a multiracial and multireligious society.

Forts and Palaces

There are quite a lot of forts, at least in the north and central part of India where we were. Was there a fear of war and insurrection? Of other guys coming down from the farther north and throwing out the current rulers, even as they had themselves done? The answer has to be yes or possibly "Huh?" Due north is the Himalayas, not much of an invasion route. Also interesting to note is that of the four original castes in India, the second-highest one was the warrior caste, or Kshatriya. We could point out that warriors, generally called "knights," were a pretty big deal in Europe as well, so this is hardly an Indian preoccupation.

The Amber Fort—it is a beautiful palace really, not a fort, the defensive fort is on top of the same hill, and when the bad guys attacked the royal residents took a tunnel up the hill to the real fort. The Amber Fort itself is about three-quarters of the way up the hill, and to get to it many tourists ride on elephants up the long set of ramps, slowly and ploddingly, and then get offloaded in the courtyard and look either embarrassed or surprised that they have actually done such a thing. The elephants look inscrutable. Our guide said his tour company stopped using the elephants about a year ago after one got spooked and crushed a tourist. I think this was understandable. Also the elephants are occasionally mistreated, get sores, get really bored, and have to wear gaudy headdresses. It is not recorded if the maharajah who built the fort, Shah Jahan, got to his palace on an elephant or more sensibly on a horse. We came up the back way in jeeps.

The fort, really palace, is a lovely, large, many-layered, many-roomed place. With lots of tourists around looking at the many rooms and wondering who took the furniture. And why they paid for the slow and uncomfortable elephant ride to get there. But the use of mirrors as inlays in the "public audience" room is really spectacular. It was good to be the emperor.

Red Fort—the other good thing in Agra besides the Taj Mahal is the Red Fort, sometimes called the Agra Fort. It is subject to the two-fort confusion. There is a "red fort" in Delhi, and there's one in Agra. They were both built by Mughal emperors, Shah Jahan and Akbar, respectively. It does look like they used the same architect. And they are both World Heritage sites. We drive past the Red Fort in Delhi but don't stop, which is too bad as it is one of only three World Heritage sites in the city. We also pass the ruins of a Delhi sultanate fortress that looks pretty interesting but we don't stop. And we see bits of the original city walls. From the bus. Next time. The Red Fort in Agra is another matter.

Here is a quick Indian history refresher, because it is not taught well in American public schools. India (and by this we include Pakistan and Bangladesh) was made of a large number of competing states, pretty much all Buddhist or Hindu, from earliest times until 1050, when the first Muslim tribes began invading from the Turkic area in the central Asian steppes. Although it should be noted that Alexander the Great and his army got as far as deep into the Punjab before inconveniently dying in 328 BC.

This first wave of Muslims, generally known as the sultans, conquered and ruled most of India for about three hundred years—1250 to 1550, converting many of the conquered Hindus and Buddhists to Islam. But this zeal for conversion did not prevent them in turn from being conquered by their brother Muslims in the form of the Mughals from north Asia. There were six "great emperors" in the Mughal dynasty, and they and then others ruled for about three hundred more years until 1850, by which time the reign had fragmented into lots of princedoms ruled by Mughal maharajahs. Many of these had been suborned by the wiles of the British East India Company who had better guns, better organization, and were happy to just get the maharajahs into debt and hire their armies and slowly take over lots of the country as forfeited collateral, in fact if not in name. The maharajahs had not discovered compound interest, it seems.

The first six guys were pretty effective. The initial emperor was Babur (the warrior not the elephant in the French kid's books although he may have used elephants) who beat the sultan's forces decisively in 1526. He was followed by Humayun, whose main accomplishment seems to have been making sure he got a great tomb. Then Akbar who was a very effective and terrifying ruler, enlarging the conquered area and building his big fort and palace at Agra in 1573, the first of the two "red forts." By this point the Mughal empire included all of Afghanistan, Pakistan, Bangladesh, and all of India but a small bit at the southern tip of the subcontinent.

The Agra Fort was both fort and royal palace, covering about two square kilometers on the Yamuna riverfront. It is largely of dramatic red sandstone, hence the name, and looks like a fort is supposed to look—tall, sheer ramparts, crenulations, firing ports, drawbridge, armored gates that occur in sets, three major layers of defensive walls and even a moat and drawbridge. The British, recognizing quality when they saw it, occupied it after they took over India and about half of it is still a military base. It is much more impressive in sheer size and grandeur than most European forts/castles—bigger, taller, more elaborate, and with far better "apartments" for the Mughal and his various consorts and children. The Taj Mahal is gorgeous, but this was the first time I had seen the Red Fort. I found it captivating.

So, too, is the story of Shah Jahan, the fourth Mughal emperor who was no slouch himself, enlarging the empire in southern India after taking over when Akbar died, and eventually finding/wedding (since his three thousand existing wives wasn't enough) a legendary Persian beauty and bestowing on her the name "Mumtaz Mahal," which means "Precious One of the Palace." She accompanied him on his military campaigns and bore him fourteen children. Whew. At the birth of number fourteen she made him promise to build her a big memorial if she died, and then promptly expired.

So he did, and then planned on building an equally grand mausoleum for himself out of black marble. But by then his four remaining sons had narrowed themselves down to one, Aurangzeb, the narrowing being accomplished by Aurangzeb killing the other three. Unless he did it all at once (the accounts are not clear) then the last brother killed must have been either a bit slow or not paying attention. Aurangzeb then informed his dad that no more treasure was going to monuments. He threw his father into house arrest in said Red Fort—with his apartment having a view of the Taj. Who says there are no romantics in the world?

City Palace in Jaipur—it's big and lovely and has many rooms and an associated museum where there are many examples of the clothing worn by the various shahs. Of special interest is the long tunic worn by the one who weighed five hundred pounds. As one might expect, the gown is large and tentlike. And there's a nice café on the grounds of the palace, which might be the best part of the place. Otherwise it's not so interesting, and all the signage in the museum is in Hindi. The Amber Fort it is not.

Temples and Churches

India is 80% Hindu, 18% Muslim, and the remaining bits are Sikh (1%), Buddhist (0.7%) and minor Jain and Christian populations. As best one can tell, much of Indian life has a higher "religious" content than that found in the West. Maybe. Evidence of religious belief as shown by religious practice is hard to document. But more on that later.

Largest mosque in Delhi—to really get in the spirit of India, we are first required to take a death-defying bicycle rikshaw ride through the narrow streets of Old Delhi. If we hadn't been on a budget-priced tour I would have thought that it was a movie set put together just for us. Crowded, people on the sidewalks, and small storefronts and on the narrow, curving streets, people pushing carts and riding in bicycle rickshaws and in tuk-tuks and even in the occasional intrepid car (fools). Every so often we stopped and sat for a moment or two, not to take pics but because the traffic was so crammed up. And then people in other pedicabs bumped into us from behind. Clearances between vehicles could be a small as an inch. Keep your hands inside the vehicle at all times.

Shah Jahan apparently did not care for wide roads and straight lines. On the other hand, he was emperor of almost all of India so he got to do pretty much what he wanted. Hence Old Delhi, which he constructed out of whole cloth and mud brick in the 1650s. The place wasn't very big when he built it but it even included a city wall, almost completely gone now. You can't be too careful.

The Brits, when they took over in 1858, had different ideas. The major urban design was laid out and significant buildings were built by two architects in particular—Edwin Lutyens and Herbert Baker, who were keen on grids and low buildings with big yards and parks and roundabouts and broad avenues. This is everything that Old Delhi is not. And it is far easier to navigate. When you're a tourist you do a lot of driving around in noxious big busses, so I know. They called it "New Delhi," which at the time it was. There, mystery solved.

After our Old Delhi trial by pedicab, we eventually arrived, slightly dented, at the Jama Masjid Mosque, built as a part of Old Delhi by Shah Jahan. Big open square plaza, people just walking around and hanging out. Not all Muslim people, as judged by the general lack of female head coverings, only a few abayas and only a couple of the full-face concealments on the women. Marble and red sandstone, built in 1656—three gates, three big domes, four towers, two very tall minarets, all constructed by hand—no power tools, no bucket trucks, no cranes, probably a lot of scaffolding, no steel-toed shoes. Impressive in an austere way. The absence of human or animal imagery, a Koran requirement, makes the decorative parts somewhat less interesting. Carved lotus leaves surround the base of columns, but that's about it.

It is said that on special holidays the mosque holds as many as twenty-five or thirty thousand people. But it is smack dab in the middle of Old Delhi with its maze of small streets and two- and three-story havelis. When I hear this, as I am still an American, I think to myself, "I wonder where they all park."

Sikh temple—we visit the largest Sikh worship site in New Delhi, the Gurudwara Bangla Sahib temple. Sikhs make up only 1% of the Indian population, but they are serious warriors and generally seem to punch above their weight in the troublemaking department. I don't know why as we never really got a good explanation of the theology. What is clear is that not only do you take off your shoes, you walk through a small trough of water to purify your feet as well as your hands, which you have previously washed. Then you walk around with wet feet. Also everyone must cover their heads, and a baseball cap won't do. A bandana wrapped as a do-rag does work, however.

The interesting thing here is that as a matter of religious commitment they run a large communal feeding program, feeding twenty thousand people a day. You don't have to be poor or a Sikh, just show up and they'll feed you, for free. Good works are good works.

The temple itself has lots of gold inside the small worship area. No images. You worship at your own speed—stand, kneel, prostrate yourself, it's all fine. There is someone reading the holy scripture in an elevated voice but this is not a "service" as Christians think of it. No requirement for daily worship, or weekly, or monthly, just come whenever. The rest of the ortho-doxy or required practice was unclear, except you have to wear a turban if you are male. And never cut your hair.

Hindu temple in Rajasthan—built by the Birla family, the second-richest family in India after the Tatas, it is new and pure shining white, constructed entirely of white marble. Striking if not awe inspiring, it also has a number of statues placed in small alcoves surrounding it of people you wouldn't have expected—Plato, Aristotle, St. Peter, Jesus, Buddha, Zeus, Zoroaster, Donald Duck. No, I am just kidding about that, but the others and many more are there, perhaps attesting to the remarkable malleability of the Hindu view of religion. It has bright stained-glass windows, with images of Shiva and Vishnu and Ganesha. It is clearly an act of devotion by the family and quite elaborate. Not many people are there.

Buddhists? We don't see any active Buddhist temples or monasteries. The Buddhists seem to have all been driven out, headed for Nepal or Sri

Lanka or to Burma where they could in turn drive out the Rohingya. We did see one large Buddha statue in Sarnath but it was built by donations from Thailand.

Wildlife

Tigers! Tigers! We are in southern Rajasthan and the Ranthambore National Park's tiger reserve for three game drives. Our team is put in big open trucks with room for twenty people—five rows of four seats, not elevated. And thus not really good sight lines for people in the middle seats. Except they won't be eaten first. It doesn't matter as there's nothing to see except lovely birds, nice small spotted deer, nice big dark sambar deer, occasional ugly wild pigs, and the odd crocodile in one of the three lakes. This could be a wildlife paradise for the predators as there is lots of prey around and no one these days like humans to kill the predators or take over their land and build forts, palaces, houses, factories and shopping malls. According to our "naturalist" guide who has worked here for seventeen years but has only a high school education, there are sixty-five tigers on this reserve, ninety leopards, and twenty-five sloth bears who we don't see as they are hiding out somewhere being, well, slothful. There are no smaller animals with teeth and claws so the deer have a good time and the few predators have a great time.

It is a more rugged place than the game reserves in Africa—a series of steep hills, canyons, and flatlands, three modest-sized lakes, a bit of a cross between high desert and second-growth deciduous forest and grassland. Right now all the grass is gold to yellow because it has been three months since the rains stopped. Great cover for tigers who are also golden yellow. There is a large ninth century fortress on top of one of the hills and it is quite impressive. But not on our list of things to see. The reserve covers 150 square miles, and it is but one of forty-eight tiger preserves in India. Tigers numbered 32,000 in 1900 and were down to about 2,000 in 1971 before Indira Gandhi stepped in and created the reserves. We were also told that she made all hunting illegal in India at the same time. Yes, all hunting, not just hunting tigers. Maybe true, maybe not, but true for the tigers who have since then slowly built their strength up to 4,000.

At the same time as the hunting ban she made owning guns illegal throughout the country. Our guide is legitimately proud of this fact without pointing out the US problems with private firearms. Since he is being polite, we are as well, and do not point out <u>that Indira Gandhi was killed</u> <u>by a gun</u>, several guns, and may have been wary of armed insurrections.

Tiger facts that may or may not be true:

» Male tigers need a range of forty square kilometers, females sixteen to twenty. Males weigh in at six hundred pounds, females four hundred pounds, neither one of whom you want to meet on a dark night when they're hungry.

» Tigers are solitary and do not hunt in packs, unlike lions. They mark their territory and do not like to see other tigers except for dates. They hunt at night and sleep in the day, or maybe sit around smoking and playing cards and rewinding their turbans.

» When mating, male tigers "do it" fifty times a day, presumably with female tigers. We are not sure who first counted this phenomenon.

» Tigers can run really fast for about 100 yards, after which they have to sit down and rest for thirty minutes. Most Americans have the same problem except for the fast part. Deer can run pretty fast and for longer periods of time/distances, although mathematically all they have to do is run fast for 110 yards. Deer may not be good at math, however. They appear at least to be good at multiplication.

» Tigers like to catch and eat sambar deer—the largest deer in Asia—as these deer for some reason cannot see past fifteen feet, and their flesh is salty and spicy. A tiger lying in tall yellow grass cannot be seen by anyone, even a deer wearing glasses, because remember he's camouflaged—all that yellow fur and stripes. So vision or lack thereof is not so strong a capacity or weakness for a deer. And as for tigers liking salt and ordering extra hot peppers on their pizza, this cannot be determined.

Off we go, fully briefed. To see a solitary nocturnal camouflaged beast somewhere in its forty square kilometer area while driving around in a noisy truck in the early afternoon, accompanied by equally noisy occupants, seems unlikely. We carefully test this hypothesis and find that it is true—we see bupkis as to tigers. We return to the lodge and have a talk by another naturalist who assures us that there are tigers. Somewhere. He has a picture of one.

Before we came here, we had several friends who said, in essence, "Oh, yeah, Indian tiger preserve. Your guide will drive around and then look at the ground and say 'pug prints' and drive around some more and stop the vehicle, and demand that you all be quiet while he listens for warning cries of the deer [Deer make noise? Who knew?] and then drive slowly around and finally decide that you just missed the tiger. Bit of a con, you know."

Our second "game drive" starts in the morning at sunrise and proceeds almost exactly as above for two hours of very bumpy and somewhat cold tooling around on rocky dirt roads. And then, mirabile dictu, we get the word from other vehicles (no one seems to have discovered radios yet, even though they all have cell phones) that we're close. And then, further mirabile dictu, after some more jouncing around and getting beaten up by overhanging branches, we actually have two large tigers about twenty-five feet away, graciously gamboling alongside the vehicles for about twenty minutes and not eating any of us. They really were tigers, not dwarfs in tiger suits—a mother and her twenty-month-old cub who looked every bit as large as she did.

Fun and impressive and beautiful in a "don't come over here, you're fine, we can see great, really, from right where we are, thanks for asking" sort of way. It is clear that they realize they haven't really any enemies in the area, even though I used to be a capitalist developer. So I am a potential enemy but I am disguised as a wildlife tourist—binoculars, pants that morph into three pieces if you zip off the legs or become a double amputee, floppy dork hat, TravelSmith 100% polyester shirt, the works. The odds of actually seeing tigers in this or any tiger reserve are probably 10%, and we hit the jackpot. I am glad that the Brits didn't kill them all off, and it's disappointing that the Chinese keep paying for dead tiger and dead rhino medicine, largely to promote sexual potency. Can't they just use the Internet or Viagra like the rest of us? It's way cheaper.

Cows! Cows! Do cows really wander around the streets unmolested, even occasionally fed? We see a lot of them, so I decide to count, when we leave the city of Madophur, the medium-sized city next to the tiger reserve. From our hotel in the center of the town to the outskirts I count 138 cows, most along the roadside, some in vacant lots, none fenced in. I also count nine camels just for the heck of it, all of them pulling carts. I did not count the many dogs and the many pigs roaming around. Yes, the cow is still a sacred cow in India. I only saw one cat in twenty days.

Birds—given that the total cat population in India is approximately fifteen, there are a whole lot of birds. Large ones like kites, vulture equivalents, soaring above every city we were in. Medium-sized ones like pigeons, everywhere because it is worshipful to feed them. Good looking ones like the common mynah (wonderful yellow eyes) and the red-wattled lapwing—a dramatic black and white bird related to African lapwings but a bit more classy. No one eats any of these because many, many people are vegetarians. We do get served chicken a lot at our meals, but never beef or pork. And dal three times a day which is a bit much even for a dal fancier like me. There is an entire Hindu temple in Deshnok near Bikaner in Rajasthan where rats are worshipped. We did not go there and no one complained. Maybe next trip.

Monuments and Mausoleums

In the US you don't see a lot of mausoleums, where people are actually buried under the floor of big public buildings. But creating such things has a long history. One of the original Seven Wonders that no one can ever remember is the Mausoleum at Halicarnassus, near what is modern Bodrum, Turkey. It was erected in 350 BC by Queen Artemisia in honor of her husband King Mausolus. It was such a big deal that all such buildings henceforth took his name. The crusaders destroyed it in 1534, probably looting it first. The queen eventually had a nice perennial flower named after her (artemisia, no less). Probably not by the crusaders who were not generally gardeners.

The best place we saw in Delhi, the Qutab Minar tower, is one of three World Heritage sites there, the other being Humayun's Tomb (below) and the aforementioned Red Fort. As befitting a tower, it is very large and round and beautiful, faced with brick and then with marble. It is tall, 238 feet tall, the highest tower in India. That is half the height of the Washington Monument, but built way earlier—AD 1368, before anyone but the original owners were living along the Potomac. It was built as a triumphal monument, a tribute the Sultan Qutb-ud-din Aibak, the first Muslim ruler of Delhi, when he conquered the last Hindu state in what was then the large (Hindu) kingdom of Delhi.

The site includes the remains of a large mosque and a whole park full of remnants of earlier mosques and gateways and the like—well maintained and somewhat restored. Over to the side is a large round twenty-foot-tall platform twice as big as the base of the Qutb, built using the standard "rubble and mortar" construction precedent, with the plan to face the final structure in brick and marble. It was started by the sultan's successor to build something twice as tall as the tower—hence the base that was twice as big. But he died, so it was never finished. And then *his* son had other things to do with the money. Tempus fugit and so on. Oh, yes, you used to be able to go up to the top of the Qutb, a bit like the Washington Monument but with no elevator. In 1981 the internal lighting failed and in the stampede to get out forty-five mostly schoolchildren were killed on the stairs.

So now it's closed. Not repaired, just closed.

Humayun's Tomb—now skip ahead five centuries from the sultans to the Mughals. Note to morticians: Muslims bury their dead, and if they are rich they build big memorials. Hindus engage in cremation and then disposal of the ashes in the nearest sacred river. Not clear if anyone in India holds wakes, or the currently popular "celebration of life."

This tomb, one of the Delhi World Heritage sites, is a starter kit for the Taj Mahal. Humayun was a great Mughal emperor two before Shah Jahan, the founder of Delhi and builder of the Taj. The tomb site is quite large with lots of grass squares defined by hedges surrounding the large marble building. This grass, generally mischaracterized as a "garden," was supposed to represent paradise. Paradise also has a water feature divided into four parts—water, milk, honey, and wine. Why wine gets a place is unclear given the religion's fairly uncompromising stance on alcohol. The building itself is impressive and you can go inside and see a small marble crypt that is not actually that interesting.

We ran into lots of lines of schoolgirls being taken on a fun outing to visit the tomb of some dead ruler of hundreds of years ago. They trooped past us in a more or less orderly file, all in blue pinafore uniforms. Most of them called out "hello" and most of us said "hello" back, thus establishing a meaningful dialogue with India's younger generation. The girls giggled. We grinned. Humayun's reaction was not clear.

The Chand Baori—on the way to Agra we were told we would stop and see a step well. I thought this was filler. And besides it didn't fit into any of my categories. And besides I had never heard of it. I figured that some guy a long time ago dug a big well with steps inside it so women in saris could walk down some dirt steps, fill a pot with water, put it on their heads, and then, using the remarkable feat of balance that many Indian women seem to master, hike back up to the top and go home and make chapatis. How interesting can this be, although it's nice to break up the long bus ride. A drive-through McDonald's might be OK as well, but that's not in the cards.

Wrong, very wrong. This was a remarkable place. Abhaneri in Jaipur where we stopped is a crumby rural village, but it's famous for having the deepest step well in the world.

The step well is a very large set of excavated squares, the topmost one thirty-five by thirty-five meters, and each subsequent one probably two meters less in dimension. Finally, you get down thirteen stories to the well part, which is not a hole in the ground exactly but a backyard swimming pool size body of water. The entire thing is not dirt, the walls are covered with careful stonework. Around three sides of the levels ziggurat stone steps have been built, every five meters or so, which serve not only as descent utilities but as dramatic decorations.

Holes in the ground, even deep ones, are not as notable as pyramids. But if you took this well and inverted it, you would have a hundred-foot pyramid, half the height of one of the pyramids at Giza. And decorated on each level with these stone steps, now arrayed as blocky shapes. Sitting in the middle of the green fields of Rajasthan. And built before AD 900. I found this remarkable—who wouldn't?

But there's more—it was also decorated around the top gallery with a series of stone carvings of exquisite detail, bearing a close resemblance to the best carvings at Angkor Wat. Wall panels with deep (five or six inches) bas reliefs of gods and demons and apsaras and buddhas and all other sorts of Asian iconography. Much of it has been looted over time, but much remains. The Indian government has only recently decided that this site needs protection, and now it has guards and a guy taking tickets, and they have restored a lot of the ground level structure as well. This was a major resting place, a "caravanserai" during earlier times. It is beautiful and not very crowded and remarkable. It needs a better publicist. And a better parking lot. The bathrooms are OK.

The Taj Mahal—there are only two things worth seeing in Agra. And to contradict that statement immediately, we should add a garden called the Mehtab Bagh. It is directly across the Yamuna River from the Taj and was designed to be an ideal viewing point, with a large pool that would exactly reflect the monument. But there was a problem—the pool was destroyed by a flood in 1987. Fixing it would have cost maybe $100K of civil work, but it has never been done. Really. Mystical India.

It is difficult to think of anything to say about the Taj that hasn't already been said. Except if your companion says, "Do you love me as much as Shah Jahan loved Mumtaz? Will you build me a Taj Mahal if I die before you?" You could say, "Sure, if you'll change your name to Mumtaz." But that is a tiny bit flippant. There is no adequate answer. The mausoleum took twenty-two years to build, is composed entirely of white marble, exquisitely decorated with inlaid precious and semiprecious stones and is very big, a fact that does not really come through in the pictures. It is the most visited site in all of India. It's also on the "New Seven Wonders of the World" list. So you say, "Of course, darling, I would be made bereft by your untimely passing" or you say, "Shoot no, where would I get that kind of money?" or you say, "Uh-huh," which is probably the only honest answer. But never mind this foolery, the Taj is a gorgeous building, a remarkable engineering and construction and decoration achievement, and a truly moving tribute to the power of love. Might even be that we need more of that these days and less of contentiousness and rancor. But what do I know?

Observing the observatory—we visit the popular site that gets my award for the dumbest tourist attraction in Rajasthan or possibly all of India—the "observatory" in Jaipur. This is a bunch of big cast masonry stuff—some two-story triangles, some one-story circles placed at an angle from the vertical, some half sphere holes in the ground sprinkled around a sort of grungy park. The creator was a midlevel maharajah named Singh and what this is not, first of all, is an "observatory" in any understandable definition of the word. It is instead a bunch of sundials and calendars, all hugely larger than they need to be, and created in 1736 after visits to other "observatories" including allegedly the Greenwich Meridian. He apparently did not pick up on the fact that measuring time by sundials had been <u>invented by the Babylonians</u> way before Christ, roughly 2,500 years previous. If he wanted to know what month it was or what day it was he could have asked the Maya <u>or other pre-Columbian cultures</u> any time after 500 BC. I hope we didn't pay a lot to get in. We did have six tour busses there, counting ours—four Chinese and two westerners. Not a lot of stuff to see in Jaipur one surmises.

Villages and Shopping

Shopping! We have small business day in Jaipur—actually two days, with a total of four visits to, in order, a jewelry factory, a blue pottery factory, a papermaking factory, and a rug and fabrics factory. The papermaking uses people instead of machines and makes nice rag paper gift bags and boxes and little five-by-eight journals with Buddha on the cover that you buy intent on suddenly becoming a gifted essayist but then realize how much easier it is just to write on your computer. The journals do not have spell-check nor do the gift bags.

Seeing all the workers submerge their arms past the elbow into vats of chemical dyes to pull out the packs of rags turning into paper was pretty disquieting. And doing it once every forty-five seconds for eight hours a day does not look like a wonderful job. Maybe the dyes are organic....

The pottery is pretty but made of quartz sand held together with some sort of "natural glue" and only fired once. Every bit of it is done by hand by the fifteen to twenty employees in the small factory. It looks like no two pieces are the same and the straight lines are raggedy. Because of the basic material and the absence of two firings, most of it breaks soon after you unwrap it, there is no Internet presence, you can't buy a "set" of anything, and porcelain and ceramic goods are so inexpensive that it is not hard to figure out that this "tradition" will soon bite the (quartz) dust. I skip the rugs/fabrics tour as I do not need a pashmina unless this is a genie who grants wishes suitable for general audiences.

Welcome back, liberal guilt, where have you been? On to the white man's burden part of the tour, which seems to be an obligation of all these adventures. For this we drive into the more rural part of Rajasthan that is easy as 70% of all Indians still live in villages and work in the fields. We leave the sanctuary of the bus and get jammed into the back of military-style jeeps where we cannot see and keep bumping our heads on the metal ceilings. We uncomfortably go down a very bumpy road and finally come to our destination. It is a one-room schoolhouse with no books, forty-four kids in eight grades, two teachers, one of whom never shows up, and not enough desks or chairs for everyone so they mostly sit on the floor. The kids are requisitely cute and we coo at them and to prove our empathy distribute erasers and socks. Socks for kids who wear flip-flops. I do not care for this and it certainly doesn't make any sense as philanthropy.

I skip the afternoon, which is an uncomfortable camel cart ride to a local village where we can see "how villagers live" and converse about their lives with them. What? Why? What is it we'd like to know—how do you like raising large plots of mustard? We have already taught their children that the rich white people come and give them gifts for nothing, what more wisdom do we have to convey—when to harvest the wheat fields? Ugh, ugh, and ugh.

In the evening we have entertainment—native touristic dancers who put pots of fire on their heads and whirl around. The dancers have been brought from Jaipur to perform for us in this pastoral rural area.

Hinduism and Its Holy Place

To use up some of our copious bus time, our guide gives us a long discourse on Hinduism, well done and pretty clear. Except where Hanuman the monkey god came from was skipped over. Not to be confused with Humayun the Mughal ruler with the big tomb. Everyone makes that mistake.

This is one confusing religion. Even my *Hinduism: A Very Short Introduction* book spends the first chapter trying to explain whether it is a religion or a way of life, and where it came from. No founder, no Bible, no Ten Commandments handed down on a mountaintop. You can't be a convert; you have to be born Hindu. While there are a number of well-known and popular gods, including Rama, Krishna, and Shiva, they all have manifestations, nine for Rama so far, about the same for the others. And they each have wives, and their wives have incarnations. You can worship any one of the big three or any one of their manifestations. But since the high being, although nameless as well as somewhat removed and disinterested, is found in all things, then anything you worship is part of that god and can be a god site. I think about the rat temple. Is each rat a god, or is it simply the class of rats? If the information we have been given is correct, then Hinduism is like pantheism without the structure. For example, 330 million gods. Why not 325,417? Who gets to decide? Who keeps track? The guide says, "You westerners name things, we worship them." These are analytical, "We like everything neat," sorts of questions that don't seem to work in Hinduism.

Is it important? Example one: Hinduism decrees a caste system that Gandhi got outlawed. However, every Sunday in the *Times of India*, there is a whole section devoted to ads for potential spouses, placed by the parents who are arranging the marriages. Every ad carries a notation of the caste of the sponsor and requests that any response have this same information, as well as the birth date of the respondent so that horoscopes can be compared. Hindu horoscopes.

Example two: Padmavati, queen of Chittor, is a figure of legend. Her existence, any record of her life and death, is not supported by anything in the historic record. Here's the accurate part: The second sultan of Delhi,

Alauddin Khalji, was a pretty good warrior as these things go. He fought off several Mongol invasions, and conquered nearby territories, including Gujarat, Ranthambore, and Chittor. He thus ended a number of Hindu dynasties.

Here is the legend part: What he really wanted was Queen Padmavati of Chittor, a Hindu. He conquered the territory and killed her husband. She, rather than submitting to an Islamic ruler, decided to burn herself to death, along with three thousand of her ladies-in-waiting, thus preserving her honor.

Here is the modern part: A Bollywood director named Sanjay Bansal has made a movie. In it there is a dream sequence where she appears to accept the advances of the conqueror Alauddin. This has outraged Hindu nationalists who accuse it of "distorting history." The chief minister of Madhya Pradesh has declared that he will ban it in his state. More radical groups have threatened to burn down any cinema that shows the film, and to cut the nose off of Deepika Padukone, the actress who plays the queen. A reward has also been offered for anyone who beheads the director. The national censorship board is reviewing the film to make sure that it is historically authentic. The unpleasant part of this is that the threats seem real. It's a legend, guys.

Varanasi—Varanasi is the holiest city in India, a combo of Jerusalem, the Vatican, and Mecca. And it sits on the River Ganges, the most sacred river in India. We ask ourselves unanswerable questions: How does a river become a god? Or in this case a goddess? The river isn't mentioned in early Hindu texts (the Rigveda or the Ramayana) and it is quite polluted near Varanasi—fecal coliform bacteria levels more than one hundred times the official India limit. But it is India's largest river by length and by volume of discharge, and the third largest in the world by discharge, although no one would have known this 2,500 years ago. It plays an important economic role in the lives of millions who live on the Indo-Gangetic Plain and make a living from agriculture. And if you are cremated on its shores you immediately achieve nirvana or the Hindu equivalent. And every Hindu is expected to come to Varanasi and bathe in it at least once in his or her life.

While water is important in Christianity (think baptism and holy water) and water is featured in Islam for its purifying abilities, there is no analogue to the powers attributed to the Ganges in any other major religion. There's the River Styx but it is imaginary. And while we're into epistemology, why is only the west side of the river sacred, and not the east side? The west has literally miles of houses/guest houses/hotels/temples/former palaces built along the banks, all called "ghats." They are slightly set back from the continuous sets of stairs that go down to and into the river. Every so often there is a gap and a narrow road intrudes so one can get down to the river through this very thickly built out western side. On the other side, nothing but a plain and the riverbank. I even see a guy galloping on a horse along this other bank, by himself. In this very crowded city, there are no structures on the east bank and only a very few people.

One interesting side note: among the ghats fronting the river is a large and impressive mosque, built by Akbar, the third Mughal emperor. Islam has nothing to do with the Ganges, and Muslims are buried, not cremated. It's kind of an "in your face" gesture by the emperor, and there it stands, still big and functioning. It is a little surprising that the radical Hindus haven't made a big deal out of it. The analogue would be building a mosque on the edge of Saint Peter's Square.

Since we don't plan on bathing in the Ganges or cremating anyone, why are we here? Largely as spectators—do they really burn corpses on its banks? Do pilgrims really bathe in it and thus cleanse themselves of all sins? Is there really a daily worship service to make sure the water continues its functions?

Yes, to all of the above. We ride in a large wooden boat resembling the *African Queen* without the wheelhouse. The diesel engine sounds exactly like Katharine Hepburn should be along any minute and help Bogart get the damn thing started. We go out in the evening and float around and watch eight pyres burning in the open along the bank at the cremation ghat, and then see what appears to be a Las Vegas guy act of seven men in bright, shiny, cream-colored jumpsuits dancing, ringing bells, singing, and whirling fire around in unison. In fact, it is Brahmins preforming the daily Aarti ritual. This is necessary to keep the river going, and has been performed every day for five thousand years. So we are told.

Until several years ago there was only one set of Brahmins doing this, but now a competing group has gone into business just down the river, with its own bells and loudspeakers, so it's a noisy set of dueling scriptures taking place under lights designed to look like umbrellas. It is interesting as showmanship, but since we don't know the language we cannot understand what is being said/chanted, and since we aren't Hindus we don't really understand the ceremony and the symbolism. And it is cold out on the river. The good news is that the ceremony works, because the river continues to flow.

We return in the morning, in another open boat, to watch people bathing. One would worry that this might be judged intrusive were it not for the fact that there are lots and lots of other boats floating around, filled with people doing same, as well as many people on the shore who are not bathers. There are more watchers than bathers. And besides, the women go in fully clothed, and the men at least wear their underwear. Titillation factor: zero. Watching people with their clothes on jump into a dirty river is not so interesting, it turns out.

You cannot park very close to the river, due to the constricted nature of the area. On the long walk back to the bus from the river we try and avoid stepping in the numerous cow patties. We try not to get run over by the numerous people on bikes and motorcycles. Fortunately, large trucks and busses are not allowed in the area around the ghats. We pass by what seems an endless chain of people begging—misshapen men, elderly widows, young girls with babies, you name it. And we attract an equally large cloud of street vendors selling postcards, toy camels, brass bells, necklaces, and whatever. They are very persistent. It is not a wholly pleasant experience. And it's still cold.

A questionable fact from our guide—there is a special bacteriophage found in the Ganges that makes the water clean and keeps it from spoiling [sic]. Despite the fact that it receives raw sewage from a number of sources, and untreated runoff, and the ashes of five hundred to six hundred corpses a day and plain old dead (uncremated) bodies of women, babies, sick people and holy men, none of whom for reasons unknown are allowed to be cremated. Unless you're Indira Gandhi who was in fact cremated and her ashes placed into the Yamuna, a major tributary of the Ganges. Despite this assurance, we did not take a bottle of Ganges water home with us.

Closing Observations

Ease of travel—overall traveling in India has become far more comfortable than when I first started going there for business in 1992. Food, hotels, bathrooms, bottled water availability, airports, roads are all better. It used to be that when I got out of the airplane on a trip to India, the minute my feet hit the tarmac I had diarrhea. Not so anymore. It is still challenging but it is also fascinating.

Tour groups—we had twenty-six people on our tour, which was too many. We ended up with several parties who were at best thoughtless or at worst addled. On a daily basis, one of this group was sure to be late to the bus every time, to touch the monuments when they are not to be touched, to fail to tip the sadhu when you have just taken an intrusive photo even though you have been told to do so (fifteen cents in rupees, not a big number), to lean over or push aside others to get the best picture, and to have to be taught each time how to turn on the listening devices that we all carry (it's the switch on top designated "on" and "off") thus delaying the rest of us who can actually tell time and read schedules. They also ask questions like:

Is that mountain natural?

Do rivers have tides?

Was there a movie about Gandhi?

This is the curse of large tour groups. Yes, it is easy to avoid, we just didn't.

Industry—after our visit to the papermaking factory there was a big discussion about how wonderful it was that the owner used lots of people and they did most of the work by hand, even ignoring machines already on the site. Preserving lousy and low paid and dead end and probably dangerous "manufacturing" jobs instead of using machines that are available just means that the Chinese will make all the paper. And the jobs will go away anyway. Ditto making pottery by hand.

If employment is such an important thing, then it should be possible to hire some more people to pick up the trash at the Taj Mahal. Lots of plastic wrappers, bits of tickets, cellophane, empty chip packets and the like. This is India's most visited tourist attraction and undoubtedly a big revenue earner, and it's trashy. What a sad thing.

But we had a great time, we saw lots of interesting stuff, and we stayed healthy. We are already plotting our next trip.

Love and kisses, Bob

Afterword: India has come a very long way since I first went there. I was in the ninth grade, with my family, and we were on a big boat cruising from Hong Kong to Naples via Ceylon, India, and the Suez Canal. It is now much easier to navigate, to stay healthy, to generally enjoy the opportunity to see such a different blend of cultures and such a long span of dramatic history. Unlike many of the places I have visited, India is actually getting better.

[22]

All Pasta All the Time

May 2018

Dear Aunt Janet,

It all started badly. But it's just another "missed airline connection with expensive rebooking scramble" horror story, so feel free to skip down a couple of pages if you are so inclined and have experienced more than enough of these yourself.

We left on Saturday but our Southwest flight was three hours and twenty minutes delayed by weather in getting in to Newark. We had a three-hour connection window with a "bargain" carrier, La Compagnie, that would take us to Paris. And then another generously timed flight on another carrier to take us to Palermo. Sicily is harder to get to than you would think.

We missed the La Compagnie flight, there was no one at the ticket desk in Newark when we finally arrived, no customer service number available except nine to five on weekdays, which this was not. We sent email. No response.

We notified the hotel in Palermo that we would be a day late, they were quick and helpful and sympathetic. Obviously they were not an airline.

Since we were going to be late, we changed the ongoing flight from Paris to Palermo on the Air France site on the Internet and paid the ticket change fee. Little did we know that we weren't on Air France, but on a code-shared piece of doo-doo airline called Transavia that has not yet discovered the Internet.

We called six hotels before getting a room for the night in Newark. We worried about quality of the manger.

The hotel dining room in the Best Western Plus was not open despite info from the front desk saying it was. They did have cheap red wine served at the bar in plastic glasses. The Coke machine had Doritos so all was not lost. We wondered what the "Plus" in the name was for.

Sunday we finally succeeded in getting the bargain airline on the phone after being on hold for thirty minutes. All tickets had been cancelled when we missed our first flight, including our return flight. Which obviously we had not missed. Goodbye bargain five thousand dollars.

Instead we bought Icelandair tix. I have always wanted to go to Iceland. Wish come true. But Icelandair didn't leave until eight-thirty Sunday evening, so we went to the next-door Wyndham for lunch, walking along the edge of the freeway as there are no sidewalks in Newark. We ate at the lovely Starlight Dining Room although no starlight was evident, it being 11:45 a.m. The menu had black piping and brass corner brads holding the plastic down. It's not often you get to see menus from the fifties, both the cosmetics and the substance. I considered ordering Jell-O salad off the menu. Instead I ordered a beer. Not available because it is not 12:00 yet. It is Sunday, you should be in church, not drinking beer before noon. I did not realize that New Jersey had become a theocratic state.

There was a huge mess in TSA screening at the airport. How many people can possibly want to go to Iceland? Fortunately we have a magic green dot on our boarding passes (biz class I guess or the native color of Iceland) so we bypass a huge line, thus it only takes us one hour to get through. Good thing we started early. Newark Airport is not a particularly fun place to hang out, in case you were curious.

Finally we're on. The airline crew wears Jackie Kennedy pillbox hats, at least the women. This is probably not in honor of the fiftieth anniversary of the RFK assassination that is coming up. This item is not for sale in the Icelandic magazine, pity. However, reindeer filet is one of the choices on the dinner menu. And there were some good movies. Unfortunately *Blade Runner 2049* is gorgeous but a completely incomprehensible mess as a story. And Harrison Ford should stop taking cameo roles in movies where he once starred.

The trip to Europe on Icelandair includes the added benefit of a stop in Reykjavik. Wow. The airline magazine boasts that Iceland is the third-windiest place on earth. The first two were not mentioned.

The Internet lists "ten windiest places on earth" but Iceland is not among them, not even tenth. It also didn't make the cut when I looked for the "seven windiest places on earth." After that I stopped looking. By the way, the consensus on the first two seems to be Antarctica and Mount Washington in New Hampshire, but there is great Internet disagreement. This is kind of like trying to answer "What are the three best beers in the world?" or "Name the three stupidest things Donald Trump has ever said."

We land with no trouble (the wind had the day off) except it's five in the morning. All around us is moldy green moss, flat, vacant, cold. No ice. Inside the airport, mostly white people. No, entirely white people. And no place to sit.

Other useful Iceland facts—*snyrtingar* means hello or possibly toilet, and is easily confused with the capital of Kashmir; thank you is *pakka per fyrir.*

Iceland looks like Kazakhstan but from our limited sample less Slavic. And less attractive, if that is even possible.

It's cold. Remember, "Ice Land." Must be a reason for the name.

We are required to go through passport control (nothing else to do with a two-hour layover, so what the heck) but it just got you into another restricted section of the airport, not into Iceland. At five in the morning the puffins are all asleep anyway. Welcome to the EU, of which Iceland is not a part.

We are in Saga class—is this really a good name? Against my will I am already part of a saga, so where's the blue cheese? Another benefit: the

Saga lounge in the airport has rocks in the floor and in the walls at various odd locations. I wonder about having rocks in my head based on my airline selection.

The best feature of the lounge other than rocks: a large video screen playing over and over a picture of several small very wan girls modeling Iceland clothes while auditioning for the local coven.

There are graphics of large birds with yellow crests, six-feet-tall pictures, decorating the walls as you head into the toilets, both sexes (the toilets, not the birds)—kind of makes you shrink up and wonder if you really need to go. Are there real birds inside the john?

And finally Sicily. The real story starts now.

General Observations

GO #1: It's more hilly than I thought, actually the place is full of hills and in some cases mountains. Big surprise—lots of mountains, or at least sharp and steep hills. And therefore valleys. Mount Pellegrino is to the immediate north of Palermo. No, the water doesn't come from there. We drove through a lot of the mountains and valleys, and it was mostly fine, but took longer than one would have thought. Especially if you ignored the directions from the rental car man who said, "Don't go this way," and made a big X on the map over the route. But then that was the only road we could find, so . . .

GO #2: It's more beautiful than I imagined. Maybe we just picked the right season, but there were flowers everywhere. Not just in careful gardens, but in the medians of all the freeways, and along roadsides. I saw oleanders in bloom everywhere, literally everywhere. And if it wasn't oleanders, it was bougainvillea. Other plants in profusion: Queen Anne's lace (*Daucus carota* for the Latinophiles) in a white and a yellow version, *Acanthus mollis*, wild petunia (either *Ruellia humilis* or *Ruellia simplex*, couldn't determine), yellow mullein with many branched stalks (*Verbascum thapsus*), dark red thistle, hollyhocks, yellow broom in profusion, centranthus, artemesia, fennel or dill, and cactus (*Opuntia* species) in bloom. And since Sicily is largely agricultural, many groves of citrus, almond, many fields of olive trees and lots of grapes in tidy rows in vineyards. In San Diego we're no slouches on roadside flowers, but this was impressive.

GO #3: The ocean is beautiful. Ever since L inadvertently (we hope) tried to kill us both by putting us on a Zodiac in twelve-foot seas in Kauai so we could go see some alleged native home sites of previous Hawaiians, accessible only on death-defying tiny inflatable and thereby also deflatable boats, we have had a solemn mutual agreement whose entire text can be quoted here: "No small boats." The definition of "small" is less displacement than an aircraft carrier. That agreement has worked fine, except that she loves boats, swims well, and is fearless. Thus we relented and took two tourist boat rides, one on a moderately sized boat off the island of Ortygia, where we were accompanied by nineteen young American women, probably college freshmen from a not very good but expensive school (USC perhaps?) who sat behind and around us and chattered the whole time about clothes, where they had bought clothes, future plans for clothes, and which of the waiters they had met were "hot." As required, they also continuously looked at their cell phones rather than the very nice shoreline with ancient sites, working fishing boats, and other bay-like things. But they were harmless in a "boy if their parents only knew what their money was paying for" sort of way, and besides the ride only lasted half an hour.

The other nautical excursion was off Taormina, just us and a boat driver who was very good and so we toured around Elephant Rock—which really does look like an elephant—and went into some small and not deep grottoes, and looked at the expensive hotels on the slopes and marveled at the amazing clarity of the water. It was better and clearer than anything I have seen in California. You could see the fish, lots of them, mostly eight to twelve inches, blue and grey and swimming in schools and fish-looking. No sharks. L jumped in and "swam with the fishes" but not in *The Godfather* sense. I monitored the distance to shore and the location on the boat of the life jackets. And drank the prosecco that was part of the deal. We each have our specialties.

GO #4: You could have put an annex to New Hampshire's White Face Lodge here—no Africans except selling beach shoes. Not hardly any brown persons either. Despite the huge hue and cry about refugees, none were in evidence. Maybe they're all in camps like in the kindly US. We could have been in Montana except that Sicily and Montana are completely different.

GO #5: There were lots of girls with lovely Caucasian skin but frizzy black hair, now dubbed "Sicily hair" by me, and black eyebrows. If not black enough, apply eyebrow pencil to make blacker and add a fine edge. Almost no blondes. We're not in Scandinavia or Montana. By the way, who sold these women all this really bad red hair dye? Red as in flaming carrot red if carrots burned. It was not subtle, and used without concern (or skill) by women of all ages. Sometime the whole head, sometimes just the top, sometimes streaks, sometimes just the bottom strands. Nice contrast with the eyebrows.

GO #6: Yet more proof if proof were needed that jeans and running shoes have triumphed everywhere: over all ages, races, sizes, and geographies. Nobody dresses up. We saw maybe two or three men in each of the major cities in coat and tie. Of course, we weren't doing business. But everyone we saw was casual-plus—slacks, shorts, jeans, sandals, running shoes, sneakers, T-shirts with logos or pictures, polo shirts, tank tops. One could have gotten by on two pairs of pants, two pairs of shoes, four shirts. And then you would be able to lift your luggage. There is laundry here and Woolite is portable. All that talk about fashionable Italians? Not in Sicily. Marcello Mastroianni has left the building. Also fat has triumphed, not just in America.

GO #7: No washcloths/face cloths in the hotels. I did not believe this when I read the advice in one of our guidebooks. Pack a washcloth? To a series of four- and five-star hotels? Really? You can always just give up and use a hand towel, but it's sloppier.

GO #8: For seventeen days, we did not eat a single piece of beef or chicken. Not because we weren't trying, it was just that everything else looked so attractive. We also did not read a newspaper or turn on a television set. Not out of policy, we just had more interesting things to do and see. It seems we didn't really miss much. And they let us back into the US despite this. I am glad there wasn't a test.

Favorite phrase of the trip: In Palermo, when we were out walking around we noticed a restaurant that was kitty-corner to our hotel. It had white tablecloths, it was full, and the menu looked interesting. The next day I went down and asked the desk person, "Does the restaurant across the street have good food?"

He answered, "All right. Why not?" Why not indeed, a useful phrase for much of Sicily.

"Shall we take the third exit on the roundabout even though it seems to lead in the wrong direction?"

"All right, why not?"

"Should we try the pasta with sardines although I have never eaten a sardine in my life?" "Should we climb the thousand steps to the Saracen Castle even though it's not in any of the guidebooks?" You can see how useful this can be. OK, enough of this, on to the pasta.

First things first: The search was to find and eat as many kinds of pasta dishes as possible in seventeen days, or "Can you eat pasta twice a day with no ill effects?" The short answer is yes. ABC agrees with me, if that matters. I found this out later when randomly watching "the news." If any of our hotels had offered pasta as a part of their breakfast buffets, I would have had pasta three times a day. One of them, the Caportigia Hotel in Siracusa, did have tomato bruschetta every morning, and so did I. Here are the findings of the experiment:

Durum spaghetti with pan fried broccoli rabe and Sicilian anchovies—sauce too thick, anchovy taste didn't really come through, but it was still great—Villa Igiea fancy restaurant, Palermo. Very good Sicilian red wine.

Fettucine amatriciana with Sicilian ham—ham looked threatening, like the "sliced pressed ham" you buy in American supermarkets but it was really good, especially with the very fresh grated parmesan. Trattoria on the sidewalk in Palermo.

Spaghetti with sardines and breadcrumbs—a couple of sardines on top, then big heap of spaghetti and bits of sardine and other stuff. Bebop Ristorante across from Grand Hotel Wagner—and another excellent Sicilian red wine, this time from a winery in the Etna DOC. This is said to be a traditional Sicilian dish, and we did see it a lot.

Spaghetti with tiny shrimp and dried tuna eggs—thin tomato sauce, hard to find the tuna eggs. Maybe this was a good thing. Lo Scopeto restaurant in Palermo near Grand Hotel Wagner.

Another night in Palermo at the fancy hotel: lobster soup with broken up pieces of fettucine in it. I decided to count this as a pasta dish, and it was wonderful. Just a hint of tomato, generous chunks of fresh lobster, and lots of quarter-inch pieces of broken fettucine. We could do that. And all the while, the background piano player was giving us a rendition of "The Girl from Ipanema." One more reason to hate piano players.

Tubetti, large cylindrical but short pasta tubes, with fresh cherry tomato quarters, and a pesto of almonds, modest garlic, and maybe a small amount of olive oil and cheese, topped with toasted sliced almonds—excellent! Small hole in the wall trattoria in Palermo near the hotel.

As a peculiar aside, L ordered a calzone, which usually looks like a large turnover in the US. In this case it was a full-sized pizza, and sitting on top of it was a somewhat conical pizza dough hat, not connected to the underlying pizza. You could pick it up to look at the pizza underneath. Or wear it. Or rip it into pieces and eat it. Or take it home to use as a Frisbee substitute. Very interesting.

Ortygia Trattoria—egg pasta in small strips with broad beans and their broth and big leafed spinach. Kind of a sort of a soup or stew but just yellow pasta, white beans, and wilted bits of green spinach—wonderful and simple.

Fancy hotel restaurant—squid ink pasta with fresh ricotta and datte-rino tomatoes (a breed of tomato that resembles a half-sized roma plum tomato and, this being Sicily, is always dead ripe) and probably olive oil. I have always wondered about squid ink but culinary cowardice has kept me from trying it. No longer! The pasta in small short tubes was a streaky black, not the sauce, which was a bit of olive oil. It tasted like, umm, pasta. Well, that's either good news or bad news depending on what you expected. It did not taste fishy or salty or like tennis shoes. It did, I was informed, make my tongue black but this wore off. So there we are.

Restaurant in Ortygia called Da Salva—L ordered fettucine with small bits of tomato, maybe a little chopped parsley, sitting in the middle of the plate, and surrounded on three sides by a half of an entire lobster, meat still in the tail and body and especially the large claw. No cracking hardware, none of those little tiny pointy things to use to pry out the meat.

However, there was a small flat fish knife that is all a determined person needs to go after it. And she did. I note that L was wearing a pristine white dress while making this attack. I suggested politely that she might want to tuck a napkin in at her neck, since there was no lobster bib. She couldn't make that work but proceeded apace and ended digging, cracking, tearing and otherwise successfully assaulting the lobster while getting nary a bit on her person. If this had been me, I would have ended up covered with lobster goo down to my sneakers.

Same restaurant, cascadere pasta with small shrimp and julienne of smoked swordfish. The pasta looks suspiciously like larger spaghetti but the waiter drew me a picture that looked like relaxed macaroni. Maybe it was what we know as bucatini. In any event, it was quite good although much fork spinning was required.

Random drop in at seafood trattoria named La Spigola for lunch after a morning of hiking and birdwatching—we each ordered pasta, L got a fabulous spaghetti *frutti di mare* with tomatoes and parsley and every kind of seafood, mostly mussels, clams, dime-sized small shrimp, pieces of some white fish, chunks of squid, etc.—we teamed up and ate it all. I got spaghetti amatriciana in a great tomato sauce with small chunks of some sort of smoked ham, also wonderful, and a couple of glasses of house red wine as good as any bottle we had had in Sicily. We debated just staying there for the rest of the day and drinking more wine. When we entered this eight-table place at one-thirty there were four tables occupied, all by real Italians, and none by tourists. Usually a good sign, and in this case it proved to be.

Rosmarino Ristorante in Taormina, first night—spaghetti with black truffles, Nubian garlic, artichoke hearts. Excellent! I didn't know the Nubians raised garlic. I didn't know there were Nubians anymore.

Second night in Taormina, restaurant along the street—fettuccine with gorgonzola, radicchio and walnuts—yummy.

Third night—large tubes with octopus and chickpeas—very good. I am learning to really like octopus. Easier if it's chopped up in bits. It also would be easier if I hadn't in January read *The Soul of an Octopus* by Sy Montgomery. A very good book.

Food observations #1: Very well, you could argue that the last discourse on pasta could have already been food observations, but read on.

After much data collection it is clear that Sicilians at least do not think that any pasta except one with red sauce needs or deserves or requires parmesan cheese to top it off. So they don't provide any and as we are trying to fit in, we don't ask. If you make the pasta the right way, it doesn't need any cheese, you stupid American. I think this is the message.

FO #2: If you go to a wine tasting location and they serve you tiny helpings of wine in thimble-sized plastic cups like you'd find holding your daily dose of pills if you were in the hospital, then the chances are not good that this will be drinkable wine. Flee.

FO #3: Why can't the Italians, of Sicily at least, make decent desserts? They make everything else so well! Then it comes to desert and common sense and good judgment just desert them, so to speak, and they decide that if a little gelatin is good, a lot is better, and while you're at it, why not take perfectly good cream puffs and douse them in not very good rum, or take lovely cannoli and add twice as much sugar as the recipe calls for? Or twice as much ricotta (and twice as much sugar) as will actually fit? Oh my, not good.

Palermo

We stayed at the Grand Hotel Villa Igiea, a fine old historic set of buildings built on a hill on the north side of the large working port, with a great view of the port and the whole harbor. A lovely swimming pool and a fabulous dining room, and a certain courtly décor to it all. Pictures of visiting and well-dressed dignitaries from the twenties and thirties decorated all the hallways. I half expected to run into Wallis Simpson rounding one of the corners.

The dinner process was initiated, both times that we ate there, with a complimentary glass of prosecco. You didn't even have to ask, they just brought it. Maybe I hadn't done enough work on this, but I have never in the US had a glass of this Italian champagne equivalent that struck me as any better than OK. Not so at the restaurant; it was crisp and cold and lovely. I even asked to see the bottle and wrote down the name—Borgo

Molino Prosecco—but I have my doubts that this will be available at the local BevMo. Probably not in Iceland either.

We walked around Palermo several times, especially the downtown part where all the neat buildings are—a great cathedral with outside decorations of Islamic motifs, all geometric, no images of living things. The explanatory material constantly points out that Sicily has a long history of being ruled by: Greeks, Romans, Arabs, Normans, French, and maybe the East India Company. Everybody got a turn. And thus the local food, architecture, culture, religion, etc., is a composite of all of these various rulers. The Greeks got the prize for longest tenure, ten centuries, and left behind the best stuff. Normans came in second.

Best cathedral/church/chapel/*chiesa*/*cappella* of the trip, and there were many: the Cathedral of Monreale. This is a small mountain village above Palermo. It translates as "mountain of the king" as I suppose it was at one point. We hired a driver and a car (which turned out to be a Porsche sedan) with a knowledgeable guide. The cathedral from the outside was fortress-like, since it began life as a fortress sitting on top of a mountain with a nice view of Palermo. Two large watch towers on the front. And since this is Norman architecture, it is very boxy, no flying buttresses, no gargoyles.

Inside it is soaring as befits a cathedral, with rows of columns, several domes, a large altar, and backdrop. The windows along the sides are quite small with no stained glass—fortress architecture again. There is virtually no sculpture anywhere other than a small altarpiece with six saints in a row. Ho hum—but wait!

While the lower walls are unornamented, the upper walls on two levels are completely covered with large mosaics of biblical scenes including much from the Old Testament. And it is all gold all the time—everything is mosaics with gold. Our guide says 250 pounds of gold were used in the artwork. It is not clear who measured this or how it was measured, remarks the analyst inside me, but it is clearly a lot of gold. Each separate scene had Latin lettering so you had a clue what it was. I got Noah and the ark right away. But Lot's wife looking back at Sodom and Gomorrah and turning into a very pure white figure of salt wasn't so immediately clear, especially as the representation of Sodom and Gomorrah in flames looked like a couple of dollhouses burning in a trash can. But that is a small quibble, the art was wildly impressive.

Attached was a cloister, largest of the Middle Ages. Lots of complicated iconography on the capitals of the columns surrounding the four sides and holding up the roof of the large courtyard. Where they grew the vegetables for the monastery, all in the courtyard. Well, it's on the side of a mountain for goodness' sake, flat land was at a premium.

And, as always, an entry for the "untrue things our guide told us." In this case he pointed out a grove of ailanthus trees near the cloister and noted that if you cooked the bark for a while it became an effective source of poison. But . . . there is nothing conclusive in Wikipedia to support this claim. Note that this tree it is much used in Chinese traditional medicine, and for making steamer baskets, which would argue against it being poisonous.

The next day we walked to the Norman Palace, which is supposedly a big deal, exemplar of the Norman style during the four centuries that the Normans ruled Sicily and much of southern Italy. You stand in line to get in, pay twelve euros each (senior discount only applies to EU citizens) and then all you get to see is a small chapel about half the size of Monreale; beautiful but very similar (125 pounds of gold?). Also a showing of seventeenth century Flemish paintings from painters who weren't good enough to make it in Brussels (Flanders? Flemville?) so they moved to Sicily. Not impressive. I wanted to see the castle and the moats and the old cannons and all that. It was disappointing.

We stopped for a beer and a pizza at a little place overlooking the Palermo Cathedral and this was better and a better deal than the Villa Igea. Happily fortified, we then walked all the way to the port and the botanic garden (Orto Botanico). Because hope springs eternal, we had sought this out, such sought-ing consisting of noticing it on the city map. We have done this with poor results in a number of locations, but are slow learners. As generally happens, it was a bunch of trees and an occasional bedraggled rosebush. I have a new plan: I am forsaking all botanic gardens not made by the English or the Americans, everyone else seems to believe that trees are what it takes, not flowers. Although truthfully none of the guidebooks even mentioned the place, which might have been a clue to someone less hardheaded. All the flowers are along the highways.

The garden was located on a street labeled Via Abramo Lincoln and immediately next to Palermo's Chinatown. Globalism in unexpected places? These are the guys bringing the shipping containers from China into Palermo harbor, full of goods labeled "Made in Italy." We persevered and walked back to our hotel (see "hardheaded" above although also it was not possible to find a taxi) for a round trip of four and a half miles. We took off our shoes and socks and laid down.

Agrigento

Palermo is on the northwest quarter of Sicily, with Agrigento and the Valley of the Temples on the south in the middle. The map shows some freeways in various places, but this may be invented, since we only found the ones on the far east side of the island. We spent a bit of time driving slowly behind other lines of cars and trucks, on hilly and twisting roads. But we had plenty of time and plenty of itinerary flexibility.

The result of this was that we finally got to Agrigento at noon rather than our plan of being there earlier. Then we walked all around the site—no little tour busses for us, by God!—for about ten kilometers in the midday sun.

Agrigento is a recommended tourist site, but despite this kiss of death well worth visiting. The clever Greeks and then the clever Romans picked a site on a ridgeline about a mile from the ocean but with a beautiful view of same. It is also possible that they wanted a defensive barrier so that the next occupiers would not be able to seize their temples immediately. There are twelve temples advertised in the park, nicely laid out and with good explanatory signs in several languages including ours.

Along about number six one begins to think about what actually qualifies as a "temple." And of course to develop a Temple Evaluation System. In simplest terms, temples with columns standing upright are better than a site with clumps of big marble lying around on the grass, and nothing standing on top of anything else. In my system, a bunch of recumbent marble or sandstone or limestone in a big mess is not a "temple." It may be a "temple site" but a temple it ain't. To qualify you really have to have at least one column standing, even a foreshortened one. And you also get points for sheer size, with the Parthenon in Athens being the best temple I have ever seen. So, a two-part designation: A–F for size and 1–10 for percent of columns still standing, compared to the original design. The Parthenon is the gold standard and gets an A-10 rating. It has forty-six columns, all standing, and arranged in the classic four-to-nine ratio. I don't think this is the golden mean but didn't check. The fact that it has been repaired or rebuilt several times is OK.

Of the twelve temples of Agrigento only six really qualify as temples, rather than temple sites. Of these six, the top ratings go to Concordia (38 columns, B-10), and Juno (19 columns, B- 7). The others range from seventeen to fifteen to seven to four. And they are all about "B" size. The only real disappointment is the Temple of Zeus, which has nothing left standing. For reference, the Parthenon, as noted above, is a forty-six-column monster. See what fun numbers can be?

Finally we have seen them all, sites and temples, and stop to sit down, have a beer, and see if gelato is any different than ice cream. No, at least not in Agrigento.

Siracusa

The first day's exploration was of Ortygia Island, an island that is approximately one hundred feet off the coast of Sicily and downtown Siracusa and connected by two wide streets/bridges to Siracusa. You could throw a baseball across this distance. The island is small and interesting with the usual neat things—a fascinating bunch of stalls arranged into a food market, with the fish probably the best part. One stand has an actual big swordfish sitting there on a cutting table, sword and all. Dozens of cuttlefish and squid, in all sizes; more ripe tomatoes again of all sizes than you ever see in the US, none of them in plastic; brilliant zucchini blossoms; cheeses; fresh fruit; and on and on. Of course, since we are staying in a hotel and not cooking anything, it's all a bit of a tease, but the ratio of actual purchasers to gawkers is probably ten to one, which seems healthy and makes the place probably authentic.

A large ruin, the Temple of Apollo, is also right there at the start of the island. In accordance with the recently developed temple rating system, this one clocks in at twenty-three pillars/columns for a rating of C-8. It is pretty well preserved and doesn't have a lot of stray blocks lying around.

The Fountain of Arethusa is a nice piece of round marble with mythical figures spouting water, located in the center of the island. This is confusing if you read about it because the original "fountain" is instead a freshwater spring near the western side of the island, but there is also this big fancy multicharacter installation.

The myth: one of nymphs of Artemis (Diana in the Roman characterization) was being harassed by a hunter named Alpheus. Diana was the goddess of the hunt, of animals, of war, of the moon, and perhaps of five card monte; the Internet is unclear. The harassed nymph, Arethusa, appealed to Diana for help but forgot to add #MeToo to the message. The helpful Diana/Artemis turned Arethusa into the aforementioned spring. The hunter, not to be put off, somehow turned himself into an underground river and thus "mingled his waters" with the now-liquid Arethusa before the whole thing arrived in Ortygia. This does not look like it was a good deal for Arethusa. Why didn't Diana just take her bow and shoot the jerk?

It does upon reflection make one observe that there is a whole lot of "boy chasing girl when girl isn't interested" in the mythology of the Greeks. Leda and the Swan, Zeus turning himself into a bull to pursue Europa, Zeus pursuing Callisto who got turned into a bear (there's an ugly surprise!), and so on. It could further be argued that if this was OK for the male gods, then it was ok for the male humans. Role models matter.

Since we had lugged our binoculars and a couple of bird identification books along in our luggage, we took a day and went to the Vendicari Nature Reserve—a four hundred-acre, fully protected rectangular property along the ocean south of Siracusa. Lots of sand and scrub vegetation and two long lagoons; it was described as a good place for migrating species and waterfowl. We got a driver, got there at ten, and saw many tour busses and people including student groups hiking into the park. Response: "Uh-oh, this doesn't look good." High school groups of bird-watchers? But with one or two exceptions, no one had binoculars.

We soldiered on and soon found that there is a "free" beach associated with and part of the reserve, a very nice beach in fact: fine sand, tiny waves, beautiful clear and warm water, long gentle slope. But the price is distant parking, a long, hot walk to get to the beach, and no facilities—no hot dog stands, no bathrooms or changing facilities, just a lovely beach. So anything you want there needs to come in on your back.

Despite this, the beach was the destination of 98% of the people we saw, and all of the school groups. We did hike around the trails and saw an egret, doves, magpies, swifts, and lots and lots of flamingoes. Impressive standing in the water although quite white in color, but beautiful in flight where their pink wings show. Like a long pink spear flying through the air.

We saw black-winged stilts, though fewer in number, a water bird with striking red feet that is equally beautiful in flight. This is the official bird of Siracusa. That's the $1000 question on Sicilian *Jeopardy*. We saw many small swifts, a dark-colored bird with a distinctive white patch on its back. Our books assured us that it was not found in Italy. We queried the bird on this but it was too busy flying around swiftly to respond.

Ragusa and Noto

Our plan of not driving except between hotels (hard to park, hard to figure out where to go, hard roads to navigate) was used again for these two World Heritage sites, with a driver and a capable tour guide named Chiara. The originals of both cities, which are probably fifteen kilometers apart although it seems longer given the twisty and narrow roads, were simultaneously destroyed in a very large earthquake in 1693. Chiara says that 80% of the residents died. When you see the "old" part of Ragusa, which resembles the icing stuck precariously on the sides of a tall irregularly rounded cake, with buildings all built right into the steep mountainside and all the internal roads being switchbacks, you can see how this could have been catastrophic. One house at the top starts to slide, it takes everything below with it. Not clear what happened to all the other cities in the area, like Modica, which probably also got destroyed, but they get no press. The residents (such as they were) rebuilt these two in the then-popular ornate rococo style, with all buildings conforming to this stylistic approach.

There are lots of churches with big paintings lining the walls and one cathedral with same, lots of "palaces" that are really just very fancy big houses for the aristocrats, lots of piazzas with city buildings and opera houses fronting them. It is hot and sunny and crowded but impressive. One of the painted ceilings in one of the churches in one of the cities had a round painting on its domed ceiling of Mary and the twelve apostles standing around, arms waving in what looked to me like they were at a rave. Jesus going to do stage diving? After a while cathedral fatigue sets in and irreverence takes over.

We walked up the street from our hotel in Siracusa to the Neapolis Archeological Park, home of the few ruins in Siracusa worth seeing. There is a large Greek amphitheater set steeply into a hillside facing the sea, which one can see from the top level. Great site, but really gummed up with new seats made of grey painted plywood and section signs. Could be a Greek theater, could be a Class B ballpark in Oneonta.

There is also a Roman minicolosseum in the park. It really does look like the colosseum in Rome, if the colosseum were one-eighth its size and sunk into the ground. The floor is not even big enough for arena football, whatever that is. But it is nicely preserved and has good signage explaining each section. However, like so much of the rest of the park, half of it is closed off. Why? The place is overrun with tourists, trust me, who each pay ten euros to get in, and half the walkways in the park have Do Not Enter signs on them. It's not because they're being renovated, no work at all is going on there. Disappointing, stupid and expensive for the product offered.

The Latomie del Paradiso is a peculiar place inside the park, rated forty-eight out of 150 attractions in Siracusa by TripAdvisor. Believe me, there are not 150 attractions in Siracusa, a pretty small town. Unfortunately Latomie does not mean garden, it means limestone quarry. "Limestone Quarry of Paradise?" Three out of four guidebooks don't list it. No quarrying going on, it is now a so-so garden, not well maintained, with wild raspberries growing out of the top of the hedges.

While one is wandering around the city, which does not take long, one inevitably comes across not one but two large modern circular churches of the 1960 era, the heyday of round churches. One is called the "Tears of the Madonna," and when you get up close to the design you can understand why she was crying, it's really ugly. The other is even less well recognized and, if possible, uglier. They are within one kilometer of each other. Probably there was there a "round church contest" in Siracusa in 1962?

Many of the souvenir stores have in their windows a set of ceramic planters, of medium size to full scale size, of two attractive heads. One is of an elegant woman and one of a man in a turban, usually the former white and the latter black. We see these all over.

Finally we ask our concierge. We are told that this is the legend of the beautiful maiden and the Turkish soldier. This was one presumes during the period when the Arabs had their turn in ruling Sicily. The young maiden was on her balcony when a handsome Turkish soldier passed by. She invited him up, a night of passion followed, but in the morning, the realization that he was leaving and besides was married and had two kids caused her some upset. So she chopped off his head and used it for a planter. For basil. It is not explained why her head has also become a planter, but it does make you think about whether there is some core violence/revenge thing in Sicily. Maybe *The Godfather* had it right?

Taormina

Located on the side of yet another mountain in northeast Sicily, this is "the most visited city in Italy." We are told this by the Taormina Chamber of Commerce and our hotel. We were not told this ahead of time, but our homework isn't always perfect. The good news is that it is a fabulous town, with a fabulous hotel and views and food and on and on. And because we are cleverly (but unknowingly) there the week before school lets out in Italy, it is not very crowded. Huzzah!

We spot a brochure for a local cooking class and under the "All right. Why not?" doctrine, sign up. We make busiate pasta by hand, starting with just semolina flour and water, plus maccheroni and orecchiette and the small one with lines in it. We cook fresh tuna baked in Italian stuff—olive oil, tomato sauce, white wine, olives, capers, parsley, fennel fronds, and it is among the best fish dishes I have ever eaten. We even make caponata with my second least favorite vegetable, eggplant, and it's very good. Besides the teacher says you can make it with potatoes.

Our room has a view of Mount Etna, second largest active volcano in the world. It actually is quite big, and steam keeps coming out of the top of it. OK, Kilauea is the most active, you don't have to go look it up. We sign up for a trip up to close to the top (10,000 feet), but we only get to about eight thousand. We drive around, we are shown lava fields, we climb into a lava tube and thankfully out again, we walk through the forest and climb several (dormant) craters. Because volcanos follow the laws of geology and not of second grade art, they are not all perfect cones. This one has three hundred craters of which we climb around in two. Not active, but steep and interesting.

Everything has a story. Jupiter was always trying to kill his sons, before they were able to grow up and kill him. It wasn't always great to be a god. One of the sons got hidden in a cave in the mountain by his mom, grew up there, and decided to stay underground, and became Vulcan, god of the underworld. Hence volcanoes.

And then there's Florence Trevelyan. An orphaned English girl of good family, she was raised by Queen Victoria but had a "liaison" with Victoria's son, Prince Edward VII, the future king. She was rusticated and ended up in Taormina, where she established a lovely English garden along the edge of the town, full of fancies and an Italian WWII two-person torpedo that was to be ridden underwater and guided by aforementioned two persons until it ran into an enemy ship. The plaque explaining this does not explain how the two riders got off before the explosion, or if they did. This may help explain why Italy did not win the war. Florence subsequently married the mayor of Taormina and led a classic English expat life. I think Victoria had given her some money to disappear.

In addition to Florence's large and lovely garden, there are beaches here. The water is very clear and clean. The weather is warm. You take a cable car to go from the hillside perch of Taormina down to sea level. The beaches are covered with two unattractive things: rocks ranging from golf ball to softball size, and hundreds and hundreds of people, most of them about as attractive as the larger rocks, but wearing small bathing clothes.

Tight small bathing clothes. Speedo has much to answer for.

We check it out and find that the small island in the small bay below our hotel was also owned by Florence—Isola Bella. Her husband bought it for her as a present—nice. One is reminded of Dorothy Parker's lament about lovers who always send her "one perfect rose" instead of one perfect limousine. To get there you take a cable car down to more or less sea level, then you walk down one hundred steps to the narrow, crowded and rocky beach, and across it to the island.

Our hotel told us at least six times about the "one hundred steps" so we figured they had complaints. We chanced it, and it turned out to be 105 steps but that's just the accountant in the back of my head. Florence planted her island generously with tropicals and built a house into the sides of it, about eight rooms in six stories, all with big windows, some with glass doors opening out erratically onto patios. Very exotic and English design.

The island is covered with a beautiful shrub called *Capparis spinosa*, which the ticket taker gave me the name of, and also said, "Capers." This is a spiny floppy thing with gorgeous pink and many-stamened flowers blooming all over the plant. No capers in evidence so I figured I misheard her or she meant to say "Thank you" or "*Gesundheit*." Later research reveals that this is in fact the source of capers, which are the flower buds. And if you let the flowers mature you get caper berries from this plant. I thought they came from Japan or the Malay highlands or somewhere English.

After walking all over Florence's quite peculiar house, and watching the small beach become even more crowded, we decide to go back and sit by the lovely pool in our hotel that has clear and beautiful water, one or two people in it, free chairs, no rocks to walk on, and a kiosk where you can order lunch and wine and charge it to your room. Not to mention a fantastic view of Naxos Bay stretching out below and Mount Etna to the west.

On our last night in Taormina, we went into the town, principally to find some more Kleenex for the trip home. You never pack enough, it seems. As we came up to the main street we noticed that large rectangular paintings surrounded by leaves or flowers had been executed smack in the middle of the street, as if part of a path. We are nothing if not observant.

Everyone was walking on the sides of the road, being careful not to step on the street art. Many people were taking pictures. Several side streets were the same, although the pictures were more elaborate—whole four-by-twelve-foot art made with bright flower petals or seeds and beans or in some cases chalk. The images were largely religious—crosses, doves, lilies, etc. We were told it was for a celebration in honor of Saint Pancreas, the saint of internal organs. At least that's what I thought they said. It turns out to be Saint Pancras. According to Beliefnet, there are saints for cancer and infertility and so on but not for internal organs.

Wikipedia seems not to agree on dates: "His feast day was entered into the Roman Martyrology as April 3; recently this was amended to July 8. More often he is celebrated on July 9, the traditional day of his martyrdom." No mention of 3 June.

We were variously informed that the procession would begin: a) at sunset, or b) in thirty minutes, or c) not today, which seemed to cover all the options. We found a small bar in the Piazza Victor Emmanuel near the church of someone or other that was the procession's destination. We had a glass of prosecco and several handfuls of peanuts. All right, why not? By nine-thirty and another prosecco, no procession had showed up, so we walked along the main procession route—no processioneers in evidence— to the cutoff to the hotel, admiring again the elaborate street decorations, the strings of lights across the small streets, and the many people out strolling and eating and drinking. We considered selling all our possessions and moving to Taormina but instead went back to our hotel room to pack.

Going home: we got to the front of the Alitalia counter in Catania, after a long, long wait during which at least three of the counter agents decided it was—we don't know—coffee break time and took off, leaving one to deal with the roughly sixty customers still in line. When it was at last our turn, we needed really hard things: two boarding passes for a ticket we had bought thirty days ago and confirmed, and to check two pieces of luggage.

"Your baggage did not make a reservation," it was announced. One pondered   a response—"I don't let it use the Internet, it just downloads luggage porn." No, better to just look befuddled, which at this point is easy. Twenty minutes and €106 later, the baggage had a reservation at least through Paris. The airline is being privatized, and whoever buys it has work to do.

One final note: because of, wait, never mind, no more explanations of airline problems, it took us three days to get back. At one point we found ourselves at Paris Orly. In the men's toilet a small sign had been placed over each urinal, just above the button you pushed to flush. It read: "*Interdiction de Boire, Eau Non Potable.*" Thinking about the necessity for this sign amused me all the way back to Iceland.

Love and kisses, Bob

Afterword: Sometimes things that start badly end well. This could not have been a better trip, and now I never have to go to Iceland—I've been there.

[23]

Lots of Cranes in Nebraska, Really?

March 2019

Dear Aunt Janet,

Why, one might reasonably ask, would an otherwise normal person leave a lovely beach house in San Diego, where the March temperature averages 68°F, the rain is essentially nonexistent, and the winds moderate when they blow at all, only to venture into the middle of Nebraska where the temperature averages below freezing, there is lots of wind, and lots of rain, and many of the rivers are frozen? To add to the attractiveness there are large, unsightly globs and piles of dirty brown snow on the ground, bordering all the sidewalks and streets.

Why indeed? Because said normal person in his general reading stumbled across a *Smithsonian* magazine article detailing a large gathering of large birds who are in the middle of a significant six- to seven-thousand-mile migration from their winter homes in northern Mexico to their summer nesting places at or slightly above the arctic circle. They take about a six-week break along the Sandhill and Platte Rivers, centering on

Kearney, NE. They are thus called "sandhill cranes" or *Antigone canadensis* although one supposes that they might as well be called northern Mexico cranes or arctic circle cranes. I guess we got there first and claimed naming rights. Why the genus is named after the daughter of Oedipus, who came to a tragic end for trying to give her brother an official burial, is not specified in any account that I could find. And none of the four cranes in the species are found in Greece, or even in Europe. But we digress.

The particularly intriguing thing about this particular bird and this trip is that there are 600,000 to 800,000 cranes who pass through central Nebraska in early spring, and this is generally acknowledged to be the largest migration of any animal on the North American continent.

Love and kisses, Bob

Afterword: Who knew this was such a spectacle? In the middle of otherwise unspectacle-like mid-Nebraska! Right in our own country, no visas and no immigration and no overnight flights. You did have to wear warm clothes and get up early, but it was assuredly worth it. I do not know if there is a "Seven Bird Wonders of the World" but if there were, this would surely be a candidate.

[24]

Mitzi Gaynor Has Left the Building, Taking Rossano Brazzi with Her

August 2019

Dear Aunt Janet,

Getting to the Southwest Pacific Takes Some Effort

Air New Zealand turns out to be a pretty decent airline. Can't say if they fly anywhere other than to and from New Zealand, generally to its capital named Auckland. Names are funny things. This two-island nation in the South Pacific, usually referred to as "little brother" by its larger and also English-colonized neighbor, Australia, was discovered in 1642 by a Dutch explorer named Abel Tasman, who named it after the Dutch province of Zeeland. He had earlier discovered the Australia island of Tasmania, and charmingly named it after himself. By the time he got to NZ, he may have decided modestly that calling it "Abelland" wouldn't work. Since he never landed, one wonders about any resemblance he may have found (or imagined) to the polders of his homeland. By the way, *South Pacific* was not filmed in the South Pacific, but on the north shore of the island of Kauai in Hawaii.

One speculates that the local residents, the Maori, probably were not sitting around saying to whomever would listen, "Gee, I wish someone would discover us, too, so we could have all the advantages of civilization like parliaments, cell phones, Snickers, and surfing." And so about 130 years later along came James Cook, in 1769 to be exact. No one was in any particular hurry, it seems. Maybe Abel didn't leave good notes.

Cook not only discovered or rediscovered the islands, but actually landed and claimed them in the name of King George III of England. Who may not have even known that he had some footloose English guy running around in a perilously small boat, looking for a way to the South Pole (Why? We ask, but no answer follows), and stopping off to discover New Zealand. Which he immediately did not name "New King George the Third Land" but left it as New Zealand. But how did he even know that was its name? Again, no answer. Besides, KG3 was about to have enough trouble with North America.

And while we're at it, no offense to our brethren in the southern seas, but why did the name stick? New Hebrides eventually became Vanuatu. Then why did the NZ folks decide—they or someone—that the locals and all their professional sports teams should be named the "Kiwis," along with a brand of black shoe polish? An extinct flightless bird, eh? That should certainly inspire terror in the hearts of our opponents. Watch out or I'll peck you! Only probably around the ankles as I can't really fly and I'm not much for jumping.

And while we're at it again, why name the capital of this misnamed country "Auckland"? Is there an "auck," perhaps another large flightless bird? Modest research, defined as looking this up on Wikipedia, says no. It is a medieval Norse term for "more" and the name got stuck on some land in England's northeast—auck land. There is even still a baron of Auckland, in the northeast of the UK. So much for engaging history.

Back to the airline. It has its business class seats arranged in four rows, all angled at a somewhat better than forty-five-degree angle inside, pointing forward so that to enter the plane it looks like you're walking into the mouth of a dragon, fitted out with two parallel rows of dragon's teeth. It is a little off-putting, although perhaps the optimum arrangement of getting biz class passengers into little podlike things so they won't bother the flight attendants more than the minimum amount and you use the space most efficiently. It works well because these really are "flatbed" seats. On other airlines this designation usually means a peculiar terrain contortion of hills and valleys that the seat goes through once you push the buttons on "recline." Much of this geometry you should not stick your hand into, the seat has a mind of its own and doesn't need your help. It finally ends up with a surface putting your head about 5% lower than your feet, and leaving several vales and moraines remaining between your head and toes. None of which match the natural peaks and valleys between your actual head and toes. You know how it's hard to walk with a stone in your shoe? It's like that except you have a roll of stones at various uncertain places in your back and legs.

The ANZ bed is not like that! It actually is flat and almost comfortable. This is airline progress. Sticking seats ever closer together and making them ever narrower is not.

It's a bit of a bumpy ride from San Francisco into NZ. I haven't gotten airsick in a very long time despite all the miles I have flown. But I began to worry. Finally I got up to go to the bathroom, mostly since it had been eleven hours on the airplane, and besides just in case I wanted to see if they had airsick bags, or if this amenity too had gone the way of good service, decent food, and good old-fashioned politeness—both from stewardesses and from passengers. Yes, they still do. The bags are printed with cutesy global stuff—the words for "vomit" in sixteen languages ("*kraikas vomito*" for example, Lithuanian if you didn't immediately recognize it)—in various typefaces, colors, and sizes, and at the bottom in quite small type, but English, it says: "If affected by motion sickness use this bag and not your carry-on." So, don't throw up in your carry-on? Probably good advice, choose the bag instead, but why not the carry-on? Isn't it your problem, not theirs? Whereas if you hurl going down the aisle trying to get to the john for which there is a line of four people, isn't that more their problem now? Wouldn't they rather, in this case, have you ralph in your backpack, assuming that you opened it and then carefully closed it when completed? It's hard to understand the thinking on this.

We soldier on, we didn't get sick, we got to Auckland and then transferred successfully to the ANZ flight to Apia. For those who don't know, which would include me before this enterprise began, Apia is not the Greek goddess of bees although she could be, but rather is the capital and only international airport of the island nation of Samoa (the country not the Girl Scout cookie) that begins our bird-viewing adventure. So there.

What? Bird-Watching? Have You Lost Your Mind?

We signed up to go on a bird-watching trip because it was focused on four southwest Pacific islands we had never been to (Samoa, Fiji, Vanuatu, and New Caledonia). As you know, we had been doing some nonserious bird-watching around San Diego and one sort of serious sortie to Nebraska to see sandhill cranes and we kind of liked it. In addition the tour group had a great name: Rockjumper. It turns out that this is a colorful South African bird and not slang for a rogue geologist. It also turns out that this is not a good way to select a tour company.

We started all this when we were on a safari trip in Africa organized by Cornell a couple of years ago—I think we sent you a letter about that. We have done several of these, and the safari camps or lodges have it down pretty well. You get up in the morning, early, and drive around looking for animals until about 0930 or so. You do the same thing in the late afternoon hours before and including sunset. And because poachers have not yet killed off all the big animals, let alone the myriad small ungulates—antelopes and deer of many kinds and sizes—you do see many animals. The way it works is that your guide generally knows the area, so he knows where the animals hang out. You drive to one of these areas or viewing spots, which are usually along a road or trail, pull off, and wait. And eventually you see something, or the guide gets a radio call from another guide, and he goes to a new location where someone has seen a lion eating a kill or a leopard in a tree. Pulls off the road and waits. It is no longer OK to chase down animals, so there is a lot of sitting and waiting time, even in the best cases.

For the Cornell trip we had the good fortune to be on a Land Rover with a skilled bird-watcher, generous with her knowledge and her binoculars. While you're waiting for the rhinos to show up, there are always birds around. We became intrigued as the birds were plentiful and colorful, and besides it was an interesting way to pass the time between giraffes.

There is also much technology to help you. Once you get started, what you want to do is not just say, "Gee, look at the pretty red bird." Instead you want to be able to say, "Look at the woodland redthroat." There are lots of printed field guides to help determine what you're looking at, and there is now a wonderful app for your cell phone called Merlin. It's way easier to carry your cell phone around than to lug a three hundred-page field guide with you. It was developed by the Cornell Ornithology Lab in 2014 and is based on the eBird reports that they have been receiving for some time. See eBird discussion below.

But creating this computer program carefully isn't easy and there's a lot of data massaging involved. The Merlin website suggests that what they have done so far is based on 650 million observations of birds, sent in to them on eBird. The app is organized into specific geographic "packs" (data sets) that you download onto your phone. Merlin currently covers 3,000+ species, but as noted later, this is only about 30% of all the world's bird species. When you run through the list of data packs, you find that the US, Canada, and Europe are very well covered, as is Central America. South America has Colombia packs, one for Chile, and one for the southeast coast of Brazil. Nothing for Ecuador, which is said to have the most species of any country in the world. Nothing for Africa—nothing. Nothing on Antarctica so penguins, you're on your own. Nothing for Russia or China or Japan. Only an "introductory" pack for India, nothing for Pakistan or Sri Lanka or Bangladesh or any of the Stans. Israel is covered, but nothing for the rest of the Middle East. There's work to be done, and since all of these apps are free, you can see why it may be a while before Vietnam and Laos are included, let alone Bolivia or Gambia. Nonetheless, this is a great tool.

Unfortunately, the SW Pacific islands are not yet in Merlin, so we carried with us Birds of Melanesia (446 pages). We identified the birds we saw the old-fashioned way: a) ask someone else who knows more than you, which for us was everyone else on the trip; and b) thumb through the book trying to match what you saw with the pictures therein. We still ended the trip with five bird pictures we could not identify.

First stop, Samoa, and if you don't immediately know where any of this stuff is, see map below. We didn't. I've never even heard of the Phoenix Islands.

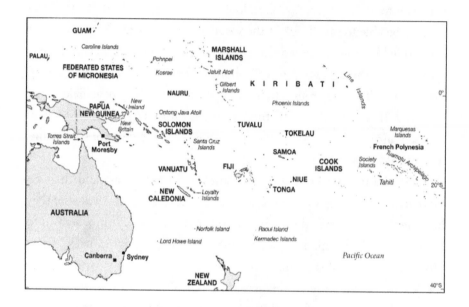

As any guidebook will tell you, and we could only find one, a Lonely Planet number that covered Samoa, Rarotonga, and Tonga, this is a small nation. It consists of two big and seven much smaller islands. We are going to Upolu, the main island where three-quarters of the two hundred thousand Samoans live. There does not appear to be any local manufacturing, and the agriculture looks disorganized with many old coconut trees that don't look tended anymore. Ditto the fields of banana trees. We went to the local market in a crumby warehouse place in downtown Apia, unimpressive unless you're looking for bananas or coconuts or cheap Chinese textiles. Usually local markets are interesting. In this one there were no—count them—no vegetables other than bananas, coconuts, and papayas. No tomatoes, no lettuce of any kind, no cucumbers, no squash of any kind, no mushrooms, no celery, no potatoes, no sweet potatoes (one of the key vegetables of every tropical diet—but not here). No dried meat or sausages or any meat at all, although there is a local fish market in a different location. And we saw lots of chickens running around the local neighborhoods, including on the road as we drove through the countryside. Also, a couple of pigs and three goats. This is not a complete census, but you get the picture. Overall the place reminds me of rural Hawaii thirty years ago, except with cell phones but, inexplicably, very few satellite antennae. It's got a surrounding reef, it's got some nice but shallow beaches, it's got a tropical climate, but somehow it lacks oomph or style. Oh well, we're here for the birds not the sunbathing, jet skiing, surfing, snorkeling, mai tai drinking, native touristic dancing, etc. Good thing. Our first step is to rendezvous with our four other bird-watching trip participants, and Erik our guide. We meet at Uncle Dave's Eco Lodge, way up the hill from town. And so it begins. . . .

It doesn't really begin well. For starters it is raining. This is the dry season. I know this from a book. For the main course, or whatever comes after starters, Uncle Dave's Eco Lodge is awful.

Notes on Dave's Eco Lodge, the good parts:

- » Great view from two-thirds of the way up the mountain on which it sits, overlooking the pretty small metropolis of Apia—except most of the time it's too misty or rainy to see anything.
- » All the windows have screens, but no AC.
- » Running water, cold only, not drinkable.
- » Two bars of soap.
- » One towel per person, no washcloth.
- » A working toilet with toilet paper.
- » A door that appears to lock, and two keys, one of which doesn't work.
- » An electric output that works, one out of three. Fortunately, we have brought a power cord with multiple sockets.
- » An "Fun Tourist Activities to Do in Apia" dated 2012/2013.
- » A map showing the two major Samoa islands, dated 2013/2014.
- » A "Guests Information" sheet dated 2018, including a prohibition on doing laundry in the room.

The not so great parts:

- » No hot water.
- » Lousy food, seriously lousy food. Take my word for it. Terrible food. And we have to eat here because we paid for it and we are outside of town and there's no way to get into town.
- » No hot water for showers or shaving or other incidental uses. Not that this is a sensitive point.
- » No coffee or tea fixings inside the room, but a hot water pot. "Care for a cup of boiling water this morning, love?"
- » No Wi-Fi or Internet—are you kidding?

I suppose I could stop there, and not mention no changes of towels or linens, the light outside the balcony that won't turn off and shines in the room all night, the inadequate curtains that don't keep the light from shining in all night, the three-foot gap between the bathroom enclosure wall and the ceiling that rather defeats the concept of privacy, no safe, no bedside light, no shampoo, no hair dryer, no bottles of water, some rickety glasses and plates but no hot plate or microwave. There really are a lot of things that you get even at a $129 per night Hampton Inn in El Centro where I recently stayed. Wow, I was not sufficiently grateful at the time.

And no hot water.

This place gets a special star for goodness in the Places to Stay portion of the Lonely Planet guidebook referenced above. Is everything else really worse? Hard to believe. It's kind of like being in jail. Or what I imagine jail to be like except I have a female roommate.

There is a bar on one side of the "dining room" in the main lodge. We ask for the wine list—blank stares all around. The well-meaning server shows us their wine cellar—four bottles of William Atkinson cabernet from Australia—and then three bottles of some white, same vintner. Because we have no standards, we drink it. Not all at once, though this is tempting. By the time our three-day stay is over, the cellar inventory has been significantly depleted and not replenished. Good luck, you next set of suckers. Our tour compatriots are not at all hesitant to drink wine, except curiously the French woman. On principle, I decline to drink either of the Samoa beers (Vailima and Taula) because they do not have either the names of or the pictures of animals on the label. What happened to Simba beer from Africa or the Thai beer—Syngha— named after a lion? There are some great bird names here—blue-faced parrotfinch, jungle myna, etc. Of course, if we run out of wine before we leave, I may relent.

Our First Day of Serious Bird-Watching

It is rainy and misty, and we had trouble finding the "reserve" where we were planning to go. Mostly because the trip leader hadn't done the advance work even though he arrived a couple of days before us. We lost an hour driving back and forth along various roads until he finally recognized the place. Then it started to rain. This sentence could be repeated probably sixteen times as describing almost every day and evening of the trip. This is the "dry" season. As noted. Could the "wet" season be wetter? Perhaps enough said.

So far as I can tell, tropical birding consists of walking along damp, muddy and/or rocky forest paths with occasional clearings and all-around thick forests of giant acacias, palms, tulip trees and other stuff that I cannot identify. As an alternative, one can walk along muddy, rocky dirt roads with rainforest on either side. They both work about the same. We stop occasionally and peer intently upward, hoping to see a small colorless bird in the treetops. Sometimes we do, then much excitement. Usually the bird gets excited, too, and flies away. Everyone but me seems to be able to identify the bird immediately, and to know where it fits in the bird-watching desirability scale which runs from Very Elusive and Beautiful to Common, Ordinary, and Found Everywhere. Of course, we are on Samoa, and things Found Everywhere here are not found at all in San Diego.

Thus, I am easy to please, and delighted to see the birds hanging out in the motel parking lot, all of which strike me as exotic—the jungle myna and the cardinal myzomela for example. The former is all black with a bright yellow eye and eyepatch, the latter has a brilliant red—and I do mean brilliant red—head and a black body. I wouldn't chase either one of these guys away from my bird feeder. There is also the buff-banded rail. Why a bird is named after an elongated piece of steel is not explained, they are short and kind of roundish but with red caps and a preference for running along the ground, kind of like quail, rhymes with rail? They also appear to have a preference for reproduction. As a test, when we were coming back from a long trip to the other side of the island, Erik our trip leader was goaded into doing a count of how many rails we saw before we got home. In the ensuing three-and-a-half-hour period, mostly spent driving moderately on two-lane twisty roads with ocean views on the right, we ended up with 126 rails sighted, almost all along the grass edges of the tarmac, and none of which we ran over. Erik said he would report this to eBird, but they would probably reject it as being an unrealistic number. I think he meant too high, but he did not elaborate.

What Is eBird Anyway?

What follows is pretty high-level bird geek talk. Feel free to speed past it. "eBird" (technically eBird.org) is a citizen scientist sort of bird data gathering app one can get on one's cell phone, for free. It allows one, nay encourages one, to make a list of birds you have seen on a particular day, time and location, presumably by looking for them rather than by accident. For example, we had one of our group of six volunteer to be the eBird reporting person. Apparently, this is de rigueur for every birding trip. The report, once submitted to the eBird website, is then added to the site's worldwide database that is used to publish articles, write testimony, put together the avian section of environmental impact reviews, etc., about the distribution and health of bird populations, specific, locational, general, historic, trending, or whatever. It does not purport to be a complete census of all the birds in the world at a point in time—how could it? It was developed and is maintained by the Cornell Lab of Ornithology, probably the most respected academic organization in the world specializing in birds.

In addition to the scientific purpose, the data is available to any eBird user. There are at least two easy ways to use it. Say you would like to know what the birds are that hang about around your home. You input your address, specify a time period for the piece of the database to query (since time began, last five years, this year, last week) and up comes a map with a bunch of circles with pointy tails. There must be an IT name for these but I don't know what it is. You click on one of these symbols and you get a

summary of all the recent reports sent in by diligent birders for that location, and access to the data in each individual report. You find that for our
address, there are lots of reports of crows, house finches, house sparrows,
mourning doves, and northern mockingbirds. Actually we already know
that because we have identified who comes to our bird feeders. But if you
were going off to Cottonwood, Arizona, and wanted to see if there were
any interesting birds there, this would be quite helpful.

Or perhaps you would like to know where in the world to find the Fiji
goshawk, because you have a particular interest in this bird. Let's assume
you're pretty slow, so you don't think it's necessarily or exclusively in Fiji.
Enter this name in the query section, and you get a worldwide map of
everywhere that any bird has been reported, not only the Fiji goshawk.
This is not very helpful until you get it that the trick is to look for the deep
purple squares, not the grey squares. Grey means something/anything has
been reported, but not your bird. Purple means only the Fiji goshawk,
or whatever you have specified. As you drill down on the purple areas
which the map helpfully lets you do, you will find that in this case that's
just Fiji. If for kicks you try the Canada goose instead, you find them
reported everywhere in North America and Europe, but nowhere in South
America. There are also reports, curiously, for said bird in New Caledonia
(lots of reports), three on the southwest coast of Australia, and one in
Vanuatu, but none in all of Asia or India.

This highlights the fact that there are one or two problems with this
application. Problem one is the quality of the reports. When I got home
and dried out, I looked up Samoa. Not many little tabs indicating a bird
report, but I clicked on one and found one of the reports our group had
sent in. It listed ten Pacific trillers, among other sightings. But we only
saw two Pacific trillers. I know, I was there. This is kind of a problem. An
even bigger lacunae is that not everyone who goes bird-watching bothers
to send in a report. Still, what is sent in is very useful for planning a trip or
for just seeing what others have reported for a specific area. eBird provides
a wonderful indicator of bird variety, but it is not really a census. It won't
tell you how many birds in the world there are. And it's obviously subject
to double counting. There could have been another report from Samoa that
had seen many of the same birds.

Anyone can participate, you don't have to be accepted or apply or whatever. The benefit for the user is this data that he or she has reported can also be simultaneously imported into his or her personal roster of birds seen, one's so-called "Life List." There are also several apps for these lists of the 10,600 species of bird currently thought to be in existence. And serious bird people, which I am not and probably never will be, talk about these, compare numbers, and discuss how many birds they need to see to complete their world list. Or their North America list. Or their list of every bird named Sam, I don't know. You check off the individual birds on your list once you have seen them. It's all on the honor system, just done for personal satisfaction, no prizes are awarded, no press releases are released, it's not even as good as becoming an Eagle Scout since you don't get your name in the newspaper.

The eBird people do exercise some quality control in the data collection. If you send in a report that you saw ten crows in your backyard on Tuesday, but mistakenly type in ten thousand, they will probably suggest that it is unlikely that your backyard was eleven deep in crows on Tuesday. Hence Erik's comments on the large number of buff-banded rails that we were going to report. And sure enough, that report didn't show up on the Samoa map—but we really did see that many.

Back to the Rainforest

We spend a lot of time in the morning walking through the alternatively thick and slightly less thick forest, a wildlife preserve with precious little wildlife in it, trying to see birds. We would especially like to see "endemics," which are birds that evolved in one place and are found nowhere else on earth. The US has relatively few, using that definition, because most US birds have wanderlust and are also found in Canada or Mexico or more exotic locations like Siberia, for example. Obviously you can only see endemics, which is generally considered a Big Deal, by going where they are. While we're happy as beginners to see any birds, our party really wants to see the less easily found endemics. We use the aforementioned tactics—slog along the trail for a while, then stop while our guide uses his recorder and speaker to scratchily play the bird call of whatever we're interested in seeing. We stand around looking vaguely upward as if we were expecting the angelic convergence to happen in the middle of a small Pacific island, and then see nothing for a generous period of time. At some point we move on and the whole process is repeated. And repeated. What we do eventually find is leeches. Not the large ones the size of several inches of a Slim Jim, but little tiny ones, about the size of a pencil lead. I suspect that the Slim Jim ones only exist in fantasy, like the piranhas that strip a cow's carcass clean in thirty seconds in all the bad Amazon horror movies. But finding a small black one on your pants leg is sobering and then rubbing your face and coming off with a small one is somewhat more unsettling. Makes you keep rubbing your face as if you were a junior professor at a bad college, trying to look thoughtful. Maybe I should stop shaving to make my face less accommodating to leeches.

Enough with the Birds, Let's Go to a Museum— At Least We're Likely to See It

On our way back from the first of our many damp bird expeditions, we prevailed on Erik to stop at the Robert Louis Stevenson Museum. Except for a slug of NFL lineman, this may be Samoa's chief claim to fame. It's a lovely wooden two-story tropical mansion, open and airy, balconies all around, with also a big botanic garden somewhat overgrown surrounding it. We took the mansion tour (we're here, it's not like we have other pressing engagements) and it was sort of interesting although big old houses are really not my cup of tea. The author is buried on the top of a local mountain, with a plaque of his poem Requiem, which begins "Under the wide and starry sky" etc., as his tombstone. While in residence in Samoa for the four years before he died, we are told that he wrote thirteen more novels in addition to his earlier successes— *Treasure Island, Robinson Crusoe, Kidnapped.* I racked my brain to think of the names of any and it came back unracked. A quick check of the Internet turned up only four, not thirteen—*The Beach of Falesá, David Balfour, The Ebb-Tide,* and *The Wrecker.* I have never heard of any of these. Literary fame is fleeting indeed.

Birds Are Where You Find Them

The next day as we were driving along the potholed but lightly trafficked beach road on the south part of the island, one of our party yelled, "Stop! Stop! Stop!" In my family this would mean that you had to throw up. On a birding trip this means, "I have actually seen a bird! Stop and let's all pile out of the van and try to scare it away!" This is an alternate to slogging through the dripping forest, and a legitimate one, with much to commend it.

So we did. In this case the incident was typical. "I think I saw a ruff!" exclaimed one of the participants. "Queen Elizabeth the First's neck support? The sound that Dennis the Menace's dog makes?" I think querulously.

"I think he went that way," says our guide, always up for a fight. He heads off away from the small lagoon and into the bush, the wet bush. The reasonable people actually look for a live bird nearby and see a white-eyed heron, a bird that meets our criteria: large, pretty, near, and still. Mr. (or Ms.?) Heron keeps poking around for fish to kill with its long and very sharp beak. Then he rises, flaps his wings and flies away—to a much nearer piece of large driftwood. He stands there contentedly, still in the lagoon but maybe fifteen feet from us, preening, turning his head this way and that, all but asking, "Is this my best profile? Can you shoot a few more?" We have no idea where the ruff (rough?) has gone to, but really, the heron is pretty terrific. To be fair, this same fire drill happens several more times, once when someone see a Pacific golden plover and a Polynesian triller, both in the middle of a soccer field for goodness' sake, and once when we see a reef heron who is walking along the shoreline trying to spear stuff of the crustacean variety. Not as good as a white-eyed heron, but still pretty damn good. I am beginning to think about specializing in herons. Also doing birding while hanging around filling stations.

On our third and final day in Samoa, of course, the weather lets up and it is lovely and sunny. We go back to the first place since it looked pretty good in the rain and is likely to look better in the sun—the Malololelei

Recreation Reserve. Big, foresty, and vacant. Sure enough, we wander around through the trails lined with wild ginger and large stands of impatiens and it is charming. We even see birds—Polynesian wattled honeyeater, Samoan flycatcher, crimson-crowned fruit dove, flat-billed kingfisher, red bulbul. I also pick up three small leaches who jump on me from the wet grass but I flick them off before they can get oriented.

At the happy hour back at the lodge we order some small frozen pizza sticks, warmed up and served with a small dish of mayonnaise to dip them in. It's almost like real food. After this delicacy is consumed, most of the folks wander off, but Tittles the local cat, a male who doesn't have any despite his name, sits down at L's feet and looks up at her. She dips her finger in the mayo and he licks it off, them immediately jumps up into her lap and meows. Since our cats are too disdainful to ever do this, it's a treat, so she feeds Tittles all the rest of the mayonnaise, lick by lick. We will make sure to explain this to our cats when we return. Get with the program. I offer to jump in her lap but she's out of mayo.

OK, What's Next? How about Another Island with a Rainforest? How about Fiji?

On to Fiji, a republic of 900,000 people and 300 islands, with most of the people on the two main islands. We reluctantly [sic] say goodbye to Samoa with its rain and crappy motel and twisty roads and fly off to Nadi, the capital of Fiji, stay there one night at the airport Novotel (hot water!! Decent food!! Hot water!) and the next morning fly on a smaller airplane to yet another green, rugged, tropical island surrounded erratically with beaches, or else with ledges or else with rocks and coral but in every case with water, hence "island." This one, Taveuni, is the third largest of the islands that make up the Republic of Fiji, formerly an agglomeration of chieftaincies and then a colony of the UK and now independent. One of the articles in the ANZ airline magazine that I read flying over noted helpfully that cannibalism had been widely practiced on these islands in the past, even the recent past, but now has been all but eliminated. "All but?"

The north half of the island has a volcano, tall but dormant, and is a wildlife sanctuary and this is its major attraction for us. Others come here to snorkel or scuba. The beaches aren't much, and the beach hotels, one of which we are staying at, are at best C minus. Ours has six young Russians staying at it. I rest my case.

Ah, the lessons of life: nothing comes without a cost, other than hang-nails and flatulence. Taveuni is billed as a paradise for birds, and for pretty much everything else small and edible, since there seem to be no mamma-lian predators of any size, not even foxes, and only one bird predator, the Fijian goshawk, who isn't really very large, kind of falcon size. But the cost is to drive a four-wheel drive truck up a rutted, bumpy, and almost unnav-igable road made of dirt/mud/unstable rock fragments while sitting in the back and holding on and praying that you really have outgrown juvenile attacks of car sickness. This is a perfect test.

We get to the top, then get out into the rain and wind, and start looking eagerly around into the thick, impenetrable tropical forest that lines both sides of the road. We are eager to see two special endemics, the silktail and the orange fruit dove. We walk slowly and damply downhill, stop-ping every ten minutes/hundred meters for Erik to play his loudspeaker, alternating with the call of the silktail and then of the orange fruit dove. They both sound chirp-like, but I presume the birds can tell them apart. Nothing shows up. We're beginning to get the routine down. At least we're walking downhill.

The tour was organized by Rockjumper, a tour organization that specializes in birding. Yes, there is one, in fact there are several such travel organizations. It is a good name, even when you find out that "rock-jumper" is a bird, noted for, yes, jumping from rock to rock. It doesn't apparently like to fly. "Their wings are very small and they do not fly very often."—Wikipedia.

The company's management sent out guidelines on how to act while birding that were clearly meant for us as novices. One strong piece of guid-ance included directions on what color clothing to wear—no black, no white, no blue, no pink, but tan and "loden" were fine. When out on a hike, which is all you do on these tours as the birds rarely show up in a conference room at your hotel, you are to be quiet so as not to disturb the birds on whom you are trying to sneak up. Since you don't see a bird every walking or waking minute, you have a lot of time to think as long as it is done quietly. So I do. "The last time I was in a small group, all dressed in shades of tan and green, carrying expensive equipment, walking quietly through the forest/jungle and looking for something elusive, and it was miserable and raining, at least I was getting paid for it." It was called being in an infantry platoon in Vietnam. L pointed out that in this case I didn't have to sleep on the ground in the rain, and the birds weren't shooting at us, just hiding. Good points.

Patience is rewarded. In each of the places to which we are going or have been, there are one or two particularly rare or elusive birds that everyone is trying to "get," which in bird land means "see" rather than shoot or capture or eat. It's a little off-putting at first, but all activities have their own jargon and this one is no exception. In Fiji it's the orange fruit dove, as noted above, a nicely round medium-sized bird of the dove family which I assume eats fruit. I cannot tell if the bird eats only orange fruit, or if it is itself orange. The second is a relatively small bird called the silktail that hides in the woods and eats I don't know what. The latter is "endemic" to this island only, not even to the whole of Fiji.

We engage in the "walk down the mountain in the rain" strategy, stopping every so often to make sure we don't have any dry spots left on our bodies, and peer around in various directions into the mist, rain, and trees. Nothing.

Finally based on some sign that is not explained, our driver who is Fijian and more than a driver, leads us off the road and into the jungle. It is thick and wet and full of trees and vines and green plants of all sorts and descriptions. I wonder what the hell is going on, he cannot possibly have seen anything in there unless he has x-ray vision. He does not lead us on a path, as there aren't any, so this is more of a ramble, stepping over fallen stuff and squatting to go under vines so as not to be garroted. Then we stop and adopt the standard birding tactic of looking curiously around and trying to see something small and dark against the largely dark and confused background. This continues for some time. I am not sure I have enough patience for this, if this is what it takes. I begin to think mean thoughts about the day, the weather, the island, our tour leader, the concept of trying to watch stuff that doesn't particularly want to be seen. In truth it's not likely you'll see anything if it's not moving.

And then suddenly there is a rustle of movement ten feet away from me and about a foot above the ground. I can see something moving, but not because I am so wonderful, but because I am standing at precisely the right place and there is a "hole" or really a small round visual tunnel of no vegetation that ends at the two black birds who are moving. Then one turns enough, and a bright white tail shows through the gloom. "It's a silktail," someone whispers. I stare at it as it moves a little and my companions all whisper, "I can't see it, where is it?" The response of "over there" isn't terribly useful but it's the best I can do. "By the tree" isn't much better since everything for 360 degrees is "by the tree" except those things that are the tree. I get probably twenty seconds before the silktails take off. No one else saw the bird for nearly that much time, but we're all pretty excited to have found even one. Does it make all the standing around getting rained on and bored worthwhile? Hard to make a blanket statement.

Some people think baseball is boring, including me, especially watching a no-hitter, so I don't. Some Americans think cricket is boring because the games last for days. And if you walk around all day and don't see any birds, that's not much fun. Seeing the silktail was pretty cool, and it's just too bad we didn't get a picture. Oh well, it's important to take small triumphs when presented with them.

Are Bats Really Birds?

One afternoon after we are back from mountain climbing in the rain, with no bird sightings, we go to the pool of our beach retreat. Several large trees border the pool, which itself is between the resort buildings and the ocean. And lo, with no action on our part, here comes a whole flood of fruit bats, flying in a cloud from the neighboring small and uninhabited island, uninhabited other than by maybe three hundred Pacific flying foxes, the birder's name for this particular bat. They fly around the water's edge of the resort in large circles for a while, and gradually settle out on the largest of the trees. Yes, hanging upside down as is their wont. They're bigger than pigeons but not threatening, just not that beautiful. No one can explain what they're doing here hanging in the tree as this isn't usual, and besides they're nocturnal and it will not be evening for another hour and the local trees aren't fruit trees. So, we just look at them and think cleverly, "WTF?" and alternatively, "That's a lot of damn bats."

On to More Fiji Islands and the Mysteries Thereof

We fly from Taveuni where it is bright and sunny in the morning as we leave, of course, and land in Suva where it is—gasp!—raining. We have been told repeatedly that this is, seasonally speaking, the "dry season" for all these islands, so this is not normal. Or everyone lies, who can tell.

Since we are here early, defined as before our rooms are ready at yet another "eco lodge," we take a local hike around the heavily wooded grounds and in the rain to see basically nothing of the bird description. Swell and wet. We all eat lunch and then the leader says we shall go off to the nearby nature preserve and see more birds in the rain. They must be somewhere? Since so far we have seen none, one wonders mathematically what the equation: (birds seen per attempt) times (number of attempts) = ? I am pretty sure that if the first term is zero, even if attempts equals infinity, the answer is still unsatisfactory.

L and I look at the weather—did I mention rain?—and hang back as our intrepid colleagues depart, binoculars and all, and then we go back to the lobby and have some tea. Two hours later, just as the rooms are finally ready, the trip participants return, and one of the saner members notes that in two hours they saw zero birds. Hence the solution to the equation listed above. We attempt to show sympathy.

How Does a Guy Get a Day Off Around Here?

Tomorrow is another day—thank you, Margaret Mitchell, but we ain't anywhere near Tara. The plan is to get up and get out of here at 0530. Yes, that early in the morning. Take a dry breakfast with us—no coffee—and also a dry lunch. Have to use up yesterday's bread somehow. Maybe we shall ambush the birds who are sleeping in and have not already flown to their daylight hiding places, locations that we clearly do not know.

During the night it rains continuously, and hard. I sleep well but keep getting awakened by the pounding rain on the tin but nonleaking roof of our "*bure*," which is Fiji for hut. We get up at 0430 to get ready for the adventure. Still raining. We check the weather forecast for Suva on the momentarily working Internet—79% chance of rain for the next two days. The Internet really does have some uses. We go down to the lobby and tell our colleagues that we are a "no" for today, maybe if it stops raining, we'll go on our own over to the local forest of all birds, known as Colo-I-Suva Forest Park. They leave. We go back to bed.

Later we have the first real breakfast in seven days, and it's great. Who knew you could get buckwheat pancakes in Fiji? And maple syrup and decent bacon and French press coffee. We sit in the lanai and play with our computers, trying to figure out the names of the birds of which L has taken pictures, many of them very good. I thought I had written them down as we went along but it's hard to write in the rain.

Around 1100 the rain seems to stop so, feeling slightly guilty, we saddle up and go over to the park, walk into it for a mile, all downhill and headed for a mythical waterfall shown on the map. I am pretty sure there will be water in it. The gods decide that that's enough and the weather changes from sunny but no birds to raining heavily and no birds. We retrace our now muddy steps, back to our *bure* and dump our wet clothing for dry but soon to be wet other clothing.

The Lost Patrol returns, after lunch (for us, not them—we share a great club sandwich with chips and several glasses of a quite acceptable New Zealand pinot. They had the standard white bread sandwich with one slice of processed cheese, and water). They did see some birds but nothing especially exciting. Plus two of the group had brought rain pants with them, and worn them. No one told us to do this—it's the dry [sic] season. The last time I even had rain pants was when I rode a motorcycle and that was more than a couple of years ago. The rain pants had gotten unbelievably muddy, and one of the better birders had fallen down twice in the mud. So: trails rugged, footing uncertain, birds few, and results muddy—great! Our decision to take the day off seemed even more sensible.

An Analytical Framework Is Introduced—And Another

The concept of cost per bird was mentioned that evening at the bar. I kicked myself for not having thought of this. Since to be here we're spending or have spent about $2,000 per day (gulp!) all in, not counting wine but including air fare, and we have seen in six days so far an average of five birds per day for whom we have verifiable photos, you can do the math. We gotta take more pictures to get our average down, but nonappearing birds complicate this effort. A different way to think about this would be minutes per bird. But that's harder as you'd have to keep track of the minutes you were out on the muddy, rocky road, standing around wondering where the birds were. When we left the nature park, the warden at the gate asked us pleasantly, "You are bird hiking?" I was tempted to reply, "Well, we sure as shit weren't bird-watching."

Every evening after a long day of bird pursuing, we all gather around a table and we go through the Checklist. This seems to be an important Bird Ritual, not previously known to us new acolytes. When the tour company sent us an email about two weeks before we were to leave, saying that they would send us the Checklist for Samoa etc. soon, we said to each other, "Geez, we know how to pack and what to bring, we're not rookies, this seems like more than a little micromanaging, we already bought all the tan and green clothes." However, the Checklist—when it arrived—was six pages, landscape orientation of an Excel spreadsheet listing down the left side every bird it was likely we would see, and across the top seventeen columns with a heading for the date of each day we would be on the trip. There were 118 birds listed, to be exact, probably assembled from eBird data. So far we have not seen anything that wasn't on the list. We have also not seen lots of stuff that is on the list.

Every evening we all sit around before dinner at the appointed time, some of us with an adult beverage, and we go down the entire list and check off what we saw, thought we saw, or even just heard on that particular day. It doesn't matter if you have seen it before—hello, common mynas—you check it off for that day. Even if you have already seen it and checked if off for each of the previous sixteen days. It is group think and based on memory. The trip leader leads it, and if he thinks he (or we?) have seen a bird, even if it was a frigatebird flying one hundred meters from us and going away, then we place a check on the "Polynesian frigatebird" square for that day. I suggested at one point that we had in fact only seen a frigatebird's nether parts, but no one seemed to think that this was in the spirit of things. Not a consensus decision. I never saw half the things that got checked off. But who cares? I suppose that you could use this checklist when you got home to update your Life List and go from 4,327 birds to 4,452. But it's your list, it's not a contest, there don't seem to be bragging rights. One of our participants did admit to being at six thousand and something birds, but he's been at this for thirty-plus years. So why do this? Like so many of the rituals of this pastime, it cannot be determined. But we do it.

One of the veteran trip members suggested that the trip leader has to turn in a "trip report" of some sort at the end of each trip, and this check-list, all filled out, is probably an important part of this; he or she doesn't get paid until the report is turned in. Maybe, I don't know. I only write down the birds that we have pictures of and the pictures are recognizable birds. No frigatebird butts. But that might be too rigorous.

More Philosophical Questions Are Raised, Some Answered

Bird geek interjection #2: Right now you're probably asking yourself, "Why am I reading this?" or "How many kinds or types or species of birds are there in the world, anyway?" Which leads us to taxonomy, which to oversimplify, is a complete list of every species of bird in the whole world. The generally acknowledged answer to the "how many species" question is 10,600 individual species. You have a choice as a birder as to which taxonomy to use, since believe it or not, there are competing ones. If you're trying to see all of the world's birds, you want a taxonomy that's easy to use. The most widely used are *The Clements Checklist of Birds of the World* and the International Ornithological Congress (IOC) one. eBird uses *Clements*, which is maintained by Cornell. The IOC list is maintained by an organi-zation called the International Ornithologists' Union, which appears to be a group of about two hundred-plus serious ornithologists. Why we need two competing lists is not clear. I suspect what's at work here are all the many reasons that humans have disputes. But I don't know, and honestly I am not that interested.

Both the taxonomies are continually updated. You might have thought that we already knew all the birds in the world, but sometimes new ones are found. More often, a species is split into several new species, based, I suppose, on better information. The Polynesian whistler becomes the Fiji whistler, the Samoa whistler, the Tahitian whistler, and the New Caledonian whistler. The differences among these are, it is somehow decided, sufficient to warrant "species" designation for each. This could be the advancement of mankind's knowledge or it could be the angels dancing with pinheads recalculation.

There is another way to ask the question, "How many birds are there in the world?" That is a much more difficult question, and perhaps from a conservation standpoint, much more important. eBird data are sort of helpful but as good as they are, they are also sporadic, erratic, and not in any sense peer reviewed. But there is another citizen science project—the Audubon Christmas Bird Count.

This is a hundred-plus year-old activity that takes place during the Christmas season, and counts numbers, not just species. It only covers North America, but has organized the country into fifteen mile in diameter circles that have stayed the same over time. Volunteers go out and spend one of the days during the availability period (14 Dec to 5 Jan each year) counting every bird that they see, name and numbers. The data provided to Audubon is thus at least consistent as to time of year counted, and consistent as to location where the birds are counted. There are about 2,500 such circles, which sounds like a lot. When you do the math, however, this amounts to 117,750 square miles, while the US has 351,905 square miles of area, so the CBC only covers a third of the country. There are only four circles in San Diego, for example. It's a big country.

Since the CBC only counts birds in a portion of one-seventh of the seven continents, it's hard to use it to estimate global bird populations. All the easiest accessible answers seem to agree on two things: a) we don't really know, for all the reasons you could guess—too many, too different, too hard to find, they fly around and don't have fixed addresses, won't respond to questionnaires, etc., and b) it is unlikely that we will ever know with any precision—for the same reasons. I would add a third, which is that we only really need to know when a species starts to become endangered. If there are 1.5 billion quelas in Africa (current estimate) then knowing if it's 1.4 or 1.6 is not of particular significance. Seeing the whooping crane population drop to twenty-three birds in 1941 set off alarm bells, and resulted in a seventy-year conservation effort, which has now raised the numbers to around eight hundred. Not perfect but better.

All that being said, the general agreement is that it's somewhere between 200 billion and 400 billion birds. That's a big range, but that's what we have. Somewhere between twenty-eight and fifty-seven birds per person, globally.

Can We Please Get Back to Seeing Birds?

We fly off to Kadavu Island. It's a large island relatively, fourth largest in Fiji, but has only one thousand residents. And as far as I could see, one bird. Flying over the island when taking off and landing, and walking up and down the main road a couple of times is not a conclusive investigation, but it looks like mostly steep hills and rainforest, occasional small huts with tin roofs, no organized agriculture, three or four C-minus dive resorts, one bed and breakfast, the small airport half the size of a standard 7-Eleven, and that's it.

The island has one dirt but real road bisecting it, and almost no roads along the coasts. Hence, we have to go to our "resort" by boat, small dive boat. We have to get in the boat by sloshing through about fifty meters of knee- to hip-deep bay, after crossing twenty meters of beach. The unenviable choice is to keep on one's boots and get them and your socks completely soaked in an environment where nothing dries. Or you can take off your shoes and socks and risk getting your feet cut up by the odd bit of coral, or stepping on a poisonous but apparently dead sea snake. We tried one of each, neither very satisfactory. The sea snake was pretty scary.

When the boat finally lands us at the resort beach, we unload from the boat into the water and squish inside. We find that there are no guests here but us. This is the high season, I have been told.

The Matana Beach Resort is essentially a dive motel, with a number of decently roomy individual cottages—maybe ten or twelve, some with two bedrooms. It is on a thin slice of beach in the northwest corner of the island. No wharf or dock, however, which seems odd. You have to carry your air tanks through the water to get them into the boat? No wonder there aren't a lot of people here.

Let's get this out of the way quickly: there is no Internet. There is no hot water for showers. While there is electricity for lighting in the evening, by the dawn Mr. Electricity has gone for an early morning hike into the mountains, apparently counting on the sun to come up and provide enough light for guests to dress and pack. There is no explanatory material in the room to say whether it's OK to put the toilet paper in the john or in the plastic waste can poised suggestively beside the toilet.

The curious fact is that all the bird hiking on Kadavu is done on the road running directly from the airport and across the small waist of the island. So why are we not staying in the vicinity, rather than in an isolated lodge miles by boat away? And then we wouldn't have to make the boots/no boots choice, and the sea snakes would be on their own.

We go for two bird hikes on Kadavu, both in the rain (*quelle surprise!*), one for three hours after we get to the island, and a second in the morning for two hours before we leave. We see one very distant, too far to photograph maroon shining parrot briefly at the end of the first hike, and nothing the second. It's as bad as Taveuni but without the long, muddy, bumpy, twisting road winding up two or three thousand feet. Instead we ride in the back of what would be a two-and-a-half-ton truck if we were in the army. At least it's covered so you only get rained on when you get out to look for birds. Swell.

After this remarkably dreary experience, we fly back to Nadi on the main island and our old friend the Novotel. It's looking better and better. Because we have the time, we take a bird walk around the perimeter of this airport hotel, which is surrounded by a nine-hole golf course with no one on it. With no effort, we see two parrot finches, beautiful green and red birds, fooling around in the bushes. More than we saw in two days on Kadavu. Not that we're complaining. To make up for this good fortune, the food that night retreated to the trip's standard of ugly, overcooked, greasy, and nasty. Well, you can't have everything.

On to Vanuatu, Formerly New Hebrides

Vanuatu is eighty-plus islands, mostly small, and 275,000 people, mostly of average size. It was initially discovered by Europeans in 1606 and then, a mere 158 years later, was rediscovered by the redoubtable Captain Cook. Perhaps someone forgot where they put it. It was so highly valued that the Brits and the French agreed to co-govern it. It eventually became independent when no one was looking.

We fly in the morning to Luganville on Espiritu Santo, the biggest island, and go to the Barrier Beach Resort. Which is wonderful. All the things that one would expect a classy beach resort to have, it has—hot water, excellent food, AC, lots of towels, Internet, etc. So it is possible here!

And to make sure that we don't get too giddy, the next morning at 0530 we go off to a rainforest conservation area an hour up the road. It begins raining. We get out at a small village and pick up a guide and begin a six-hour trek among trees and pasture full of very much cow dung and some rainforest, all randomly arranged. We don't see much, and at one point even become separated from our group as the trip leader charges off heedlessly after a fruitless stop to look for birds, leaving L and me behind. We wander after them but lose the trail and finally end up shouting into the trees. We are reunited, no thanks to the trip leadership. Not fun, not professional. Next time I am taking a compass and a map. Perhaps small arms.

On the morning when we are leaving the only really nice hotel we have stayed in, one of our party spots something out near the reef edge that defines the lagoon. It resembles an elongated brown slick of sludge on the water but instead it is a manatee, two manatees (mother and calf) inside the reef and within fifty meters of the shore. Our team is very excited, especially for some inexplicable reason our noncommunicating French person. I guess they are fine but compared to some of the colorful birds we have managed to see, this seems a very unattractive contribution of nature to the library of marine mammals. And it's not a bird. I am sure of that.

But alas (or thank goodness) we can't stand there forever watching mom and kid cruise chunkily back and forth, doing nothing much. We have to get to our fourth country, New Caledonia.

Airport Transfers, South Pacific Style

We are to fly from Luganville on the island of Espiritu Santo, Vanuatu, to the airport in Port Vila, the capital of Vanuatu, strangely located on the much smaller island of Etafe. Although we are going on the same airline, Air Vanuatu, on to Noumea, New Caledonia, on our next flight—a mere two hours away—it is not possible to check the luggage through or to get the two necessary boarding passes at once. Yes, we are changing countries, but I do seem to remember flying from Country A to Country B a time or two in my life before this, and it all worked just fine. But not here. Sometimes air travel has come to resemble the stations of the cross.

As a bonus there is the three hour-plus layover that does not offer much opportunity for gaiety or even commerce. It's a very small airport. We plunk ourselves down in the small nonenclosed café, chiseled out of the space of the check-in area for international flights, order beer (Tusker, pretty good) or Cokes (pretty Coke-like) and hope that the terminal security guys don't kick us out. We may have to buy more beer, we've already bought the entire inventory of "Eta" brand potato chips, except for the "chicken flavor" ones. I meditate on what this flavor infused into a potato chip can be. Roast chicken, Kentucky Fried Chicken, chicken à la king, Kung Pao chicken, coq au vin? Meanwhile our leader decides we should stay here—at least we all have chairs—and he will go off into town and bring back pizzas, and merrily takes orders for same. I am pretty unsure if the large flat square pizza boxes have gotten to Vanuatu, and I am almost certain that the insulated aluminum foil carriers have not, and anyway him walking back into the airport carrying a bunch of pizzas on his shoulder could possibly start a riot, although whether it would be by people anxious for real American [sic] pizza or trying to escape the frightening figure that he would cut we cannot say. And we still have two and a half hours before we can even check in.

Finally, New Caledonia

There is a lot of talk in developmental economics about the "curse" of wealth. Generally stated, the thesis is that it isn't good for a country to be endowed with lots of oil or gold or what have you; it breeds corruption and the money stays with elites or goes out of the country—the average citizens don't benefit. I don't really have a strong view on this, retreating to the all-purpose answer for everything: "It depends." But New Caledonia has 25% of the world's nickel deposits, in a reasonably small island nation of 300,000 people, and the difference from the other three island nations where we have stayed is striking. For example, all the roads here are paved. There are real buildings, and several of nine or ten stories. There are traffic lights, and traffic. There are no chickens alongside the roads. It is a pleasant change. There is also a very large nickel smelting facility on one of the bays that we pass, and it is ugly in a standard industrial way. Nothing's perfect.

We stay at Le Lagon, a Novotel manqué hotel that is not in fact on the lagoon, but several blocks down the street from it. It advertises itself as three stars and the number one hotel on TripAdvisor for Noumea, three years in a row. Recent years. I have not checked this reference, but there is a nine-story Hilton a block and a half down the street, fronting on the water. Le Lagon has hot water but no Internet. This is the best hotel in Noumea? Three days to go before we can go home.

We take a day off even though it's raining and decline to fly over and back to the small nearby island of Lifou, which has a special little bird called the silvereye. The travel book spends all of one and a half pages on Lifou and mentions nothing but diving and snorkeling. We stay in Noumea and it rains like crazy, but we have a long languorous lunch of excellent French food in a restaurant sitting on pilings in the bay. My goodness, you can actually get very good food in at least one of these islands, and fine French wines to boot—you'd never know it if you stuck with Rockjumper.

The final day, we go to the Blue River National Park, home of the famous and hard to see and endangered cagou, a largish grey/white bird, flightless and for some reason an emblem of New Caledonia. Also, endemic. Its distinguishing characteristic is an elaborate crest on the top of its head. The crest is normally flaccid, but when inflated (or erected—we're not entirely clear on the biology here) it's pretty impressive and is a feature of both males and females. This all has to do with mating, of course, as does so much of the display of the bird world, and biology in general. We are fortunate to see this bird in two different settings in the park. It's fine, and is considered an accomplishment. To celebrate, we have our by-now traditional cheap lunch of a white bread sandwich, one slice of cheese, and water. No mayo, no chips, occasionally an apple.

A Final Observation, Thank God

So what exactly is bird watching? A hobby? A pastime? A recreational sport? A fitness pursuit? A competition? An obsession? An intellectual interest? A relentless quest to see birds, undeterred by weather, terrain, or common sense? And the rarer the bird, the better. Common, widely available, easily visible birds are of no value.

This trip has been unbelievably bird focused. The best analogue I can come up with is that it is a little like being a decent but not exceptional Little League ball player, probably in the "good field, no hit" category, and suddenly being thrust into a starting spot on the Yankees. You know the name of the game, and you know the rules of the game, but you have not spent years deeply submerged in the incunabula of mechanics and species differentiation and migratory patterns, and the names of famous player and authors and the characteristics of each ballpark and each pitcher and each hitter in the league. All the others around you know all this, and discuss it endlessly among themselves in the dedicated language that inevitably grows up around any human specialization, baseball or bird-watching. And they speak of little else. No one even mentions President Trump once! Actually that was OK.

Obviously, someone cares that the Polynesian orange-bellied flycatcher has now been split into six species: the Samoan orange-bellied flycatcher, the Fijian orange-bellied flycatcher, the Vanuatu orange-bellied flycatcher, the New Caledonian orange-bellied flycatcher, the New Zealand orange-bellied flycatcher, and the Tahitian orange-bellied flycatcher. If you thought that you "had" the bird on your Life List, you now have to decide which one it was that you "had." This means you need to have quite good records on where and when you "got" it. Then you correct your Life List and add five more damn birds to it that you still need to get. These directives come out from the gods of taxonomy reasonably frequently and sometimes are as long as twenty pages. After all, they have 10,600 species to work on improving. And someone, many someones, are sending in all these eBird reports. There is much that is attractive in wandering about the forest in a leisurely fashion, looking for interestingly colored avians. Just not in the rain.

After sixteen days away, with thirteen days of rain, bad hotels, and worse food, I was so glad when I got back to San Francisco that I planned to drop to my knees and kiss the ground. Only you can't do that at a modern airport; you're in a jetway and in a passageway and in a building and in a customs line. So I kissed the gate attendant.

Love and kisses, Bob

Afterword: Mitzi Gaynor and Rossano Brazzi were the stars of the Rodgers and Hammerstein musical South Pacific. *It was made into a movie that was filmed in Hawaii, not in the South Pacific. I can only conclude that they knew something I didn't know.*

Acknowledgements

We created AES Solar with nothing but some investment capital provided by AES and Riverstone. I was the first employee of what grew to be about 150 people in eight locations around the world. In five years we built fifty different solar plants totaling almost 550 Mw of electric capacity, financing them each with a lot of nonrecourse debt and some modest sponsor equity. This would never have been possible without the talents and dedication and grinding hard work of all of these people. I have listed their names below, and I am deeply grateful to each of them personally.

Dave Amico, David Anson, Carter Atlamazoglu, Greg Boryan, Javier Barcelo Brito, Erik Bue, Olga Bukharina, Paul Burdick, Carolina Canaveras, Luigi Capussela, Irene Chiao, Enrique Collado, Becky Cranna, John Crosson, Julien Desgranges, Dan Diamond, Maya Enright, Aneliya Erdly, Liviu Floroaie, David Flory, Francisca Fontana, Ellen Ann Gallup, Patricia Garffer, Julia Georgieva, Bonnie Guo, Tony Haramis, Luis Herrera, Denyu Hristov, Pauline Idogho, Aina Jumabaeva, Stacie Kim, Evy Kopsidas, Apostolos Kotsaris, Luis Laguna, Marcelo Lando, Federica Lombardi, Juan Lopez, Jeni Lorenz, Frederick Marchand, Giancarlo Matias, Maya Melnikovskaya, Roberto Minguez, Tim Montgomery, Tania Morabito, John Motta, Janay Mullin, Srinivas Nagabhirava, Lola Namazova, Carlo Nannetti, Mai Nguyen, Corinne Onetto, Su Lin Ong, Kristen Panerali, Ben Parry, Claudio Pisi, Jon Poley, Matteo Quatraro, Olivier Renon, Patty Rollin, Satya Sai, Obed Santos, Emil Simionov, Maria Taft, John Turner, Angelina Tutino, Marc Van Patten, Jai Verma, Rich Watson, Neil Watlington, Olga Zelenova.

About Robert F. Hemphill

Mr. Hemphill for much of his career was employed at AES, a global electric power generating and distribution company, where he served as Executive Vice President and Chief of Staff to the CEO. Hemphill was one of the three executives who began the company in 1981, growing it from a million dollar six person start up. AES owns and operates 38,000 MW of power plants in 21 countries around the globe, is publicly listed on the NYSE, and had approximately $18 billion of revenues in 2013.

Recently, Hemphill was the founder and CEO of AES Solar Power Ltd from its inception until his retirement in December 2013. The company, formed in March 2008, is a joint venture of the AES Corporation and Riverstone LLC, an energy focused private equity fund. AES Solar is a leading developer, owner and operator of utility-scale photovoltaic solar plants connected to the electric power grid. These installations, ranging in size from less than 2 MW to more than 250 MW, consist of large arrays of land-based solar photovoltaic panels that directly convert sunlight to electricity. Under his leadership, the company designed, permitted and constructed fifty-one solar plants (526 MW) in seven countries: Spain, France, Italy, Bulgaria, Greece, India and the US.

He has also been a senior policy official at the Department of Energy and Deputy Manager of Power at the Tennessee Valley Authority.

Mr. Hemphill graduated Magna Cum Laude from Yale University and earned an MA from UCLA and an MBA from George Washington University. He served as an airborne infantry officer in the US Army in Vietnam, and in the Special Forces.

His first book, *Dust Tea, Dingoes and Dragons*, was published in 2014 and won the National Indie Excellence Award for Humor, three Gold Awards from the Nonfiction Authors Association (Humor, International Business, and Travel), and was a San Diego Book Awards finalist in the "memoir" category.

His interests include geraniums, unsuccessful participation in Final Four pools, sporadic exercise, competitive duck cooking and tribal art.